THE CITY LIBRARY
SPRINGFIELD, (MA) CITY LIBRARY

Discarded by
the City Library

THIS MATERIAL
DOES NOT CIRCULATE

ICONS OF HIP HOP

**Recent Titles in
Greenwood Icons**

Icons of Horror and the Supernatural: An Encyclopedia of
Our Worst Nightmares
Edited by S.T. Joshi

Icons of Business: An Encyclopedia of Mavericks, Movers, and Shakers
Kateri Drexler

ICONS OF HIP HOP

An Encyclopedia of the Movement, Music, And Culture

VOLUME 1

Edited by Mickey Hess

Greenwood Icons

GREENWOOD PRESS
Westport, Connecticut • London

Library of Congress Cataloging-in-Publication Data

Icons of hip hop : an encyclopedia of the movement, music, and culture / edited by Mickey Hess
  p. cm. – (Greenwood icons)
Includes bibliographical references, discographies, and index.
ISBN-13: 978-0-313-33902-8 (set: alk. paper)
ISBN-13: 978-0-313-33903-5 (vol 1: alk. paper)
ISBN-13: 978-0-313-33904-2 (vol 2: alk. paper)
 1. Rap musicians—Biography. 2. Turntablists—Biography.
 3. Rap (Music)—History and criticism. 4. Hip-hop. I. Hess, Mickey, 1975–
ML394. I26 2007
782.421649'03—dc22   2007008194

British Library Cataloguing in Publication Data is available.

Copyright © 2007 by Mickey Hess

All rights reserved. No portion of this book may be reproduced, by any process or technique, without the express written consent of the publisher.

Library of Congress Catalog Card Number: 2007008194
ISBN-10: 0-313-33902-3 (set)   ISBN-13: 978-0-313-33902-8 (set)
        0-313-33903-1 (vol. 1)   978-0-313-33903-5 (vol. 1)
        0-313-33904-X (vol. 2)   978-0-313-33904-2 (vol. 2)

First published in 2007

Greenwood Press, 88 Post Road West, Westport, CT 06881
An imprint of Greenwood Publishing Group, Inc.
www.greenwood.com

Printed in the United States of America

The paper used in this book complies with the Permanent Paper Standard issued by the National Information Standards Organization (Z39.48-1984).

10 9 8 7 6 5 4 3 2 1

Contents

List of Photos — vii

Volume One

Foreword, *Jeru the Damaja* — ix

Preface — xiii

Introduction — xvii

A Timeline of Hip Hop History, *Nicole Hodges Persley* — xxi

Kool Herc, *Wayne Marshall* — 1
Grandmaster Flash, *H.C. Williams* — 27
Roxanne Shanté, *Thembisa S. Mshaka* — 51
Run-DMC, *Jeb Aram Middlebrook* — 69
Beastie Boys, *Mickey Hess* — 91
MC Lyte, *Jennifer R. Young* — 117
Eric B. & Rakim, *Shawn Bernardo* — 141
Public Enemy, *George Ciccariello-Maher* — 169
Salt-N-Pepa, *Athena Elafros* — 193
Queen Latifah, *Faiza Hirji* — 217
The Geto Boys, *Jason D. Haugen* — 243
The Native Tongues, *Aine McGlynn* — 265

Volume Two

Preface — ix

Ice Cube, *David J. Leonard* — 293
Dr. Dre and Snoop Dogg, *David Diallo* — 317

Nas, *Susan Weinstein*	341
Wu-Tang Clan, *Jessica Elliott and Mickey Hess*	365
Tupac Shakur, *Carlos D. Morrison and Celnisha L. Dangerfield*	391
Notorious B.I.G., *James Peterson*	417
Lil' Kim, *Aine McGlynn*	439
Outkast, *T. Hasan Johnson*	457
Eminem, *Katherine V. Tsiopos-Wills*	481
Missy Elliot, *Joi Carr*	503
Jay-Z, *T. Hasan Johnson*	529
Kanye West, *Todd Dills*	555

Interviews:

Let 'Em In: An Interview with DJ Premier, *Shamika Ann Mitchell*	579
Word Up: An Interview with DJ Scratch, *Shamika Ann Mitchell*	591
Afterword: The Twenty-Four Most Overlooked MCs in Hip Hop, *Masta Ace*	603
Selected Bibliography	609
Notes on Contributors	613
Index	621

List of Photos

DJ Kool Herc (page 1) speaking at a news conference to launch "Hip-Hop Won't Stop: The Beat, The Rhymes, The Life," the first ever hip-hop initiative at the Smithsonian's National Museum of American History in New York, 2006. © AP Photo/Henny Ray Abrams.

Grandmaster Flash (page 27) performing live at Wembley Arena in London, 1985. © S.I.N / Alamy.

Roxanne Shante (page 51). © David Corio.

Run DMC (page 69), ca. 1985. Courtesy of Photofest.

Beastie Boys (page 91), 1998. Courtesy of Photofest.

MC Lyte (page 117). Courtesy of Photofest.

Eric B and Rakim (page 141). © Waring Abbott / Alamy.

Public Enemy (page 169). Courtesy of Photofest.

Salt n Pepa (page 193), ca. 1994. Courtesy of Photofest.

Queen Latifah (page 217). Courtesy of Photofest.

The Geto Boys (page 243) arrive at the 2004 Source Hip-Hop Music Awards at the James L. Knight Center, October 10, 2004 in Miami, Florida. © Orlando Garcia / Getty Image.

De La Soul (page 265), one of the founding members of the Native Tongues posse, along with A Tribe Called Quest, the Jungle Brothers, Afrika Bambaataa, and others. © David Corio.

Ice Cube (page 293). Courtesy of Photofest.

Dr. Dre and Snoop Dogg (page 317), 1993. Courtesy of Photofest.

Nas (page 341), 1994. Courtesy of Photofest.

Wu Tang Clan (page 365), 2000. © Kevin Winter / Getty Images.

Tupac Shakur (page 391), 1996. Courtesy of Photofest.

Notorious B.I.G. (page 417), ca. 1997. Courtesy of Photofest.

Lil' Kim (page 439) in the pressroom at the 2006 MTV Video Music Awards in New York. © AP Photo / Tammie Arroyo.

Big Boi and Andre 3000 (page 457) pose in front of the three awards they won at the 46th Annual Grammy Awards, 2004. © AP Photo / Reed Saxon.

Eminem (page 481), 2000. Courtesy of Photofest.

Missy Elliot (page 503) performs during the 2003 MTV Europe Music Awards in Edinburgh, Scotland. Courtesy of Photofest.

Jay-Z (page 529) rapper and CEO of Def Jam Records, 2001. Courtesy of Photofest.

Kanye West (page 555) performs "Jesus Walks" at the 47th Annual Grammy Awards in Los Angeles, 2005. © AP Photo / Kevork Djansezian.

Foreword

I grew up in the seventies and eighties in East New York, Brooklyn, where summertime meant playing freeze tag, kick the can, and skelly in the streets. Seventy-nine was the year that changed my life forever. "Rapper's Delight" was played so many times on my grandmother's stereo that it became part of me. So much so that I know all the words by heart to this day. It was *The Great Adventures of Super Rhymes,* not Slick Rick (that is the generation following mine) that had me hooked like Benji from the Alice Childress novel *A Hero Ain't Nothin' but a Sandwich* the first time he tried smack. That would be the summer that would change the course of my life or rather put me on the right course. A new family moved onto the block that summer. There was a young mother named Debbie and her young son. I forget his name, but the story goes like this.

It was the last block party of the summer and a bunch of dudes we had never seen before were standing in front of the building where the new family was living, clearly friends and family of the new family. The older guys were up in arms because in those days a group of young black men on your block that did not live there usually ended up in some sort of physical confrontation. Dirty looks and ice grills were exchanged and had the block hotter than an Eskimo in the desert. But before it could escalate, some guy that looked like JJ from *Good Times* called several of the kids indoors. Here we go ...

The block party had just started and it was going to get shut down already. A few minutes passed and the door of the building flung open but instead of sticks, bats, chains, and other popular tools of destruction, the strangers came out carrying huge speakers. Speakers? All of a sudden fear had become curiosity. I was about eight at the time and had never seen speakers so big. And I grew up in a party house! I wanted to get a better look so I got closer. The young men kept their focus on hooking up the speakers, concentrating on the task at hand. By this time a pretty decent crowd had gathered but they seemed not to notice—like they had done this a thousand times. I had heard stories about block parties with gigantic speakers playing music you could hear for miles and kids dancing in the street. But I had never witnessed it firsthand. All we ever did at the neighborhood block party was play hide and seek, round up, catch and kiss, and eat all the different kinds of food everybody's mother was cheffing up on the grills. And as far as music, people put their stereo speakers on the porch and played Marvin Gaye, Bob Marley, jazz, salsa, and music from their native lands. It was sort of like a musical jambalaya, and every few steps you discovered a new flavor.

The scene that was being set up this summer afternoon looked like something I had heard of, the new music that I heard the older kids around the way talking about. Of course! It was unfolding before my eyes.... I couldn't believe that I was about to see hip hop with my own two eyes—I was so excited that I couldn't move. Out came the milk crates, a piece of plywood, turntables, and last but not least an extension cord from the first-floor window. When they hooked up the power cords it was like watching one of those old-school Frankenstein movies when the scientist hits the lifeless pile of spare parts with a million volts of electricity, but instead of a hideous monster a different beast was awakened. A few of the strange dudes grabbed the mic and started spittin' the flavor. Rhymes like "dang diddy dang di dang da dang ding, my meat taste better than Burger King . . . " or was that the song they were playing? Whatever it was, they had me mesmerized. I had never seen live DJing or MCing, never heard of Kool Herc, Grandmaster Flash, or any of the godfathers of hip hop. That was my first true hip hop experience. Of course after that everyone wanted to know the people who brought real hip hop to East New York. The JJ-looking kid's name was David and from what I remember he became an instant block star. What a way to move into a neighborhood! My aunt and some of the older kids on the block became friends with David and his homeboy Charles and started a little crew. Well, they seemed like a crew to me. They had sweatshirts with their names ironed on them and they DJed parties around the hood. My aunt had to babysit me so I was their official mascot. As wack as that sounds, I thought it was the bomb.

I started writing my own rhymes and got my big break at my aunt's birthday party the following summer. When I look back, I must have sounded ridiculous. I was only nine or ten years old but it was official to me: I was an MC. The next few years went by and I listened to anything hip hop, memorized every record, and battled my sister on the porch so I could sharpen my skills. The mid-eighties rolled around and hip hop had become the dominant street culture. MCs got more complex with their flows. Kool Moe Dee taught us about safe sex. Rakim taught us how to spell "emcee." Kool G Rap showed us how to paint pictures with rhymes on the canvas of the mind. KRS-One showed us that the most brilliant mind was the criminal mind. Run-DMC took hip hop worldwide and sucker MCs could never touch the mic again. Whodini gave us five minutes of funk that lasted all the way through the new millennium. Doug E. Fresh made beats with his lips. The Fat

Boys ate everything in sight. There was Big Daddy Kane, the Jungle Brothers, 3rd Bass, Biz, and so many different MCs we would need a whole book to name them all. There were the MCs that influenced my style. Because biting was a cardinal sin, I had to take a little from Melle Mel, a little from Grandmaster Caz, and all the other great MCs and form my own style. Jeru the Damaja style ...

People always ask me where I see hip hop going in the future. I must admit I loved the days when MCs weren't all about only getting paid. And your skill was the currency that made you the richest cat in the hood. But all things must evolve, even things we wish could stay the same. So what do I see for the future of hip hop? Hip hop *is* the future.

Long live hip hop.

—Jeru the Damaja

Preface

Choosing the twenty-four most important hip hop artists of all time is no easy task. From Kool Herc to Kanye West, *Icons of Hip Hop* spans four decades of MCs and DJs, old-school pioneers and new-school innovators, to profile the figures who have made hip hop music what it is today. Hip hop music, once considered a passing fad, continues to thrive and evolve more than thirty years into its history. *Icons of Hip Hop* presents the stories of twenty-four important figures who have contributed to the music's development and success.

Our profiles begin with Kool Herc and Grandmaster Flash, two DJs who established hip hop's musical foundation with their invention of breakbeats and turntable scratching. These hip hop pioneers collected funk and soul records and transformed their record players into instruments that created new sounds through backspinning and scratching. These turntable techniques, along with digital samplers and drum machines, form the backbone of hip hop music. The sounds that DJs like Herc, Flash, Afrika Bambaataa, Pete DJ Jones, and Grandwizard Theodore invented have been built upon by three decades of DJs and producers, from Rick Rubin and Jam Master Jay to Eric B and the Bomb Squad to DJ Premier, DJ Scratch, Dr. Dre, and Kanye West.

At Kool Herc's block parties in the 1970s, the DJ was the focal point of the performance, and the MC, or rapper, served chiefly to call the crowd's attention to the DJ and to entice people onto the dance floor. As early MCs like Coke La Rock and Busy Bee began to develop more complex rhyming routines, the MC came into his own. Famous MC battles, such as the 1982 competition between Busy Bee and Kool Moe Dee, took rhyming to a new level as these MCs sought to win over the crowd with their rhyme structure, wordplay, and wit. Whether hyping up the DJ or boasting about his or her own skills on the mic, the MC was always a crowd pleaser. With the 1979 release of Sugarhill Gang's "Rapper's Delight," the first hip hop record to reach mainstream radio worldwide, the rapper became the face of commercial rap music.

"Rapper's Delight" also introduced mainstream listeners to the terms *rap* and *hip hop*. The song begins with the words, "I said a hip hop...." From that early moment in hip hop history, when *rap* and *hip hop* were used in the title and first lines of the same song, the meanings of these two terms have been debated. When many fans and artists talk about hip hop, they explain that it is a culture that expands beyond music to include four central elements: graffiti art (aka tagging or writing), b-boying (aka break dancing, popping, and locking), DJing (aka turntablism, or mixing, cutting, and scratching records), and MCing (aka rapping or rhyming). On his song "9 Elements," KRS-One expanded this definition to include five more elements: beatboxing, fashion, language, street knowledge, and entrepreneurialism. In his lyrics to "9 Elements," KRS makes the distinction that to rap is merely an action that anyone can take, but "Hip hop is something you live." Both terms, hip hop and rap, however, are used to describe music. To distinguish between the two forms, the term *hip hop music* is often used to designate a song that holds true to hip hop's orginal aesthetic rather than appealing to a pop audience, and the term *MC*, as opposed to *rapper*, is often used to designate a hip hop vocalist who holds true to this same aesthetic. In an exclusive interview for *Icons of Hip Hop*, Roxanne Shanté explained the difference between MCs and rappers: "Rappers need videos, MCs don't."

Although Shanté eventually did make a video, she first made her name going head-to-head with other MCs in the street. Her record "Roxanne's Revenge," hailed as one of hip hop's first answer records, took rhyme battles into the recording studio as she responded to a single, "Roxanne, Roxanne," by the group UTFO. Roxanne initiated a series of answer records from several different MCs, and extended hip hop's competitive element to recordings and radio airplay. Video airplay would become even more important to Run-DMC, whose visual imagery of black fedoras, gold chains, and unlaced Adidas sneakers would introduce hip hop fashion to MTV audiences. As hip hop culture moved into mainstream outlets like MTV, listeners sought to preserve the original culture by making distinctions about which songs counted as "real hip hop" and which were created for crossover success on the pop charts. In the mid-1990s, MC Hammer dropped the "MC" from his name, claiming he was in the business of entertainment rather than hip hop, in response to criticisms that his pop hits like "U Can't Touch This" were selling out hip hop culture. Debates about what characteristics consitute rap or hip hop rage on today as artists like Defari claim to make "real hip hop" rather than pop rap.

Ideological distinctions aside, however, rap music is an inextricable part of hip hop culture. Artists and listeners will continue to argue about which MCs are making music to make money and which ones do it out of a pure love for hip hop, but even as these debates continue, we should remember that the shiny suits and diamond grills we see on MTV and BET in the twenty-first century are as much a part of hip hop as the Kangol hats and Fila jumpsuits worn by hip hoppers in New York City parks in the 1980s. Rather than debating which figures belong to rap and which to hip hop, *Icons of Hip Hop* showcases the inventions and innovations of twenty-four musical icons from 1973 to 2007. Even at two volumes, however, our icon profiles are not comprehensive. As with any collection, there are omissions. Throughout the book, however, we make connections to other MCs, DJs, and producers whose stories intersect with the twenty-four figures we have chosen. Each profile discusses and cross-references other artists connected with the icon at hand. A foreword from Jeru the Damaja, a rapper included in Kool Moe Dee's list of the top fifty MCs of all time, credits the artists who influenced his rhyme style. Nicole Hodges Persley's timeline of hip hop history highlights the innovations of artists like Kurtis Blow and Schoolly D, icons who are not included in our twenty-four in-depth profiles. An afterword by veteran rap artist Masta Ace lists the twenty-four most overlooked hip hop icons, who are worthy of further study. Exclusive interviews with Masta Ace, Roxanne Shanté, Mystic, and Kool DJ Red Alert, included in the Roxanne Shanté profile, provide a firsthand account of the development of the first female MC to spark a national trend. And finally, Shamika Ann Mitchell's exclusive interviews with DJ Premier and DJ Scratch give further attention to producers, the people behind the music, as icons.

The scope of *Icons of Hip Hop* is intentionally broad in that we seek to profile old-school orginators as well as new-school innovators, devote attention to the different regions that have contributed to what hip hop culture has become in the United States, and recover the stories of lesser-known artists. As the editor, I sought to pay homage to those artists, like Ice Cube and Eminem, who typically come to mind when hip hop is mentioned, but also to call attention to groups like the Native Tongues and Eric B. & Rakim, that haven't matched Ice Cube's sales but that rank high on many fans' lists of the best rappers of all time. In short, the twenty-four artists profiled in these two volumes were chosen based on their unique contributions to the development of hip hop music, style, and culture: Grandmaster Flash made the turntables an instrument, Eric B. & Rakim created more complex rhyme flows, MC Lyte proved that women could rap with aggression, Outkast shifted attention to Southern hip hop, and the Native Tongues provided a much-needed critique of hip hop culture itself. Each essay ends with a section on the legacy of the artists, which emphasizes their influence on hip-hop today and their importance to hip hop in the future. We include producers and DJs as well as MCs, fan favorites as well as platinum-selling artists, women as well as men, and Atlanta and Houston as well as New York and Los Angeles. With this approach to selecting its subjects, *Icons of Hip Hop* presents a historical and cultural framework for hip hop that extends to current or emerging artists, unearths the histories of important artists from outside hip hop's mainstream, and examines the varied and ever-changing forms of the music.

Each of our twenty-four profiles features in-depth coverage of the artist's life and work, highlighting the artist's influence in making hip hop music and culture what it is today. The profiles are supported by several sidebars that place the icons within cultural and historical context. The sidebars highlight such issues as hip hop's homophobia, vegetarian rappers, hip hop and Islam, the mafia, horror films, fashion trends, musical innovations such as turntable scratching and digital sampling, legal issues, and hip hop's culture of death. There are certain consistent themes to the sidebars, such as regional scenes (Houston, Memphis, and Canada), and hip hop's intersections with other musical forms (rock, jazz, blues, and metal). Each profile also includes a discography and list of resources for further research. Broad in scope and distinctive in detail, *Icons of Hip Hop* is an excellent resource for the student or casual listener as well as the true hip hop head.

—Mickey Hess

Introduction

Jeru the Damaja ends his foreword to this volume by reminding us that hip hop keeps on evolving. This is an important consideration because many critics long for a past era, complaining that hip hop has changed too much. A common and unfortunate version of the story claims that hip hop began in the 1970s as an innocent form of self-expression, and became corrupted by money, violence, and sexism as its artists left behind New York City street corners for MTV videos. This ideal of a purer, unadulterated hip hop is complicated, though, because hip hop has never been any one thing. Several of hip hop's pioneers sought to make money from their music, and several MCs heard on today's radio are dedicated to making quality songs. Because hip hop began in South Bronx parks and on street corners instead of in a major-label recording studio, fans and artists are nostalgic for a purer moment in time, when hip hop music wasn't heard in McDonald's commercials and the Pillsbury Doughboy had never considered rapping to sell crescent rolls. Corporate record labels have bought into hip hop, but they haven't bought it up; the individual, entrepreneurial spirit that drove hip hop's early years is alive and well in independent labels like Swishahouse, Stone's Throw, and Hieroglyphics, and rappers themselves have become CEOs of larger record companies: Jay-Z heads Def Jam, Scarface heads Def Jam South, and Dr. Dre has built his Aftermath label into a rap dynasty. In its thirty-plus-year history, hip hop has gone worldwide. It has become big business. Yet the music remains alive today because hip hop has never meant any one thing. The music has never stagnated because artists are constantly inventing new forms and responding to clichés in their music, constantly seeking to one-up their peers. If real hip hop were truly defined by the shape it took in the 1970s, then hip hop would not be alive today.

Nas' album *Hip Hop is Dead* (2006) blames hip hop's commercialism for killing off what was vital about the original culture, yet on this same album Nas brags in his lyrics about seeing his face on the side of Sony's promotional trucks. Full of such contradictions, the album's bold and provocative title sparked a lot of response, including an on-air debate between old school rapper (and pioneering female MC) Monie Love and Southern rapper Young Jeezy on Love's radio show on Philadelphia's WPHI-FM on December 7, 2006. Monie Love supported Nas in pining for hip hop's good old days while Young Jeezy asserted that hip hop is alive and well in the South and that Nas disrespected the new breed of Southern hip hop artists by declaring the music dead. Nas certainly wasn't the first person to declare hip hop dead because it has moved too far away from where it began. Yet although some critics claim that real hip hop was killed off by hyperconsumerist gangsta rap and its fascination with shiny jewelry, expensive cars, and sexy dancers, a more accurate history reveals that hip hop has long embodied these contradictions between culture and commerce. Political, consciousness-raising rap has existed, and continues to exist, alongside thug rap and party rap. Niggaz Wit Attitude, Compton, California's gangsta rap pioneers, shared a bill with De La Soul, Amityville, New York's Afrocentric-conscious rap pioneers. When these two groups were paired for a U.S. tour in 1988, hip hop was young enough that their sharing the bill made sense: after all, they were both rap groups. Almost twenty years later, hip hop music has expanded to include several specialized subgenres, and a conscious rapper like Talib Kweli would seem terribly out of place opening for a gangsta rapper like 50 Cent. It would be like Bob Dylan opening for Black Sabbath in the 1970s.

The secret to the unlikely pairing of N.W.A. and De La Soul lies in the themes of N.W.A.'s "Express Yourself" and De La Soul's "Me Myself and I": Each of these groups believed that hip hop is about being yourself, not fitting into a current trend. What all hip hop subgenres share is a love of beats and rhymes, and the value of the individual perspective. N.W.A. rhymed about drug dealers, gangs, and guns because that was part of the reality they witnessed in their South Central Los Angeles neighborhoods. De La Soul were from a relatively affluent background, by comparison, so they rhymed about going to high school, and about the fact that they didn't fit the mold of what it meant to be a rapper. In their video for "Me Myself and I," the three members of De La Soul are failing Professor Def Beats' class in rapping because they don't wear gold chains and they can't adopt an aggressive pose for the camera. Instead, De La Soul wore their Day-Glo colors and black Africa medallions, and showed listeners an alternative definition of what it meant to be hip hop.

De La Soul were not the first rappers to reinvent the model of hip hop style. Run-DMC did it before them by ditching the flashy, disco-style costumes of Kurtis Blow and Whodini and putting on blue jeans, gold chains, and unlaced Adidas sneakers. N.W.A. had done it with black dungarees, Lakers' caps, and dark sunglasses. In his book about country music, another American music form where authenticity is hotly debated, Richard A. Peterson defined authenticity as fitting the model while at the same time proving not to be a copy of that model (95). In hip hop music, artists must constantly reinvent the model of real hip hop by responding to it from their own unique perspective. The Fat Boys rhymed about food. The Geto Boys and Outkast opened up hip hop to the South. MC Lyte, Queen Latifah, and Lil' Kim responded to hip hop's aggressive sexuality from a female perspective. Kanye West, the son of university professor Donda West, made it okay to be middle-class. Eminem and the Beastie Boys adapted an African American form without mimicking it or taking credit away from those who created it. These artists made hip hop their own by imbuing it with their own reality and writing and delivering lyrics in a style that reflects that reality by preserving regional dialect and slang to tell the story of the place that they come from.

Yet even with these musical innovations and new perspectives, even as hip hop has spread across the United States with vibrant scenes in Miami, Houston, Atlanta, the San Francisco Bay Area, Chicago, and Memphis, and even as Hip Hop's popularity grows in Germany, South Africa, Australia, and Japan, certain aspects of its original model remain. Hip hop traces its roots back to African griots and the bad-man legends of folklore figures like Stackalee. Hip hop music grows out of Jamaican DJs boasting and toasting, out of the dozens, snaps, "ya mama" jokes, and playground chants heard from girls playing double Dutch. Hip hop music grows out of the blues, jazz, funk, rock, rhythm and blues, and disco. Its heroes are Muhammad Ali, Malcolm X, Madam C.J. Walker, and Angela Davis. Its closest predeccesors, lyrically, are Gil Scott-Heron and the Last Poets. Rhythmically, it draws from James Brown and Rick James. But just as its drumbeats and bass lines are adapted from other music forms, hip hop has in turn influenced today's rock music and dancehall reggae, and has left an indelible mark on pop music, culture, fashion, and language. Because hip hop values individuality in the way Snoop Dogg and E-40 speak, the way Lil' Kim and Outkast dress, and the way Kanye West and Dr. Dre make beats, it preserves individual style even as it all becomes a part of hip hop.

In that respect, *Icons of Hip Hop* seeks to mirror the range of perspectives that makes hip hop what it is. My perspective on hip hop's history is only that, my own. I grew up listening to hip hop in Eubank, Kentucky. My friends and I lip-synched to U.T.F.O.'s "Roxanne, Roxanne" at the sixth grade talent show. Dubbed cassette tapes of Too $hort and the Geto Boys were passed around my middle school like contraband. I used to scope out Pirate's Cove, the mall arcade, for someone over eighteen who looked cool enough to buy me the uncensored version of Eazy-E's *Eazy-Duz-It* or N.W.A.'s *Straight Outta Compton*. Failing that, I settled for the Kmart censored versions, where "motherfuckin'" became "crazy-lookin'" and "Fuck tha Police" was left off entirely. I was a white kid in Eubank, Kentucky, listening to censored rap cassettes my mom bought me at Kmart. I grew up listening to hip hop, and I continue to listen to it, write about it, and teach it today. In editing this collection, I strived to recruit contributors whose perspectives I value, even when they do not match my own. I believe that *Icons of Hip Hop*, like hip hop itself, greatly benefits from this range of perspectives, and that the collection represents both a wide range of artists and varied approaches to thinking about them.

—Mickey Hess

WORK CITED

Peterson, Richard A. *Creating Country Music: Fabricating Authenticity*. Chicago: University of Chicago Press, 1997.

A Timeline of Hip Hop History

Nicole Hodges Persley

1973   Jamaican American DJ Kool Herc creates the breakbeat by isolating the most exciting instrumental break in a record and looping that section so that the break played continuously. The breakbeat becomes the cornerstone of hip hop music. At his legendary block parties, Herc powers his turntables from street lamps, running extension cords from the outlets to his speakers and turntables. Herc pioneers a revolution in DJ technique with his mobile sound systems; rather than rely on a venue's sound system, Herc owned his own equipment, and could move from spot to spot in the city.

1973   The Lockers dance group is started in Los Angeles by Don Campbell, the inventor of the locking dance style, in which a series of faster moves are linked together by points of freezing in one position, or locking into place. Members of the Lockers include Don "Campbellock" Campbell, Fred Barry (who went on to play Rerun on the popular sitcom *What's Happening?*), and Adolfo "Shabba Doo" Quiñones (who went on to play Ozone in the films *Breakin'* and *Breakin' 2: Electric Boogaloo*. Locking began in the 1960s as a dance form associated with funk, but it became a hip hop dance style and heavily influenced the creation of hip hop dance forms like popping and breakdancing.

1975   The MC is born from the call and response routines between DJs and the audience. Kool Herc and Afrika Bambaataa borrow from the African and Caribbean traditions of boasting and toasting to talk over breakbeats and move the crowd to action. Hip hop's most famous DJ calls such as "And you don't stop" and "Yes, yes y'all" begin. Busy Bee is one of the first MCs to work with DJs to get the crowd moving. He becomes one of the first MCs to freestyle rhymes, and one of the first to work with a DJ to record his rap routines.

1977   The Rock Steady Crew is founded by Jojo and Jimmy D in the Bronx, New York. The b-boys of Rock Steady use dance as a way to combat problems with rival gangs in the Bronx. The term *b-boy* (and *b-girl*) is used to describe these new dancers who move to the breakbeat in a series of flowing poses. One of the most famous members of the Rock Steady Crew is the b-boy Crazy Legs, who started his own chapter in 1981 in Manhattan. Other important members of Rock Steady Crew are Frosty Freeze, Take One, Little Crazy Legs, and Ken Swift.

1979   Sugarhill Gang releases "Rapper's Delight," considered the first rap record. Although the Fatback Band's "King Tim III (Personality Jock)" was released just prior to "Rapper's Delight," making it the first rap record ever released, its commercial success and cultural impact did not match Sugarhill Gang's "Rapper's Delight," which became a worldwide hit.

1980   Kurtis Blow becomes the first rap artist to release a full-length album on a major label when Mercury releases *Kurtis Blow* on the strength of the success of singles like Sugarhill Gang's "Rapper's Delight" and Kurtis' own "Christmas Rappin'." Kurtis' second single, "The Breaks" broke into the top five on the U.S. R&B Chart, making him the first solo MC to achieve commercial success.

1981   Graffiti artist Fab 5 Freddy, who is later the host of MTV's *Yo! MTV Raps*, is shouted out in Blondie's song, "Rapture," which is a number one hit in the UK and United States. Blondie's Debbie Harry, who raps the shout-out to Freddy, is an icon of New York's punk and underground art scene of the 1980s, and "Rapture" bridges these two cultures similarly to Jean-Michel Basquiat, a graffiti artist turned art star. Prior to his work on *Yo! MTV Raps*, Fab 5 Freddy produced the music for and had a lead role in 1982's *Wildstyle*, which is considered the first hip hop film.

1981   Turntable scratching is featured on Grandmaster Flash's "The Adventures of Grandmaster Flash on the Wheels of Steel," one of the first rap records to capture the sounds of live DJ scratching.

1982   The famous battle between Kool Moe Dee and Busy Bee takes place at Harlem World in New York City. Kool Moe Dee wins the battle and becomes famous for his unique vocal style and his ability to freestyle rhymes. Kool Moe Dee goes on to found the rap group Treacherous Three with Special K and DJ Easy Lee, and he later stages another famous battle with LL Cool J.

1982 — Grandmaster Flash and the Furious Five release "The Message," which is arguably the first "conscious" rap song. "The Message" includes the famous hook "Don't push me 'cause I'm close to the edge." The song depicts conditions of poverty and disenfranchisement and becomes an icon of hip hop music and culture for many who hear it because it expresses the frustrations of the urban communities where hip hop developed.

1982 — Afrika Bambaataa and the Soul Sonic Force release *Looking for the Perfect Beat* on Tommy Boy Records. The album, featuring the cut "Planet Rock," becomes the first rap record to use synthesizers and an electronic drum machine. Bambaataa samples electronic music from European group Kraftwerk in this song and creates a hip hop classic as well as a new base for electronic dance music. Digital music genres such as house and electronica also consider this song a part of their histories.

1984 — Run-DMC's self-titled debut album is released, and their music video for "Rock Box" is the first rap video on MTV. Run-DMC starts two important fashion trends in hip hop: hard-shell Adidas shoes and gold rope chains.

1984 — U.T.F.O. records the song "Roxanne, Roxanne," which disses a fictional woman who doesn't respond to the group's advances. The song incites a string of response records, including the Roxanne Shanté (Lolita Shanté Gooden) song "Roxanne's Revenge," which sold over half a million copies. Adelaida Martinez, calling herself The Real Roxanne, responded to Gooden in the song "Romeo," and several other MCs, male and female, weighed in with their own responses. By some estimates, the Roxanne Wars created nearly 100 response records to U.T.F.O's original song.

1984 — Fresh Fest is the first national hip hop tour in the United States and the first tour to galvanize a diverse group of rappers together under a single billing. It is one of the most successful tours of hip hop music, appearing in over twenty-seven cities across the United States. The roster includes acts such as Run-DMC, Roxanne Shanté, Kurtis Blow, Whodini, and the Fat Boys. The tour grosses almost 4 million dollars. In 2005, the Fresh Fest returns as an old-school summer concert series featuring many of the headliners that opened in 1984.

1984	Rick Rubin and Russell Simmons form Def Jam Records, initially selling records out of Rubin's dorm room at New York University. Def Jam's first two releases are LL Cool J's "I Need a Beat" and the Beastie Boys' "Rock Hard." The 1985 film *Krush Groove* is based loosely on Rubin's and Simmons' lives as hip hop producers and label executives. Simmons hired Blair Underwood to play himself while the Beastie Boys, Run-DMC, and several other Def Jam artists appeared in the film as themselves.
1985	Doug E. Fresh and the Get Fresh Crew release "The Show." Doug E. Fresh, the original human beatbox, goes on to work alone as a beatboxer, MC, and producer. The Get Fresh Crew included Slick Rick (formerly known as MC Ricky D), Barry B, and Chill Will.
1985	Tipper Gore's group PMRC (Parents' Music Resource Center) demands a ratings advisory for explicit lyrics in rock and rap music. The goal of the PMRC is to create a system that can alert parents to the explicit content of rock 'n' roll and rap records. Gore appealed to traditional American family values. The PMRC pushed for a rating system similar to the film rating system but instead secured a requirement for record companies to mark their products with the label "Parental Advisory: Explicit Lyrics," also known as the Tipper Sticker.
1986	Run-DMC's *Raising Hell* is the first platinum hip hop album. On "Walk This Way," a hit single from the album, Run-DMC collaborates with rock legends Aerosmith to produce a rap cover of their 1975 classic "Walk This Way." The single both rejuvenates Aerosmith's career and catapults Run-DMC to platinum status. The song is considered one of the first crossover hits in rap music, reaching the Top 5 on the *Billboard* music chart.
1986	Salt-N-Pepa's *Hot, Cool & Vicious* album debuts, bringing new attention to female MCs with platinum sales and a Grammy nomination. "The Show Stopper" is a response to Doug E. Fresh and the Get Fresh Crew's "The Show," "Tramp" addresses male promiscuity, and their breakout hit, "Push It," a B-Side to "Tramp" single asserts female sexuality and desire.
1986	A battle over the true home of hip hop begins between KRS-One and Boogie Down Productions and Marley Marl's Juice Crew. MC Shan's lyrics in "The Bridge" (1986) point to Queensbridge. In Boogie Down Productions' "The Bridge Is Over" (1987), however, KRS-One argues that the Bronx is the home of hip hop. The battle continues in over ten records

A Timeline of Hip Hop History

featuring exchange responses from the Juice Crew and Boogie Down Productions.

1986　Ice-T's "Six in the Morning" becomes a hallmark of West Coast gangsta rap. Ice's rhymes about Los Angeles gang life build from the style of Philadelphia's Schoolly D, who spoke about gang life on "Gangster Boogie" and "P.S.K. (What Does It Mean?)."

1986　Def Jam releases the Beastie Boys' *Licensed to Ill*. Former skaters and punk musicians, their mix of hip hop, rock, and punk create a new sound for hip hop music. The Beastie Boys are the first white rap group to have success in the genre, and their hits "No Sleep 'til Brooklyn" and "(You Gotta) Fight for Your Right (to Party)" propel their sales past the mark set by their mentors and Def Jam labelmates Run-DMC.

1987　Eric B. & Rakim produce the hip hop classic *Paid in Full*. Rakim presents a laid back and sophisticated new style of rapping that mimics jazz riffs, while Eric B. creates his own innovations as a DJ. Together, the team raises the stakes in the rap game because they create more complex rhymes and sample schemes in their work. Today, many MCs cite Eric B. & Rakim as one of the top rap groups in history. Hip hop magazine *The Source* named Rakim the best MC of all time.

1987　Public Enemy's *Yo! Bum Rush the Show* is released. The album gives a sample of Chuck D and Flavor Flav's black radical commentary on social issues that will be more pronounced on *It Takes a Nation of Millions to Hold Us Back*. Boogie Down Productions releases *Criminal Minded*. BDP's DJ Scott La Rock is killed this same year.

1988　*Yo! MTV Raps* is born. The show is so popular that it is soon split into a weekday afternoon format, hosted by Ed Lover and Dr. Dre, and a two-hour Saturday night format, hosted by Fab 5 Freddy. The show features rap videos, interviews with rap artists, skits, commentary, and trivia about the artists from the hosts. The show is one of MTV's most successful shows, running for seven years. It serves as an outlet for rap stars to promote their records to a large audience.

1988　Will Smith and DJ Jazzy Jeff win the first Grammy presented for rap music. The song "Parents Just Don't Understand" goes gold. Will Smith and DJ Jazzy Jeff go on to record several albums together that receive numerous awards. They are known for their fun-loving party raps and produced mostly dance hits, although Jeff is considered a turntable pioneer (he invented the chirp scratch and was the first to record a transform scratch). Their albums *Rock the House* and *He's the DJ, I'm the Rapper* also feature beatboxing from Ready Rock C. Together, Jeff and the Fresh Prince go on to star in a television sitcom, *The Fresh Prince of Bel Air*. Smith later stars in films such as *Independence Day* and *I, Robot*.

1988	N.W.A.'s *Straight Outta Compton* becomes a breakthrough gangsta rap album. The album is released by Priority Records but is not supported commercially. Independently, the album sells over 2 million copies underground. MTV does not support the album due to its controversial subject matter. Songs such as "Fuck tha Police" and "Straight Outta Compton" are regarded as threats to law enforcement. The group's gangsta status is solidified with this album based on their subject matter of violence, guns, and antigovernment rhetoric.
1989	Queen Latifah's *All Hail the Queen* debuts. "Ladies First" becomes an anthem for women's rights, projecting a feminist agenda and demanding respect. The song features guest vocals from a British MC, Monie Love.
1989	De La Soul releases *3 Feet High and Rising*. Their eclectic sound samples from country, folk, and rock music and their vibe of love, peace, and knowledge gets them labeled "hippies" and offers an alternative to gangsta rap. They are part of the Native Tongues collective with artists Afrika Bambaataa, Monie Love, Queen Latifah, the Jungle Brothers, and A Tribe Called Quest, to bring positive Afrocentric lyrics to the forefront of hip hop music with hits such as "Me Myself and I."
1990	The Miami group 2 Live Crew releases the album *As Nasty as They Wanna Be*, which is the first album in America to be declared legally obscene. Their song "Me So Horny" becomes a hit. The group's albums receive parental warning labels for sexually graphic content. Their use of the Roland-808 drum machine lays the foundation for the Miami bass sound and much of Southern rap music. 2 Live Crew member Luke Skyywalker (Luther Campbell) is sued by director George Lucas for using the name of a Star Wars character as his stage name. He is forced to change his name to Luke for performances.
1990	Vanilla Ice becomes one of the most successful white rappers in a genre of music dominated by African Americans. His song "Ice Ice Baby" is the best-selling rap record of the year, selling over 15 million copies and pushing MC Hammer out of the top spot on the charts. The song is nominated for a Grammy, but fans turn on Vanilla Ice after journalist Ken Parish Perkins exposes

lies in his official SBK Records artist biography. Ice later appears on reality television programs such as VH-1's "The Surreal Life."

1991   Death Row Records is founded by Suge Knight and Dr. Dre in Los Angeles, California. The label houses some of hip hop's biggest stars, such as Dr. Dre, Snoop Dogg, Tupac, MC Hammer, and many others. Suge Knight becomes famous for his ruthless business savvy and is feared in the music industry because of his alleged unethical business practices. Dr. Dre and Suge work together until Dr. Dre leaves the label to pursue other endeavors in 1996.

1991   A Tribe Called Quest releases its sophomore album, *The Low-End Theory*, a fusion of rap, jazz, and R&B. Their positive style is deemed an alternative to much of the violent and misogynist lyrics in rap music at the time. The popular group joins artists such as De La Soul, Digable Planets, and Arrested Development in creating progressive, positive, and political rap music without gratuitous sex, violence, or obscenities.

1993   Dr. Dre's *The Chronic* goes platinum. Though Dr. Dre had introduced his new protégé Snoop Doggy Dogg on the song "Deep Cover" from the *Deep Cover* soundtrack, *The Chronic* catapults Snoop to fame and solidifies Dr. Dre's post-N.W.A. career as a producer and MC. The album's success sparks a beef with Dre's former N.W.A. bandmate Eazy-E, who disses Dre and Snoop on his EP *It's On (Dr. Dre 187um) Killa*.

1993   Conservative activist C. Delores Tucker begins her boycott of rap music. Tupac Shakur and Ice Cube fight back by attacking her in their songs. Reverend Calvin Butts boycotts gangsta rap at station WBLA in NYC.

1993   Wu-Tang Clan releases its debut album, *Enter the Wu-Tang (36 Chambers)*. In signing with RCA, the nine-member Wu-Tang Clan negotiates an unprecedented deal that allows each member to record freely as a solo artist outside the group's obligation to RCA.

1993   Queen Latifah's album *Black Reign* produces the hit "U.N.I.T.Y.," which wins a Grammy award for Best Solo Performance and positions Latifah as one of the most successful female MCs in hip hop history. She is a rapper, writer, producer, and model, and one of the first rap artists to star in her own television sitcom. Her show, *Living Single*, airs for five years. She also wrote and produced the show's theme song and served as an executive producer. The show opened up opportunities for Latifah to become one of the most sought-after actresses in

	Hollywood. In 2004 she departs from rapping to record a jazz album that also receives critical acclaim.
1994	Tupac Shakur is shot five times in the lobby of a recording studio in New York. Tupac survives, and blames his shooting on Notorious B.I.G. and Bad Boy Records. His shooting starts a rivalry between Bad Boy Records and Tupac's label, Death Row. The tensions continue to escalate between the two labels and their artist, resulting in several battle songs between artists such as Tupac, Biggie, and others.
1994	The Atlanta-based rap duo Outkast release their debut album *Southernplayalisticadillacmuzik*. The group consists of Big Boi (Antwan Patton) and Dre (Andre Benjamin). The two artists are known for their eclectic style of dress, their creative use of samples, and retro references to groups like Parliament Funkadelic, Prince, and Sly and the Family Stone. Their original sound, which incorporates Southern drawl, regional references to local color, and fun pop culture samples, marks a break in bicoastal hip hop sound and ushers in a new Southern sound for rap, which influences groups such as Goodie Mob, Joi, and Bubba Sparxxx.
1995	Eazy-E dies of AIDS in Los Angeles, California. The rapper enters the hospital complaining of chest pains and breathing problems and is diagnosed with an advanced form of AIDS. After suffering from AIDS-complicated pneumonia, he slips into a coma and dies just days after he is admitted.
1996	Tupac Shakur is shot in Las Vegas, Nevada while riding in a car with Death Row Records owner Suge Knight. Two men pull up on the car and shoot at the passenger's side where Tupac is riding. Tupac is shot four times and Suge Knight receives minor injuries. The two are rushed to a local hospital where Tupac dies six days after the shooting. A number of conspiracy theories surround the shooting, including Knight's involvement in the murder and Tupac's faking his own death.
1997	Notorious B.I.G. is killed in a drive-by shooting. Biggie was leaving a party hosted by Vibe Magazine. Though many conspiracy theories have linked his death to the East Coast versus West Coast hip hop rivalries, no evidence has been produced to support these claims. Smalls is considered today to be one of the greatest MCs in the history of hip hop music. He is survived by his wife, singer Faith Evans, who sang the chorus on his hit "One More Chance."
1999	Eminem releases *The Slim Shady LP,* produced by Dr. Dre. The album goes multiplatinum and marks the beginning of a long

history of collaboration between Eminem and Dr. Dre, including *The Marshal Mathers LP* in 2000 and *The Eminem Show* in 2002. Eminem goes on to produce work for several other artists signed to Aftermath including 50 Cent, Missy Elliot, and D-12. Eminem creates his own label, Shady Records, as a result of his success, all under the umbrella of the Interscope records empire.

1999 — Lauryn Hill is the first female hip hop artist to be nominated for ten Grammy awards. Her album *The Miseducation of Lauryn Hill* (1998) wins Album of the Year. She wins five of her ten nominations. On February 9, 1999, she also is the first rapper to grace the cover of the politics and news weekly *Time* magazine, dedicated to "The Hip-Hop Nation." Hill is later sued by groups of songwriters and producers who worked on the album and were not properly credited.

2000–2001 — After years of hip hop beefs being solved with bloodshed, Jay-Z and Nas take things back to the old school and fight with MC skills. After one of Jay-Z's MCs, Memphis Bleek, puts out a sound strikingly similar to Nas's, a war of words ensues. Nas, the senior of the two rappers, checks the new MC, takes offense, and the battle is on. Jay-Z steps in for Bleek and the fight turns to Nas and Jay-Z battling for the title King of New York. Nas wins by popular vote at a local NYC radio station.

2003 — Eminem is the first hip hop artist to win an Oscar. His song "Lose Yourself" from the movie *8 Mile* wins in the Best Song category. He does not attend the awards. Eminem plays the lead role in the film based on his life growing up in Detroit. The film is produced by Brian Grazer, who also produced the hip hop spoof *CB4* featuring Chris Rock.

2005 — Hip hop producer-turned-rapper Kanye West graces the cover of *Time* magazine's August 21, 2005, issue. He chronicles his rise to the top of the hip hop charts in 2004, his debut album *College Dropout*, which sold more than 3 million copies, and his relationship with Roc-a-fella Records. West is later nominated for ten Grammy awards in 2005 and wins three. He steals the show with a performance of his own death and resurrection staged while singing his hit "Jesus Walks." West produced for artists such as Jay-Z and Cam'ron.

2006 — Three 6 Mafia wins a Best Song Oscar for "It's Hard Out Here for a Pimp," featured in the film *Hustle and Flow*. The Memphis rap group is the only rap act in the category, the second rap group ever to win for Best Song, and the first African American group ever to win in the category. (Eminem won for "Lose Yourself" in 2003.)

2006　Lil' Kim gets a five-mic rating from *The Source* magazine for her album *The Naked Truth*. This is the highest rating for an MC. Kim begins a prison term for lying to a federal grand jury about a 2001 shooting.

© AP Photo/Henny Ray Abrams.

Kool Herc

Wayne Marshall

Few individuals can claim a life story that so closely parallels hip hop's narrative arc as Clive Campbell, better known as DJ Kool Herc. Often considered the movement's founding father and an innovator of the musical and cultural practices that have since swept the world, Kool Herc embodies hip hop's roots and routes, its booms and busts, its struggles and triumphs. From his childhood in Kingston, Jamaica, to his coming of age in the Bronx, from his rise as a streetwise, peerless DJ to his decline in the wake of hip hop's new forms and commercial success, from his drug addiction in the 1980s to his recent return as standard bearer and spokesman, Herc's tale can be read as a thread running through hip hop history. Although his story has been told and retold and sold many times over, often making it difficult to extract the truth from the myths, the representations, and the press releases, Herc has been generous in granting interviews over the years, and his myriad recollections, as well as those of his peers, provide a strong outline for understanding his role as an architect and inventor, as one who forged so many of the forms we recognize today as hip hop.

TRENCHTOWN ROCK: CLIVE CAMPBELL'S KNOTTY REGGAE ROOTS

Clive Campbell was born in 1955 in Kingston, Jamaica, the first of six children of Keith and Nettie Campbell. He spent his early childhood living in an area of the city known as Trenchtown, the same storied public housing scheme and concrete jungle that produced such reggae luminaries as Bob Marley, Peter Tosh, and Alton Ellis. Clive's father worked as a foreman at Kingston Wharf garage—a respectable, working-class job that eventually allowed the Campbells to move to Franklyn Town, a lower-middle-class neighborhood where the family had their own house and yard. It was while living in the government yard of Trenchtown, though, that Herc got his first taste of the powerful sound systems he would later emulate as a Bronx-based DJ.

Although Herc has at times denied the influence of Jamaican-style DJing on his own performance practice, arguing that the Bronx audiences he played for demanded a more local style, he has also acknowledged how being a witness to Kingston sound system dances deeply informed his sense of the power of music and of the DJ in particular—not to mention his sense of what was cool (e.g., suavely dressed, well-respected gangsters and rebellious, ratchet-knife-wielding rude boys), as much as that may have needed recalibration upon moving to the Bronx. When asked about his musical influences by a reporter for the *Jamaica Observer* (Jackson), Herc broke from his typical list of American performers and disc jockeys and instead named such Jamaican greats as Prince Buster, Don Drummond, the Skatalites, Big Youth, U-Roy, and sound system pioneer Clement "Coxsone" Dodd.

It was at these dances—or just outside them (since, due to his age, he often had to settle for spying through holes in the zinc fences that enclosed the dance halls)—where young Clive got his first glimpses of sound system culture. He would watch the sound systems' crews wheel in speakers and amplifiers on handcarts, the vendors set up their wares and stew up some curry goat, the gangsters and rude boys and dance hall queens strut their stuff before passing through the gate. But then, seeing was often less important than hearing the sound systems at work—and one need not get too close to hear the selectors and DJs do their thing. Whether Clive was sitting just over the fence or in his family's home down the road, there was no avoiding the engulfing sonic presence of the neighborhood dance. His body vibrating along with the heavy bass and his ears tickled by the well-designed systems' crisp highs and clear midrange frequencies, he developed a taste for the power and clarity of sound produced by the systems' custom-crafted components. Later, seeking to reproduce this aesthetic with his own system in the Bronx, Herc would distinguish himself from his contemporaries and vanquish his rivals.

Beyond hearing the sound of the systems, of course, Clive also heard the music they played, as well as their style of playing it. It is worth noting that Clive left Jamaica before the term *reggae* gained currency and before the style that it describes emerged from rocksteady, the soul-infused balladeer tradition that followed ska's lead out of American influences and into a distinctive Jamaican synthesis of foreign and familiar styles. So the music that Clive would have heard emanating from the dance halls in his youth comprised a mix of exciting, new local forms—often infused with the ebullience of independence, granted in 1962—and imported favorites, especially soul and R&B sides. Although Jamaican popular music increasingly expressed a localized aesthetic over the course of the 1960s, cover versions of American pop songs remained staples of the local recording industry, stylistic nods to rock, soul, and R&B abounded, and the sounds of black America never totally fell out of favor in the dance halls, though foreign-produced records no longer constituted the bulk of the sound system repertory as they had in the 1950s. Indeed, sound system performance practice, for all its uniqueness, can itself be traced to so-called foreign sources—in particular to African American singers and disc jockeys, though one might ask, given the prevailing cultural politics of the day, what would be considered foreign from a Pan-Africanist or Black Power perspective.

By the mid-1960s, Kingston's mobile sound systems had already eclipsed a long-standing tradition of live band performance in Jamaica. Although the island's talented musicians continued to contribute crucially to the creation of Jamaican music, after the rise of the sound systems many musicians found themselves working in recording studios to produce the very recordings that would be played at local dances. The success of the sound systems was due in part to the entrepreneurial acumen of early soundmen such as Coxsone Dodd and Duke Reid, both of whom parlayed their success throwing dances and parties into their own music industry mini-empires, building recording studios, pressing records (at first for dances and later for sale to the public), and establishing labels with international audiences and musical legacies that continue well into today's digital dance hall world. When Dodd first began playing the latest, hottest R&B records for patrons of his parents' liquor store, soon expanding the operation to a makeshift dance hall, what he was doing looked a lot like what Herc would do in the Bronx years later. And when Dodd hired King Stitt to talk over the records, shouting out friends and associates, bigging up the sound system itself, and exhorting the audience to dance and buy food and drinks, Stitt sounded a lot like Herc and his partner (and fellow Jamaican immigrant) Coke La Rock would later sound.

Of course, King Stitt's performances were steeped in the same Jamaican slang and patois poetics that Kool Herc and Coke La Rock would largely have to shed in order to reach their Bronx peers. And Stitt was called a DJ, not an MC—despite the fact that he rarely, if ever, operated the turntable. (In Jamaican parlance, the person who actually plays the records, cueing them up and pulling them up, is called the selector.) Stitt's designation as a DJ, though—and the continued use of the term DJ to describe a nonsinging vocalist in Jamaica—makes an important connection between Jamaican sound system practice, early hip hop performance, and the main influence that both forms share: African American radio disc jockeys and their jive-talking, rhyme-slinging, rhythm-rolling style. Having for years tuned into American radio broadcasts that could reach Jamaica from as far north as Memphis or Cincinnati, the earliest Jamaican DJs borrowed liberally from the smooth signatures, scat singing, and catchy cadences of radio legends such as New Orleans-based Vernon "Dr. Daddy-O" Winslow and his many followers across the South, not to mention such influential figures as Tommy "Dr. Jive" Smalls and Douglas "Jocko" Henderson. In something of an ironic twist, Herc and Coke La Rock would later synthesize what they had absorbed from these Jamaican versions of African American disc jockey performance with the New York–based descendents of the same models, including such white disc jocks as Wolfman Jack and Cousin Brucie, both of whom Herc cites as early influences on both his talkover style and his American accent. Rather than riding the beat with a constant flow of syncopated syllables as rappers have since the late seventies, Jamaica's DJs of the sixties and early seventies and hip hop's earliest DJs and MCs would pepper songs with short phrases, often in the form of rhyming couplets, employing the latest slang (including scat-filled routines), and often in a relatively free manner—that is, without relating too directly to the rhythm of the track playing on the turntable (but frequently connecting to the track's theme or to specific lyrics or connotations the song may have).

Thus Herc's exposure to American music far preceded his actual move to the United States at age twelve. In addition to hearing popular R&B and soul songs on the radio and at sound system events (never mind Jamaican versions of these songs and styles), he also heard such music at home, for his father's collection included records by Nina Simone, Nat King Cole, and country singer Jim Reeves, while his mother had been sending the family the latest James Brown and Motown records, among other soul and pop fare, since she moved to New York in the mid-sixties. Like many a Jamaican migrant, Nettie Campbell was also sending money to her family, working as a dental technician while attending nursing school. She would soon send for her eldest son, who would eventually be followed by his siblings and father. When Clive arrived in New York on a cold winter night in 1967, he may not have realized how useful his practice sessions with his parents' records would turn out to be.

THE BOOGIE-DOWN BRONX AND CLIVE'S KOOL NEW ACCENT

Although the number of West Indian residents grew steadily in New York during the late sixties and throughout the seventies, due in part to British anti-immigration acts passed in the sixties and the U.S. 1965 Immigration Act, which abolished national origins as the basis for immigration legislation, Clive Campbell's experience shows that a critical mass had not yet crystallized so that borough culture could reflect such foreign infusions as Jamaican-ness or so that notions of blackness could include Anglo-Caribbean or Latin Caribbean versions. Far from the aura of quasi-exotic cool that it carries today, being Jamaican in the Bronx during the 1970s carried such a stigma that some young immigrants found it better to conceal their backgrounds. Not only would Clive have to lose his accent to fit in among his new peers, he would have to lose his "hick" clothing as well, including the boots, or "roach killers," for which he was ridiculed at school. Although Clive denies that he ever hid his Jamaicanness, he puts the situation in perspective by recalling a particularly telling example of how this harassment would play out in his new neighborhood: "At that time [the early 1970s], being Jamaican wasn't fashionable. Bob Marley didn't come through yet to make it more fashionable, to even give a chance for people to listen to our music. . . . I remember one time a guy said, 'Clive, man, don't walk down that way cause they throwing Jamaicans in garbage cans'" (Chang 72). Of course, for a young man in a working-class family, adopting a new accent was, in a certain sense, a lot easier than finding a new wardrobe.

Having honed something of an American accent by singing along to his parents' records, Clive continued to mold his voice upon moving to the Bronx, tuning to the distinctively American enunciations of Cousin Brucie and Wolfman Jack as well as their African American contemporaries, including Chuck Leonard and Frankie Crocker, on such stations as WWRL, New York's most popular "black music" station at that time. Adjusting his accent to be intelligible to classmates, by the time he began attending classes and playing sports at Alfred E. Smith High School, few of his peers would have identified Clive as a Jamaican—or even thought about throwing him in a garbage can. Indeed, a prodigious weight lifter, a track medalist, and a fierce basketball player who could dunk the ball with ease, Clive Campbell, standing over six feet tall at this point, would soon be crowned with the first part of his new name: "Herc," short for Hercules.

The "Kool" part of Clive's new name arose from his early adventures as a graffiti writer. Running with a crew called the Ex-Vandals, alongside such soon-to-be legends as Phase 2, Super Kool, and El Marko, Clive originally adopted the tag Clyde as Kool since "Clive"—not an uncommon name in Jamaica—continued to serve as yet another marker of his foreignness. Because so many of his peers would call him by the more familiar Clyde, he eventually embraced it himself. And as seen in the name of fellow crewmember Super Kool, the term *Kool* (with a *k*) had already attained no small currency among Herc's peers. Clive himself identifies the special spelling with the cigarette brand that bears the same name and specifically with a television commercial for the brand that so exuded cool (with a *c*) that Clive was inspired to adopt the appellation. So "Clyde as Kool" morphed into "Kool Herc." It was a name both chosen by Clive and suggested by his peers, a name that seemed to symbolize Clive's new Bronx self, and a name—especially given its recognition value as a local graffiti tag—that would soon serve him well as a self-promoting DJ. (He would bill himself, and be billed, alternately as Kool DJ Herc, which—as evidenced by predecessors such as Pete DJ Jones—was a common way to designate oneself a DJ at the time, and as DJ Kool Herc, which is now the more conventional form. Similar to naming practices among reggae artists, one hears echoes of Herc in the names of subsequent DJs such as Kool DJ AJ and Kool DJ Red Alert.)

For all its modesty, Kool Herc's first party has become an event of mythic proportions. A back-to-school fund-raiser for his sister Cindy, it was held in August 1973 in the community center or rec room of the building where the Campbells lived: 1520 Sedgwick Avenue in the West Bronx. Knowing that her brother had DJ ambitions and, moreover, that he knew how to get the most out of their father's powerful PA system, Cindy asked Herc to DJ the party. In preparation, Herc bought about twenty new records to add to his small but growing collection. An astute observer of local party dynamics since his mother began taking him to events around New York in the late sixties, Herc had developed a fine sense of what a young Bronx crowd would want to hear. This did not stop him, however, from attempting to represent his roots by dropping some of the "big tunes" that would have sent a dance in Kingston into a frenzy. But at that time in New York, a time when West Indian immigrants could be singled out for cruel harassment, Jamaican music was still shunned as too "country" or degraded as "jungle music" by many African Americans, a good number of whom, as first- or second-generation rural migrants from the South, still sought to distance themselves from a "hick" past. When Herc's reggae selections were received coolly, the savvy young DJ played the sort of soul and funk hits, full of Latin-tinged percussion breaks, that he knew would go over well among his West Bronx peers. Thus the same chameleonic process that Herc embraced to change his accent, his name, and his sense of self now extended to his performance practice as he adapted Jamaican sound system techniques for his funk-oriented audience, shouting out and bigging up the crowd in local slang over the records people wanted to hear. The strategy worked: The room filled with young dancers and a feeling of exuberance; Cindy made enough money to buy herself a new set of clothes; and a buzz went out across the West Bronx about DJ Kool Herc, his serious sound system, and his funky record collection.

As word spread, soon the Campbells were filling the rec room on a regular basis, and new possibilities opened up for the young entrepreneurs. The parties' attendees were—especially at first—relatively young, many of them high school students. As a new generation of kids who had largely managed to escape the height of gang violence in the Bronx but who inhabited a decaying, dangerous environment all the same, they were eager to find a relatively safe place for the sort of recreation Herc was offering. As less violent, though often no less competitive, style wars increasingly supplanted gang wars among Bronx youth, Herc's parties seemed to herald a cultural sea change for the borough. By the summer of 1974, Herc was throwing block parties on Sedgwick Avenue, attracting a sizeable, multigenerational following and often playing until daybreak. When the crowds grew too large for the block, Herc moved the party up to Cedar Park at 179th Street and Sedgwick, tapping into the city's power supply, and thus began the storied parties in the park that have been commemorated in hip hop lyrics ever since. By 1975, after a number of successful all-ages dances at the Webster PAL (Police Athletic League), Herc was playing regularly in clubs, beginning with a gig at the Twilight Zone so impressive in its draw that he was offered a weekly residency at the Hevalo, a venue that not long before had shooed Herc away for passing out fliers. As demand for Herc grew, he would go on to play at many of hip hop's early hot spots: the T-Connection, the Sparkle (formerly the Executive Playhouse), the Audubon, the Monterey Center, the Godfather's Club, and the Galaxy 2000. Notably, although most of the clubs had their own sound, Herc would always bring in his own indomitable system, which, in a nod to a Hanna-Barbera cartoon, he had dubbed the Herculoids.

Along with the Herculoids, Kool Herc was also usually accompanied by the Herculords, a group of supporters and performers who assisted him in various ways. Among the Herculords were such DJs and DJ/MCs (since they often handled both turntable and microphone duties) as Coke La Rock, Clark Kent, Timmy Tim, LeBrew, and the Imperial JC. Herc also had a number of women in the crew, among them some of the first female MCs: Pebblee-Poo, Sweet and Sour, and Smiley. Many of the Herculords—male and female—also doubled as dancers, providing an instant critical mass when it was time to get things going. This was the dawn of what became known in the eighties as break dancing, though the local term was b-boying, named after the b-boys (alternately defined as "break boys," "beat boys," "Bronx boys," "Boogie Boys," etc.) whom Herc would specifically encourage to dance when he played the popular, percussive breaks from the day's funk hits. Ever the embodiment of hip hop, Herc himself had background as a dancer, having gotten down in his younger days at such spots as the Puzzle, an experience which no doubt informed his selections as a DJ. (Once he assumed the role of soundman, however, he tended to stay behind the boards—except on occasions when he would watch the door to make sure the money was flowing as it should.) In addition to these multifaceted performers, the Herculords also included a number of devoted dancers, among them some of the earliest and most accomplished b-boys: Sau Sau, Tricksy, and the Nigger Twins (aka Keith and Kevin, later known simply as the Twins).

By 1976, Kool Herc and the Herculords/Herculoids were the toast of the Bronx. He had developed an iconic style to match his status, having graduated from wearing "roach killers" to sporting dress shoes and sharp slacks, leather jackets and fur coats, and, when he wasn't rocking a medium-sized Afro, a signature cowboy hat and big, round, dark sunglasses. On Herc's hulking frame, hip hop's larger-than-life fashion sense seemed to find the perfect model. Herc and his crew attracted audiences from across the borough and beyond, including some curious, young upstarts (such as Afrika Bambaataa and Grandmaster Flash) who would eventually challenge Herc's dominance. They would only do so, though, by beating Herc at his own game, for, by this point, he had set the template for what was beginning to be called hip hop.

HOW HERC BECAME A HIP HOP HERO: SOUND, SELECTION, AND STYLE

The three main qualities that came to define Herc's style—and, later, that of hip hop DJs more generally—were already present when he threw his first party: (1) his sound, that is, the system through which he played his records; (2) his selection, that is, the repertory of records he played; and (3) his style, that is, the way he played the records.

Herc's sound system was simply incontestable. Of course, he had the good fortune to have a father who decided to sponsor a local R&B group and so had purchased a Shure PA system and a mighty Macintosh amplifier to power it. When Herc figured out how to wire the system properly and really make it pump, his father was so grateful that rather than punishing him for playing with the prohibited equipment, he proposed a father-and-son business, allowing Herc to use the system for his parties while enlisting him to play between breaks at the R&B group's shows. With incomparably heavy bass, sparkling highs, and clear mids (i.e., middle-range frequencies), Herc would taunt any fellow DJs who dared show up at his parties, sometimes emphasizing the separate frequency bands while discussing his system's strengths. In terms of sheer sonic presence, none of Herc's colleagues could compete. He famously drowned out Afrika Bambaataa at an early battle, embarrassing and upstaging the East Bronx challenger. And although Disco King Mario was known for a similarly superb system, he traveled in different circles than Herc and his presence was rarely felt in the hip hop scene—with the notable exception of the time Mario loaned Bambaataa an amp for a battle with an easily vanquished

DJ Breakout. Having such a system also meant that Herc was not a DJ for hire: He was a soundman with his own system and he needed neither promoters nor club owners to help him do his thing, throw his parties, run his business.

Like many of his enterprising peers, Herc also invested a good deal of his early earnings back into his system, maintaining a state-of-the-art edge over his competitors. Although hip hop's myth of origins often emphasizes the crushing poverty of the Bronx and the resourcefulness of young people who, abandoned by the state and the system, made do with what was available, such a story also tends to downplay the degree to which hip hop's pioneers borrowed and hustled and saved in order to obtain what they needed to make their art and their living. Often what they needed, such as turntables and sound systems, was not easily available and did not come cheap. It was largely through hard work, family assistance, and entrepreneurial acumen that such trailblazers as Kool Herc built a system, a culture, and, if so fortunate, a stream of steady revenue.

If anything could rival Herc's sound system, it was his impeccable record selection. Herc quickly earned a reputation as a DJ with singular taste. Rather than the commercial confections that found favor on the radio and in the clubs throughout the seventies, Herc played more obscure records: good, hard, funky music that, for him and his neighbors, seemed to tap more directly into the zeitgeist. It was no coincidence that the music Herc and his peers wanted to hear was the music of Black Power, of militant pride, and of continued calls for social and economic justice in the post-Civil Rights era. Notably, these were not the songs one typically heard at that time on the radio, even on "black radio," which increasingly devoted its programming to disco and other styles associated with the upwardly mobile black middle class. As "black and proud" artists and bandleaders such as James Brown refined soul and R&B into a sparer, harder style that came to be called funk, tightening up the rhythms and focusing on riffs and repetition, one common feature of such songs that caught the imagination of the listening (and dancing) public—especially the b-boys of the Bronx—was the use of bare-bones, percussion-heavy, in-the-pocket drum breaks (i.e., solo passages during which the drummer would accentuate and play with but not diverge too far from the basic beat). Such breaks often took the place of the instrumental solo in rock or pop or jazz, occurring after the second chorus or the bridge, though sometimes they constituted a much larger portion of a track. Rather than a melody-based solo, as was conventional in previous pop genres, funk breaks were rhythm-centric passages, performed on drum kits and hand drums—typically, the bongos and congas that had been absorbed into American music via Latin Caribbean traditions—and occasionally featuring a bass line and/or regular riffs or hits from other instruments in the ensemble. These breaks—soon to be known around the Bronx as breakbeats—emerged as a staple of the genre, and b-boys would save their most impressive, acrobatic, and competitive routines for these explosive moments.

Always a keen observer of dance party dynamics, Herc noticed the excitement such breaks could generate. It was an insight that would lead to Herc's major aesthetic innovation: the isolation and repetition of the breaks. He began to seek out records simply for their breakbeats, regardless of whether the rest of the song was something one would want to hear. Like his Jamaican sound system predecessors, Herc attracted an audience that came specifically to hear his special selection of records. Similarly, one might compare Herc's battery of breakbeats to Coxsone Dodd's catalog of riddims, the instrumental tracks recorded at Dodd's Studio One in the late sixties that have served as the basis for an enormous number of reggae recordings. Herc's "breaks records" not only came to constitute what is essentially a b-boy canon, they also established the foundational repertory of the hip hop DJ. Because so many subsequent DJs sought out the same records they heard played by Herc, a great number of these tracks—many of them relatively obscure, though many of them hits—now stand as touchstones of early hip hop. Moreover, these same breaks became favorites of sample-based hip hop producers in the eighties and nineties, further affirming their status and ingraining their familiar rhythms and timbres in the hip hop imagination. Though it may take a hip hop or funk aficionado to recognize many of the names on these records, they have so deeply permeated the sound of modern hip hop, pop, and electronic music that few would find their strains unfamiliar. Some of Herc's favorites included the following: James Brown's "Give It Up or Turnit a Loose" (and other cuts from *Sex Machine*), Booker T and the MGs' "Melting Pot," Michael Viner's Incredible Bongo Band's "Bongo Rock" and "Apache," Babe Ruth's "The Mexican," Baby Huey's "Listen to Me," Dennis Coffee's "Scorpio," Mandrill's "Fencewalk," Jimmy Castor's "It's Just Begun," Bob James's "Take Me to the Mardi Gras," Aretha Franklin's "Rock Steady," and Rare Earth's "Get Ready."

Although Herc was known for letting records play before and beyond their breaks (sometimes, to the consternation of some observers, including the wack or undesirable parts, or all the way to the end of a track), perhaps his most lasting legacy is the practice of isolating and extending these breakbeats, transforming the fleeting, funky moments into loops that could last for many minutes. Eventually, by employing two turntables and two copies of a record, Herc developed what he called the merry-go-round technique. Dropping the needle back to the beginning of the break on one record just as the other was about to end, and repeating the process ad infinitum, Herc could keep a break—and a crowd of b-boys—breaking for as long as that particular section would work. Though the hip hop story has enshrined Herc as the first to isolate and repeat breakbeats in this way, it should be noted that Herc's technical proficiency was never exactly heralded, and so his focus on and liberation of the break should perhaps be understood more as an aesthetic than a technical achievement. Later DJs, such as Grandmaster Flash, influenced by Herc's model but more virtuosic in their control over the turntables and mixer, would improve on the formula, moving beyond drop-the-needle imprecision by backspinning, scratching, and cutting the records while cueing them via monitoring headphones, thus allowing one to mix breaks more seamlessly into one another and to isolate shorter and shorter sections for repetition(see sidebar: The Mixtape).

As an element of style, Herc's less-than-seamless stop-and-start approach to selection draws yet another connection to reggae performance practice.

The Mixtape
Shamika Ann Mitchell

There is a distinction between a private mixtape audiocassette, which is usually intended for a specific listener or private social event, and a public mixtape, or party tape. While the former usually has sentimental value (they are often given as expressions of affection), the latter consists of a live recording of a club performance by a DJ. Originally, cassette tapes (reel-to-reel, cartridge, and audiocassette) were dubbed by DJs to serve as a standby or segue between songs, but hip hop DJs forever changed the meaning and significance of the mixtape. In hip hop's founding years, there was no major media outlet for the music; radio stations or programs, magazines, television programs, and even professional recordings with a hip hop format were nonexistent. In response to this void, mixtapes became the platform to give the music exposure. Also, because these artists did not have recording contracts, the mixtapes became a source of revenue for the DJs. In the 1970s, pioneer hip hop DJs such as Kool Herc, Grandmaster Flash, Afrika Bambaataa, and DJ Hollywood would often sell recordings of their club performances via mixtapes. In addition to live performance recordings, some DJs would also make customized mixtapes. These custom mixtapes were often pricey (as high as $1 per minute in some cases) but highly collectible.

The mixtape begins its evolution in the late seventies and early eighties, and DJs started featuring rappers or MCs, sometimes featuring more rapping than DJ mixes of popular or original songs. Although in the 1980s hip hop was often labeled a fad, it was slowly becoming established as a recording industry with a legitimate fan base, which was to the advantage for hip hop DJs in particular. Hip hop–based media outlets were still slow to come (except for some major cities), which provided a market for mixtapes. It was not until the 1990s that making and selling mixtapes became a full-fledged business for the hip hop DJ. DJs were able to use their mixtapes to establish a brand or trademark of their music. While some DJs were a draw because of their mixing abilities, others were popular for their exclusive access to unreleased songs by artists. The first mixtape DJ to have a recording contract with a major label was Kid Capri, who released his first album, *The Tape,* in 1991 on the Cold Chillin'/Warner Brothers label. Several other DJs have since followed suit, including Funkmaster Flex, DJ Clue, DJ Kay Slay, and DJ S&S.

> For the discriminating consumer, mixtapes now come in varieties. In addition to the aforementioned exclusives, mixtapes will also highlight a DJ's ability to mix by blending beats from one song with the vocals from another. Freestyles or unscripted rhymes from a respected rapper are also popular attractions. Arguably, the most interesting evolutionary aspect of the mixtape is that it is now released only in CD format; however, the term *mixtape* remains a permanent fixture.

Whereas hip hop DJing—partly related to its roots in disco and the club scene—has since developed in a manner that privileges smooth, beat-matched transitions between tracks, reggae selecting has remained a style more defined by stark cuts and mixes. This is often the case even when a selector is juggling, or mixing sequentially, several songs on the same underlying riddim: when a popular song receives requests for a pull up, the selector rewinds it, usually suddenly and audibly, and lets it play again. Reggae-style selecting arises partly out of the constraints of using a single turntable, which is another reason that talkover-style DJs played an important role, filling in between songs and keeping the audience's attention rapt. Such an approach, like Herc's own orientation, prizes the effect that a popular song or "big tune" will have, seeking to repeat this effect again and again, rather than the effect that a series of smoothly mixed songs would achieve over the course of an evening. Further, one might hear Herc's emphasis on drum and bass, the isolated elements in so many breaks, as another connection to the reggae tradition, which has long cherished the power of sparse, heavy grooves. And, of course, the storied technique of soaking records in the bathtub to remove their labels in order to stop competitors from "stealing" one's signature songs is another practice that hip hop's pioneers borrowed from their Jamaican precursors. Indeed, it was Herc's father, well familiar with sound system lore, who advised him to protect the identity of his records in this manner and thus protect his cache with a clientele who came explicitly to hear Herc's special selections. (Grandmaster Flash gives a conflicting account, claiming he was the first hip hop DJ to use this technique.) Finally, Herc's use of effects, especially the echo and reverb he famously, and generously, applied to his and his fellow DJs' and MCs' vocals, also appears to have been inspired by sound system style and dub reggae aesthetics.

Despite paying respects to Jamaican originators and considering hip hop and reggae to be cousins, Herc himself has denied that reggae-style DJing informed his own approach (see sidebar: Hip hop and Reggae). When asked whether Jamaican "toasting," a term often used to describe early reggae DJ/talkover style, had any influence on his performance practice, Herc typically disavows any such thing, noting that he could not play reggae in the Bronx, and instead credits African American vocalists such as James Brown or Jalal Nuriddin of the Last Poets, the proto-rapper on *Hustler's Convention* (1973),

Hip Hop and Reggae
Wayne Marshall

Although histories of hip hop typically begin by acknowledging Jamaican-born Kool Herc as founding father, they often proceed as if Jamaicans stopped moving to New York or infusing hip hop with West Indian accents, raggamuffin flows, and dub aesthetics. A closer listen reveals a sustained, if not intensifying, relationship between hip hop and reggae. Not long after the release of the Sugarhill Gang's "Rapper's Delight" in 1979, dance hall DJs Welton Irie and General Echo recorded their own reggae-inflected versions of the song. And New York-based rappers were making militant references to "I and I" and Bob Marley as early as 1980 on Brother D and Collective Effort's "How We Gonna Make the Black Nation Rise." By 1985, rap's most commercially successful groups, such as Run-DMC and the Fat Boys, were incorporating reggae into their songs.

On 1987's *Criminal Minded*, Scott LaRock sampled classic riddims while KRS-One borrowed dance hall melodies for his verses and hooks and peppered his rhymes with a heavy dose of patois—in the process driving a number of reggae references deep into the hip hop lexicon. In the late 1980s, a slew of fast-rapping, flip-tongue DJs such as Daddy Freddy and Asher D were innovating a hybrid style called raggamuffin hip hop that would echo in the riggity-riggity rhymes of Brooklyn-based acts such as Das EFX and the Fu-Schnickens in the 1990s, not to mention 1990s pop phenoms and "miggity-macks" like Kriss Kross or LA-based acts like the D.O.C. and his producer, the "diggy-diggy" Dr. Dre. Considering that New York and Miami have been among the biggest sites of Jamaican-U.S. migration, it's not surprising to hear 2 Live Crew rap about *punaany* and reference various dance hall hits on their "Reggae Joint" (1989), but even such quintessentially West Coast releases as Dre's *The Chronic* (1992) features patois interludes and raggamuffin flows (listen to Daz on the chorus of "Lil' Ghetto Boy").

Top reggae releases have been staples in hip hop DJs' crates since at least the early eighties, but the early nineties saw a surge of dance hall hits enter the hip hop canon, including tracks by Chaka Demus & Pliers, Shabba Ranks, Super Cat, Cutty Ranks, and Buju Banton (many of whom also issued hip hop remixes of their most popular songs), while the early 2000s have introduced stateside listeners to hip hop–generation dance hall DJs such as Sean Paul, Beenie Man, Vybz Kartel, Sizzla, and Elephant Man (a number of whom have been signed to hip hop labels). In the wake of these crossover waves, hip hop artists have increasingly incorporated reggae style into their own local lingo. Again, certain centers of the Jamaican diaspora such as Brooklyn (and New York more generally) have played host to the most dance hall–derived flows. Reflecting their cities' reggae-infused soundscapes, acts such as Smif-N-Wessun (aka the Cocoa Brovaz), Heltah Skeltah (and the Boot Camp Clik more generally), Biggie Smalls, Busta Rhymes, A Tribe Called Quest, Black Star (especially Mos Def), Method Man, the Fugees, and a great many others—not all of whom have family connections to the West Indies—have borrowed both from reggae's stylistic bag of tricks and from its pan-African/anti-imperialist politics and/or rude boy/gangsta stance. With advances in travel and information technologies further facilitating exchange, hip hop and reggae will no doubt continue their long-standing relationship.

---

with providing the inspiration for rap's vocal styles. Even so, descriptions of Herc's and his Herculord comrades' vocalizations often paint them more akin to such reggae DJs as U-Roy than to the rhythm-riding MCs of the late seventies, such as Cowboy and Melle Mel, Busy Bee and Grandmaster Caz, who are generally acknowledged as among the first rappers. In contrast to these early MCs' beat-centric approach, strewing syllables on strong beats and syncopated accents alike and often rhyming on the final beat of each measure, Kool Herc and Coke La Rock were known for declaiming more freely over the beat. Employing short stock phrases, often in the form of rhymed couplets, and with improvised references to the situation at hand, Herc and the Herculords would shout out their own names and those of their friends, urge b-boys to dance, and project their larger-than-life, cooler-than-cool personas through the latest local slang and catch phrases: "Rock on, my mellow!" "To the beat, y'all!" "You don't stop!"

Although it seems likely that many of Herc's techniques were inspired by his acquaintance with Jamaican sound system style, similarities between his approach to DJing/MCing and reggae selector/DJ methods might, in the end, be better understood as a product of the common roots of the two—such as African American disc jockey practice—than any sort of intentional synthesis. It is possible both to underestimate and overstate the degree to which Jamaican practices informed hip hop, and so Herc's reluctance to embrace a reggae-centric myth of origins is instructive. Indeed, a number of hip hop historians have distorted the picture at times, falsely asserting the Jamaicanness of Grandmaster Flash (whose parents are Bajan) and Afrika Bambaataa (of mixed Bajan and Jamaican parentage) and even the Incredible Bongo Band (which featured Nassau-born bongo player King Errisson among the studio musicians assembled by bandleader Michael Viner, but no Jamaicans; interestingly, their "Apache" was re-issued by a Jamaican record label, perhaps sowing the confusion). Herc has not let his interviewers forget how difficult it was for a boy in the Bronx to be Jamaican in the early seventies. He has repeatedly underscored the Americanness and African Americanness of hip hop. Given his commitment to teasing out the truth amid such complex cultural circumstances, Herc's testimony offers the readers and writers of hip hop's narrative a number of insights into how hip hop's cultural politics and modes of expression differed from those of reggae, funk, rock, and disco, among other contemporary formations.

FROM OLD SCHOOL TO NEW GUARD: THE CHALLENGES OF COMMERCIALIZATION

In the early and mid-1970s, Kool Herc's style—from his mobile sound system to his break-laden selections to his slang-steeped talkover—distinguished him from local competitors as well as from the rapping-and-mixing disco DJs of the club scene, but as a new generation of DJs and MCs borrowed (and in some cases, improved upon) Herc's techniques and as hip hop proved to be a commercially viable music genre in its own right, Herc found himself increasingly out of the limelight and unable to adapt to or capitalize on what amounted to a serious shift for hip hop.

Perceptions of an underground/commercial divide in hip hop long predate the advent of recorded rap as popularized by the Sugarhill Gang's "Rapper's Delight" in 1979 (see sidebar: Undergound Hip Hop). Whereas disco DJ luminaries, such as Pete DJ Jones and DJ Hollywood, catered to an older audience in the clubs of the Bronx and other boroughs, Herc and his ilk were seen as representing the street, playing to young, high school age audiences in

---

Underground Hip Hop
H. C. Williams

In hip hop, the term *underground* is a medal of honor. Artists who sign with independent labels seek to avoid the corporatization of hip hop, and typically identify themselves as underground. For them, it is more important to be true to the music rather than selling out to the recording industry—though, admittedly, in the independent label there is still a world of merchandising and promotion. Hieroglyphics is an underground group but they still tour internationally and sell DVDs, T-shirts, and posters like commercial hip hop groups. In this sense, underground hip hop is just a smaller version of the corporate world, yet underground artists do tend to maintain more control over the production and marketing of their music, which affords them more control over their sound and style.

Underground artists focus on the presentation of personal style to gain clout and support as well as develop an audience. It is through style that they get their music into circulation rather than through music videos. It is crucial to understand that "underground" signifies not just rappers (MCs), but also DJs, break dancers, and graffiti artists. For these other artists, style is their key to that medal of honor. Unfortunately, even in the underground these other artists do not receive the same publicity as MCs.

One characteristic of underground hip hop is the rapper's approach to his or her topic, which is deeper than the ideas of rims, bitches, and hoes, and the shimmering bling around necks and fingers that are hot topics of recent commercial rap. However, just as the hardships of growing up poor surface in commercial rap, this idea of deprivation appears frequently in underground hip hop—but the underground artist does not mention privation offhandedly. If the MC discusses a harsh upbringing, it will likely be the focus of the track. Where mainstream MCs such as Jay-Z use their impoverished backgrounds to build rags-to-riches success stories, underground MCs often continue to promote their poverty as a sign that they remain true to the underground and haven't sold out.

Many underground artists might say they differ from the artists who appear on TV because they remain true to the roots of hip hop, or those musical and fashion styles or performance values that are old school. Along with serving as a way to showcase one's style, hip hop was originally the means by which the underprivileged usually male youth vented his frustration with the system and the way that system withheld from him and those like him the opportunity to achieve in a corporate world. Immortal Technique addresses this problem in "Harlem Streets" from the album *Revolutionary Vol. 2*. Non Phixion also express their contempt for the system in the album *The Future Is Now*; especially on the track "There Is No Future."

Although corporations have commodified hip hop, using rap to sell shoes and cell phones, some artists refuse the money and fame to keep alive the old-school ideals of hip hop. Whether the artist is keeping it real by refusing to cede control to the recording industry, maintaining loyalty to old-school hip hop, or staking his or her claim to the best rhyme style rather than the most expensive jewelry, underground hip hoppers are proud to be called so and would be offended if they were mistaken for supporters of commercial hip hop.

---

parks, community centers, and small, rough-and-tumble clubs in the Bronx. Not only did these two camps of DJs play to different clienteles in different venues, they also, by and large, played different records in a different manner while employing divergent styles of vocal engagement with the music and the audience. Although there was some overlap in terms of repertory, the shiny, schmaltzy disco selections popular on the radio and in clubs were, in the early hip hop imagination, generally opposed to funk's syncopated, percussion-heavy breakbeats. In contrast to Herc's pull-ups and needle drops, disco DJs favored smooth segues from track to track. They also tended to rap in a more mellifluous style, relating directly, if casually, to the steady beats of the music they were playing, and stringing together long, verselike presentations of their own sets of stock phrases rather than the freer, more fragmentary interjections of the Herculords and their streetwise colleagues. The next generation of hip hop DJs and MCs, led by Grandmaster Flash and Afrika Bambaataa and their respective crews, would synthesize these distinct stylistic strands, refining (if not outright commercializing) "street" style while bringing a harder edge to the smooth surfaces of club rap and disco DJing.

The combination would prove a winning one, in the mass market and the street alike, leaving behind originators such as Herc while moving hip hop into unforeseen territory.

Hip hop's second generation took the template that Herc had so solidly set and ran with it. Afrika Bambaataa followed in Herc's footsteps by amassing a record collection unparalleled in terms of eclectic, electric breakbeats, while Grandmaster Flash elevated the art of DJing far beyond merry-go-round needle dropping, building on the innovations of Grandwizard Theodore—generally credited with having discovered and refined the practice of scratching—in order to scratch, cut, and mix his selections with punch and precision, sometimes while spinning around or using body parts other than his hands. As other DJs and crews such as the L Brothers (featuring Grandwizard Theodore), DJ Breakout, and Baron (of Funky 4 fame), and Kool DJ AJ made the field an increasingly competitive one, showmanship and technical skill grew in importance as ways to distinguish one's act from the pack. MCs as well as DJs had to sharpen their skills and refine their acts to make a name for themselves, especially as the men and women on the microphones, rather than the turntables, became the new focal point for hip hop performance. As big name DJs such as Flash literally placed their MCs in the foreground at parties and shows, moving them from behind the DJ table to the front of the stage, MCs began to develop more elaborate routines. Relieved of any DJ duties, MCs developed their storehouses of shout-outs and rhymes into longer verses (both composed and improvised) and sometimes into full songs and group routines, enhanced with choreography, matching uniforms, and props of various kinds.

MCs became the focus of attention and the primary draw for audiences, outshining the DJs who, nonetheless, often retained the top name on marquees and fliers. Drawing on the smooth and steady rap style of disco DJs, the proto-rap spiel of the Last Poets and Gil Scott-Heron, various other American and African American oral traditions (including, as mentioned above, radio disc jockey practice), and refining and further stylizing the street style of the Herculords, MCs such as Cowboy and Melle Mel, who worked with Flash and later comprised half of the Furious Four, advanced the art of MCing in their performances, riding the beat more explicitly and developing increasingly sophisticated rhyme schemes and group routines. These more intricate, showy performances were often saved for later in the evening, with the early hours of the party still focusing on the DJ and his selections and featuring short, often improvised exhortations from the MCs.

Before long the number of MCs and crews of rappers exploded. Kid Creole and Scorpio rounded out the Furious Four before being joined by Raheim (who defected from the Funky 4 after losing a battle to Flash's crew) to become the Furious Five. K.K. Rockwell, Keith Keith, Jazzy Jeff (a different artist than Philadelphia's DJ Jazzy Jeff, who worked with the Fresh Prince), Rodney Cee, and Busy Bee made up the rotating cast known as the Funky 4 (or the Funky 4+1 when pioneering female MC Sha Rock joined them).

Grandmaster Caz, formerly known as DJ Casanova Fly, commanded the microphone and turntables alongside DJ Disco Wiz before forming a group called Mighty Force with Whipper Whip and Dot-a-Rock (both of whom would later help comprise the Cold Crush Brothers and then the Fantastic 5). Caz developed a strong set of rhymes and routines during this period, a number of which found their way into Sugarhill Gang's breakthrough single (including the line "I'm the C-A-S-A-N the O-V-A and the rest is F-L-Y," spelling Caz's former tag). As the story goes, Big Bank Hank, despite not being an MC himself, was approached by Silvia Robinson of Sugar Hill Records to record some of the rhymes she heard him reciting at a pizzeria where he was working. Because Hank was serving as a manager and promoter for Caz and Mighty Force, he already knew many of Caz's rhymes—as did many hip hop devotees at that time—and he had privileged access to Caz. Not realizing the record would be an enormous hit, Caz allegedly gave Hank free reign to pick through his rhyme book, and with their smash single the Sugarhill Gang soon outstripped all other MC crews in terms of notoriety. Some twenty years later, Caz would record "MC's Delight," an attempt to set the historical record straight.

Caz's influence as an MC did not stop with Sugarhill Gang's appropriation of his well-known rhymes, for his work with the Cold Crush Brothers served to push the art of MCing to greater heights of wordplay and into flashy, well-rehearsed routines. Invited by DJ Charlie Chase to help with auditions for Cold Crush, Caz was convinced to join the group himself. Alongside Charlie Chase, DJ Tony Tone, Easy AD, Almighty Kay Gee, and Jerry Dee Lewis (JDL), Caz helped forge a distinctive group style for Cold Crush, involving intricate, back-and-forth interplay between the MCs and melodic, sing-along passages that often found the members harmonizing together. The high theater of the Cold Crush Brothers' performances presented a formidable challenge to rival crews such as the Fantastic 5, and their rapid-fire, interlaced rhymes carried forward into the dynamic routines of such acts as Run-DMC—as well as more recent groups, such as Jurassic 5, who essentially serve as a living tribute to Cold Crush style.

The late seventies also saw the rise of a number of strong female MCs. Joining the eminent Sha Rock on the scene were Lisa Lee (who played with Bambaataa and who, along with Debbie D and Sha Rock would later form the trio Us Girls), Little Lee (who worked with DJ AJ), and Herc's mainstays Pebblee-Poo, Sweet and Sour, and Smiley. A few women got into the DJ business as well, among them DJ Wanda D (an early member of Bambaataa's Zulu Nation) and Pambaataa (who was ushered into the scene by Grandmaster Caz). Like many minority members of the early hip hop scene, such as Latinos and West Indians, female performers were sometimes subject to harassment or ridicule, but generally they were respected, protected, and promoted.

Even as Herc's prominence was waning with the ascension of new DJs and MCs, new styles and forms, he continued to enjoy success as a dominant force on the scene. Thoughout the mid to late seventies, while new doors were opening for hip hop's next generation, Herc was still regularly rocking parties with the Herculords and Herculoids. Indeed, even as some of hip hop's first recording stars were emerging, Herc was still earning more money by throwing parties than a gold-record-holding MC. There was little incentive, then, for Herc to get into the record business. Moreover, before hip hop recordings had proven successful as a commodity in themselves, it made little sense to someone like Herc or Flash to take the aesthetic leap of making a record out of other records. For originators such as Herc, hip hop was not something you could put on a record; hip hop was a party in the park, a social event, a practice rather than a product. Few thought the experience could translate to recordings at all, never mind into a commercially lucrative form. Thus, not only did upstarts such as Flash and Bambaataa present figurative and literal battles for Herc—who won a number of such battles before finally being outshined—but the advent of rap recordings sounded a death knell for the hip hop DJ more generally. Most early rap recordings did away with the DJ entirely, employing instead—as was traditionally the case in studios—a house band to replicate the breakbeat-derived accompaniments for MCs' routines. The recession of the very role of the DJ spelled serious trouble for Herc, and as hip hop moved further into the club scene, with some DJs booking themselves at multiple venues in a single evening, the days of the self-sufficient hip hop sound system seemed numbered.

The year 1977 stands as a watershed both for hip hop and for Herc. For one, it was the year of the great summer blackout in New York. By many accounts, the looting of stores specializing in electronics and audio equipment resulted in yet another explosion of competing crews, each with their own state-of-the-art systems. It was also the year that Herc was stabbed while coming to the aid of a friend at one of his own parties at the Sparkle. Sustaining several wounds to his side and his palm, Herc was hospitalized for weeks and admits to withdrawing from the scene for some time thereafter. He returned still serious about his business and about maintaining the vibe he had cultivated for so long, but by the early eighties things were changing in the world of hip hop. With a few rap hits on the charts and a humming media buzz around break dancing and graffiti, mainstream arrival—in both economic and cultural terms—seemed like a real possibility for hip hop, and the music and film industries displayed no little interest in exploiting the scene's vibrancy for commercial gain. Although he continued to sharpen his skills, collect the hottest breaks, and bring new talent into his crew, Herc never got involved with commercial recording. It is unclear, at any rate, whether he had the desire or the ability to do so: For Herc, hip hop was always about making a party move, not about showboating or vocalizing with a band of studio musicians. He was getting older, as was his audience, and the movement that he had helped to shape and form was now growing at a startling rate and going in unexpected directions.

HERC'S DECLINE AND FALL, CLIMB AND RETURN

In something of a symbolic turn, Kool Herc appeared as himself, complete with cowboy hat, tasseled jacket, and round, dark sunglasses, in the film *Beat Street* (1984)—the second attempt to market a movie about hip hop to mainstream America. Arriving in theaters shortly after *Breakin'* (1984), *Beat Street* was set in New York and clearly drew on the documentary-style realism of *Wild Style* (1982) and *Style Wars* (1983) even as it indulged in Hollywood cliches (see sidebar: *Wild Style*). Tellingly, Herc does not play an active DJ in

---

Wild Style
Shamika Ann Mitchell

Released in 1982, *Wild Style* is considered a cult classic, and is credited with giving hip hop larger exposure and introducing it to a new audience. Although the film centers on the lives of fictional characters, one particular draw to the film is its cast. Part documentary, part screenplay, the film's cast list reads as a Who's Who of old-school hip hop, and showcases notable pioneer hip hop figures who have achieved icon status. Legendary DJs Grandwizard Theodore and Grandmaster Flash make appearances, as do the famed rappers Busy Bee and Grandmaster Caz, the pioneering rap groups the Cold Crush Brothers, Fantastic Freaks, Double Trouble, and the breakdancing b-boy troupe the Rock Steady Crew. In addition to these key figures, the film stars as its protagonists the legendary subway graffiti artist "Lee" George Quinones and Sandra "Lady Pink" Fabara, the queen of the New York City graffiti scene (she was the only known female graffiti artist at that time). Graffiti masters Dondi, Zephyr, and Daze were also represented in the movie. An important highlight is rapper Fab 5 Freddy, who in conjunction with producer-writer-director Charlie Ahearn not only helped to create *Wild Style* but also plays the hip hop impresario Phade. The film has a documentary character in that the narrative follows these outlaw graffiti artists through New York City's train yards. To Ahearn's credit, he was able to film in the actual train yards after receiving permission from the New York City Metropolitan Transit Authority (MTA); this is a significant accomplishment, especially for an independent filmmaker.

Wild Style is the precursor of later hip hop films *Krush Groove* (1985) and *Breakin'* (1984). While both of these films achieved greater commercial success, the authenticity and integrity of the hip hop cultural depictions were both questioned and criticized. As commercial films, *Krush Groove* (Warner Bros.) and *Breakin'* (MGM) introduced hip hop culture to an even broader audience and were being shown in major movie theatres across the nation. However, *Wild Style*'s uniqueness comes from its grassroots status and the raw talent and energy of the featured artists, who, with the exception of a few, perform as themselves in the cast lineup. *Wild Style*'s soundtrack is still considered a classic as well.

the film so much as a broker of sorts, a manager of his own club, which is given a reggae-tinged title, the Burning Spear, and dressed up tiki-room style with graffiti-inspired placards interspersed among the South Pacific kitsch. Herc stands as a towering figure in the film, and he invests the role with proper authority. Upon being told that the aspiring DJ (and lead actor) deserves a shot at playing at the Burning Spear since he's "the best DJ in the Bronx"—an irony that would not have been lost on the man who previously claimed that title—Herc replies, curtly and pointedly, "Better be." Indeed, if no longer the "best DJ in the Bronx," Herc is portrayed in the film as a major tastemaker, and his name carries enough weight that when dropped to the manager of the Roxy, for whom the lead actor would also like to audition, it's enough to convince him to go see the young DJ play at the Burning Spear. Even so, it's clear that Herc's function in the film is to pass the torch to a new generation, endorsing the young, up-and-coming DJ rather than reigning as king of the scene. Perhaps his marginalization in the film's portrayal, despite Herc allegedly requesting—and receiving—a more prominent role, was appropriate: 1984 was the same year that the Stardust Ballroom played host to what many considered Herc's last jam. Hip hop had set sail, and Kool Herc, formerly the ship's captain, had missed the boat(see sidebar: Hip hop goes Hollywood).

Hip Hop Goes Hollywood
Wayne Marshall

Early representations of hip hop on film have proven seminal in shaping popular perceptions of what hip hop is all about. The first films featuring hip hop artists and practices not only exposed new audiences to graffiti, break dancing, DJing, and MCing, they also crystallized the very idea that these forms were linked together and comprised a cultural whole. Starring actual practitioners doing what they do best, *Wild Style* (1982) and *Style Wars* (1983) essentially served as documentaries and how-to manuals, providing an intimate look at the role hip hop, especially graffiti, played in the lives of young people in New York. These two films informed a spate of Hollywood productions that followed, most of which tended to cast actors in starring roles despite also featuring some b-boys and b-girls and a number of early rap stars.

Set in LA, *Breakin'* (1984) was Hollywood's first attempt to cash in on hip hop's sudden cultural cachet. Inspired by *Breakin' and Enterin'* (1983), a German-produced documentary on hip hop in Los Angeles, *Breakin'* offers a look at LA's vibrant and distinctive scene, especially with its focus on such regional dance styles as popping, ably demonstrated by Adolfo "Shabba-Doo" Quinones and Michael "Boogaloo Shrimp" Chambers. The plot revolves around the conflicts between the worlds of artistic dance and the new breed of competitive street dancers. Followed months later by a much derided sequel, *Breakin' 2: Electric Boogaloo*, Hollywood's first hip hop film would soon be bested by *Beat Street* (1984), Harry Belafonte's New York–based version of cross-class relationships and the power of hip hop style.

Opening with stark images of urban blight, *Beat Street* (1984) places its narrative more squarely in classic hip hop territory: New York City, especially the Bronx, complete with burned-out buildings and graffiti-covered trains. Despite some stylization, including "graffiti" painted by set designers, the film represents the era's style fairly well. The characters are dressed in the day's staples: Kangols, bomber jackets, track suits, Puma sneakers. When an aspiring DJ lands a gig at a fictional club run by Kool Herc, he meets an uptown choreographer, and a class-conflicted courtship ensues. For all its strengths, including some riveting b-boy battles between the Rock Steady Crew and the New York City Breakers, *Beat Street* suffers from faults similar to *Breakin'*, presenting a slightly cartoonish, canned picture of hip hop that condescends as it celebrates and affirms stereotypes even as it critiques prejudice and inequality.

Representing a cultural and commercial transition for hip hop, *Krush Groove* (1985) shifted focus from underground parties and public spaces to stars and studios, and its drama revolves around economic exploitation more than class prejudice. The film was a promotional vehicle for Def Jam Records: it featured performances by the label's star roster of Run-DMC, Kurtis Blow, LL Cool J, the Fat Boys, and the Beastie Boys. With its myth-making and savvy self-promotion, *Krush Groove* may, in some sense, best represent the hip hop film, proving the potential of the music-video-meets-biopic—a popular format for such films ever since, from *Streets Is Watching* (1998) to *8 Mile* (2004).

Herc's story takes a dark detour in the mid to late eighties. He began selling and smoking crack cocaine, developed an addiction to the powerful drug, and found himself living in a building known as the Hallways of Horror. In 1987, he was arrested for selling to an undercover agent and spent some time in jail. "My father had died, my music was declining and things were changing," Herc recounts, "I couldn't cope, so I started medicating. I thought I could handle it, but it was bigger than I was" (Gonzales 150). Some of the same rap recordings that would document a bleak, crack-ravaged New York—such as Boogie Down Productions' *Criminal Minded* (1987)—would also represent hip hop's strongest embrace of reggae style to date. A lot had changed since the early seventies, including the arrival of hundreds of thousands of Jamaicans in New York, among them the notorious drug-running posses whose cool-and-deadly pose would provide new images of and ideas about Jamaicanness. By the late eighties, it seemed quite possible, if not persuasive, to represent the Bronx in a patois tongue. Ironically, Herc embraced crack right alongside his hip hop brethren but missed out on the open celebration of the very heritage he had decided to downplay years before.

Eventually, Herc pulled himself out of his slump and began seeking the statesman status he deserved. He literally cleaned himself up, appearing clean-shaven with short hair (but still those dark glasses), and gradually began growing some small dreads. As the wider world came to recognize hip hop as a vibrant, brilliant, poignant set of cultural forms, Herc once again found himself credited as a founding father—though, in the early days of such recognition, such praise was more commonly lavished from Europe or Japan than in the United States. Herc's status climbed steadily over the course of the nineties, and he found himself the subject of numerous interviews, a prominent guest at conferences, and, in something of a twist, a coveted collaborator on some commercial recordings. Billed as the Master of Ceremonies, Herc appeared on several cuts, including the intro and outro (called "Herc's Message"), on *Super Bad* (1994), an album by Public Enemy's Terminator X. Significantly, the liner notes refer to Herc as "The Godfather and Founder of Hip Hop," signaling a grander acknowledgment of the role Herc played. A few years later, the hip hop–influenced "big beat" duo, the Chemical Brothers, invited Herc to open one of their concerts in London. Herc's voice, seemingly sampled from his live set, figures prominently on a track called "Elektrobank" from the group's massively popular second album, *Dig Your Own Hole* (1997). And although Herc's role on the track is to introduce the Chemical Brothers in classic MC style, the recording surely served to introduce Herc to a new generation of listeners around the globe.

Herc may still be better known abroad, but his stateside profile has been rising with the spate of hip hop retrospectives now regularly appearing on television, radio, and in book form. With his hair grown to shoulder length and his physique as Herculean as ever, he still casts a long shadow. Occasionally wearing a Jamaican-style tam to contain his dreads, Herc's intermittent slippage into a West Indian lilt seems a lot less out of place than it once might have. Like his old-school comrades, Flash and Bambaataa, Kool Herc occasionally plays shows as a DJ, appearing as a guest of honor at various events and concerts in major cities around the United States and the world. In 1999, for instance, Herc performed at a CMJ (College Music Journal) convention party at CBGB's in New York, apparently playing—among other selections—a fair amount of classic eighties house records, showing that he's still got open ears, unconventional tastes, and deep crates. Despite being so sought after, however, Herc has continued to live humbly since his fall from the top of the Bronx party scene. Upon hearing in 2004 that Herc was working at Federal Express to earn a living, the Roots' Ahmir "?uestlove" Thompson proposed a foundation, established by successful hip hop artists, to offer substantial awards to hip hop's undercompensated pioneers.

If proper credit (especially in monetary terms) has been a long time coming, Herc is at least now widely recognized as the trailblazer he is, and he has increasingly found himself serving as a spokesman for the old school and for hip hop more generally. Among other public acknowledgments, Herc was the first to be recognized at VH1's "Hip Hop Honors" ceremony in 2004. He wrote the introduction to Jeff Chang's *Can't Stop Won't Stop: A History of the Hip-Hop Generation* (2005) and appeared at several tour stops to talk about the book, his past, and hip hop's present. He appeared on NPR's *Fresh Air* in the spring of 2005, discussing his role as "father of the breakbeat" with Terry Gross, and he had a cameo in the video for Jin's "Top 5 (Dead or Alive)" (2005), a song that pays homage to hip hop's greats and begins with the line: "It started out with the legendary Kool Herc." Back in Jamaica, Herc has also been acclaimed for his accomplishments, serving as yet another proud symbol of the small island's big influence. In addition, at a time when, due to its cultural prominence, hip hop–related gear can generate as much revenue as record sales, Herc has endorsed and promoted since 2005, alongside fellow pioneers Afrika Bambaataa, Grandmaster Caz, Melle Mel, Busy Bee, and Sha-Rock, an old-school-oriented clothing line, Sedgwick and Cedar, named after the intersection where he threw many of his most storied parties. In early 2006, Herc was among the hip hop luminaries donating records, turntables, and other objects of significance to an exhibit to be housed at the Smithsonian's National Museum of American History.

The consensus around Kool Herc's position as hip hop's most eminent architect is, ultimately, perhaps the greatest tribute he could hope to receive for so strongly shaping one of the most powerful and popular cultural movements of the modern era. Clive Campbell's life story provides a parable parallel to hip hop's own. His name lives on—and not just in song. The historical record will remember Herc not only as hip hop's founding father but as one of its shining sons.

See also: Grandmaster Flash, Eric B. & Rakim, Native Tongues

WORKS CITED

Chang, Jeff. *Can't Stop Won't Stop: A History of the Hip-Hop Generation.* New York: St. Martin's Press, 2005. 7-85.

Gonzales, Michael A. "The Labors of Hercules." *The Source* 100 (January 1998): 144-150.

Jackson, Kevin. "DJ Kool Herc: Hip-Hop Pioneer." *Jamaica Observer.* 8 October 2004. <http://www.jamaicaobserver.com/lifestyle/html/20041007T170000-0500_67281_OBS_DJ_KOOL_HERC__HIP_HOP_PIONEER_.asp>.

FURTHER RESOURCES

Davey D. "1989 Interview with DJ Kool Herc." *Davey D's Hip-hop Corner.* 19 May 2003. <http://www.daveyd.com/interviewkoolherc89.html>.

Fricke, Jim and Charlie Ahearn. *Yes Yes Y'all: The Experience Music Project Oral History of Hip-Hop's First Decade.* Cambridge, MA: Da Capo Press, 2002.

Hebdige, Dick. *Cut 'N' Mix: Culture, Identity, and Caribbean Music.* London: Comedia, 1987.

Katz, David. *Solid Foundation: An Oral History of Reggae*. New York and London: Bloomsbury, 2003.
McCord, Mark. "Kool DJ Herc vs. Pete DJ Jones: One Night at the Executive Playhouse." *Wax Poetics* 17 (June/July 2006): 84-94.
Stolzoff, Norman. *Wake the Town and Tell the People: Dancehall Culture in Jamaica*. Durham and London: Duke University Press, 2000.
Waters, Mary. *Black Identities: West Indian Immigrant Dreams and American Realities*. New York: Russell Sage Foundation Books, 2001.

© S.I.N/Alamy.

Grandmaster Flash

H. C. Williams

It is rare to come across a true hip hop fan who is not familiar with the name Grandmaster Flash. One member of hip hop's holy trinity (along with DJ Kool Herc and Afrika Bambaataa), Flash helped create the phenomenon that came to be known as hip hop. These pioneers' efforts ignited the cultural dynamite that hip hop has become, blasting into all aspects of corporate, artistic, and even philosophical life. Break dancers had their boomboxes and flattened cardboard, graffiti artists had their backpacks full of Krylon spray paint, and MCs, or rappers, provided the verbal pyrotechnics. But hip hop's roots lie in the realm of the DJ and his turntables. Born Joseph Saddler, Grandmaster Flash was a whiz with electronics, and since he could not afford higher quality equipment, he built his first sound system himself, finding more basic elements and tweaking them to improve performance. Because he knew electronics so well, he was able to modify his wheels of steel and dazzle listeners with breakthrough techniques, manipulating the records in original ways. Some argue that his apprentice, Theodore Livingston (Grandwizard Theodore) invented the scratch, but without Joseph's scientific approach to turntablism (another term for DJing), including prescratching techniques like cutting and backspinning, Theodore would not have made the chirping noises that became scratching. In this sense, Flash is the father of the scratch, which has become a movement of its own in the DJ world. Flash was also the first DJ to introduce acrobatics during his set, manipulating the records from behind his back, using his feet or his mouth on the mixer, and performing other outlandish physical feats that are known today as body tricks. These fancy, flashy movements enriched the audience's experience and may have influenced the development of the break dancer. After more than thirty years, the Grandmaster continues to influence the world of hip hop in many ways, from educating striving young musicians to insisting that hip hop should incorporate all musical genres and radiate love. His technical savvy and modifications, his larger-than-life personality on stage, and his desire to push hip hop to (and beyond) its limits—all these aspects of his style and career make Flash an indispensable icon of the genre. Without his myriad contributions to the movement, especially to turntablism itself, hip hop would not be the international cultural phenomenon that it is today.

HERE'S A LITTLE STORY THAT MUST BE TOLD: JOSEPH SADDLER'S FIRST LOVE

Joseph Saddler was born on January 1, 1958, in Barbados. He was the fourth child of five, and the only boy. When he was still a baby, his family relocated to the Bronx in New York City. Because he was so young, he did not enter America with the telltale signs of his Caribbean roots, so he did not have to practice speaking without an accent, modify his dress, or undergo any of the other changes that Clive "DJ Kool Herc" Campbell had to in order to fit in with his peers. No one could sense Joseph's hick roots, so he escaped the ridicule Clive Campbell faced as a young man in the Bronx.

Joseph may have avoided trouble from his prejudiced schoolmates, but home was an entirely different matter. While generally well behaved, Joseph had an insatiable curiosity that often left him with a sore backside. But if he had not continued his mischief as soon as the bruises healed, the man we know as Grandmaster Flash might not exist.

Whenever his father left for work, he always warned Joseph that he had better stay away from a particular closet in the Saddler home or he would have trouble sitting for a few days (Miller 72). This seems like saying, "Whatever you do, don't touch that big red button over there!" When humans are faced with these situations, we always seem to desire to do the one thing we are not supposed to do. This is what happened in Joseph Saddler's case. Curiosity, combined with the willingness to have his hide tanned, compelled Joseph to plunder the secret contents of the closet. He would retrieve a chair from the kitchen so he could reach the doorknob (which speaks to his age at the time) and open the creaky door to discover piles of neatly arranged, categorized records, pristine in their original sleeves. Ebullient, Joseph would choose from a variety of artists, such as Frank Sinatra, Aretha Franklin, Led Zeppelin, Glen Miller, James Brown, and Thin Lizzy. He would slide records from various genres onto his father's phonograph and, amid his mother's reminders of what would happen if his father caught him, dance all over the living room, lost in the loose rhythms, pulsating beats, and provocative vocals.

Joseph intended to put away all the records before his father returned from work, but he rarely put them back in the same order, so he received his promised beating. One day Joseph dropped several 78s, which shattered into many irreparable pieces. His father's blows had extra zeal that night. Yet Joseph continued to raid the collection, in love with the vinyl circles and the magic he felt when the needle of the phonograph slid along their grooves. The impetus for sneaking into that closet—curiosity—also drove the other half of Joseph's first love. His father's fancy stereo captivated him, and what most fascinated him was the small red light in the bottom center of the system that glowed when the stereo had power. This tiny light triggered Joseph's love of and intense interest in electronics—without which he would never have made the technological innovations he produced once everyone knew him as Flash. When he was a little older, Joseph often sneaked into his sister's room, disassembling her hair dryer and any other small appliances he could find, trying to figure out which parts served what function, and then attempting to put them back together. Sometimes he was not successful. When he failed to return the appliances to their original condition, his sister complained to their parents that he had rummaged through her things because certain electronics mysteriously quit working.

Rather than punish him for secretly dissecting the small appliances, his parents realized his budding passion could become a solid source of income, so they enrolled him in Samuel Gompers Vocational High School where he could discover how appliances work without forcing his sister to walk around with wet hair. He soon progressed to bigger, more complex equipment, though he was wise enough to search junkyards around the Bronx for appliances that were already inoperative so he would not risk breaking the family's stove or refrigerator. Joseph had latched onto a practical interest in electronics that he would build into a career, but no one in the Saddler family could have possibly predicted just how he would decide to put his knowledge of electronics to use.

GOOD TIMES: THE BLOCK PARTY, DJ KOOL HERC, AND SADDLER'S FIRST SHOW

When Joseph was fifteen, he began attending block parties in the neighborhood. At the time, DJ Kool Herc was the only one using the turntable as an instrument. Herc played the turntables by cutting, mixing, and looping sections from different records in front of a live audience. There were DJs in discotheques all over New York, but they typically played popular music and did so without rearranging or altering the songs at all. Kool Herc was different—he would look for obscure records of all genres in search of a song or part of a song that was funky enough to make the crowd get down. Later, he, Flash, and Bambaataa all made separate and regular trips to Downstairs Records on Forty-third Street to go through the process that became known as digging (George 2004, 107). Of course, they each went to other stores as well, but they still sought the same unusual music. In the record stores they would flip through crates of records, sometimes for hours, to find any album, in any genre, that might contain something worth using in a routine, even if it were a short break in one song. But Herc was the only artist playing unfamiliar tracks for the crowds in the early seventies—so he may be more of a godfather of hip hop than a father. He was the only one doing hip hop; the other members of the trinity were only just beginning to understand the art and form their own identities as DJs.

The block party of the 1970s was a phenomenon in itself. It was free to everyone, and children as well as seniors attended with equal enthusiasm. The DJ would bring his sound system and beg someone with a first-floor apartment to let him use it as a power source. If the tenant refused, the DJ and his crew would break a lamppost and have unlimited electricity—courtesy of the City of New York. The party would last at least six hours, and although today's police officers are suspicious of large outdoor parties, the officers at the time loved the gatherings because everyone was in the same place. The entire community was involved. A local grocery store would provide free concessions. Big-time drug dealers would bring hot dogs and fruit juice. The stickup kids, who liked to prove their masculinity by stealing anything and fighting everyone, would take the day off. Instead of settling disputes with physical violence, young men (and a few women) would form crews and use dancing to battle over territory, over the claim to superiority, or sometimes just to fool around or let off steam. The small house shows and neighborhood block parties provided a safe place to hang out for teens and twenty-somethings, a place where they could let down their guards, drop the aggressive facial expressions, and chill as they jammed to the beats. At the block parties they had nothing to prove in terms of the gang violence that climaxed right before these parties became popular. Everyone was there to enjoy the music, the dancers, the MCs, and if anyone brought beef, they were expected to settle it through a hip hop battle. Occasionally, breaking crews would get carried away during a battle and it would turn into a brawl, but for the most part, would-be gangsters expressed their masculinity and frustration through hip hop performance. The block party was, in some sense, revolutionary in taming a volatile youth culture while simultaneously providing free entertainment to people who could likely not afford to pay for it.

In 2004, hip hop comedian Dave Chappelle threw a block party in the Bedford-Stuyvesant neighborhood of Brooklyn. He invited many hip hop musicians, including Lauryn Hill and the Fugees, Kanye West, the Roots, Erykah Badu, Common, Mos Def, Talib Kweli, and others. Chappelle recorded the experience as a documentary, *Dave Chappelle's Block Party*, which was released in theaters in March 2006. The film was a great success, but neither the film nor the party itself can compare to the unofficial regularity and spontaneity of the seventies block parties. Chappelle's party was meticulously planned with a schedule of events, and the songs to be performed were chosen well in advance. Block parties in the 1970s were loosely organized. Of course, DJs often had a planned order of records they used in a set, but one day they might play the first third of the set, and the last half on another. Otherwise, the events were unpredictable and improvised, like the jazz that captured the hearts of the previous generation, and the mellow nature of the scene was one of the characteristics that made the block party popular.

Joseph Saddler was infatuated with Kool Herc's performances at these block parties. He used to scrutinize Herc's methods, noticing aspects he wanted to imitate as well as potential flaws that could be improved to make the show even more effective at pleasing the crowd. After watching several of Herc's parties, Joseph went scavenging to find parts to assemble to create his own sound system. With his background in electronics, he was able to use more affordable components and modify them to do things that some store-bought equipment was not even designed to do at the time. In some ways, his vocational training enabled him to put together a sound system that surpassed the others. In terms of speaker power, though, no one had a system that could match the chest-shaking power of Herc's, but with regard to versatility and innovation, Saddler had them all beat. When he finally obtained and revamped the necessities, Saddler began practicing in his bedroom for hours each day. He was developing his own style, theories, and technical innovations, which would all prove to be fundamental to the formation of today's hip hop. He spent over three years perfecting techniques that opened the door to drastically new approaches to DJing.

Before Flash could wow the crowd with his manipulation of records, he had to have a mixer and a set of turntables. He started out with a Sony MX 6 microphone mixer. He went to Radio Shack and got the necessary parts to adjust the mixer so it could handle the level of electricity coming into it from the turntable. The turntables are as essential as the mixer (see sidebar: Turntables). Flash spent several years working with various brands, trying to find the perfect table. He tried Pioneer, Fisher, and Magnavox, but none got

Turntables

Nicole Hodges Persley

In hip hop music, the turntables are often referred to as the wheels of steel or tables and are considered an instrument to be played by cutting, mixing, and scratching to create new sounds from existing recordings. In order to use turntables as an instrument, DJs must have two turntables, with direct-drive and pitch control, and a mixer with a cross-fader that allows the DJ to mute one turntable while allowing the other to play through the speakers. The use of a cross-fader allows the DJ to play one copy of a record forward while he or she spins a second copy of the same record backward to the beginning of the desired section; this creates a seamless repetition, or loop, of a sound that may play only once on the original record. The turntables must have a stylus and cartridge that set into the grooves of the vinyl records in order to scratch, and the turntable must allow the DJ to spin the record backward to isolate and repeat specific sections of a song. This technique of mixing and cutting is enhanced by the addition of scratching, in which the DJ moves the record back and forth across the needle to slow down, speed up, and distort existing sounds on the record.

The method of scratching was invented by Grandwizard Theodore and has been mastered by turntablists around the world. The scratching action performed by DJs allows breaks to be set in the music that are signaled by a rough, raspy scratching sound produced when the stylus hits the vinyl. The DJ then rubs his fingers back and forth in a scratching action while the record is spinning. The scratch will not work unless the DJ replaces the rubber mats that come standard under most turntables with what are called slip mats. These mats are generally made of felt and allow the vinyl records to spin freely instead of stopping on the rubber. One of the most popular models for hip hop DJs is the Technics SL-1200, which was very popular in the late 1970s and is still preferred by many DJs of the twenty-first century. Though today certain hip hop DJs rely on CD technology and music software such as Pro-Tools, many DJs still prefer to use turntables and mixers.

Further Resources

Denning, Jack. "Two Turntables, a Cheap Sampler and a 4 Track." *Tape Op*, No. 5.
Schloss, Jeff. *Making Beats: The Art of Sample Based Hip-Hop.* Middletown: Wesleyan UP, 2004.
Weheliye, Alexander. *Phonographies: Grooves in Afro-Sonic Modernity.* Durham: Duke UP, 2006.

---

the job done to his satisfaction. In an interview with Davey D, he explained that when he first began observing DJs, he noticed that they did not care about beats per minute, which meant that sometimes when the DJ transitioned to a different record, that record would be too fast or too slow compared to the previous one. Flash also noticed how well the break in the song, the section usually past the halfway point that consists only of the bass or drums, hyped up the crowd. Kool Herc was the first one to realize this, so he often played a set thick with breaks from all kinds of songs. But what bothered Flash was the fact that the break was usually only ten or fifteen seconds long. In an interview for ThaFormula.com, he said, "That pissed me off!" He wanted the part of the song that energized the audience to last longer, so he started working on a way to make this possible.

The result was Saddler's quick mix theory, which involved backspinning (rewinding the record without moving the needle or making a sound) and what he called cutting. After years of practice, Saddler found the courage to perform at his first block party. He gathered his equipment and took it to 63 Park Avenue on 168th Street. In an interview with Sally Howard, he described the audience's response to his technique: "They just stood there . . . and I went home and cried for a week." Though Herc had already been using duplicate records to extend a break, Saddler was the first to make this the core of his routine. The crowd did not understand—who would immediately boogie down to a song that was just a small part of the song repeated over and over? Saddler felt he had worked all those years for nothing. Luckily, audiences would begin to catch on and he would soon rock each party 'til the break of dawn. But this did not happen overnight.

Flash also invented the clock theory, which is a relatively simple concept that made it possible to immediately set the needle down on the right track. He would mark the record with tape or a crayon so he knew exactly what part of the record he wanted to use. Many current DJs have adopted this technique to streamline the mixing process, making it another breakthrough method that still influences the art. At some point, though, Flash and others needed a way to protect their wax from other DJs who wanted to buy the same records. So DJs began dunking their records in bathtubs to remove the labels. There are contradictory sources regarding which DJ was the first to do this. In Jeff Chang's *Can't Stop Won't Stop*, Herc is credited as the first DJ to do this, taking advice from his father. However, in a Nelson George interview in which Herc, Bambaataa, and Flash all participated, Flash claimed responsibility for inventing this delabeling, and although some sources cite Herc as the first one, he did not deny Flash's response (George 2004, 48).

THE L BROTHERS: PRE–FURIOUS FIVE FLASH TEACHES AND LEARNS

In the beginning of Flash's career, observers noticed how quickly Saddler flipped his style and started calling himself Flash. The title Grandmaster came from Saddler's love of seventies kung fu flicks. Bruce Lee, king of kung fu as America knows it, was honored with the title Grand Master. It is not clear whether his peers gave Flash this title or he crowned himself, but either way, the name stuck, and it came to signify a legend.

Before he worked with the Furious Five (the group he was with when he started recording albums), Flash worked with the L Brothers—"Mean" Gene Livingston, Claudio Livingston, and their little brother Theodore (later known as Grandwizard Theodore). They practiced in Gene's room where Flash kept his equipment. Gene repeatedly told Flash not to let his little brother touch the decks. According to an interview conducted by Davey D, Flash believes Gene said this because he could not personally grasp what Flash was trying to do with the records. It was, after all, uncharted theoretical and technical territory; no one had done what Flash was doing, so it was hard for most people to understand. But Flash noticed Theo watching everything he did as he played, so when Gene left for work, Flash grabbed a milk crate for the little guy to stand on so he could reach the tables. The young boy became Flash's first apprentice, but Flash could only teach him when Gene was away. Despite this setback, Theo picked up quickly and was one of the first people who comprehended the ideas behind what Flash sometimes calls his formula. In a future performance, Theo would finally get to unveil his talents in public, and from there a fruitful career was born.

Once they had played a few small gigs and were comfortable in front of a crowd, Flash pulled Mean Gene aside at a show. He tried to convince Gene to let his brother play the turntables because that would be something unique about them among the other fledgling groups and would bring them notoriety in the Bronx scene. Flash had persisted on this for a while, and this time, Gene reluctantly assented. Flash produced the same milk crate Theo had used to learn the secrets of Flash's modus operandi. As soon as the crowd realized the young Theo was about to do something with the turntables, they set down their juice, stopped eating their burgers, and paid full attention. Would he just fool around and look cute up there with the big boys' equipment? Would he break part of the system? Would he play the records like an inexperienced child plays a drum set, by hitting parts randomly and making a racket?

As soon as Theo began tearing up the records like a veteran, the crowd went crazy. Theo's movements looked natural; he had fully embraced his mentor's philosophy and instruction. This did not please his older brother. Theo outshined Gene that day, and Gene was unhappy in anyone's shadow. According to Flash's remarks in interviews, this is the scenario Gene had feared and what drove him to keep his brother away from the turntables. But Flash could not stand the idea of depriving anyone interested in turntablism from learning as much as he could teach them. Even today, Flash seeks out inquiring minds, making it a major priority to educate people about the DJ's purpose and abilities, as well as providing an accurate history of hip hop as someone who has been in the trenches from its inception. He explained to Max Woodworth of the *Taipei Times* that the DJ is the root of the culture even though rappers have all the attention, and attempts to pass on hip hop's original values—physical nonviolence, open-mindedness, incorporating music from all colors and creeds, and doing it for love instead of the big record deal—to the younger generation. Flash is so determined to stay connected with youth that he has expressed his desire to open a school for kids who want to become DJs. Theo was his first student and was incredibly sharp and successful. His performance in the park, balancing on a chipped milk crate, was a catalyst for both his and Flash's careers.

Before Theo's surprising performance, though, the group mostly played at modest house parties and small discos. It was during this period that Flash met Pete DJ Jones, a veteran disco DJ who entertained the older crowd. Flash studied Jones's performance and realized that he somehow mixed one record into another more seamlessly than Herc did. While Herc simply started a song by dropping the needle on a groove in the record, Jones had a precuing system that resulted in smoother transitions. Flash asked Jones several times if he could play on his system, and when Jones finally agreed, Flash discovered something amazing about Jones's setup. He had rigged his system so he could listen through a pair of headphones and hear the other turntable, the one not playing at that moment, before the crowd did. Armed with this new technological opportunity, Flash went home and got to work.

FLASH GETS HIS RECORDS STRAIGHT: MIXERS, BREAKS, AND MISTAKES

After discovering how Pete DJ Jones could change from one turntable to the other without skipping a beat, Flash set out to build his own version of Jones's system. Flash created what he called the peek-a-boo system. Mixers were equipped with a toggle switch. In the center position, it was off. When he clicked the switch to the left, only the left turntable was audible. When he clicked it two times to the right, he isolated the sound from the right turntable. His invention has been refined and is now called a cross-fader. The new version of his system involves a slot on the mixer. The DJ uses his fingers to slide the fader from side to side. In the standard DJ style, when the fader is on the right, the right turntable is the only one producing sound, and vice versa (the other option is hamster style, which is the opposite—when the fader slides to one side, that turntable's sound cuts out). Being able to switch between tables by sliding a knob instead of clicking a switch is one change that made it possible for DJs to do more than basic mixing, namely scratching, with more complexity. For the turntablists who focus on scratching, the cross-fader is indispensable and usually needs replacement once a year, depending on the quality of the part, because it is basically the piece of the mixer that makes scratching possible. The more complex forms of scratching a DJ performs, the sooner the cross-fader is exhausted, because the scratch's complexity is proportional to the number of times the DJ moves the fader.

Flash's manual installation of the peek-a-boo system is just one of many mechanical modifications he made to the wheels of steel that expanded the opportunities available to the DJ and paved the way for the DJ's more recent focus on manipulating records to create new sounds.

To be able to bring all his ideas together, Flash needed a turntable with the right belt drive and amount of torque. He wanted a table that would accelerate from completely stopped to full speed in at least half or a quarter of a revolution. This was crucial in tying together all his different methods to produce a premium quality performance, which included the ability to extend a ten-second break indefinitely. He finally came across a turntable that would work. It was an ugly silver table made by the Technics company, the SL-20. Ten years later Technics created the SL-1200, which became the standard turntable for serious DJs. The brand is cited in several hip hop songs, such as KRS-One's "Real Hip-Hop," and the model is even mentioned in tracks by Defari, Kool Keith, and others. Armed with a pair of turntables that would become the DJ standard, a mic mixer modified to work with his decks and fitted with his peek-a-boo system, and the modest speaker system he had obtained, Flash had everything he needed to play for a crowd. Still frustrated by the brevity of most breakbeats, Flash decided to use duplicate copies of the same records on his decks. With his peek-a-boo modification, he could play the smallest part of a song if he wished, then click over to the other table, which had the record cued to start at the beginning of the same tiny part, and thus continue that part of the song, repeating the process as long as the crowd was feeling it.

Flash was not the first turntablist to use duplicate records to lengthen the breakbeat. Kool Herc, the true pioneer of the art, employed what he called his merry-go-round technique. Herc would play the record on one table and then place the needle on the spot where the break began on the other record as the first break ended. The process of switching between the same two records to keep part of a record playing, first accomplished by Herc and then refined by Flash, is known as looping. Unfortunately for the real live DJ, digital technology now exists that makes it possible to loop part of a song, often called a sample, by simply pushing a button or two. Though Herc was the first to loop records, Flash added precision to the process, eventually blending separate records together so smoothly most could not recognize when one ended and the other began. He had seen Herc use his own technique in parks, but according to Jeff Chang's account it was not as clean as Flash wanted his routine to sound. Sometimes Herc got off beat or dropped the needle a little too far before or after the break, but no one in the audience cared, if they even noticed. His music was so new and different that most people may not have even realized these were mistakes.

Occasionally, early hip hop performers would pretend to make a mistake, such as a breaking move that involved presenting the illusion that the dancer had started a move and messed up or forgot, when it was really an intentional stall or freeze for dramatic effect. Flash's first performance in the park, before he became Flash, was a disaster, in part because people did not understand what he was doing, and perhaps some of them thought the record was skipping. A few months later audiences realized that this was no mistake—it was a technique. To audiences accustomed to the smooth transition between records played by radio disc jockeys and dance club DJs, Flash's scratches may have initially sounded like a mistake. Before hip hop, the sound of a needle scratching a record had been associated with clumsiness. Flash's new techniques, however, made scratching rhythmic and musical. He played the turntables as an instrument, and made the sound of a needle scratching vinyl a key component of hip hop.

Even though Herc's method of looping was not always clean, he still got the party kicking and the b-boys dancing. Herc often chose breaks that were heavy in bass or drums, making his superior speakers pulsate. If it was funky, he used it. Generally, breaks in traditional songs only involve the bass and drums, the rhythm section of the tune. Herc's picks always pleased the crowd, and as the preference moved from an early James Brown style to the tighter, more rhythm-oriented funk tracks, the best breaks became increasingly heavy on the bass line. The hip hop audiences loved it, and although their approval is inescapably tied to how well the DJ flipped his wax, part of their pleasure must relate to this more rhythm-driven music.

HOW LOW CAN YOU GO? HI-FI SCIENCE: HIP HOP, DRUMS, BASS, AND TURNTABLISM

The hip hop generation might be the first to connect more strongly with rhythm and bass than rhythm and blues. Hip hop fans love nothing more than a trunk-rattling bass line pumping from customized car stereos. Since Herc's use of breakbeats drove the crowd mad, listeners have gradually developed an auditory palate that prefers hard drums to guitar strums. This thirst for low frequencies may be the source of the techno DJ, whose work is principally appreciated for the bass lines. This might seem unrelated to hip hop, but techno DJs are close cousins, for several reasons. Of course, there is the obvious fact that both DJs use a mixer and two turntables as their instruments. Second, there are several crossover DJs who play hip hop and various offshoots of techno interchangeably (the most prominent of these is DJ Shadow). Also, there is the ragga DJ. Ragga is a form of techno that mixes the complex, frenzied, urban-meets-African-bush style of jungle music with reggae. Just as hip hop owes some credit (acknowledged or not) to the Jamaican selectors, the ragga DJ would not be here if not for those selectors. These DJs work with standard jungle beats and weave in vocals that speak to reggae roots. One example is the album *Tribute to Haile Selassie* by Congo Natty. Along with jungle noises like screaming monkeys and allusions to urban life (cf. Bob Marley's "Concrete Jungle"), Congo Natty adds in vocal snippets such as "Exodus," "Jah—Rastafari," and a brief inclusion of the reggae neoclassic, "Ring Da Alarm."

The DJ's set is composed of far more blues, funk, classic R&B, or soul than blasting brass or hair-band vocals that sound harsh, hoarse, and manic compared to the mellow, hip, funky vocals on more popular records. A well-known exception to this distaste for higher pitched instruments is a saxophone solo by Tom Scott, from the album *Honeysuckle Breeze*, which was the main melody in the 1990s hip hop classic "They Reminisce Over You (T.R.O.Y.)" by Pete Rock and C.L. Smooth. Perhaps it is hip hop's respect for jazz that allowed a sax solo to become immensely popular among its fans. That same saxophone solo reappeared in a recorded mix called *Sex Machine Today* by J-Rocc, a member of the Beat Junkies, which is one of the most active and talented crews of turntablists that exist today. This crew, which includes J-Rocc, Babu, Melo-D, and Rhettmatic (along with other charter members such as Tommy Gunn, D-Styles, Shortkut, DJ What?, and others) has probably taken Flash's prescratching methods and Grandwizard Theodore's additional exploration of the subgenre further than any single DJ in the world. One turntablist who comes close to being that single DJ is Q-bert, a member of the Invisibl Skratch Piklz, which include Q-bert, Shortkut, Yogafrog, and at one time, Mixmaster Mike, who now DJs for the Beastie Boys. These DJs are often cited as the crew who initiated the turntablist culture. Q-bert's scratching style is so quick and clean that it boggles the mind how it is humanly possible to move one's fingers that fast without turning the track into mush. He is so venerated in the circle of veteran turtablists that he received a lifetime achievement award at the 1998 DMC Championships (see sidebar: DMC World Championships).

Q-bert looks for inspiration by trying to think about what kind of music aliens are playing on more advanced planets, and he (along with Mixmaster

---

DMC World Championships
H. C. Williams

Some DJs practice the same routine for years, attempting to work their way up from the regional DMC competition to the DMC World Championships. The goal is understandable; the winner is declared the best DJ on the planet and can brag and gloat until the following year, when he or she must defend that title. In 1981, Tony Prince, a European radio DJ, began playing DJs' mixtapes on his show—which, at some point, became the *Disco Mix Club Show*. He worked at one of the only nationally broadcast stations, and his show attracted 50 million listeners, according to the DMC Web site. He began receiving thousands of tapes from DJs seeking national exposure. Prince decided he had tapped into a fledgling musical movement and wanted to see it fly, so he left his job after twenty years and coerced his wife, Christine, into joining in his new venture, whose goal was to help DJs gain the success that was at their fingertips.

DMC did not begin their World Championships competition until two years into their official work. Their original goal was to form a DJs-only record label, and in February 1983 they became the first label licensed for this purpose. They also put their savings into a magazine, *Mixmag*, that accompanied monthly mixes (or "megamixes," a phrase they coined) produced by and sent to subscribers. The magazine was a strong influence on demand for DJs and helped create a niche for them in the music industry. They soon published *MIXER*, the American version of *Mixmag*, which rekindled the demand for U.S. DJs.

In 1985, DMC launched the World Championships so DJs could showcase their talents while hearing what the rest of the world's DJs were up to. According to their Web site, they "gave birth to 'Turntablism'" through this competition—which is definitely debatable. Either way, the competition did move from electronic/techno/club DJing toward turntablism and scratching. It became the ultimate DJ battle.

Further Resources

DMC Discography. http://www.discogs.com/label/DMC.
DMC World Championships Vol. 1 and 2. DVD. DMC World Pictures.
DMC World. Official Web site. http://www.dmcworld.com.
Interview with Tony Prince. Rapnews Online. http://www.rapnews.co.uk/?p=419.

Mike) believes that scratching is a form of communication with extraterrestrials (see sidebar: Wave Twisters). For an example of Mike's work, listen to the Beastie Boys' 1998 album *Hello Nasty*, which includes the Grammy Award–winning track "Intergalactic," as well as "Three MCs and One DJ," the song that introduced Mike to Beastie Boys fans. This song echoes a remark made in *Scratch*, as Bambaataa speaks of his wish to see the art go "intergalactic," which could be that next level or new frontier that DJs are searching for. The idea that the sounds made when a turntablist scratches can—and do—communicate with aliens is definitely not a typical American's belief, but Q-bert is recognized in the turntablists' royal court as being the best, bar none. It seems far-fetched, but maybe that kind of perspective is what it takes to master such chiseled, controlled, and frenetic finger work(see sidebar: Invasion of the Pickle Scratcher).

Turntablist is another word for DJ. Babu of the Beat Junkies coined the term, writing "Babu the Turntablist" on his mix CDs, and the concept took over this niche in the DJ world. A turntablist is typically more concerned with doing things to the records than simply mixing albums, which is why those DJs who focus on scratching wish to be called turntablists instead of disc jockeys (a term that refers to radio show hosts who play one whole song after another) or even selectors—the Jamaican term for DJs—because the selector

Wave Twisters
H. C. Williams

Wave Twisters is a forty-five-minute visual manifestation of DJ Q-bert's groundbreaking 1998 album of the same title, and the first movie whose central focus and inspiration is scratching itself. Released in 2001, *Wave Twisters* uses multiple forms of animation, set to match the sampling and scratching on the CD, to produce a sensory supernova. Comparable to the Beatles' 1968 animated film *The Yellow Submarine* in its hallucinogenic simulation and George Lucas's *Star Wars* movies in its sci-fi/extraterrestrial milieu, *Wave Twisters* begins in "inner space"—inside the diamond of a turntable needle. The protagonist, Inner Space Dental Commander, is accompanied by the old-school character Grandpa, the streetwise Honey, and the R2D2-meets-Duracell Rubbish. The evil Lord Ook and his sinister sidekick, Red Worm, conspire to suppress hip hop's four lost arts—break dancing, graffiti, MCing and DJing. The Dental Commander et al. are thus on a quest to save the old school, and their only weapon is a Wave Twister—a watchlike mini-turntable that emits deadly rays when triggered by scratching.

But do not let this linear plot description fool you; there is no traditional dialogue whatsoever and rarely do the characters even move in ways we consider normal. The only dialogue comes from samples that conveniently include words, though they are often only phrases (e.g., "say ah," "surrender your . . . "). Yet somehow the plot approaches linearity and the careful observer still understands the action—despite the fragmentary, nonsensical presentation that is expected in postmodern media.

The use of sampling, in both the animation and Q-bert's original music, is another postmodern characteristic of the film. The CD, like the movie, is a collage of samples that allude to both old and new. From a fifties-era dental hygiene commercial to pieces from new hip hop songs and electronic noises (beeps, etc.), Q-bert does not discriminate. Allusions to pop culture—also a postmodern quality—constantly appear. Q-bert samples video games, anime, movies, and more. The animators parallel his allusions with an homage to the 1980s video game Donkey Kong, a parodied version of the Norton Antivirus software called Disc Doctor, and other references to American pop culture.

---

is also more concerned with playing the record, though the selector will play with the needle, pull the record back to make a sound that resembles scratching, and do other small things to spice up the experience.

The turntablist, when working alone, will typically have one turntable playing a beat or an instrumental track. On the other table, the turntablist will have a record made up of samples or battle breaks (short sounds recorded back-to-back specifically for the DJ). The most basic sample is a high-pitched swooshing noise called a crash, and when the turntablist wants to show his

Invasion of the Pickle Scratcher: DJ Q-bert
H. C. Williams

In 1985, DJ Q-bert (Richard Quitevis) began manipulating records after meeting Mixmaster Mike, who later joined Q, D-Styles, Shortkut, and Yogafrog to form the Invisibl Skratch Piklz, considered the most influential turntablist crew. Q-bert approaches turntablism as if he always has more to learn, and this mentality keeps him continually perfecting his craft. Q-bert transformed the turntable into a versatile instrument, scratching recordings of violins, saxophones, and steel drums, and thereby applying a new technique to what had been chiefly manipulation of vocals, drums, bass, and guitar. Q-bert explored the uncharted territory of the turntable, taking turntablism to a different galaxy. As Q-bert explains in the documentary *Scratch*, he views scratching as a language he uses to communicate with more advanced life forms on distant planets.

Although underground hip hoppers can be notoriously secretive about the tricks of the trade, Q-bert has logged endless hours teaching turntablism to anyone ready to learn. He created two how-to videos: *Complete Do-It-Yourself (Volume 1: Scratching, Volume 2: Skratch Sessions)*. He has also taught many seminars in turntablism and was a main force behind Scratchcon, the first conference for scratching, which consisted of performing and teaching young musicians with itching fingers. In an art that had become selfish and secretive, Q-bert's desire to spread knowledge made many new DJs and showed the old ones a valuable lesson too.

Further Resources

Campos, Samantha. "King of Scratch: Turntable Master Innovator, DJ Q-bert." *Maui Time Weekly*. 3 June 2004.
Desuasido, Riche-Van, Eric Ignacio, et al. Dirs. *DJ Q-bert Live: Australia, Asia*. 2005. DVD. Thud Rumble Pictures.
Mayo, James. "Like a Record, Baby: Q-bert and the Invisibl Skratch Piklz Put a New Spin on the DJ Craft." *Westwood*. 13 January 2000. https://den.secure.newtimes.com/issues/2000-01-13/music2.html.

---

technical prowess, he often works with this sample because it is basic enough for listeners to hear exactly what he is doing to the sound. Other samples vary widely from grunting and animal noises to lines from kung fu flicks. The majority of the samples on the record consist of: (a) phrases the DJ can play to brag about his skills or diss his opponent during a battle; (b) single words in the hip hop lexicon (e.g., *fresh*, *word*), and (c) most significantly, original shout-outs and classic DJ staples, such as "Make 'Em Clap to This," "Good Times," "September," or just about anything James Brown sang. What is important is the fact that these DJs, who are taking this element of hip hop to a new level, are not leaving behind the songs and phrases they heard themselves as the culture grew.

As an important side note, in the movie *Scratch*, the DJs cite Grandmaster DST as the "originator." In 1984 he performed the song "Rockit" with Herbie Hancock, and the show was televised. Because many of today's premier turntablists are concentrated on the West Coast, they were likely not exposed to the (pre)scratching DJ until they saw DST on television. This is the most logical reason why they would cite DST, rather than Theodore or Flash, as the pioneer in cutting and scratching. But they do give props to their predecessors, whether they refer to the first televised scratching DJ or to the ones who really opened the doors. One of the fundamental old-school keywords is *respect*. Hip hoppers should respect everyone, even crews they battle, even people who bite their style, even the guy who stole their cab yesterday. This is part of hip hop's original philosophy. Flash and Bambaataa may have shaken things up a lot from Herc's view, but all three have much love and respect for each other. These new DJs respect their roots, where they came from—when they design their own records and choose their own sounds to sample, they still pick James Brown, Chic, Earth, Wind and Fire, and other classics. They also record samples of old-school MC shout-outs and pieces of dialogue that directly relate to the origins of hip hop, including references to Islam/Black Power and Rastafarianism/Jamaica. They respect their roots, which, according to some people, go back to the Jamaican selector and his sound system.

If that is the case, then hip hop came full circle in Stephen Marley's compilation and release of *Chant Down Babylon*, an album that layers Bob Marley's original vocals over hip hop beats and artists who contributed their own messages to each track. The album features some of hip hop's most popular and pure (i.e., not pop hip hop) artists, such as Rakim, Guru from Gangstar, Lauryn Hill (married to Bob's son, Ziggy), MC Lyte, Chuck D, and others. The blend of reggae riddims and striking bass lines, the old soul rebels and the new ones, and the philosophical stance of Bob's rude rock reggae mixed with the philosophy of today's urban sounds, is truly a milestone in the development of hip hop itself, as well as serving as another sign that today's hip hoppers do not want to dismiss what they have learned and inherited; they want to pass it all on to the next generation.

FLASH AND THE FURIOUS: PSEUDO-DJ, "STEPPING LIGHTLY," AND MISADVENTURES WITH SUGAR HILL

Grandmaster Flash was rocking the parties and dropping the science that would later become the hip hop DJ's central source of growth, but, as Steven Stancell (116) mentions in *Rap Whoz Who*, everyone was so focused on what he was doing to the records that no one was dancing. So he set out to find someone to provide a vocal and contrasting aesthetic element to his performance. His first MC, Keith "Cowboy" Wiggins, had a deep, sexy voice that kept the fly girls coming to the shows, and his classic shout-outs were so engaging that Flash sought out more MCs to pump up the jam.

The next MCs to join the group were the Glover brothers: Melvin "Melle Mel" and Nathaniel "Kidd Creole." They called themselves Grandmaster Flash and the 3 MCs. Soon after that Flash began working with a Vox drum machine and they became Grandmaster Flash and the 3 MCs with the Beat Box. The beatbox was originally a piece of electronic equipment, but the term has come to signify using one's mouth to simulate the sounds created by that machine. Shortly before Scorpio, aka Mr. Ness, joined the group to form Grandmaster Flash and the Furious Four, a cop-turned-promoter named Ray Chandler approached Flash at St. Ann's Park. He suggested that Flash should find a venue at which he could perform regularly, thereby maintaining a solid fan base. Flash was open to the idea, and when they came across the right club they called it the Black Door because the entrance door was painted black. After a few months of performing amid increasing problems from the stickup kids, Chandler enlisted a posse of ex–Black Spades to serve as security. They were known as the Casanova Crew and were led by a guy named Tiny.

Scorpio joined the mix of performers in leather-studded jumpsuits, but a short while after that the group split up to pursue various projects. In 1974, Bobby Robinson of the independent Enjoy Records recruited Flash and requested that he make a record with his MCs. Just before they went into the studio, Rahiem (formerly a member of the Funky Four) joined Flash after the Five defeated his crew in a battle, and they finally became Grandmaster Flash and the Furious Five. Armed with the sense of completion derived from forming a six-member group, and their signature style of rhyming—tossing phrases back and forth to create sentences, and using more intricate and lyrically complex diction—Flash and the Five marched into the soundproof room and recorded "Superappin'" for Enjoy.

The single was not as successful as both Robinson and the group had hoped. By some accounts, it was Robinson who dropped them from the label because of the album's poor reception; others claim that Flash and the Five left Robinson because they were dissatisfied with the amount of radio play for the record. Either way, Flash and his crew left Enjoy Records. Sylvia Robinson (no relation), a no-nonsense talent agent and co-owner of Sugar Hill Records (responsible for the first hip hop record, "Rapper's Delight") approached Flash one Tuesday after his regular gig at Disco Fever. She told him that she could get their music on the back of a popular record by a group called Freedom, and their first single with Sugar Hill, also called "Freedom," saw more success than their work under Bobby Robinson. It looked like the group would finally get a turn in the spotlight. But unfortunately, the beam of light that brought them national recognition also left (most of) them in the dark.

There were signs of this upcoming blackout from the beginning. Flash's mixing and unique treatment of the records were recorded for the album by the studio's house band. According to Chuck Miller, Flash complimented their ability to reproduce sections of other songs and make it sound so much like his own work, but in several interviews, including with Nelson George and ThaFormula.com, he has stressed the role of the DJ as the originator and backbone of hip hop and has emphasized the fact that the DJ rarely gets the recognition he deserves.

Not only did Flash praise the house band for reproducing the music he made, but he also said that the situation was actually a good thing. He was able to stand in the control booth with a 600-pound sound engineer named Jerome. His exposure to Jerome's work prepared him for future ventures in production. Indeed, once he was again a solo artist, he put the bulk of his energy into production, working with such hip hop legends as Russell Simmons and Chris Rock. This speaks to Flash's ability to adapt to the flux of demands in hip hop's development. In *Can't Stop Won't Stop*, Jeff Chang quotes Flash as recognizing hip hop's own incessant reinvention: "It was either you survive and you go with the changes or you get left back" (128). Before hip hop's tenth birthday, the DJ was already being marginalized, despite the fact that his name continued to appear first in flyers and ads. Because of the beatbox—which Flash himself popularized—and additional technology, the producer could imitate the DJ more easily than ever. Any studio with the proper equipment could now produce the illusion of a DJ, which is impossible for the MC, whose role became more significant as a result. The fact that Flash was on the other side of the glass from his first days at Sugar Hill should have (and might have) prepared him for the role Sylvia Robinson assigned to him—a passive, silent observer whom she kept around because his name increased record sales, and whom she expected to stay silent (this is not personal opinion; future legal battles would officially reveal her sentiment).

Flash did, however, have the opportunity to cut a record that focused solely on the DJ and what he was capable of when an MC was not rhyming over his orchestration. "The Adventures of Grandmaster Flash on the Wheels of Steel" (1981) was the first record of its kind, and it paved the way for other DJs like Jazzy Jay and Grandmaster DST to record their own DJ-centered tracks (and in fact, DST's song was "Rockit," the selection he performed on television that ignited a new generation's interest in the art of the DJ). In e-mail correspondence with me, Chuck Miller discussed the details of the actual songs Flash used in the set, calling the record

> a mélange of pop sounds, funk music, British rock and fragments of rare beats and tracks. The mix includes such Sugarhill tracks as Spoonie Gee and the Sequence's "Monster Jam," the Sugarhill Gang's "8th Wonder," the instrumental track from "Rapper's Delight" (actually a clone of Chic's "Good Times"),

and Flash and the Five's "The Birthday Party," along with Blondie's "Rapture," Queen's "Another One Bites the Dust," the Incredible Bongo Band's "Apache," a spoken-word section from a concept album by the Hellers, and a radio clip from a *Flash Gordon* episode. There had been medleys before, but usually it involved an artist singing two songs together in a four-minute span (i.e., the Lettermen's "Goin' Out of My Head"/"Can't Take My Eyes Off of You"), or they involved knockoff medleys of 20 pop hits as sung by a single studio group (e.g., Stars on 45 or Gidea Park).

This was an invaluable chance for Flash to show listeners everywhere what the DJ really sounds like and to prove something the whole world had been told. As an added bonus, his eclectic choice of sounds inspired a new generation of DJs, who sampled an amazingly wide variety of songs, dialogue, and other forms of noise.

There was, then, a catalyst for this day spent in the studio cutting and scratching, and the resulting slices of vinyl that emerged from the wax press. Fab 5 Freddy was all over hip hop culture. He began as a graffiti artist, then played a pivotal role in uniting the uptown and downtown music scenes and went on to fulfill other roles in the creation and expression of hip hop. During the period in which he was showing New Yorkers what was going down on the other side of town, he brought the platinum-topped Deborah Harry (lead singer of Blondie) to one of Flash's shows. She listened intently and watched him work for the entire show, and as Flash was breaking down his equipment, Fab 5 Freddy approached him to tell him that Harry was so impressed by his skills that she might pay him tribute on an upcoming album. A few months later, "Rapture" leaped to the number one spot and took Flash's reputation with it. Harry's unforgettable lyrics, "Fab 5 Freddy told me everybody's fly" did more than simply give Flash a sound reason to create his "Adventures" record. This part of Blondie's song became a DJ favorite, and DJs everywhere sampled pieces of it to demonstrate their loyalty to what came before them.

Although they had a loyal fan base, Flash and the Five were not taken seriously because they still did not take their songs seriously, choosing shallow ideas over and over as subject matter. Sylvia Robinson decided to change that, and the result was "The Message," released in 1982. As the first hip hop song to move beyond boasting about good times and including lighthearted shout-outs, this was the song that made the critics and editors begin paying attention to hip hop. And, as the title suggests, the song had a message. In a 1996 issue of *Goldmine*, Chuck Miller hinted at the poignancy of the song, noting that its "lyrics told of a New York that wasn't all parties, cars and women—a dark commentary reminiscent of the soliloquies of Gil Scott-Heron and Bob Dylan" (74). The track served as dynamite that razed a mountain of chest-puffing to build a highway for hip hop as a vehicle for sociopolitical commentary (e.g., Run-DMC, Public Enemy, Common). The song also led to VH1's recent recognition of Flash and the Five for the direction in which they steered the movement. The song is still influential, as is evidenced by Mos Def's 2004 single "Close Edge," in which Mos incorporates part of Melle Mel's ominous chorus, "Don't push me 'cause I'm close to the edge," to ground his own grim portrait of city life.

Despite its success and influence, there is a blemish on this song's otherwise perfect complexion. Though Flash and the Furious Five were credited on the album cover, they were barely involved in making or recording the single. Most of the rhymes came from Duke Bootie (aka Ed Fletcher, the studio percussionist), and Melle Mel was the only member of the group who even made it on the track. Flash had been around long enough to worry about this: In his experiences, he had learned that once a group makes a record with only one or two of the actual musicians on it, the breakup is soon to follow. So he worked hard to get all his MCs on the track, but Sylvia Robinson complained that he was using too much studio time. Then she stopped them completely because she wanted the track to be Sugar Hill's next single. Their next few records had similar issues with credit. Melle Mel usually got credit when he rhymed, but often the Five's names were listed whether or not they contributed to the song. Flash soon began his search for a new label, and Sylvia took him to court over the right to the name "Grandmaster Flash and the Furious Five." The judge ruled that he could keep his original title and Sylvia could continue to use the same name, minus the "Flash."

Flash had already left Sugar Hill when they released "White Lines (Don't Do It)," but with the song credited to Grandmaster and Melle Mel, there are people who even today wrongly believe that Flash contributed to the song. After that, the group split up, some staying with Sylvia and others moving on. Flash had signed with Elektra, and when Sugar Hill folded he asked everyone to join him on that label. The result was their reunion album, *On the Strength*, which was technically impressive but did not sell well, so Elektra dropped the group. A few months later, Flash learned that Cowboy, his first MC, was extremely sick, and a couple days later, two weeks shy of his thirty-ninth birthday, Wiggins died from complications of AIDS. The funeral was virtually the last place the group was together. After continuing solo work, they came together for a tour and appeared on Duran Duran's cover of "White Lines," but nothing was the same without Cowboy. They never reunited to perform again.

MAD SCIENTIST: FLASH SPEAKS ON HIS LEGACY AND THE RESULTS OF HIS EXPERIMENT

Flash may be more popular today than he was at the time of "Rapper's Delight" when he was the DJ all the record companies wanted to sign. His official Web site—www.grandmasterflash.com—lists his most recent achievements and honors. The list only goes back to 1998, so Flash may have even more on his résumé than the many accomplishments already listed (though it is hard to imagine what else there is to accomplish). He was the DJ for Chris Rock on his HBO show; he played at the Super Bowl; he played in front of the Queen of England. He was given a key to Cincinnati; a street in New York bears his name, and there is a plaque on a wall in the Bronx at 161st Street that recognizes his induction into the Bronx Walk of Fame. He and the Furious Five were recently nominated for induction into the Rock and Roll Hall of Fame (making them the first rap group to achieve this status), but when Max Woodworth interviewed him, Flash said the plaque was a greater accomplishment than the nomination.

Even after worldwide recognition, he still feels most honored when it comes from his own neighborhood, and this perspective holds true for the majority of artists who grew up in various versions of the ghetto. For them (at least the nonpop hip hop artists), respect and support from the community, and the satisfaction that comes from performing and feeling like it meant something to someone, are chief sources of motivation and inspiration. This is the way of the old school, which Flash fully supports. The new school, on the other hand, while still positive in some ways, disappoints or frustrates Flash for several reasons. When asked by Davey D, Sally Howard, and others about his views on today's hip hop, Flash responded with virtually the same answer: He does not like where hip hop has gone and is going, and he blames the record industry and commercialization for pushing it in that direction. In the interview with Davey D, which took place within days of Tupac Shakur's death, Flash explained his ideology the following way: He, Bambaataa, and Herc all planted the seed of hip hop, and it grew into a huge tree with many branches and leaves, or possible subject matter. For Flash, anything is hip hop if it has a beat with someone rhyming over it, and where the artist is from or what the song is about has absolutely nothing to do with whether or not it is hip hop. He thinks that there is too much focus on one side of the tree (the violent, reactionary, poppin' gats side) and not enough diversity to do justice to the whole concept of hip hop as a manifestation of diversity. Flash blames the music industry for this situation because, to him, companies do not seek out originality. They seek out a different version of the chart-topping artist at the other company.

Flash also points a finger at the music industry for being responsible for the violence that seems more prevalent, or more noticeable, in hip hop music. In his conversation with Davey D, he explains that hip hop is aggressive by nature. The goal is to get the crowd hyped up, and excitement can lead to violence in any scenario. But according to Flash, the record companies encourage East versus West and other squabbles because their artists act like guests on the *Jerry Springer Show* dissing each other. Flash explains that artists simply need to step back and evaluate what it is they are doing and why. In this interview, Flash is polite, but critical when he discusses the record industry. In another interview, that restraint is absent. He is direct and concise: "Corporate America has damn near forgotten the DJ" (ThaFormula.com). Because of new technology that makes it possible to reproduce the DJ's contributions, the live DJ has become obsolete in many contexts.

This issue is probably a major influence on the development of new movements in turntablism, which make the DJ's performance so complex that too much would be happening if someone rapped over it.

Flash is not completely negative about what hip hop has become. He recognizes that there are still artists trying to push the limits and approach the whole scene in a more productive way, and he is excited that it has grown into an international phenomenon. He has said several times that he feels lucky to be still alive so he can witness hip hop's explosion. At times Flash's passion can seem melodramatic, as with the interview with Max Woodworth when he mentions his desire to "instill [hip hop's] history" into the minds of the younger generation. In the same interview, he makes an even more grandiose declaration, expressing the belief that he is "a prophet of hip hop." Flash was one of hip hop's progenitors and has seen the culture grow and transform; he has seen the musical genre remain true to its roots and branch off into new territory. Though Flash did not predict the multifaceted nature that hip hop music would take on, he does know its truth and continues to spread its word so that others might hear his message and find their way in the dark until the power that they will create comes on.

See also: Kool Herc, Native Tongues, Beastie Boys, Wu-Tang Clan, Dr. Dre and Snoop Dogg

WORKS CITED

Chang, Jeff. *Can't Stop Won't Stop: A History of the Hip-Hop Generation.* New York: St. Martin's Press, 2005.

Flash, Grandmaster. Interview with Davey D. http://www.daveyd.com/interviewgmflashchronicle.html.

Flash, Grandmaster. Interview. ThaFormula.com. http://www.thaformula.com/grandmaster_flash_-_backbone_of_hip_hop_day_5.htm.

Flash, Grandmaster. Interview with Sally Howard. http://www.viewlondon.co.uk/home_feat_int_grandmaster.asp.

George, Nelson. "Hip-hop's Founding Fathers Speak the Truth." In Murray Forman and Mark Anthony Neal, Eds. *That's the Joint! The Hip-Hop Studies Reader.* New York: Routledge, 2004.

Miller, Chuck. "Two Turntables and a Microphone: The Story of Grandmaster Flash." *Goldmine* 432 (December 1996): 72-74, 88, 90.

Miller, Chuck. E-mail correspondence with the author. 24 August 2006.

Stancell, Steven. *Rap Whoz Who: The World of Rap Music Performers, Producers, Promoters.* New York: Schirmer Books, 1996. 115-118.

Woodworth, Max. "Commence the 'Philoso-jam.'" *Taipei Times.* 18 March 2005: 13. 1 August 2006. http://www.taipeitimes.com/News/feat/archives/2005/03/18/2003246789.

FURTHER RESOURCES

Flash, Grandmaster. Interview. http://www.la-groove.com/archives/00169.php.

Flash, Grandmaster. Official Web site. http://www.grandmasterflash.com.

Fuchs, Cynthia. DVD review. http://www.popmatters.com/film/reviews/s/scratch-dvd.shtml.
George, Nelson. *Hip Hop America*. New York: Penguin, 1998.
Pray, Doug, dir. *Scratch*. 2001. DVD. Palm Pictures.

SELECTED DISCOGRAPHY

Special thanks to Chuck Miller for his help in compiling this list.

Grandmaster Flash and the Furious Five

"Superrapin'/Superrapin' Theme" (single). Enjoy, 1979.
"The Adventures of Grandmaster Flash on the Wheels of Steel"/"The Birthday Party" (instrumental). Sugar Hill, 1981.
"Gold"/"Back in the Old Days of Hip-Hop." Elektra, 1988.
"Magic Carpet Ride"/"On the Strength." Elektra, 1988.

Grandmaster Flash

"Girls Love the Way He Spins"/"Larry's Dance Theme." Elektra, 1981.
"U Know What Time It Is." Elektra, 1987.
"All Wrapped Up." Elektra, 1987.
"The Official Adventures of Grandmaster Flash." Strut, 2002.
Spoiler Talks DVD Series: Grandmaster Flash. 2003. DVD. Subetage. [Note: This release is limited to one copy, which can be borrowed free of charge from the Spoiler library in Vienna.]
"The Flash Mash." Sirius Radio, 2001 to present.
Closing of Commonwealth Games: Manchester, England, 2002.
Hosted MTV Video Music Awards: Miami, 2005.

© David Corio.

Roxanne Shanté

Thembisa S. Mshaka

Roxanne Shanté was the sole female member of a hip hop collective known as the Juice Crew, formed by hip hop godfather Marley Marl in the borough of Queens in New York City. The Juice Crew was composed of Big Daddy Kane, Masta Ace, Kool G Rap, MC Shan, Craig G, Intelligent Hoodlum, Marley Marl, Roxanne Shanté, and Biz Markie, who beatboxed for Roxanne on stage (see sidebar: The Human Beatbox). Before each of these stars went on to successful solo careers, the Juice Crew produced "The Symphony," one of

The Human Beatbox
Mickey Hess

Human beatbox is a term used for performers who vocally mimic the drumbeats and samples used in hip hop music. Beatbox pioneers include Doug E. Fresh ("the Original Human Beatbox"), Ready Rock C, the Fat Boys' Darren Robinson (aka the Human Beatbox), K Love (the first female beatboxer to be recorded) and L. Each of these beatboxers created a style all his or her own. Biz's song "Make the Music with Your Mouth, Biz" showcased the unique beatboxing/humming/singing style that Biz made famous on stage with Roxanne Shanté and the Juice Crew. Doug E. Fresh's style was marked by rapid-fire tongue-clicking noises integrated with deeper bass sounds he made by putting the microphone to his throat. The Human Beatbox's routine included rapid inhalation and exhalation, which created the "uh-huh-uh-huh" sound that marked many of the Fat Boy's songs.

Ready Rock C, who performed with DJ Jazzy Jeff and the Fresh Prince, was also known as the Human Linn Drum, taking his name from a drum machine often used in eighties and nineties hip hop production. Ready Rock is featured prominently on the group's first two albums, *Rock the House* and *He's the DJ, I'm the Rapper*, where he used his voice to mimic video game sound effects and the theme song from the television sitcom *Sanford and Son*, which he even did "underwater," adding gurgling noises to his beatbox routine. His versatile beatbox work is best showcased on tracks like "Rock the House," which features the Fresh Prince rhyming not over music, but over sounds created by Ready Rock C. When DJ Jazzy Jeff and the Fresh Prince won rap's first Grammy for *He's the DJ, I'm the Rapper*, Ready Rock C became the first beatboxer to receive such an accolade. After that album, however, he no longer performed with the group. In 1997, he sued Will Smith (the Fresh Prince) over royalties for his work, claiming he held rights as a cowriter of several of the group's hit songs.

In the early 1990s, beatboxing became less prominent on records and became a part of old-school hip hop that was left behind in the mainstream. Certain groups, however, continue to support beatboxing as an essential part of hip hop music. In 1993, De La Soul featured Biz Markie's beatboxing on their song "Stone Age," which commented on the old-school techniques of turntable scratching and beatboxing that had disappeared from the popular hip hop landscape. Although beatboxing is not as central to hip hop as it once was, it remains part of the music's history and represents an artist's desire to keep hip hop true to its roots. In 2004, the Beastie Boys invited Doug E. Fresh onto the stage to beatbox during their performance of "Time to Get Ill" at Madison Square Garden. Current beatbox innovators include Razhel and Matisyahu, who blends hip hop styles with reggae. In the world of pop music, Justin Timberlake developed his own beatbox routine for concerts and songs.

hip hop's first posse cuts (songs that showcase several members of a crew by allowing each MC to have his or her own verse). The Juice Crew stood together to claim that Queens was the true home of hip hop. In 1986, MC Shan released "The Bridge," which incited KRS-One's Bronx-based group Boogie Down Productions to release "The Bridge Is Over," leading to a series of answer records between these two camps. Two years earlier, however, fourteen-year-old Roxanne Shanté spawned the phenomenon of the answer record. While the other members of the Juice Crew all are hip hop icons in their own right, Roxanne was catapulted to fame upon the 1984 release of "Roxanne's Revenge," a song that responded to U.T.F.O.'s "Roxanne, Roxanne," the lyrics of which described an encounter with a fictional woman named Roxanne, who coldly resisted the group's advances.

The lyrical exchange between U.T.F.O. and Roxanne Shanté eventually spawned between 30 and 100 answer records; many of these releases were from start-up labels, or self-financed, or saw only local airplay, so a definitive count is difficult. The Roxanne Wars phenomenon became so phenomenal that the song overshadowed the songmakers; Roxanne Shanté (Lolita Shanté Gooden) is often confused with the Real Roxanne (Adelaida Martinez), another female MC who recorded an answer record, claiming she was the actual woman who became the topic of U.T.F.O's song. Shanté's place as an icon, however, is not limited to the success of her first single. She is a pivotal MC and a pioneering female lyricist. Her uncompromising lyrics, rapid-fire delivery, and searing vocals confirmed that women rappers could be as aggressive as their male counterparts and still be commercially viable. As the "Queen of the Twelve-Inch," she realized unprecedented sales with "Roxanne's Revenge," selling over a quarter million copies in New York City alone. A critical part of Shanté's legacy is her talents as a merciless battle MC. With "Roxanne's Revenge," she set the standard for answer records, sometimes also called "dis records," used to settle conflicts in songs rather than in the streets (this is where the term "bangin' on wax" comes from).

What began as Shanté's offer to call out U.T.F.O. on vinyl for failing to appear at a concert opened a floodgate of lyrical wars that have produced many memorable hits (see sidebar: Beef). The departure of Ice Cube from N.W.A. spawned "No Vaseline," aimed at Eazy-E and the other remaining members of the group. LL Cool J figuratively came for the head of West Coast rhyme kingpin Ice-T with "Jack the Ripper." In the 1990s, the beef turned bloody—and deadly—as both 2Pac and the Notorious B.I.G. lost their lives to real bullets flying amid the lyrical shots fired in songs like 2Pac's "Toss It Up." Hip hop's most celebrated battle of wills and skills transpired between Nas and Jay-Z in 2001, beginning with Jay-Z's lacerating single "The Takeover" from his album *The Blueprint*. Nas answered powerfully with "Ether" from his *Stillmatic* LP, and was proclaimed the pound-for-pound victor by the streets and the airwaves. All the rumors, rancor, and media attention that swirls around battle rhymes today tipped with "Roxanne's Revenge" in 1984.

Beef
Susan Weinstein

Beef, or conflict, is integral to hip hop culture, or at least an inevitable outcome of the intense competition that has been part of the movement from the time that DJs around the Bronx had to fight for a limited audience in order to earn both reputation and, if at all possible, a living. Add to this the long tradition of verbal humor and competition in African American genres like toasting and the dozens (aka "yo momma" jokes), and the existence in hip hop of battle, and sometimes beef, makes sense.

While Tupac Shakur and Biggie Smalls' beef remains the most sensational—and ultimately, the most devastating—others caused a lot of talk in their day, such as Queensbridge's Juice Crew's beef with the South Bronx's Boogie Down Productions. Around the same time, Kool Moe Dee squared off with a new young rapper named LL Cool J, claiming that LL had copied his style. Each of these beefs ended peacefully. The Juice Crew/BDP beef waned when BDP's Scott La Rock was shot dead in an unrelated incident and KRS-One became involved in his Stop the Violence movement. LL got the last strong shot in at Kool Moe Dee with "To the Break of Dawn"; Kool Moe's response, "Deathblow," was considered unimpressive, and LL was considered by fans to have won the battle.

Beef continues to be part of hip hop. Indeed, 50 Cent has made beefs an integral element in his career plan. And beef can be a positive thing, if it challenges artists to hone their skills (as both Nas and Jay-Z acknowledge happened with them) and helps everyone sell more records. So far, fortunately, the cautionary tale of Tupac and Biggie seems to have kept most later conflicts from getting out of hand; that may, ultimately, be one of these two artists' most significant contributions to hip hop.

Further Resource

Spirer, Peter. *Beef* (video series). Image Entertainment, 2003.

Upbeat party rap had met its match, and Shanté made it clear that all bets were off.

As the sole female in the world-renowned Juice Crew, Shanté trademarked the notion of a female MC flanked by men who assumed the roles of big brothers, protectors, and posse members. For better or for worse, this construct has indelibly shaped the introduction and longevity of female rap artists to audiences on a global scale. After the arrival of Shanté, many women broke onto the rap scene with a male producer or DJ as a front man (à la Salt-N-Pepa and DJ Hurby Luv Bug or Eve and Swizz Beats' Ruff Ryders collective), or another prominent male solo MC, as in the case of Lil' Kim and Notorious B.I.G., Yo-Yo and Ice Cube, Foxy Brown and Nas, or the Conscious

Daughters and Paris. For women rappers, credibility and capability have been inextricably tied to their associations with men. Roxanne Shanté's affiliation with the formidable, well-rounded Juice Crew contributed greatly to this paradigm.

Roxanne was incredibly young when her career began; she was performing and recording at thirteen. She not only "gave birth" (as she liked to boast in her rhymes) to a generation of female MCs; she also ushered in the age of the teen rap prodigy. Prior to the explosion of Shanté, black music had only seen this type of child star in R&B with Little Stevie Wonder and Michael Jackson. Her only counterpart in terms of age was perhaps LL Cool J, who signed to Def Jam at fifteen. Eazy-E, in fact, tried to capitalize on the appeal of the teenage rapper by using his youthful looks and small stature to claim he was "only fifteen," a tactic he describes in the lyrics to his debut album *Eazy-Duz-It*. Hip hop artists Another Bad Creation, Kriss Kross, Lil' Bow Wow, and Lil Romeo are beneficiaries of the trail Shanté blazed, and the lessons she learned (the hard way) about the music business.

Although Roxanne Shanté's time in the spotlight was brief, her influence is still felt today. She is a hip hop pioneer who developed an aggressive rhyme style that remained feminine. In an exclusive interview for *Icons of Hip Hop*, Masta Ace of the Juice Crew reflected on Shanté's style: "She was the homegirl of the crew but she could hold her own. You didn't wanna get into a verbal thing with her, she had jokes. She got respect from all the artists on the label. She really started it all for all of us with her record 'Roxanne's Revenge.' She was real outspoken. I was just trying to look and watch and learn. She carried her everyday persona onstage with her and would speak her mind in a minute."

THE JUICE CREW: STRENGTH IN NUMBERS

Along with Roxanne Shanté, Marley Marl's Juice Crew sparked the careers of Big Daddy Kane, Kool G Rap, and Masta Ace. Marley Marl served as producer and impresario for the crew in much the same way that Dr. Dre would later do in working with the new artists he signed to Death Row and Aftermath Records, including D.O.C, Snoop Dogg, and Eminem. In 1987, Marley Marl recorded "The Symphony," the posse cut that featured the early work of Masta Ace and Big Daddy Kane. Kane was new to the rap scene and without a single, much less an album of his own. The unproven rapper with the swagger to call himself Big Daddy was unknown when he dropped his classic verse on "The Symphony," the song that launched his career and made him one of the most respected and popular artists on Cold Chillin'. With a crisp, deep voice and the ability to rhyme at a leisurely pace or at what sounded like lightning speed, Big Daddy Kane was among the genre's most versatile MCs. Equal parts battle rhymer, sex symbol, and Five Percent Nation black nationalist, KANE was an acronym for King Asiatic Nobody's Equal.

Kane's lyrical superiority was evident on his debut album, *Long Live the Kane* (1988) . The album generated the undeniable hip hop classics "Raw," "Ain't No Half Steppin'," and "Set It Off." His classic 1989 follow-up, *It's a Big Daddy Thing*, cemented Kane as a force to be reckoned with in the genre at that time, with bass-heavy, soul-sample-based slow jams like "Smooth Operator" on the one hand, which sampled the Mary Jane Girls' "All Night Long"; on the other end of the spectrum, Kane would rip verses packed with articulate, fully enunciated, lacerating metaphors and punchlines on records like "Warm It Up, Kane," and "I Get the Job Done." Both *Long Live the Kane* and *It's a Big Daddy Thing* reached the Top 5 of Billboard's R&B/Hip-Hop Albums chart.

Kane also had the total package going for him: In addition to being an MC who could destroy anyone on the mic in a battle, he was politically astute, taking a pro-black stand on tracks like "Word to the Mother (Land)" and "Rap Summary (Lean on Me)." Big Daddy Kane was tall, dark, and handsome with a striking physique, extremely charismatic, and blessed with considerable dance ability. He kept up with the furious pace of his dancers, Skoob and Scrap, in videos and on stage at his electrifying concerts. A regular on the biggest sold-out tours throughout the late eighties and early nineties, Kane was known to go all out during live shows, stripping down to spandex biker shorts for the ladies, even soaking in a Jacuzzi. He was a fixture during the height of the New Jack Swing era, led by super-producer Teddy Riley. This ultimately worked against him toward the sunset of his career as a recording artist, when party raps and love raps gave way to gangsta rap. Kane, once the epitome of cool, suddenly was perceived as over-the-top and corny, posing shirtless on his album cover for 1991's *Taste of Chocolate*, wearing a silk robe on the cover of *Daddy's Home* (1994), and appearing in Madonna's photo book, *Sex*. Big Daddy Kane ultimately leaves a legacy of unparalleled writing ability and disciplined delivery across many styles of MCing. He was recognized at the 2005 VH1 Hip-Hop Honors.

Along with helping to spark Big Daddy Kane's career, "The Symphony" featured one of the first recorded verses from Masta Ace. Twenty-one and fresh out of college, Ace saw a flyer about a rap contest at a skating rink, awarding studio time with Marley as first prize. Ace jumped at the chance. In an exclusive interview for *Icons of Hip Hop*, He told the story vividly: "It was at United Skates of America in Queens. The first prize was six hours of studio time with Marley Marl. For Marley, I was 'the guy who I had to give these hours to,' and that took a year—but he was feelin' me enough to have me come back, and eventually I ended up on his compilation album."

That appearance on the now classic *In Control, Vol. 1* led to Ace's fortuitous cameo on a song that featured three other incredibly talented unknowns, Craig G, Kool G Rap, and Big Daddy Kane. Ace ended up filling in on "The Symphony" for the Juice Crew's MC Shan. "Shan was supposed to be on there," noted Ace, "but he felt he was playin' himself by being on the song with a bunch of cats with no albums out. 'The Symphony' crowned us the Juice Crew." If Marley's contest was the door that opened Masta Ace's career, Shan's ego blew the door off of it. Because Shan declined to drop a verse on "The Symphony," Ace became part of the hardest crew of MCs in New York at the time, on a label packed with heavy hitters. Ace was among the second generation of Cold Chillin' stars along with Biz Markie, Kool G Rap, Granddaddy I.U., DJ Kid Capri, and the Genius (who later changed his name to GZA and formed Wu-Tang Clan). Ace collaborated with Cold Chillin's first lady, Roxanne Shanté, writing three songs for her *Bad Sister* album.

Before it was popular for East Coast MCs to pay homage to or integrate West Coast production, Ace did both. Signing with West Coast–based label Delicious Vinyl, he released *SlaughtaHouse* in 1995, effectively unifying the sounds of each coast on one record. He achieved commercial success with his group Masta Ace Incorporated, whose album *Sittin' on Chrome* generated standout hits "Born to Roll" and "The I.N.C. Ride." Ace proved himself to be a progressive MC amid many a misogynist. At the peak of gangsta rap's woman-hating zenith, Ace went against the grain and opted to hand women the mic instead of degrading them with it by including Lashae and Paula Perry in the I.N.C. Over the course of his fifteen-year-plus career, Ace has recorded five albums and continues to tour the world performing a wide-ranging repertoire of driving, thought-provoking songs.

At the same time Ace was linking East and West Coast rap with his production style, his fellow Juice Crew member Kool G Rap was writing rhymes that would influence the hip hop subgenre that came to be known as gangsta rap. Before Los Angeles erupted with gangsta rap, before the Notorious B.I.G. dubbed himself Frank White (after the ruthless drug dealer in the cult classic film *King of New York*), there was Kool G Rap, an MC of uncompromising skill and laserlike visual descriptions. G Rap was as hard-core as any rapper had been up to the point at which he arrived on the scene in 1986.

The "Kool Genius of Rap," born Nathaniel Wilson and based in Queens, New York, started out as the rhyming half of Kool G Rap and DJ Polo, releasing the single "I'm Fly/It's a Demo" on Cold Chillin' before being anointed a member of the Juice Crew as a featured artist on "The Symphony" along with Kane, Ace, and Craig G. He recorded his first three albums with DJ Polo before they parted ways in the early nineties. Kool G Rap's rhymes were gritty tales of graphic, indiscriminate violence, told with the detail and wit of a master storyteller. He relayed the code of the streets as well as the consequences for disrespecting that code with an unmatched degree of cold intensity. His voice, curt and textured like gravel, was unmistakable due to his lisp. One might think that a speech impediment would handicap a recording artist, but this only added character and depth of feeling to his songs. Records like "Streets of New York," "Erase Racism," "Road to Riches," and "Poison" were irrefutable proof that Kool G Rap meant business, and he had plenty of examples, weapons, and warnings for anyone within the sound of his voice.

G Rap was a rapper's rapper: He spat each verse as if his life were hanging in the balance. He told the hideous truths about the game, the streets, and the music industry. He never held back, and though he only enjoyed moderate chart and commercial success, he continues to be widely regarded as the East Coast ambassador of hard-core street rap, and indeed a forefather of gangsta rap overall. Artists who modeled themselves after or deeply respected G Rap, including Fat Joe, Big L, Talib Kweli, Big Pun, and fellow Queens natives Nas and Mobb Deep, invited him to appear on a string of collaborations in the new millennium, generating momentum that unfortunately went unfulfilled for his comeback release, 2002's *The Giancana Story*. The songs for which he is remembered best from his formidable career are "Ill Street Blues" from the classic album *Live and Let Die* with DJ Polo and "It's a Shame," from his only Billboard R&B/Hip-Hop chart-topping album, the solo release titled *4,5,6*.

THE HOMEGIRL OF THE CREW

Lolita Shanté Gooden was born November 9, 1969, and grew up in Queensbridge Projects, the largest public housing development in America. Her father was an alcoholic. She was surrounded by drugs, hustlers, and violence. She wanted to be a lawyer when she grew up, but in the meantime, she would pass the time in her courtyard performing choreographed steps and hand games in girlhood round-robins, the prepubescent ritual that, in essence, is a precursor to the rhyme circles MCs compete in known as ciphers.

Shanté was innocent, but a quick study. In an exclusive interview for *Icons of Hip Hop*, she recalled being eleven years old when she recognized she "had a knack for rhyming" in the round of her asphalt jungle: "When it came to my turn I was very creative with my rhyme," she muses. "I started going project to project and battled for money. Hustlers would come and pick me up and ask me to battle for them." Indeed, Shanté was making a name for herself throughout the borough of Queens as a ferocious competitor, the freestyler to beat. Thus, her career began.

While Shanté was petite in stature with a high-pitched voice, she had an attitude and persona that were larger than life, belying her thirteen years. She never wanted to be a recording artist. "I wanted to be a lawyer when I grew up," she says. Ironically, she would wind up the victim of her own management, who took advantage of Shanté's status as a minor throughout her five years in the spotlight. "Those five years felt like twenty-five years," notes Shanté upon reflection. "I lost so much of my childhood, my innocence."

According to Shanté, much of that innocence was lost to Fly Ty, the head of Cold Chillin' Records. Shanté notes that Ty held the roles of "manager, road manager, booking agent, accountant, and father figure." With all her business being handled by one person, Roxanne was never fully informed about how much she made for the label to which she was signed. To date, she still doesn't know how many records she sold. "Roxanne's Revenge" was number one for three weeks and in the Top 10 for more than four weeks. "Some say 400,000 units, but it has to be more." Roxanne says that she has "very few good memories of [Cold Chillin' President Lenny Fischelberg], noting that he was "often causing a lot of separation within our crew."

This includes the way Cold Chillin' handled their contractual relationship with producer Marley Marl. Marley was the exclusive producer for the Cold Chillin' label, but he too was not seeing the income he deserved. Eventually, Marley took legal action. Ace remembers it well. "Marley was getting beat [out of pay] like the rest of us. He took Cold Chillin' to court and won the rights to the music he produced through a settlement that also allowed him to work with other artists. Once he got out of the contract, he produced LL Cool J's multiplatinum album, *Mama Said Knock You Out*. His obligation is to pay the publishing. I haven't been accounted to since 1990. That's where he messed up with all of us." Roxanne spent a total of eight years reclaiming her lyrics and masters as well.

Masta Ace attests to the unscrupulous practices of Fly Ty and Fischelberg. Ace wrote songs for Roxanne on her *Bad Sister* LP, and as her up-and-coming label mate, he observed how she and MC Shan, the label's marquis players at the time, were treated.

> Fly Ty was Shanté's management, and he was the CEO of Cold Chillin' so he was raping people—getting paid on both sides of the table. I was the first artist not to sign to with them for management, and Ty had an attitude with me about it. [Big Daddy] Kane got wise and went to [Russell Simmons's] RUSH Management. Biz left too eventually and got new management (see sidebar: Biz Markie). Lenny Fischelberg was the president. Dudes were barely making ends meet, but he had a yacht, his wife had mink on at the Christmas party. They had everyone's publishing. Eventually Lenny was beating Ty out of money too, because Ty was [known as] "Stay High Ty." He was using drugs.

Roxanne was being issued a weekly paycheck, as was MC Shan. Ace views this tactic as the label's way of avoiding paying her what she actually earned. It was common practice at that time to pay artists with homes, cars, and the trappings of success rather than paying them fairly and disclosing earnings with regular accounting statements. Cold Chillin' was no different. Ace continues, "The weekly appeasement of a check was meant to pacify her. That was the way they kept her and Shan at bay. They bought Biz [Markie] a 735 BMW after 'Just a Friend' exploded; they bought his house, studio equipment, and a car. What they bought was most likely a fraction of what he and other artists were owed."

Ace was witness to Shanté's formidable mic presence. It's what set her apart from her peers, both male and female, and part of what made her a hip hop icon. "When you talk about female MCs, you have to start with her," Ace insisted during our interview. "There were women before her, but none that

Biz Markie
Mickey Hess

Biz Markie, also known as the Diabolical Biz Markie, the Ambassador of Hip Hop, and the Clown Prince of Hip Hop, began his career with the Juice Crew in 1985, beatboxing for Roxanne Shanté at her concerts. Only fifteen at the time, Biz made a name for himself as a beatboxer, DJ, and MC. He released his first solo album, *Goin' Off*, in 1988. Backed by the singer TJ Swan, Biz beatboxed and rhymed on songs like "Make the Music with Your Mouth, Biz" and "Nobody Beats the Biz," which borrowed its title and chorus from a slogan for a New York City electronics store called the Wiz. "The Vapors" tells a story about the different reactions Biz and his friends got from people in his neighborhood before and after his hip hop stardom.

Still active in music, Biz has maintained his position as a hip hop icon even though he may be best known for his catchy pop hit "Just a Friend" and for the 1991 sampling lawsuit that nearly destroyed his career. Biz sampled portions of Gilbert O'sullivan's "Alone Again (Naturally)" for his song "Alone Again," and when O'sullivan won a subsequent lawsuit, Biz's 1991 album *I Need a Haircut* was recalled from stores. Biz's career survived the lawsuit and the unprecedented fine levied against him by Judge Kevin Thomas Duffy. Always the clown, Biz referenced the lawsuit in the title of his 1993 comeback album, *All Samples Cleared*.

While he has slowed in releasing albums over the past decade, Biz remains a hip hop icon who DJs in clubs and guests on the albums of other rap artists. In 2001, he toured with the inaugural Spitkickers Tour, along with Talib Kweli, De La Soul, Jurassic 5, Dilated Peoples, and Pharoah Monch. Biz has guest starred on albums by De La Soul and the Beastie Boys, and in 2005 he starred on the VH1 reality show *Celebrity Fit Club*, which puts actors and musicians in a weight loss competition. Biz, who is known for scratching turntables with his belly at concerts, lost forty pounds, more weight than any of his competitors.

Further Resource

Biz Markie Official Website. www.bizmarkie.com.

---

did it on record, on video, and had her impact. She made other females want to rhyme, and she took on guys. She wasn't trying to be hard or overly masculine. She was the round-the-way girl who could rhyme and cuss you out at the same time. Debby Deb, Sequence, they were party rappers. Roxanne is a point of reference for women as hip hop artists. She was definitely the first to get respect from men on the streets. She's the first woman who could go up against any male in a battle."

But on wax, she'd come for another woman and in so doing, make history. The story of the battle of the Roxannes usually starts at the point where Shanté offered to cut "Roxanne's Revenge" for Mr. Magic, Marley Marl, and Fly Ty, who had promoted a U.T.F.O. concert that the group never showed up for. Veteran on-air personality and hip hop cultural icon Kool DJ Red Alert was the disc jockey who was the first to play "Roxanne, Roxanne" by U.T.F.O. on the radio. His choice of this song was far from accidental. Red Alert was in the mix at 98.7 KISS New York in 1985. The label serviced him with the U.T.F.O. twelve-inch single "Hangin' Up." Red Alert thought its B side, "Roxanne Roxanne," sounded better: "They wanted to promote 'Hangin' Up,'" he recalls. "I didn't care for the A side, so I flipped it over and played it." He even took a little heat for it from Fred Maneo, the president of U.T.F.O.'s label, Select Records. Maneo thanked Red Alert for playing the record, but chided him for playing the wrong side. "During this time, if anything new and exciting came on during my mix, it would circulate through all the schools because the kids would tape my show and talk about it all week long." By the time a week elapsed, the word was out all over the city about U.T.F.O.'s new song. Red Alert had his answer: he had broken a hit.

    U.T.F.O. (Untouchable Force Organization) was made up of Mixmaster Ice, the Educated Rapper, Doctor Ice, and Kangol Kid. The group exploded with their track about Roxanne, the fictional girl who refused to give them the time of day. They performed throughout the New York City area on the heels of their smash hit. But when U.T.F.O. canceled on Mr. Magic, who was the disc jockey for New York's WBLS, Roxanne took up the fight on vinyl. However, according to Red Alert, by the time Marley Marl brought a tape of "Roxanne's Revenge" to Mr. Magic to play on the air on that fateful Sunday night, he was on a different station, WHBI 105.9. The song caused a commotion that rippled through a then very small, tight-knit rap industry. Shortly after the debut of "Roxanne's Revenge," Red Alert visited the offices of Russell Simmons at Def Jam Records and RUSH Management. At the time, Simmons managed reggae artist Jimmy Spicer, rapper Spyder D, and others. Spyder was at the office the day Red Alert came by. Spyder came to play a song for Russell recorded by his then-girlfriend, Sparky D. The song was "Sparky's Turn," an answer record tailor-made for Shanté that was released on Nia Records. A fourteen-year-old girl had ushered in a concept of lyrical rivalry that was far from friendly. Red Alert watched the rivalry develop from the stage as Sparky D's DJ. Red Alert considers Shanté to be a cornerstone of MC battling. "Shanté was the one, no lie. Sparky was the underdog because Shanté sparked the whole thing. Before Shanté's battle records, there was only 'The Showdown,' a record featuring the Furious Five versus the Sugarhill Gang. But it was a friendly record between label mates, designed to promote each group at one time."

    The lyrical contest between Roxanne and Sparky was so popular that they toured together and performed their respective battle rhymes on the same bill. Red Alert hit the road backing Sparky, who even cut him the song "He's My DJ." While hip hop beef has escalated to tragic outcomes in recent history,

Red Alert notes that at that time artists kept their attacks on record, and it rarely spiraled out of control because "entourages were not so big that they could rev things up between camps." Sparky D never released her own album, but Roxanne was on a roll. Red Alert described "Roxanne's Revenge" as an explosion that "made her presence felt." "Queen of Rox" got people to the dance floor in clubs all over the city. By the time "Bite This" came out, "everybody was for Shanté," recalls Red Alert. "She was making a stamp for herself."

QUEEN OF ROX

Shanté cut five twelve-inch singles after "Roxanne's Revenge": "Runaway," "Queen of Rox," "Bite This," "Def Fresh Crew" (with Biz Markie), and "Fly Shanté." Shanté was a headliner in her own right, and she performed tirelessly, even while pregnant with her first child at age fourteen. She rocked the stage while visibly pregnant, sparking protests in some cities. "Mothers would be picketing me, saying I was promoting teen pregnancy," she recalls. Though by all indications from her lyrics, Shanté was bold, brazen, and in full control, the reality of her life was the polar opposite. In her interview for this essay, she explained that she had no choice but to perform under those conditions. She had emancipated herself as a minor at age sixteen. Without parents to guide or protect her, she looked to a man to fill the void. She got involved with an older man who rendered her powerless with physical and psychological abuse. A seemingly indestructible young woman was imprisoned by the abusive, exploitive relationship she was in. It certainly impacted her view of men as untrustworthy and dangerous. This sentiment was echoed time and again in her songs like "Brothers Ain't Shit," which Shanté says includes her favorite rhymes.

"My boyfriend at the time was eighteen years my elder. He was the father of my child. When our son was born, I needed to present my emancipation documents to leave the hospital with my baby. My boyfriend withheld those documents and dangled them before me whenever I threatened to leave him. This went on for three years. The only way I could raise my child was by staying with him." Shanté's own father was an alcoholic. She would not comment on her mother's absence, but it caused Roxanne to emancipate herself so she could provide for herself on her own. Being a child whose parents were not in her own life, she could not conceive of being an absentee mother.

In addition to her problems at home, she was also being exploited creatively. In the studio, she freestyled her rhymes for her early recordings. The lyrics to "Roxanne's Revenge," "Bite This," "Runaway," and "Queen of Rox," for example, were never written down, yet people in the studio with her would sign their names to her work as the writers of those songs. She was told to split her concert earnings with Fly Ty and Marley Marl equally, and did so, ignorant of the pay scale for DJs and producers when she was the top-billed artist. Shanté trusted no one. She would bring her child to the venue and keep her eyes on him throughout her set. "I would hand my son to the bodyguard, perform, leave the stage, then get my son back and go to the hotel. It was really me against the world onstage." What audiences who watched her perform were actually witnessing was a volcano erupting.

Shanté toured the world on the strength of these hits with the Juice Crew. She headlined the Fresh Fest Tour as the only female on the bill with LL Cool J, Public Enemy, and Eric B. & Rakim. She signed with Columbia Records and released her debut album, *Roxanne*, in 1988. It contained the hits that made her a household name throughout ghettos of America. She followed with her second and last album of new material in 1989, *Bad Sister*, which she recorded with the Cold Chillin' label. At this point in her career, she performed songs written by Big Daddy Kane, "Go on Girl" and "Have a Nice Day," both of which were hits.

Roxanne Shanté notes her collaboration with Rick James as the highlight of her career and her proudest moment as an artist. She and James recorded "Loosey's Rap" when she went to his home in Buffalo, New York, to meet and record with him. They recorded the song that became a number one R&B smash and a Top 10 pop hit on the first night of her stay. But she was his guest for another two weeks. James taught her about the ups and downs of the business, mentoring her on its pitfalls. She was enthralled by all the plaques, awards, and wealth he had amassed, an outcome vastly different from her experience as a recording star. "I was in awe of his house for another two days." Their collaboration culminated in a shared bill in which Shanté and James performed at the Apollo together. Hip hop had become all the rage, giving traditional funk and R&B a run for its proverbial money on the black music scene. Roxanne recalls her first look at their names on the Apollo marquee. In her view, it serves as a metaphor for the divisive tendencies of the music industry in relation to generations of black musicians. "I saw 'Roxanne Shanté and Rick James' on the marquee. I was like, 'Wow, look at that!' My mother and manager told me to have the venue change it to put his [name] on top, out of respect for an artist who had paved the way for me. Young artists get caught up being the one with the hot record of the moment, and I wanted to show Rick James respect."

Cold Chillin' was a subsidiary of Warner Brothers Records. Because she was a minor when she signed, it was written into her contract that her education would be financed by the label, with no limit on the amount of tuition paid or term of subsidy. In an ocean of hopeless circumstances, this was Shanté's blessing in disguise. She feels that this clause was a way for her handlers to assuage their guilt; she also asserts that they all underestimated her and never thought she would pursue education on a long-term basis. No one involved with Shanté's career believed she would take early retirement at eighteen, but that is exactly what she did. "They thought I would get strung out and end up having more babies," she laughs. "But God had a bigger plan for me, so I socked it to them."

Roxanne was eighteen years old with two children when she realized she was exhausted from being used by the rap industry and abused by her boyfriend. She had come to associate rhyming with being abused and mistreated. While she issues a disclaimer of "not being a religious fanatic," what she describes about her prayer after five years of growing up too fast and hurting too much was for her a miracle. "I woke up one morning and decided I didn't want to rap anymore; I had a distaste in my mouth for it. I was in an abusive relationship with this man and my label, the people I created with, they all let me travel the world with him, get black eyes from him. We were all supposed to get rich together, buy nice houses, and rise up out of poverty together. I realized that if I was no longer a commodity, they would let me go. I asked God to order my steps. I walked out of my house, and I ended up at the steps of Marymount University."

Shanté registered and took courses at Marymount. She also did undergraduate study at Cornell, but eventually returned to Marymount where she earned a doctorate in psychology, becoming Dr. Roxanne Shanté. Now thirty-three years old, she heads up a thriving psychology practice in Manhattan. Her upbringing and experience as an abused teenage mother informs her practice. The majority of her clients are women in or recovering from abusive relationships and mothers fighting to regain custody of their children. She is in the process of obtaining certification as a Court Appointed Special Advocate (CASA) for the State of New York. And she has not given up on her dream of becoming an attorney.

She had a taste of the legal profession during her ordeal to secure her master recordings. Her story is an example of the arduous journey to ownership of one's own intellectual property after years of being misled and shut out with respect to the status of one's work.

THE LEGACY OF ROXANNE SHANTÉ

Shanté is often regarded as a gifted performer but not necessarily the author of her own material. Fellow Juice Crew MC Big Daddy Kane did in fact write for her, but not until her second album; the hit songs that put her on the map were of her own creation, arrangement, and design. They were made up in the moment while recording, just like her round-robin cheers in the Queensbridge projects had been. Shanté's lyrics are a bold testament to how raw the creativity of hip hop was, often going from the streets or the mind right to tape, skipping a rhyme book altogether. She is an example of a "writer" whose pen was the microphone, whose paper was the reel-to-reel studio tape. Kanye West and Jay-Z count themselves among artists like Shanté who rarely write down their lyrics—not only to protect them from being misappropriated, but as an extension of the griot style of storytelling, a tradition of musical expression rooted in the drum and born on the continent of Africa.

This method of creation presented a problem for Roxanne Shanté: Since she freestyled much of her work and was naive about the mechanics of publishing and royalties, instead of protecting her lyrics from being copied by another rapper, never writing them down served to make her vulnerable to intellectual property theft. She never signed contracts with her producers or managers, yet many of her handlers claimed writing credit on her songs beyond the scope of their actual contribution. "Other artists were listed as writers on my music because they were present in the studio," she notes incredulously years later. She did not realize anything had been stolen from her until she began to educate herself about the industry from which she retired:

> I went to every seminar and skills class so I could find out what was stolen from me. I went back to my producers and asked them to present a contract. I never signed contracts, so they could not come up with them. When I told them if they falsified contracts, I would fight them in court, they'd offer me a thousand dollars to sign my rights away. I thought to myself, "They really think I am stupid!" Once I saw that these guys were the same deceitful people they were when I was rapping, I decided to take it all. I wrote down the addresses to every house I'd been to for parties, meetings, or celebrations and if they belonged to anyone who claimed to own my music, I put a lien on those addresses. Then I waited for them to attempt to refinance or sell. To their surprise, there my name would be on the title search. Eventually, they would contact me. I would ask them what they intended to do with "our house." One person actually said, "It's my house, not our house!" I reminded them that they bought the property with the money they made pretending to be me. I ended up owning all my masters.

In 2005, Shanté sued Janet Jackson for using her voice without permission on her album, *Damita Jo*. Shanté discovered her voice saying the infamous words, "so fresh" from her song "Def Fresh Crew," which also features Biz Markie. As an artist who spent most of her career having her work exploited, she is now vigilant about protecting her assets and intellectual property rights. One of the ways she does this is by leaving her name off as the owner. She has found that "being a black woman that owns her masters makes people want to find ways around paying," so she lets those who seek the use of her music do the research to find and contact her. If they don't, once she discovers any misuse, she addresses it. Upon recording "Like You Don't Love Me," neither Jackson nor anyone in her camp looked for Shanté to get permission. By the time Shanté had sent an invoice for payment, the infamous wardrobe malfunction (in which Jackson's breast was exposed) had taken place at Super Bowl 38. "Her people said she was going through a lot, so I waited, figuring they would get around to paying me," she recalls. Months passed. Shanté called. Then she was told by Jackson representatives that the sample was not even her voice. "That's when I got upset," said Shanté. "Anyone who knows hip hop music knows that's my voice; they may think it's from 'Nobody Beats the Biz,' but it is actually from 'Def Fresh Crew,' which I own. It wasn't something I preferred to do but at that point, after being insulted, I brought the suit."

In the meantime, Shanté had gotten into the voice-over business after retiring from music, performing in animated programs and films. She had voiceprints made to authenticate her characters and prevent impersonation. She went a step further while she was getting her voiceprints made. "Something told me to have one made of me rhyming. I sent a copy to Ms. Jackson's people. No response." So she started to research Janet Jackson's property holdings in search of the right to place a lien against the royalties she was owed. "Word leaked to her attorney that I investigated some of her real estate. Right before I placed the lien, the check came." Shanté is unequivocal about her stand to protect her musical legacy. The days of others using her creativity are long over. She is the embodiment of information in action for artists who want to protect and benefit from their work. On her Myspace.com home page, she pledges her commitment to answer questions to help any artist avoid the path she traveled.

Unlike many unsung heroes and heroines of hip hop, Shanté won great acclaim while she was actively recording and touring as a skilled lyricist and dynamic performer. She did not have to wait until she was deemed a "pioneer" to receive the respect she was due. She does not count herself among the "angry old-school rappers" who gave hip hop its start. "I have been through and survived so much. I had my time, I did it very well, and no one can do it like me again. I'm in the history books for it. I take the titles and accept them all. It's their turn now; I couldn't be 'the one' forever. Am I upset at how women are representing the music today? Yes. Am I upset that they have sex shows instead of live shows? Yes I am. But I dote on the fact that I gave birth to those female MCs." Shanté likens commercial rap music and hip hop to respective "children of the same mother; one lives a lavish life, the other is still struggling." She calls herself an MC and draws a line of distinction between MCs and "rappers," a line that the corporatization and mainstreaming of hip hop music via entertainment industry has necessitated. "An MC will move a crowd without a hit record. The rapper *has* to have the song to move the crowd; without the song the audience could care less what rappers have to say. Rappers need videos, MCs don't," Shanté laughs.

The far-reaching impact of Roxanne Shanté is deftly exemplified by Mystic, a female MC who paid homage to Shanté in 2006 in her guest verse for the remix of "I Love Being a B-Boy" by the Crown City Rockers. Even today, women artists must be vigilant about keeping the history of their contributions to the art form of MCing top of mind. As the sole female on a song full of male rhymers, Mystic embraces the charge of representing the ladies, just as Shanté did two decades before: "I love bein' a b-girl even now that I'm grown." Mystic, who was discovered by dance hall artist Jamal-Ski and toured the world with Digital Underground, has made a name for herself without being the first lady of any one crew. Though she cut her teeth on MCing and is a prolific lyricist, Mystic is acknowledged as an equally skilled vocalist as well. The Grammy-nominated artist had this to say when asked to reflect on the impact of Roxanne Shanté: "What is so amazing about her is that she was just a fly chick; she never compromised herself in her rhymes. When I heard her for the first time, it was like, wow—a *female* who was dope at battle rapping! There was no way you could miss her and she was just as dope as the dudes!"

Mystic echoes Roxanne's own sentiment about the exploitation of women in rap, but from another angle: "We had so few women at that time, but their voices were so loud. It's a shame that so much [current rap] music has men giving out directions [to women] on how to degrade themselves: 'Shake this,' 'drop that.'" Mystic's observation stings with irony: Despite their volume in the genre today, women's voices are being drowned out by the sexually explicit, completely disrespectful content of their male counterparts. Add to the equation the hypersexualization of female artists by their handlers and record labels, and you have a sonic landscape that is imbalanced at best and insidiously dangerous at worst. As women rappers' voices are muted by chauvinist marketing and lyrics lacking substance, the assertive, womanist ring of Shanté's voice continues to echo with unparalleled power. This power to raise her voice in a crowd of men, to rise above the abuses and injustices handed to her by such men, is her legacy. In her short career, Roxanne Shanté left an indelible mark on hip hop, creating the mold for bold MCs of any gender, setting a standard of freestyle improvisation for all comers to meet. And today, she is a beacon for any artist who was exploited and seeks redress for publishing rights, master recordings, and monies owed retroactively. Shanté experienced the worst exploitation imaginable and emerged victorious by using the legal system to her advantage. Her perseverance in the recovery of her intellectual property is both an inspiration and an admonition to protect one's creativity at all costs. The industry did not break Roxanne Shanté. In fact, she broke away from it and thrives today as an entrepreneur, psychologist, and hip hop activist, serving on the board of directors for the Hip-Hop Association. Shanté is truly a hip hop icon.

See also: Queen Latifah, Nas, MC Lyte, Lil' Kim, Salt-N-Pepa

WORKS CITED

Kool DJ Red Alert. Interview with the author. March 2006.
Masta Ace. Interview with the author. June 19, 2006.
Mystic. Interview with the author. May 11, 2006.
Shanté, Roxanne. Interview with the author. February 24, 2006.
Shanté, Roxanne. Profile at Myspace.com. www.myspace.com/roxanneshante.

FURTHER RESOURCES

Bynoe, Yvonne. *Encyclopedia of Rap and Hip-Hop Culture.* Author, 2004.
Chang, Jeff. *Can't Stop Won't Stop: A History of the Hip-Hop Generation.* New York: St. Martin's Press, 2005.
Guevara, Nancy. "Women Writin' Rappin' Breakin.'" In William Eric Perkins, ed. *Droppin' Science: Critical Essays on Rap Music and Hip-Hop Culture.* Philadelphia: Temple UP, 1996: 49–62.
Paniccioli, Ernie and Kevin Powell, eds. *Who Shot Ya? Three Decades of Hip-Hop Photography.* New York: Amistad, 2002.
Pough, Gwendolyn. *Check It While I Wreck It: Black Womanhood, Hip-Hop, and the Public Sphere.* Boston: Northeastern UP, 2004.
Strong, Nolan. "Roxanne Shanté Files Lawsuit Against Janet Jackson." *All Hiphop News*, October 2004. http://www.allhiphop.com/hiphopnews/?ID=3624.
Strong, Nolan. "Roxanne Shante: An Incredible Journey." *All Hiphop Features*, September 2004. http://www.allhiphop.com/features/?ID=914.

SELECTED DISCOGRAPHY

Roxanne. Columbia Records, 1988.
Bad Sister. Cold Chillin', 1989.
Greatest Hits. Cold Chillin', 1995.
The Best of Cold Chillin'. Landspeed, 2005.

Courtesy of Photofest.

Run-DMC

Jeb Aram Middlebrook

Run-DMC defined what a hip hop icon was and would be to future hip hoppers and rap fans. What made Run-DMC special and ultimately iconic was their ability to tell the story of the American dream through the perspectives of three young black males from Hollis, Queens, and to tell the story in such a way that the world would listen. The marketing decisions made by Run-DMC's management team, including Bill Adler, Rick Rubin, and Russell Simmons, were key to positioning Run-DMC as an icon in their own time and into the future. Run-DMC's management harnessed the possibilities and influence of mass media and new recording technologies to make Run-DMC an icon in the minds of millions of consumers globally. Run-DMC, as a group and management team, enacted myths of Americana within a uniquely hip hop context to model on a corporate level what would become popularly known as the hustle, and produced a double framework of authenticity and crossover appeal that would serve hip hop icons and fans long after their reign.

Celebrity making has a long history in America, but Run-DMC not only helped to redefine how a hip hop act could use new technologies and media to create a career in music, they also helped to redefine the notion of celebrity in America. They broke barriers of who was allowed to be seen and heard on a mass scale. Important to this discussion is the story of how Run-DMC earned the respect and trust of the people from the inner city of New York that they claimed to represent, while at the same time gaining respect and trust from the music industry and advertising executives who gave their music global reach and signed their checks. How Run-DMC managed this cross-cultural appeal in business and marketing is the story of their iconic status, and helped define early in hip hop history what made a hip hop icon.

Run-DMC was one of the first to introduce the notion of a hip hop brand; the notion that a brand identity could exist separate from and beyond the bodies of the rap performers. Run-DMC ultimately became bigger than any one of its members—Run, Jam Master Jay, or DMC. The advent of music videos, which were both a new medium for music and a music marketing strategy, created new possibilities for artists in the mid-eighties. MTV debuted in 1981 and provided musicians a place to be seen as well as heard, but the lack of videos from black artists was an issue, and it was not until Run DMC's "Rock Box" in 1984 that MTV aired a rap video. The significance of rock music to Run-DMC's sound and subsequent commercial appeal is also significant in terms of race, class, and representation. Run-DMC's ability to guarantee authenticity and crossover appeal by combining rap and rock is a story about different sonic and racial worlds coming together and sometimes colliding. Run-DMC successfully branded themselves across multiple commercial markets and in this way drew on American myths that spoke to people across race and culture in the United States (and globally). They earned the respect of scores of White rock fans, scores of black and brown rap fans, and scores of fans in between. Their approach to making music was a conscious and lucrative marketing strategy by Def Jam Entertainment, Run-DMC's management, and was foundational in terms of defining and cementing Run-DMC's iconic status (see sidebar: Def Jam: Rap Enters the Mainstream). The rap-rock merging in combination with the strategic use of media by Run-DMC, in terms of videos, touring, and print media—as well as the prioritization of rock music videos on MTV in the mid-1980s—led Run-DMC to have the first rap video on MTV with "Rock Box" in 1984, followed by the hugely successful "Walk This Way" in 1986. These factors, among others, ultimately positioned Run-DMC to define what an icon was on their own terms.

MIC CHECK

In the years leading up to Run-DMC's debut, the world witnessed kids memorizing the scenes in *Wild Style* and *Breakin'*, and copying the dance moves and mural styles they saw in film and on TV. By 1982, hip hop had arrived in full force and was the hottest thing on the scene at hip clubs like the Roxy.

Def Jam: Rap Enters the Mainstream
Jeb Aram Middlebrook

Before the rap label Def Jam became known to the world in 1984, the two founders, Russell Simmons and Rick Rubin, had their own projects. Russell Simmons, brother of Joseph Simmons (later known as Run of Run-DMC), was juggling management and production, making beats, and throwing shows. Early on, Russell managed his brother Joseph as DJ Run; Run worked with Kurtis Blow, the first hip hop artist to record a full-length album on a major label (in 1979). Russell had a keen eye for talent, and positioned himself as an artist manager and developer with his own company, Rush Management. Rick Rubin, meanwhile, was running a small record label, Def Jam, out of his NYU dorm room von University Place in Greenwich Village. His musical aesthetic matched Russell's: huge beats, minimal melody, and aggressive vocals. Russell saw the Def Jam imprint on the record "It's Yours" by T. LaRock and Jazzy J, and wanted to meet the guy who'd made the beat. Russell and Rick met and their partnership as co-owners of Def Jam ensued. They both rebelled against the smooth R&B that typified black music on the radio at the time; and both embraced the rebel attitude that hip hop embodied. As Russell put it, they both saw that there was more in common between AC/DC and rappers than between rappers and Luther Vandross. By the time Russell became co-owner of Def Jam, he had already penned a record deal with Priority Records for Run and his group, Run-DMC. Their first album, *Run-DMC* (1983), would become a hip hop classic. Russell continued to manage Run-DMC from within Def Jam and helped to successfully guide their career and branding on Priority Records. Russell's goal with Run-DMC was to sell "black teenage music" to black teenagers, as well as to mainstream America. For Russell, ghetto attitude came as second nature to many of the early MCs, but his view was that they didn't see their theatrics in their own lives. They would polish it up for mass consumption by wearing what Rick James or a rock band would wear. Run-DMC represented a brand that saw what was happening in the street and stayed true to it. "I've always thought it takes a bit of a suburbanite—as we were, coming from Queens—to see the power in ghetto culture," Russell said (Simmons 69). The third Run-DMC album, *Raising Hell* (1986) on Priority Records, following *King of Rock* (1985), proved to be the tipping point for hip hop—the tipping point that would thrust hip hop onto the world stage and give people a glimpse of what hip hop could and would be. *Raising Hell* was the album that raised the stakes of hip hop while burying the Bronx. Rhyming skills on the corner could not hold weight against MCs with publicists, tour managers, and image consultants—especially when the rap group was Run-DMC and the management was Russell Simmons and Def Jam.

Work Cited

Simmons, Joseph. *It's Like That: A Spiritual Memoir*. New York: St. Martin's Press, 2000.

There, British expatriate Kool Lady Blue created a sensation booking DJs, MCs, graffiti writers, and break dancers in weekly celebrations of hip hop culture. The Bronx was the place to be for hip hop. Soon a second generation of performers emerged. Soon the promise of cash and prestige brought new promoters, bookers, mangers, and performers to the scene. Then the artists of Rush Management, including Kurtis Blow and Run-DMC, arrived to change the rap game forever. It was time for the Bronx to sit down, and for Queens to stand up.

Run-DMC became a pioneer in New York City rap. The group was formed by Joseph "Run" Simmons (born November 14, 1964), Darryl "DMC" McDaniels (born May 31, 1964), and DJ "Jam Master Jay" Mizell (January 21, 1965 – October 30, 2002). The trio originally performed as Orange Crush in the early eighties, and renamed themselves Run-DMC in 1982 after graduating from St. Pascal's Catholic School. They had known each other as children in the Hollis district of Queens in New York City. Run-DMC circulated demos in the underground mixtape circuit and eventually signed to Profile Records for an advance of $2,500, immediately scoring a U.S. underground hit with "It's Like That" (see sidebar: Mixtape Promotion). It was the single's B side, "Sucker MCs," however, that began to turn Run-DMC into an icon.

Mixtape Promotion
Shamika Ann Mitchell

Before and after the advent of leaking albums on Internet file-sharing sites in the late 1990s, many rappers used the mixtape industry to their advantage by releasing unofficial tracks to create interest in a forthcoming album. As the mixtape became a marketing tool in the 1980s, reputable mixtape DJs began to use their clout to attract premier rappers to perform on their mixtapes. This is advantageous to both the DJ and the rapper; while the DJ has exclusive access (which helps to guarantee sales), the rapper is able to stay true to his roots as a street artist and maintain his credibility. One mixtape form that rose to popularity in the late 1990s hails from the South. Called "slow music" or "screwed," the songs are played at significantly slower speeds by a process originated by the late legendary DJ Screw, who hailed from Houston. Many Southern-based DJs are adding scratches and cuts to these screwed mixes, essentially chopping up the song; these songs are called "screwed and chopped."

Because mixtapes were also used as demo tapes for rappers, they became viable outlets for new artists to get exposure. Even today, mixtapes are credited with playing a crucial role in a number of major rappers' careers. As a promotional and marketing tactic, mixtapes not only help to generate interest in a rapper's upcoming project (especially for one who has taken a hiatus) but also keep the artist relevant and contemporary until the next album is released. In addition, several rappers have made efforts to release mixtapes in addition to their commercial studio releases; two rappers who are best known for this are 50 Cent and Cam'ron. Because mixtapes are considered to be the entry level of hip hop, the street buzz they generate is essential to introduce an artist. Most important, mixtape sales are also a reliable indicator for anticipating an artist's success. Furthermore, an artist who is successful on the mixtape circuit will have better chances of securing a profitable recording contract. Because of their influence and widespread impact, mixtapes are an invaluable resource to both record industry executives and artists alike.

The mixtape business and phenomenon originated in New York City, and it has only within recent years spread to other major American cities. Still, New York City's mom-and-pop music stores and street vendors reign as the premier mixtape retailers. The notoriety mixtapes have received over the years has prompted the Mixtape Awards, founded by the late Justo Faison. The Mixtape Awards celebrate artists and DJs alike for their efforts. From a commercial perspective, many corporate giants are using the mixtape's appeal to promote their products. One of the most successful mixtape campaigns is the And-1 Mixtape Tour, which features streetballers in a national basketball tour. For several years, not only has And-1 managed to promote their products via the mixtapes, but they also have Frito-Lay's commercials and a reality television series of the And-1 Mixtape Tour on ESPN.

"Sucker MCs" became a popular phrase in rap slang, a term that separated the real MCs from the fake ones. It signified an important stage in hip hop, where rap parlance was elevated to the level of pop speech and quickly distinguished those who lived hip hop from those who just listened to rap. Many critics say that the single "Sucker MCs" marked the birth of modern hip hop. Its sound was bare-bones, involving no instruments aside from a drum machine and a turntable, and Run-DMC provided the iconic fashion image of the b-boy, or break dancer: street clothing, chiefly sportswear, and street language. Following the success of "Sucker MCs," Run-DMC's album went gold in 1984, the first time a rap album achieved that level of sales. Run-DMC's mainstream popularity allowed them to take their act on the road, touring extensively throughout the United States and Europe. With their album sales, music videos, and concerts, Run-DMC quickly became the face of rap music in the popular imagination. In 1985, they extended their work to film, appearing in *Krush Groove*, a Def Jam vehicle that showcased performances from Run-DMC, The Beastie Boys, Kurtis Blow, and other artists signed to the label.

IT'S TRICKY

"It's tricky ..." ran the second track on Run-DMC's best-known album, *Raising Hell* (1986). DMC said the song was about how the hip hop industry can be complicated for a young black artist (Coleman 35). Run-DMC represented street poetry revamped, plugged in, amplified, and marketed. Jay, Joe, and Darryl were from Hollis—a working-class community for upwardly mobile blacks. These aspiring entertainers, however, acted as if the neighborhoods south of the Grand Central Parkway, west of Francis Lewis Boulevard, north of Hollis Avenue, and east of 184th Street were the South Bronx—dangerous, crime-ridden streets. The microphone, the amplifier, allowed them to live out these fantasies at high volume. DJ Run, aka Son of Kurtis Blow, lived the performer's life as early as eighth grade. DMC, calling himself Grandmaster Get High early in his exposure to music, smoked joints and drank quarts of beer in the basement of his parents' house while they were at work or asleep. These were DMC's practice sessions on the turntables. The street life of Hollis was filled with private houses rather than the apartment buildings of the Bronx, and Joe and Darryl experienced supportive and financially secure family lives. The group's third member, Jam Master Jay, was born in Brooklyn and moved to Hollis with his family when he was ten years old.

Early on in Run-DMC's development, Russell Simmons (Run's brother) took it upon himself to promote the group. His goal, however, was not to make rap music with Run-DMC. He wanted to make black teenage music. And more important, Russell wanted to make successful black heroes, which he felt he did with Run-DMC and Kurtis Blow (Cepeda 49). Realness trumped being positive for Russell, however, and what defined realness according to Rush Management meant playing on some notion of the street. Run explained that their contemporary, Eazy-E of N.W.A. (Niggaz Wit Attitude), couldn't rap because he was truly a gangster (Quinn 73). A strategic embrace of the street, but with a calculated distance, was the signature for Run-DMC: to represent hip hop as it existed in the street, but without living the street life. The group idolized the Cold Crush Brothers, a street phenomenon in early eighties New York hip hop, but who faded into the background without the major push received by groups and labels such as the Sugarhill Gang (who received industry backing for their single "Rapper's Delight" in 1979). In 1983 Cold Crush records were not garnering fan support, and the doors were open for something new.

"Our whole thing," DMC says, "was to be like the Cold Crush Brothers." (Coleman 31). Run-DMC, however, wanted to produce the best show, the best rhymes, and the best DJ, and come with more beats than anybody. Cold Crush were Run-DMC's idols, but Run-DMC also wanted to be better than Cold Crush. In 1984 things were going well for Rush Management, the biggest management company in hip hop. Russell Simmons had Kurtis Blow and Whodini, as well as the Fearless Four. Russell also had a hip hop band called Orange Krush that included Davey DMX, Larry Smith, drummer Trevor Gale, and singer Alyson Williams, which helped form the early sound that Russell would take into the studio to later develop Run-DMC.

According to Simmons, Run-DMC's greatest asset was that they never aspired to be bigger (Simmons 64). They aspired to keep it real, close to the street, when that wasn't yet considered important in rap. And that attitude allowed them to outdistance all other rappers in the eighties. Rappers at the time would tell it differently. Rush Management had the handle on technology, and technology—including drum machines, amplifiers, radio, and television—is what would prove to be a boon for Run-DMC, and for hip hop in general (see sidebar: The 808). Grandmaster Caz recalled that Run-DMC was the cutoff point between the era of Grandmaster Flash and the Furious Five, Cold Crush, Funky 4+1, the Fearless 4s, the Fantastic 5s, and hip hop after that (Fricke and Ahearn 328). The pre-Run-DMC era had advanced hip hop from its bare basics, according to Caz, from a baby movement, in the park with speakers and plugging into light poles. While the Sugar Hill record label pinched pennies—denying artists drum machines and new

The 808
George Ciccariello-Maher

The Roland TR-808 drum machine is a legendary piece of hip hop production equipment. Immediately rendered obsolete upon its release in 1980 by the superior sound and sampling technology of the Linn Drum (the Linn LM-1), the 808 was an unlikely candidate for fame. But the combination of a relatively low price tag ($1,000 compared to $5,000 for the Linn) and a classic (if notably artificial) sound made the 808 a must-have for such rap originators as Run-DMC, Eric B. & Rakim, Boogie Down Productions, and Public Enemy. Specifically, the 808 featured a deep bass kick that made it an essential ingredient of the rap sound of the mid-1980s.

Despite the fact that the 808 appeared in the work of Japanese electropop group Yellow Magic Orchestra as early as 1980, it would be through the influence of rap artists more than five years later that a younger generation would come to venerate the 808 sound. In fact, it was only after Roland had ceased production of the 808 that its popularity peaked. The 808 would find a place in the early gangsta rap of N.W.A. and its later G-Funk offshoot in the work of Dr. Dre, Warren G, and Snoop Dogg. It would even find popularity in the more mainstream hip hop of the Beastie Boys, DJ Jazzy Jeff and the Fresh Prince, Sir Mix-a-Lot, and Vanilla Ice, as well as in several genres of electronic music.

Seminal Bay Area rapper Too $hort also made use of the device on his earliest songs, and Outkast made the 808 popular in the South, resulting in the contemporary predominance of an 808-type sound in the related genres of Southern crunk (e.g., Lil Jon) and Bay Area hyphy (e.g., E-40). Kelis's 2006 hit "Bossy," a track that not coincidentally includes an appearance by Too $hort, explicitly hearkens back to the 808 era: "I'm back with an 808."

turntables when asked—Def Jam invested in equipment. This is what made Def Jam different, and one reason they ultimately survived and excelled in the trickiness of the industry.

Run-DMC arrived on the cusp of a significant moment in hip hop history. In the scramble for new rap acts to get signed to major recording contracts, many acts attempted to follow in the footsteps of James Brown and other funk acts of the 1970s—big costumes, elaborate stage shows, big crews. The trend toward co-optation of rap by the mainstream was often perpetuated by rap acts themselves. In an effort to be commercially viable, many acts switched their styles from house party and corner raps to radio-friendly jingles in hopes of appealing to a mainstream demographic. Out of this environment came Run-DMC, who invigorated and reinvented the whole rap genre. From their early countercurrent putdown, "Sucker-M.C.'s," it was obvious that Run-DMC was lean, mean, and ready to do business. Following up "Sucker-M.C.'s" with a second breakthrough single, "Rock Box," Run-DMC asserted that they were not one-hit wonders, and they would not attempt to follow the music industry cookie cutter mold. Ira Robbins of *Rolling Stone* called what Run-DMC was doing by merging rap and rock "forging a new musical alliance that shattered racial barriers" (53). To many, they were Run and D from the Hollis hood; for many more they were hip hop's ambassadors to the world.

SON OF BYFORD

The track "Son of Byford" on *Raising Hell* was an homage to origins. Byford was the first name of Darryl "DMC" McDaniel's father (though, as chronicled in the 2006 VH-1 documentary "My Adoption Journey," DMC later discovered he was adopted). Run DJed at a young age for his brother Russell's first rap act on Rush Management, and the first solo rap act to appear on television—Kurtis Blow. Run began his study of music in his family's attic. There he played with a drum set his father bought him when he was ten. A neighbor, Spuddy, gave him lessons. Run and Russell benefited from a supportive family, as well as a supportive community. Hollis was populated with black working-class neighbors and bustling main street with stores and movie theaters. It had a small-town feel, with everyone inevitably running into everyone else, according to Run-DMC. It was a small, remote enclave for the black working class and the children these hard-working parents hoped would have easier lives. The families of Run, Russell, and D did their best to afford their boys the best opportunities and support as they grew up. D's brother Al, for example, one day led D into the basement. Al had purchased a second turntable (to add to a record player the brothers already had) and a $50 mixer, and had set up DJ equipment on a table. Run's drum equipment and D's turntables represented, in part, the privileged life that was afforded these two members of Run-DMC. The equipment (both drums and turntables) became a major part of Run and D's daily routines and afforded them early opportunities to hone and perfect their musical skills.

Run first got into music at around the age of ten after hearing radio station WBLS. It introduced him to a world beyond Hollis, Queens—in terms of both music and life. From that point on, Run tried to express himself through music, dubbing himself "DJ Joe." He taped songs from the radio, attended block parties where residents played guitars and drums, and banged away on the drum set his father, Daniel, had bought and installed in the attic. Daniel supported Joe's dream. An attendance supervisor for New York City's Public School District 29 and professor of black history at Pace University by night, his father had spent the second half of the 1960s as part of the civil rights movement. Now in the late 1970s, Joe saw his father reading aloud from *Hamlet*, espousing the value of a college degree and traditional nine-to-five jobs, and reciting his own politically charged poetry. Joe's mother, Evelyn, also supported his hobby of playing drums and writing song lyrics. An artist with degrees in sociology and psychology from Howard University (where she had met Joe's father), Evelyn worked as a recreation director for the city's Parks Department.

Russell (born October 4, 1957) shared a bedroom with Joe on the second floor of their home in Queens. Their father tried to get Russell a job working at a hog dog store in Manhattan's West Village. Russell quit this job, dreaming of the dangerous and extravagant life of drug dealers he witnessed on his block. He chopped up coca-leaf incense, claiming it was foil-wrapped cocaine, and attempted to sell it when he could. Russell needed money to support his expensive clothing habit. He wore lizard-skin shoes, sharkskin pants, and Stetson hats, and afforded them by selling (and using) drugs. He kept twenty 5-ounce bags of drugs in the bushes in front of the house, and he spent his nights in fancy nightclubs downtown, ignoring his parents' rules and guidance. By his senior year in high school, spring 1975, Russell was involved with drugs. He started attending City College of New York in Harlem in the fall of 1975. He was supposed to be studying to become a sociology teacher, but drugs took over. Angel dust was his drug of choice and he spent his days in the City College student lounge and going to Harlem's hottest clubs each night (Ronin 14). Russell's reckless abandon and partying in Harlem of the 1970s mirrored the musical culture of the Harlem of the 1950s—when bebop was all the rage and Harlem was the site of late nights of music, drugs, and creative passion. To some, Russell was a lost youth, a problem child. To others, he was in training for the biggest job of his life.

In autumn 1977, Russell found a passion beyond drugs and partying. He came home talking about a party he had attended in the Harlem nightclub Charles' Gallery. He'd seen a DJ mix two copies of P-Funk's single "Flashlight," and a young man named Eddie Cheeba, holding a microphone, tell a crowd of blacks and Puerto Ricans, "Somebody, anybody, everybody scream!" He told his parents he thought he could make money promoting shows like the one at Charles' Gallery. He stopped selling weed and recruited schoolmates Rudy Toppin and Curtis Walker (who then rapped as Kool DJ Kurt Walker) to help him throw parties. With Russell as the mastermind and leader, the three friends printed thousands of flyers and stickers, rented halls and charged admission, and changed Curt's stage name to Kurtis Blow. Soon Russell's flyers claimed the Harlem-bred Kurtis Blow was really "Queens's #1 rapper." Creating the image required to market hip hop acts—even if it bordered on twisting the truth—would become Russell's trademark and would prove to be invaluable in his later marketing of Run-DMC. This business model would be key to making Run-DMC into a hip hop icon and would echo in hip hop history afterward as record labels sought to play up (or invent) street aspects of a hip hop act's credentials. But no business model survives without adequate financial backing. Russell came home one night in his promotional career complaining that no one had come to one of his events and he had lost all his money. His dad urged him to treat this as a lesson and focus on school again, but his mom handed Russell $2,000 in $100 bills she kept in her personal savings and encouraged Russell to continue. This was just another example how for Run, Russell, and Darryl support from their families and communities was crucial to their development and success as artists and entrepreneurs and proved that not only are icons made, they are also nurtured and cultivated.

DEF JAM

One day Russell heard "It's Yours," a record by T. La Rock & Jazzy Jay, and loved it. In a story he recalled for hip hop journalist Nelson George, Russell noticed that while "It's Yours" was distributed by Street Wise Records, it had a little logo on it that read "Def Jam" (Simmons 77). One night at a club DJ Jazzy Jay came over and asked Russell if he wanted to meet the man who'd made "It's Yours." Jazzy Jay walked Russell over to this stocky, long-haired Long Island white kid. This was the man behind Def Jam, and in terms of entrepreneurial spirit and love for music, Rick Rubin and Russell Simmons had a lot in common. Rick's inspiration to make rap records was Russell's audio production on "Rock Box"—a strict, layered drum track that proved to be the hit from the Run-DMC debut album *Run-DMC* (1984). Producing the street attitude was crucial to Russell. The raw energy of rock and the rebellion of rap proved to be a perfect combination on "Rock Box" and became the musical bridge that connected Russell and Rick and encouraged their coproduction on Run-DMC's third album, *Raising Hell* (1986).

Raising Hell followed several rigorous months of Run-DMC touring, many nights of which were spent writing and then performing the songs that would make the album. The intensity of a live tour performance was thus translated onto record. Doubled with Russell and Rick's loud, sometimes chaotic sound, the albums begged to jump out of the speakers when played. "Our main goal with *Raising Hell* was to have the best tape of anyone else's being sold," D of Run-DMC recalls (Coleman 33). The mixtape circuit was big at the time. Prior to Run-DMC, people bought a lot of Cold Crush tapes. DMC's goal was to have the fullest sounding tape available to hip hop fans. With significant financial backing from successful touring, Def Jam invested in vinyl with Run-DMC and albums, not tapes, were produced. Combining the technological edge with the sonic edge captivated the eyes and ears of the public. This project of pushing the creative envelope while remaining true to a band's image was a trademark of Def Jam during its first golden era, from approximately 1986 to 1990. Using this formula, Def Jam developed several of the most important acts in hip hop history that each cultivated their own individual sound, rather than attempting to copy pop acts. During this period, Def Jam handled acts including LL Cool J, Public Enemy, Slick Rick, and the Beastie Boys. At the same time, Rush Management was involved in breaking Run-DMC for Profile Records, and Whodini and DJ Jazzy Jeff and the Fresh Prince for Jive Records.

MY ADIDAS

Run-DMC was a marker of post-Bronx hip hop—taking it from the local to the global. This was most visible in how Run-DMC adopted and exploited the idea of the hip hop brand. The first single from *Raising Hell* was "My Adidas," with "Peter Piper" on the B side (see sidebar: My Adidas: Hip Hop and Brand Loyalty). The group claimed they took the beat from the street and put it on television. And that's what happened. Many artists at the time of Run-DMC's rise played it safe, according to Run-DMC. When Kool Moe Dee, Treacherous Three, and Grandmaster Flash went into the studio they held back, tightened up their rhymes, and cleaned up the track with splicing and add-ins of lyrics. Just as Run-DMC wore street fashion onstage in the form of white Adidas and black leather suits with fedoras, they attempted to match their rhymes and attitude with the passion and energy of MCs on the street corner or at the house party. This wasn't pioneering. Run-DMC just did on vinyl what rappers before them were doing on mixtapes.

Today, in 2006, the trajectory of hip hop recording has reversed. Mixtapes are again hugely popular (making one wonder if they ever really went out of fashion), in large part because of the proven success of guerrilla marketing of street CDs, as modeled by 50 Cent and G-Unit. 50 Cent testified to being mentored early on by Jam Master Jay of Run-DMC (50 Cent's debut single, "Wanksta," was produced by Jay). 50 said that Jay saw him as a kid who was trying to get out of the game, and Jay respected that. As a result, 50 said, Jay "put him on," or recorded him on CD (50 Cent 163). It was the strategic use of technology in 50 Cent's time, as in Run-DMC's time, which helped lead both acts to being on the cusp of hip hop production and, more

My Adidas: Hip Hop and Brand Loyalty
Jeb Aram Middlebrook

Branding was and is a crucial component of getting any rap project into the hands of the buying customer. Making the customer believe in the product, as one would a myth, is the key to brand loyalty. The Run-DMC song "My Adidas" is sometimes characterized as crass commercialism. Run-DMC did not set out to brand Adidas, however. The group said that they wore Adidas and then everyone else started wearing them; but they didn't want people to dress like them. They just wanted people to like their beats and rhymes. An Adidas sponsorship deal did come, in 1985, but after Run-DMC had toured extensively with the song "My Adidas." The story goes that the group had everyone hold their Adidas up at a tour date at Madison Square Garden. Someone at Adidas had heard about the group and sent a rep out to the show. A sponsorship deal ensued. Adidas followed the street trend of wearing Adidas. They exploited Run-DMC's popularity to sell more shoes. In this case, the building of an iconic brand worked for the benefit of both Run-DMC and Adidas; both brands fed off each other. What was different and iconic about Run-DMC, however, was that their brand influence developed on their terms. The Run-DMC brand forced large companies, including Adidas, to adapt their advertising and marketing in the direction Run-DMC dictated—a direction that was black and urban, which was new to large companies and marketing firms at the time. Run-DMC was iconic because they lived and branded a street lifestyle true to their native Queens but marketable enough for Wall Street. In this way, they set the stage for product placement and brand loyalty in hip hop long after their time.

important, distribution. In this regard, the Internet has proven recently to be an important site of marketing and distribution for up-and-coming mixtape DJs and rappers in 2006, who mix and remix the words and music of popular rap artists to make a name for themselves.

Hip hop branding on a mass scale was largely an invention of Run-DMC. Other artists on Def Jam in the 1980s felt the power of Run-DMC's cultural branding. It was clear that when it came to white Adidas, Run-DMC was not loyal to the brand, but rather the brand was loyal to Run-DMC. Shifting the terrain of cultural appropriation, Run-DMC did what they did and America followed. Significantly, Adidas capitalized on what became a trend of rocking shell-toe Adidas and promptly signed Run-DMC to a promotional deal. It was nothing new to use a black image to sell products. Images of black people abounded in advertising at the turn of the century and into the 1950s, particularly in racist ads that tied blacks to food preparation and cleaning products. From soap to laundry detergent to pancake mix, images of blacks have been used to show how products might serve the American public. In the case of Run-DMC, however, the group would show America another meaning for the word *serve*. In hip hop slang, "to serve" means to get the best of an opponent in a face-to-face battle of wits or moves. One could say that Run-DMC served the American marketing industry in more ways than one by developing a marketable and lucrative brand, on their terms.

What was different and iconic about Run-DMC was that their brand influence was self-directed and extremely widespread. The Run-DMC brand forced large companies, including Adidas, to adapt their advertising and marketing in the direction that Run-DMC dictated. Other companies at the time, like St. Ides malt liquor, similarly understood the symbolic importance of being attached to a hip hop brand. For a long time, brewing companies like St. Ides had targeted black, urban, working-class communities. Until the mid-1980s, malt liquor was popularly associated with an older black population. Hip hop, particularly the rap groups Run-DMC and N.W.A., changed that. These groups started to brandish and name-check malt liquor in publicity material and on record, particularly Olde English 800. These did not begin as endorsement deals but rather as what one critic called "de facto product placement," or name dropping based on preference, not payment. The de facto product placement by rappers in 2006 of Cristal—a high-end champagne—is a case in point. Cristal executives openly admit to not courting (and in some cases not wanting) the business of the hip hop elite; however, the popularity of Cristal among the top rappers, and those fans that aspire to live the rapper's lifestyle, made a big enough financial impact that Cristal has been forced to adapt to the urban market. Run-DMC was the forerunner of this type of relationship with big business. The group was unique because they lived and sold a lifestyle. They retooled the notion of rags to riches to fit their demographic—black, young, urban. Their lifestyle was street to *riche*; and the concept of the high life took on new meaning.

Run-DMC's contemporaries noticed their impact. Reggie Reg of the Crash Crew said they wanted to do what Run-DMC was doing at the time. He remembered Run-DMC opening for the Crash Crew at a show in Broadway International. He described the new, streetwise persona conveyed by Run-DMC: "We was not allowed to do stuff like that on Sugarhill.... We couldn't curse on Sugarhill" (Fricke and Ahearn 328). With the arrival and increasing ascendancy of hip hop with Run-DMC, a consumer-driven market developed. Companies like Adidas and St. Ides, and later Nike, McDonald's, Cristal, and so on embraced hip hop culture. What Run-DMC dictated in the rap business was a careful balance between street culture and entrepreneurialism. They took the corner hustle to the hip hop industry board room and beyond.

WALK THIS WAY

Run-DMC broke further into the mainstream on both sides of the Atlantic in 1986 when, at Rick Rubin's suggestion, they released the heavy metal–rap collision "Walk This Way." Its distinctive video caught the imagination of audiences worldwide, and the single rocketed into the U.S. Billboard Top 10 (see sidebar: Hip Hop Video: The Importance of Run-DMC's Visuals to 1980s MTV Viewers). The success of this single had been predicted by the earlier singles "Rock Box" and "King of Rock," both of which fused rap with rock. By 1987, *Raising Hell* had sold 3 million copies in the United States, becoming the first rap album to hit the R&B number one mark, the first to enter the U.S. Top 10, and the first to go platinum. Run-DMC also became the first rap act to have a video aired by MTV, the first to be featured on the cover of *Rolling Stone*, and the first nonathletes to endorse Adidas products.

Hip Hop Video: The Importance of Run-DMC's Visuals to 1980s MTV Viewers

Jeb Aram Middlebrook

The iconic status of Run-DMC depended as much on their image as their sound. Run-DMC was responsible for the first rap video on MTV—"Rock Box" from their debut album *Run-DMC* in 1984. If video killed the radio star, it made the rap radio star; and Run-DMC was the group to capitalize on the use of image to sell the group. The album *Run-DMC* went gold (500,000 copies sold), a testament to the rotation it received on MTV as well as on radio. Run-DMC's style and sound achieved national reach through television in way that was unprecedented for rap music. The group's second album, *King of Rock* (1985), was also promoted through a video for its lead single. The video "King of Rock" featured Run and DMC vandalizing the rock hall of fame, a visual statement that rap would be the new rock for the 1980s and Run-DMC would be its forerunners. Run-DMC broke down more walls with their video for the hugely successful "Walk This Way." This 1986 video collaboration with then-struggling rock band Aerosmith helped promote the single from their third album, *Raising Hell*. The album would also become the first rap record ever to go platinum and eventually triple platinum, in part from the immense reach that the video had nationally and globally. The video began with Aerosmith vying for sonic supremacy in adjacent studios—Aerosmith with rock guitars, Run-DMC with heavy bass drums and Jam Master Jay's record scratch. Aerosmith eventually breaks through the wall, struggling for recognition in the song. Ultimately, Run-DMC takes over the rock stage and rock audience Aerosmith commands in the video, offering yet another visual statement that Run-DMC would replace the rock icons of the past. The power of the video was cosigned by MTV. "Walk This Way" was nominated for two MTV Video Music Awards for Best Stage Performance Video and Best Overall Performance in 1987 and was consistently recognized by MTV through 2006 as being among the top videos and top songs of all time.

There were numerous hits on *Raising Hell*. But none hit harder than their first worldwide smash, "Walk This Way," a cover of the Aerosmith rock classic featuring group members Steven Tyler and Joe Perry. Rick Rubin's rock approach combined with Russell Simmons' street aesthetic for Run-DMC was a big reason why the album ended up selling 6 million copies in the United States and approximately 10 to 11 million copies worldwide. "Walk This Way" was the album's second single but the first video, and arguably a main reason the single rose to the top of the charts so quickly. Television as a vehicle for music advertising and marketing came into its own with MTV (the music television of the 1980s). A station based on the promotional videos supplied by record companies, MTV obtained virtually free programming with which they could garner revenue from advertisers. MTV was successful because they made treasure out of relative trash content, effectively reusing and recycling promotional throwaway videos as stock footage for their prime-time rotations. This was before videos became a major budget item for an artist's career and could expect to go for upward of $300,000 or more. Before Run-DMC, MTV had focused exclusively on rock videos. "Rock Box," the hit single from Run-DMC's debut album, *Run-DMC*, claimed the spot as the first rap video on MTV. Its rock flavor and simplistic bass-and-kick-drum eased its way into the MTV rotation. "Walk This Way" is sometimes erroneously credited with this achievement because of its incredible crossover with rock fans globally.

"Walk This Way" was something special, however. The beat from the Aerosmith song was one that Run-DMC had always rapped over in their Hollis neighborhood, but they didn't know the group's name at the time. Run and D had their own rhymes over the beat but once in the studio, they were told to do Aerosmith's lyrics as a cover song. How far rock and roll would take them from their rap roots was a question the group negotiated even during the recording of the track. Jam Master Jay—the recognizable visionary of the group—claimed early on that "Walk This Way" had the potential to be a hit. Despite having their own lyrics on the track and not wanting to follow their contemporaries in writing pop tunes for radio, Run and D went into the studio and recorded Aerosmith's words. The lyrics, as they were recorded, did not match the Aerosmith vocals. Whether or not "Walk This Way" sounded like Aerosmith, it sounded like a hit to everyone.

The record "Walk This Way" was a rebirth and a birth, according to D (Coleman 36). The song made room for acts like the Beastie Boys, Kid Rock, Limp Bizkit, Korn, and P.O.D., and forever changed the sound of rock, period. Most rock bands today, for example, emphasize the second and fourth beats in a four-beat measure. Boom-boom, clap. Boom-boom, clap. This is the echo of Run-DMC and more specifically "Rock Box," their first rock-rap record. Rock for Run-DMC was street. The group recalled that they had rapped over rock beats in the streets of Hollis. Rock signified being hard, or tough, and that was the image the group intended to portray. D mentioned that other rap groups didn't use rock as much because they didn't know how. The balance of street and mainstream, rap and rock, black and white was mastered by Run-DMC. They matched wailing guitar lines with sparse but forceful drum machine beats and turntable scratches. Rap-rock, Def Jam, and Run-DMC sounded like rebellion to music listeners everywhere in the mid-1980s.

The Def Jam logo—one of the most memorable logos in the rap game according to Russell Simmons—was Rick Rubin's work. Ironically, Rick thought when rappers said "death" (which in the eighties was a slang term of affirmation), they were really saying "def" (Simmons 80). Russell said that white rock and roll or alternative people or suburban people coming into hip hop culture—their version of the black ghettos is always more dramatic. This would become clear also as Def Jam label mates the Beastie Boys, burst onto the scene as an all-white rap group with beats and mannerisms that were loud and raucous, à la Run-DMC. Being from middle-class Hollis, Queens, Russell considered himself outside black ghetto culture. This outsider position perhaps allowed him to have a critical distance to hip hop culture and maybe an overly dramatic view of the ghetto as he saw in other ghetto outsiders. Ironically, Jason Mizell, whose life was eventually claimed by the street, was the only member of Run-DMC who was actually from the street. Rick, Russell, Run, and D, on the other hand were like many of their fans, a hip hop journalist once wrote; they were outside of street culture. But as Russell observed, they brought something special to hip hop because of that. They heard hip hop. They loved hip hop. But their point of entry into hip hop was different, and they manifested it differently. Rick Rubin, for example, emphasized the volume of the guitar riffs and big bass drums, making the records louder. Russell made the ultimate ghetto beat record and breakthrough for Run-DMC, "Sucker M.C.'s," with no bass line and sparse drums. Admittedly, Russell approached "Sucker M.C.'s" differently than someone from Harlem or the Bronx would have at that time. For Russell and Rick, Run-DMC could be both rock and roll and rap at the same time, largely because both were parts of youth culture. It wasn't about race at that level, Russell said, but an energy and attitude that rock and rap shared. Run-DMC did this without being calculated, but by being honest about what they liked and wanted to achieve musically. According to Russell, "The band and I weren't concerned with reaching blacks or whites, but with making new sounds for people who wanted to hear them" (Simmons 80). These sounds, these expressions, of a mediated ghetto voice echoed around the world. Technology, television, media were the master's tools, and as of 1984 the tools were in the hands of three black youths from Hollis, Queens, with a passion for big beats and street poetry.

IS IT LIVE

The album *Raising Hell* was the culmination of worldwide tours spanning 1984 and 1985 and a film debut in *Krush Groove*. Run-DMC wrote the whole album on the road. "That's why it was so dope," DMC says. "We would write a song every night after a great performance, so we had a lot of energy and momentum going" (Coleman 32). They translated the aliveness and movement of touring onto record in 1985, over the course of three months in Manhattan-based Chung King studios. Rick Rubin was brought in to work formally with Run-DMC on the project. He took the group to his dorm room at NYU and showed them around. It seemed like Rick had every rock record in the world, DMC said. Russell promoted Run-DMC with black hats and leather to give them an iconic image—à la Michael Jackson's glove or Cyndi Lauper's hair, according to Russell. The black hat and leather look reportedly came from a day when Russell, Run, and D went to pick up Jay in his neighborhood. Jay came out of the house with a full leather suit and black hat on. Russell told Run and D from then on, they would wear what Jay wore. Russell hoped the rock sound and ghetto style would reach both the street and the substantial white audience, both of which identified with rock's raw, rebellious attitude (Cepeda 47).

The impact of this new look for Run-DMC can be seen in a photo shoot of Run-DMC's appearance on the television pilot of *Graffiti Rock*, a dance show that was supposed to be a hip hop version of *American Bandstand* (1952) or *Soul Train* (1971). The show was not picked up for a TV run, but the pilot aired on WPIX Channel 11 in New York City. In one famous picture by photographer Martha Cooper, rap contemporaries the Treacherous Three are poised for a freestyle battle with Run-DMC, with a crowd looking on. Run-DMC virtually leaps off the page with their stylized poses and shiny leather jackets. They were cool, they were hip, and they were conscious of always being on camera. Run-DMC gave the feel of already being celebrities, the "if you don't know ... now you know" look. It's no coincidence that Run-DMC's influence and global reach would cause young people interviewed in Germany six years later to name Run-DMC as the only rap act to achieve wider recognition in the years between 1984 and 1989. This is one major reason Run-DMC can be considered the icon's icon in hip hop. They are the preeminent example of a rap group that became so successful as a commercial brand that they effectively erased from international public memory rap groups that came before, after, or during their time. When you win a battle as a hip hop icon, you not only beat your competition, you record over them.

RAISING HELL

Run-DMC responded to the frenzy over their music on record. The title track, "Raising Hell," carried the influence of the Beastie Boys, white boy hip hop contemporaries and label mates to Run-DMC. Rick Rubin produced the Beastie Boys' classic *Licensed to Ill* and thus production tracks jumped from

Run-DMC projects to Beastie Boys projects. "We learned that punk rock is just as hip hop as Afrika Bambaataa is. And you can be silly and still be dope," D said (Coleman 37). The Beastie Boys opened for Run-DMC on tour, warming up all-black audiences for the pivotal rallying cry, "Whose house? Run's house!" The house was actually brought down at one tragic event at a Run-DMC show in Long Beach, California, in 1986. The group wasn't even onstage when several gangs decided to fight inside the concert arena. The *Los Angeles Times* covered it as a fight between Latino and black street gangs, which injured thirty people—some people were reportedly struck with metal chairs, wooden sticks, and, in one instance, a fire extinguisher. The fact that the *LA Times* put the word "rap" inside quotation marks in the coverage was a telltale sign of how the media thought about the music and culture—rap was questionable. According to Russell, gang shootings were happening all over LA at the time, but because this particular incident happened at a concert venue, it went from being gang violence to being rap violence.

When concert violence in the late eighties became an issue to the media, politicians, and parents, Run-DMC was rapping about how kids should go to school or church. Even back then, with black hats and leather pants on, Russell said, they were talking about being good and God-fearing. The push by Rush Management for Run-DMC to rhyme about positive things did little to soothe the rising insecurities that were fed to the American public by the same television, radio, and press outlets that Run-DMC relied on for their popularity. The perception of rap violence affected the concert business because it made parents keep their kids from coming out. It also made kids afraid to come out. The insurance companies and the buildings raised their fees so high that it became impossible to take tours on the road. This was the angst and artist censorship from which early gangsta rapper Schoolly D rose in Philadelphia in 1986, followed by N.W.A. in 1988, and the Death Row camp led by Dr. Dre and Snoop Dogg in the 1990s. Today in 2006, the popularity of "trap rap" or rap glorifying the world of crack cocaine dealing (often occurring in *traps*, or crack houses) is banking ironically on the notion of rap violence as a selling point.

Run-DMC showed rappers and fans that there was a way to be hard without glorifying violence. They dealt, however, with the American media, which pegged them as dangerous black thugs, especially after the Long Beach event. Run-DMC witnessed how tenuous and media-dependent iconic status could be. Oftentimes their media coverage spoke louder than the group. At the height of the *Raising Hell* tour, Run-DMC's publicist found the need to distance the group from the street—from the gangs that supported the music since the group's beginning and who clearly had bought enough tickets for the Long Beach concert to cause a full-scale riot inside the venue. This careful balance between catering to the mainstream and to the street, assuaging the police and the street gangs simultaneously, was and is an art, an art that challenges the best MCs and managers—especially those who (like Russell Simmons) sought to produce not rap, but black teenage music led by positive black role models.

PROUD TO BE BLACK

In 1985, while Run-DMC was recording *Raising Hell* and promising to overturn American music and celebrity culture, President Ronald Reagan promised to overturn over 100 years of civil rights achievements. Deindustrialization, crack cocaine, and slashes in funding for public education and afterschool programs dropped on the block as Reganomics, and Run-DMC under the tutelage and support of future label mates Public Enemy dropped the final track on *Raising Hell*, "Proud to Be Black." On this track, Run-DMC took seriously their duties as role models, as set out by Russell. DMC said, "We knew that there was power in this music. We could teach, we could innovate, we could inspire and motivate. We made it cool to put messages in lyrics" (Coleman 34). Notably, few rappers before Run-DMC, and certainly none selling at the same level, bragged about going to college. The group recognized that they could make education cool. In this way they could make a difference in their Queens neighborhood and around the world.

Run-DMC said that the song "Proud to Be Black" was influenced by Public Enemy, whom they often hung around with. Public Enemy didn't have any records out, but Run, Jay, and D would still go to their radio station, WBAU in Long Island, to connect. Chuck D was like a father, mentoring and educating the up-and-coming members of Run-DMC. The group admittedly wanted to make an album that Chuck would like with "Proud to Be Black." The members of Run-DMC all went to college and "Proud to Be Black," they said, was more about education than about being black. The year 1986 marked a transition for Run-DMC and for hip hop in general. From the perspective of Run-DMC at the time, the options in their Hollis neighborhood were either to be a basketball player or a drug dealer. The question of opportunities for black males has echoed and re-echoed since Run-DMC's reign. Rappers in 2006 still pose the question to their listeners: "Which will it be—the basketball or the crack rock?" Even though Run and D weren't immersed in street life, their image as Run-DMC—as celebrities who remained connected to the streets where they grew up—gave them a degree of respect in Hollis that was not afforded other groups.

Many of their friends were convicts, murderers, and drug dealers, but they remained connected to these people even after the industry success of the group. Run and D would stand on the corner and smoke weed and drink beer in broad daylight with people from the neighborhood. People celebrated Run-DMC as a neighborhood success story—seeing someone from the block on TV delivering a positive message to the people eased the acceptance of Run-DMC as one of Hollis's own. Run-DMC was influential and iconic in this regard because they showed in their day-to-day interactions the hip hop truism "It's not where you're from, it's where you're at."

THE AFTER PARTY

Run-DMC was at the top of the rap game with their album *Raising Hell*. But they couldn't stay there. Subsequent recording efforts failed to maintain their position at the forefront of rap, as their audience flocked to the hard-core political sounds of Public Enemy and N.W.A. Run-DMC's albums *Tougher Than Leather* (1988) and *Back from Hell* (1990) contained a few tracks ("Beats to the Rhyme," "Pause") that were reminiscent of their earlier heyday, but the momentum for Run-DMC had waned. In the nineties, DMC and Run both experienced religious conversion. Their involvement in rap faltered, but singles continued to emerge sporadically, notably "What's It All About," which sampled the Stone Roses' "Fool's Gold." Despite an obvious effort to make 1993's *Down with the King* their major comeback album, with production assistance offered by Pete Rock, EPMD, the Bomb Squad, Naughty by Nature, A Tribe Called Quest, and Rage Against the Machine, and guest appearances from KRS-One and Neneh Cherry, it was hard to convince a new generation of fans that Run-DMC was as legendary in the 1990s as they were in the 1980s. Nevertheless, *Down with the King* enjoyed a respectable commercial run and, true to form, the trio enjoyed an unexpected UK chart-topper five years later with a Jason Nevins remix of "It's Like That."

Following *Down with the King*, Run-DMC's extended studio hiatus lasted until April 2001 with the release of the star-studded *Crown Royal*. Tragically, the following October, Jam Master Jay was shot dead at his recording studio in Queens. Some speculate whether Jay's involvement in a failed cocaine deal led to his murder in October 2002 (Ronin 2). New York's Power 105 DJ and former "Yo! MTV Raps" host Ed Lover accused the rap label Murder Inc. founder Irv Gotti and Ja Rule of being behind Jay's shooting because he had worked with 50 Cent after Murder Inc. blacklisted him. These theories have not been supported by police investigation, however, and Jay's murder, like those of Tupac and Notorious B.I.G, remains unsolved. After the death of their bandmate, Run and D declared Run-DMC officially over. Both went on to record solo albums, and the success of Run's show *Run's House* on MTV and DMC's "My Adoption Journey" on VH-1 in 2006 spoke to the adaptability and lasting power of the Run-DMC brand and legacy, despite the group's end.

RUN-DMC'S LEGACY AND CONTINUING APPEAL

Writing of white 1920s jazzmen such as Bix Beiderbecke, LeRoi Jones (now Amiri Baraka) explained the appeal of jazz to white Americans in the music's "profound reflection of America" (Cepeda 224). Hip hop, especially with Run-DMC, operated in a similar way. Listening to their music was a way into understanding America better. Run-DMC's sound, with the help of producers Rick Rubin, Russell Simmons, and Larry Smith, was unrelenting. Their style and attitude, with crisp black hats and sleek leather coats, was unshakeable. Run-DMC's music did not demand, it commanded people to listen. Run-DMC was the undeniable sonic manifestation of murdered, enslaved, raped, and exploited souls rising up to break speakers, bust moves, drink 40s, wave college degrees, and exclaim, "Whose house?" And kids from all backgrounds, around the world, wanted to be just like them.

So what did the era of Run-DMC and *Raising Hell* mean for America? It meant that the idol, the hero, the icon for youth across the country would become black, male, and urban. The gangsta aesthetic would rule and everyone would wonder what they could do, if anything, to be down. The politics of Run-DMC manifested in their ability to stay true, to be honest, in the face of industry pressures to clean up and act right. They asserted themselves as a consciously black group, committed to the uplift of the black community, while also acknowledging that they could reach fans around the world that felt their expression of humanity and proclamation of "I am." This defined power. This defined the hip hop icon. This defined Run-DMC—the icon's icon.

See also: Beastie Boys, Public Enemy

WORKS CITED

50 Cent with Kris Ex. *From Pieces to Weight: Once Upon a Time in Southside Queens.* New York: Pocket Books, 2005.

Cepeda, Raquel. *And It Don't Stop: The Best American Hip-Hop Journalism of the Last 25 Years.* New York: Faber and Faber, 2004.

Coleman, Brian. *Rakim Told Me: Hip-Hop Wax Facts, Straight from the Original Artists, The 80s.* Somersville, MA: Wax Facts Press, 2005.

Fricke, Jim, and Charlie Ahearn. *Yes, Yes Ya'll: Oral History of Hip-Hop's First Decade,* Oxford, UK: Perseus, 2002.

Quinn, Eithne. *Nuthin' But a "G" Thang: The Culture and Commerce of Gangsta Rap.* New York: Columbia University Press, 2005.

Robbins, Ira A. *The Rolling Stone Review: 1985.* New York: Rolling Stone Press, 1985.

Ronin, Ro. *Raising Hell : The Reign, Ruin, and Redemption of Run-DMC and Jam Master Jay.* New York: Harper Collins, 2005.

Simmons, Joseph. *It's Like That: A Spiritual Memoir.* New York: St. Martin's Press, 2000.

FURTHER RESOURCES

Adler, Bill. *Tougher Than Leather: The Rise of Run-DMC.* Los Angeles: Consafos Press, 2002.

Chang, Jeff. *Can't Stop Won't Stop: A History of the Hip-Hop Generation.* New York: St. Martin's Press, 2005.

Forman, Murray, and Mark Anthony Neal, eds. *That's the Joint! The Hip-Hop Studies Reader.* New York: Routledge, 2004.

Foucault, Michel. *The Archaeology of Knowledge and the Discourse of Language.* New York: Pantheon, 1972.

Frank, Thomas. *The Conquest of Cool: Business Culture, Counterculture, and the Rise of Hip Consumerism.* Chicago: University of Chicago Press, 1997.

Holt, Douglas B. *How Brands Become Icons: The Principles of Cultural Branding.* Boston: Harvard Business School Press, 2004.

Kings of Rap. Visual Entertainment, 1998.

Krush Groove. Dir. Michael Schultz. Warner Bros., 1985.

Kun, Josh. *Audiotopia: Music, Race, and America.* Berkeley: University of California Press, 2005.

McDaniels, Darryl. *King of Rock: Respect, Responsibility and My Life with Run-DMC.* New York: St. Martin's Press, 2001.

Mitchell, Tony, ed. *Global Noise: Rap and Hip-Hop Outside the USA.* Middletown, CT: Wesleyan University Press.

Ramos, George. "30 Injured at Long Beach Concert; L.A. Show Off." *Los Angeles Times,* 18 August 1986: 1.

Ramsey, Guthrie P. *Race Music: Black Cultures from Bebop to Hip-Hop.* Berkeley: University of California Press, 2003.

Ronin, Ro. *Raising Hell: The Reign, Ruin, and Redemption of Run-DMC and Jam Master Jay.* New York: Harper Collins, 2005.

Run-DMC Homepage. 4 April 2006. http://www.rundmcmusic.com.

Run DMC Lyrics. The Original Hip Hop Lyrics Archive. 4 April 2006. http://www.ohhla.com/YFA_runDMC.html.

Simmons, Joseph. *It's Like That: A Spiritual Memoir.* New York: St. Martin's Press, 2000.

Simmons, Russell, and Nelson George. *Life and Def: Sex, Drugs, Money and God.* New York: Three Rivers Press, 2001.

Thigpen, David. *Jam Master Jay: The Heart of Hip Hop.* New York: Pocket Books, 2003.

Together Forever: Run-DMC Greatest Hits. Film. Arista, 2003.

Tougher Than Leather. Dir. Rick Rubin. New Line Cinema, 1988.

SELECTED DISCOGRAPHY

Run-DMC. Profile, 1984.
King of Rock. Profile, 1985.
Raising Hell. Profile, 1986.
Tougher Than Leather. Profile. 1988.
Back from Hell. Profile, 1990.
Down with the King. Profile, 1993.
Crown Royal. Profile, 2001.
Greatest Hits. Arista, 2002.
The Best Of. BMG, 2003.
Ultimate Run-DMC. Arista, 2003.

Courtesy of Photofest.

Beastie Boys

Mickey Hess

The Beastie Boys are one of hip hop's most innovative and adaptable groups. They have blended hip hop with punk, dub, instrumental rock, and alternative, while maintaining the music's integrity by keeping hip hop at the core of what they do. They have gone from the hard rock and Budweiser-driven *Licensed to Ill* to speaking out against misogyny in lyrics. They have moved from New York to Los Angeles and back again, and started their own record label and magazine. They discovered LL Cool J, made out with Madonna, and organized a series of concerts in support of Tibet. With *Licensed to Ill*, they built a new sound from Run-DMC's merger of rap and hard rock that would become a blueprint for future rap-rock acts such as Limp Bizkit, Korn, and Linkin Park (see sidebar: Hip hop and Rock), but they abandoned this sound to consistently experiment with new forms of music. They were the

---

Hip Hop and Rock
Mickey Hess

Rap and rock music first merged with Rick Rubin's production on Def Jam albums. Def Jam promoted Run-DMC's rock-based sound in singles like "King of Rock" and "Rock Box." Before Run-DMC, hip hop tracks had been constructed primarily using R&B, soul, jazz, and funk records. The blending of rap and rock propelled Run-DMC to MTV airplay for audiences that consisted of rock listeners, and prompted a new wave of crossover hits from groups like the Beastie Boys, who picked up on Run-DMC's formula. Another Def Jam group, Public Enemy, was included in *Spin Magazine*'s list of the top 100 punk groups of all time.

In 1984, Run-DMC took their use of rock music further in their collaboration with Aerosmith on "Walk This Way." The song is essentially a cover of Aerosmith's 1975 original with the addition of Jam Master Jay's scratching and with the verses rapped instead of sung. Aerosmith's Steven Tyler and Joe Perry contributed vocals and guitar to the song, and appeared in the video, in which Run-DMC and Aerosmith practice in two separate rooms with only a thin wall between them. The groups play louder and louder until Tyler ultimately breaks through the wall, signaling the end of a split between the worlds of rap and rock.

In the early 1990s, DJ Muggs picked up where Rick Rubin left off, incorporating sounds and styles from alternative rock into his production for the groups Cypress Hill, House of Pain, and Funkdoobiest. Butch Vig, who produced Nirvana's seminal record *Nevermind* and founded the band Garbage, remixed House of Pain's "Shamrocks and Shenanigans." This new blend of alternative rock and hip hop was showcased on the soundtrack of the 1993 film *Judgment Night,* which was an experiment in collaborations between rap and alternative rock groups. The soundtrack mostly paired alternative rock groups with rap groups. It featured Cypress Hill backed by Sonic Youth and Pearl Jam, Sir Mix-A-Lot backed by Mudhoney, Del the Funky Homosapien backed by Dinosaur Jr., and De La Soul backed by Teenage Fanclub.

Such collaborations paved the way for a new sound called rap-rock. In the late 1990s, rap-rock came to describe groups like Limp Bizkit, Linkin Park, and Bloodhound Gang, rock bands who employed the hip hop elements of turntables and rap vocals in their music. Limp Bizkit's Fred Durst and Bloodhound Gang's Jimmy Pop Ali alternatively sing and rap on albums, while Linkin Park uses two vocalists: one singer and one MC. All three bands use DJs, who bring in hip hop scratching with the band's traditional bass, drums, keyboard, and guitar. Rock bands Sublime and Korn also employ DJs. While early records from Run-DMC and the Beastie Boys acknowledged rock's influence on hip hop sounds, these newer bands brought hip hop's influence into rock. Often, the lines blurred between rock and rap acts. Kid Rock released hip hop albums and toured with Too Short before he hit it big with a signature rap-rock sound that brought hip hop into play with Southern rock and even country music. Limp Bizkit featured DJ Lethal, formerly of the white rap group House of Pain. Everlast, former MC from House of Pain, released a rock album called *Whitey Ford Sings the Blues*.

---

first white breakthrough act, and maintained credibility after Vanilla Ice's discrediting and throughout Eminem's success.

When Eminem released *The Slim Shady LP* in 1999, he had to contend with the discredited image of Vanilla Ice, the white rapper who had lied about his background in the official bio he released to the press. Attempting to match the biographies of his black contemporaries in hip hop, Vanilla Ice claimed he had grown up in the streets rather than the suburbs (see sidebar: Vanilla Ice). The scandal over Ice's fake bio reduced the hip hop credibility of white MCs. Eminem describes in his lyrics his struggle for acceptance as a white hip hop artist, even as he admits that his identity gains him a wider audience among white listeners. While he makes clear that he is not another Vanilla Ice, he claims to have been mistaken for a Beastie Boy by a fan. Five years before Vanilla Ice released his debut album, *To the Extreme*, a white hip hop group, the Beastie Boys, shared a stage with Run-DMC and Public Enemy. The Beastie Boys' career spans over twenty years. They survived the Vanilla Ice scandal, influenced Eminem, and remain one of hip hop's best-loved groups. They are recognized as hip hop icons, not as white rappers who made it.

The Beastie Boys are Mike D (Michael Diamond, born November 20, 1965), MCA (Adam Yauch, born August 5, 1964), and Adrock (Adam Horovitz, born October 31, 1966). The Beastie Boys' music career began in 1979, when fourteen-year-old singer Michael Diamond formed a hard-core punk group called the Young Aborigines with guitarist John Berry and drummer Kate Schnellenbach. In 1981, bassist Adam Yauch joined the group, which was then renamed B.E.A.S.T.I.E. Boys (the name is an acronym for Boys Entering Anarchistic States Through Internal Excellence). The Beastie Boys played their first show on Yauch's seventeenth birthday. This original lineup released one album, 1982's *Pollywog Stew*, on the independent New York punk label Ratcage. The Beastie Boys also were featured on the Ratcage compilation *New York Thrash*. While Diamond and Yauch founded the group, the third member of the lineup for which the Beastie Boys are best known is Adam Horovitz, who first played in another punk band called the Young and the Useless, who would open shows for the Beastie Boys.

Vanilla Ice
Mickey Hess

Although Vanilla Ice was not the first white artist to achieve crossover success with hip hop (the Beastie Boys preceded him in 1986 and 3rd Bass in 1989), his performance marked the first time a rap artist had used being white as a gimmick. Vanilla Ice was marketed as a white artist who maintained credibility in the black community. The name Vanilla Ice and the title of his first single, "Play That Funky Music (White Boy)," played on the fact that Vanilla Ice was white, while his official artist biography from SBK Records claimed that Ice had a criminal background and gang affiliation. The bio even claimed that he had been stabbed in a gang fight. Ice's biography seemed to fit with the stories of many black gangsta rap artists who were his contemporaries, but his true background was revealed by Ken Parish Perkins of the *Dallas Morning News*, who on November 18, 1990, published a story that disproved much of what SBK had claimed about Ice. According to Perkins, SBK press materials "portray a colorful teen-age background full of gangs, motorcycles and rough-and-tumble street life in lower-class Miami neighborhoods, culminating with his success in a genre dominated by young black males" (1A). In reality, Rob Van Winkle, who performed as Vanilla Ice, spent his teen years primarily in the Dallas suburbs and was not as involved with crime as his bio had claimed.

After the media scandal surrounding his fake bio, as well as related scandals over his sampling of the Queen and David Bowie song "Under Pressure" for his hit single "Ice Ice Baby," and his borrowing the chorus chant from an African American fraternity, Vanilla Ice has never produced another album to break the Top 40. On 1998's *Hard to Swallow*, he switched his style to the rap-rock sounds of groups like Limp Bizkit and Korn, who were selling well at the time. Even with this change, he has never been able to live down his Vanilla Ice persona. He recorded a rap-rock cover of his hit "Ice Ice Baby," and he most recently resurfaced as a reality television star, appearing on the WB's *The Surreal Life*, a show that groups former celebrities as roommates, and on NBC's *Hit Me Baby One More Time*, on which one-hit wonders compete in performing their old songs. On an episode of *The Surreal Life*, Vanilla Ice complained about hip hop fans not being able to forget his debut album and subsequent discrediting. He spray-painted over artwork depicting his image from 1990, saying, "Die."

Further Resources

Hess, Mickey. "Hip-Hop Realness and the White Performer." *Critical Studies in Media Communication* 22.5 (2005): 372–389.
Perkins, Ken Parish. "Under Raps: Hot Pop Vocalist Vanilla Ice Shrugs Off Conflicting Versions of His Background." *Dallas Morning News* 18 November 1990. 1A.

These bands were heavily influenced by the energy of punk bands Bad Brains, Black Flag, and Reagan Youth. These punk roots would serve the Beastie Boys well in bringing a distinct energy to hip hop, a fusion of punk chaos, rock excess, and hip hop lyricism. Later in their career, the group would use their punk roots to gain credibility in the alternative rock era of the early 1990s, when groups like Sonic Youth and Nirvana brought punk and its influence back into the mainstream. The Beastie Boys would rerelease their punk albums as a compilation titled *Some Old Bullshit*, record new punk tracks for their albums *Check Your Head* and *Ill Communication*, and release an EP of all-new punk tracks, *Aglio E Olio*.

After Horovitz joined the group in 1983, the Beastie Boys released an EP, *Cookie Puss*, which moved away from the punk styles of their first record and toward the emerging genre of rap. *Cookie Puss* also indicated the humor the Beasties would bring to hip hop. The title track set a prank phone call to a Carvell ice cream shop to a beat. The EP also featured a reggae track, "Beastie Revolution," which British Airways borrowed for use in a television commercial, prompting the Beastie Boys to sue. The group won $40,000 in this copyright lawsuit, but in the years to come, they would become the defendants in sampling lawsuits from artists like Jimmy Castor and James Newton.

As teenagers in the music scene in New York City in the early 1980s, the Beastie Boys were exposed to the tail end of punk's heyday, as well as the new sounds of Grandmaster Flash, Afrika Bambaataa, and Kool Herc. They played at the legendary punk club Max's Kansas City on its last night in business, and Public Enemy played some of its first shows opening for the Beastie Boys. Their position on the border of these two music movements allowed the Beastie Boys to create a distinctive sound, borrowing and adapting the sounds and styles they liked from both punk and hip hop. The Beastie Boys met Rick Rubin, a white producer who was making hip hop records in his dorm room at New York University. Rubin, along with Russell "Rush" Simmons, founded Def Jam Records, the label that signed Simmons's brother's group Run-DMC, as well as T La Rock, Public Enemy, LL Cool J, and other burgeoning stars. The Def Jam sound was distinctive because of Rubin's use of hard rock drums, bass, and guitar, as opposed to the funk, R&B, and soul bass lines from which other hip hop records were mostly built. The Sugarhill Gang, for instance, had hit it big with "Rapper's Delight," with a bass line sampled from Chic's "Good Times." Rather than sampling from Kool and the Gang, James Brown, and Parliament Funkadelic, Rubin constructed hip hop tracks using AC/DC, Led Zeppelin, and live guitar from Def Jam's resident metal band, Slayer. Rubin worked initially as part of the Beastie Boys' stage show, as DJ Double R, but he soon left behind the turntables to work primarily in the production booth. Onstage he was replaced by a DJ named Dr. Dre, who would go on to cohost *Yo! MTV Raps*, a pivotal TV series in widening hip hop's fan base (Dr. Dre should not be confused with the Dr. Dre who founded N.W.A. and pioneered the West Coast gangsta rap sound). In the studio, Rubin's production proved key to defining the Beastie Boys' sound, and influential to the future of hip hop (see sidebar: Def Jam Records Today).

In 1984, Def Jam released the Beasties' *Rock Hard* EP. This record featured the first Beastie Boys songs that could be classified as true hip hop. Their vocal

---

Def Jam Records Today
Mickey Hess

Def Jam, one of the first hip hop labels to produce a steady stream of crossover hits, was founded by Rick Rubin and Russell Simmons. Originally, the label was run out of Rubin's NYU dorm room, but with the success of groups like Run-DMC, the Beastie Boys, and LL Cool J, Def Jam soon became an industry powerhouse. However, this sudden rise to success took its toll on Def Jam. The Beastie Boys left the label after only one album, citing contract disputes and their mistrust of Simmons and Rubin. Later that same year, Rubin left Def Jam as well to form his own label, Def American.

Def American shifted its interests, releasing fewer hip hop albums than rock and heavy metal. On August 27, 1993, Rubin celebrated the "Death of Def" by conducting a funeral for the hip hop slang term *def*, which was over ten years old and which had become so popular that it was included in the tenth edition of *Webster's New Collegiate Dictionary*. Rubin retitled his label American Recordings and went on to release a 1994 comeback album, also titled *American Recordings*, by country music legend Johnny Cash, introducing the Man in Black to a new generation of listeners via the music video for "Deliah's Gone." Before Cash's death in 2003, Rubin worked with him on two more albums, 1996's *Unchained* and 2003's *American IV: The Man Comes Around*. Working with Rubin, Cash covered Nine Inch Nails' "Hurt," Soundgarden's "Rusty Cage," and Beck's "Rowboat," among others. Rubin also released two notable hip hop albums on American Recordings: Kwest tha Madd Ladd's *This Is My First Album* (1996), and Milk's *Never Dated* (1994), which featured a guest appearance from Ad-Rock on "Spam." In 2004, Rubin reemerged from the studio to appear in the video for Jay-Z's "99 Problems," a song Rubin produced.

Russell Simmons, in the meantime, continued to run Def Jam Records and became an entertainment mogul, expanding from music to produce HBO's Def Comedy Jam and Def Poetry Jam, franchising "def" while Rubin retired it. Simmons launched a clothing line called Phat Pharm and worked with his wife, Kimora Lee Simmons, to produce a women's line, Baby Phat.

Today, Def Jam continues to be a viable label and brand. They have released important albums by Method Man, Redman, Ghostface Killah, and Lil' Kim. Sony Playstation produced two video games, Def Jam Battle and Def Jam: Fight for New York, which feature current Def Jam artists as boxers. Currently, Jay-Z is Def Jam's CEO, and its sister label, Def Jam South, is headed by Scarface of the Geto Boys.

styles had developed in the direction of their mentors Run-DMC, but Ad-Rock, Mike D, and MCA, as Horovitz, Diamond, and Yauch now called themselves, added their own touches. They adopted Run-DMC's manner of rapping hard, shouting or spitting each line so that each word sounded crisp and distinct, rather than delivering the smoother, almost singsong vocals of earlier MCs from Sugarhill Gang, Kurtis Blow, and the Furious Five. Like Run-DMC, the Beasties often joined together to belt out the last word of a line, giving their rap extra emphasis. Listening to Run-DMC's song "Is It Live?" and the Beastie Boys' "Rhymin' and Stealin'" highlights this technique. Another vocal influence can be heard in Run-DMC's "My Adidas," where DMC whines "Nowwww" between lines. Ad-Rock would adapt this whine on the song "Paul Revere," which begins, "Nowwww, here's a little story that I gots to tell." This nasal glide is something the Beastie Boys would make their own on *Licensed to Ill*. Their voices weave in and out of each other, each of them contributing to a line, rather than delivering separate verses. On "The New Style," they incorporated a barbershop quartet feel to the final verse, with two members mock-harmonizing as the other MC delivered his verse. This was a flow they would abandon on *Check Your Head*, where they tended to alternate verses, and return to on *To the Five Boroughs*, intermingling their vocals again. Onstage during their 1998 *Ill Communication* tour, the Beastie Boys often recited the chorus from the Nice & Smooth song "Harmonize," chanting "This is the way we harmonize" between their own verses.

Along with their records, energetic live concerts have always been a part of the Beastie Boys' appeal. At the beginning of their hip hop career, the Beastie Boys toured with Run-DMC as well as Madonna during her *Like a Virgin* tour. Madonna, who kicked the Boys off her tour because they became too rowdy for the young girls who made up a large part of her fan base, claims she remembers making out with Adam Yauch in a dressing room. The Beastie Boys showcased their live performance style in an appearance in *Krush Groove*, a 1985 film dedicated to showcasing Def Jam's stable of talent: Run-DMC, Beastie Boys, Fat Boys, and LL Cool J. The film depicted the rise of Def Jam amid the seedy nightclubs and shady business dealings of rap's early days as a commercial form. The Beastie Boys also appeared in the Run-DMC film *Tougher Than Leather* (1988), which is noteworthy for Beastie Boys fans because they perform "Desperado," a song not released anywhere else. This song features an early version of the dramatic pause the Beasties would incorporate into songs like "The New Style," "Intergalactic," and "Ch-check It Out." On "Desperado," the music stops in mid-song, and Mike D begins his verse a capella: "M-I-K-E-D-E-E-E."

The Beastie Boys built from the rhyme styles of Run-DMC, and credit Run, DMC, and Jam Master Jay for their contributions to the *Licensed to Ill* album. In 1986, though, the Beastie Boys emerged from Run-DMC's shadow. Run-DMC had proven hip hop's potential for continued crossover success with their albums *King of Rock* (1985) and *Raising Hell* (1986), and now the

Beastie Boys emerged with their breakthrough album *Licensed to Ill*. The Beastie Boys were significant in extending Run-DMC's fusion of rap and rock, and also as the first white hip hop group to achieve commercial success. The Beastie Boys have acknowledged their debt to Run-DMC in several interviews and in the liner notes to their CD anthology *The Sounds of Science*, where MCA describes watching Run-DMC record vocals in the studio and being "amazed" (6). "Slow and Low," a track on *Licensed to Ill*, was a Run DMC song that the group had chosen to leave off their *King of Rock* album. Yauch asked if the Beastie Boys could record it for *Licensed to Ill*, and admits that they only changed two lines of the lyrics. Run-DMC is also credited with coming up with the idea to reverse the drum track on "Paul Revere," giving the song a distinctive backward sound. In 2005, at the *VH1 Hip-Hop Honors*, the Beastie Boys paid tribute to the influence of their mentors and Def Jam label mates, Run-DMC.

The Beasties made their mark with Def Jam Records, recording *Licensed to Ill* under the supervision of Rick Rubin, Russell Simmons, and Run-DMC. Beyond helping to shape their sound, Def Jam was influential in developing the Beastie Boys' image, as they adopted frat-boy personas that fit with the hard rock music Rubin brought to their records. This image is most prominent on *Licensed to Ill*'s first and biggest-selling single, the seminal "(You Gotta) Fight for Your Right (To Party)," and it is an image the Boys have worked hard to live down. The Beasties became involved with hip hop just as it was becoming a viable business and producing consistent crossover songs. Their affiliation with Run-DMC, Russell Simmons, and Def Jam gave them credibility, and their pranks and personas made them fun and accessible, and just edgy enough to piss off your parents.

While it is tempting to see rap's first white superstars as ready-made for crossover success, there are different accounts of the role race played in the Beasties' reception. Nelson George credits *Licensed to Ill* with creating a "racial chauvinism ... making the Beasties the first whites (but hardly the last) to be accused of treading on 100 percent black turf" (66). At the same time, George contends that rap culture never was exclusively black culture, that it was never "solely African-American created, owned, controlled, and consumed" (57). In one incident in the 1980s, the Boys themselves seemed almost ignorant of their minority status. Former Beastie DJ Dr. Dre told *Spin* magazine about a Beastie Boys performance at New York's Apollo Theater, during which Ad-Rock yelled to the crowd, "All you niggers wave your hands in the air!" (Light 153). Although this type of crowd incitement is common for hip hop artists, Dr. Dre claims he could feel an immediate cooling in the audience's reception of the Beasties, who were so much a part of hip hop culture that in the excitement of performing they forgot they were still outsiders. Dre says that the Beasties used the term "not maliciously, but out of warmth for their audience" (Light 153). Dre claims the incident is recorded on videotape, but the Beasties maintain that Dre made up the story. Whether true or not, the incident became a footnote to the Beastie Boys' long history of acceptance in hip hop.

The Beastie Boys' interaction with black artists has been key to their career. DMC and Q-Tip agree that the Beastie Boys have maintained fans' acceptance because they don't try to be black (McDaniels and Kunz 84). They focus on who they are. Yet even as they don't focus on their white identities by making it a gimmick, as Vanilla Ice did with his name and his first single, "Play That Funky Music (White Boy)," the Beastie Boys do address racism. On *Paul's Boutique*, for example, they challenged racism on two songs, "Lookin Down the Barrel of a Gun" and "B-Boy Bouillabaisse." For the majority of their career, the Beastie Boys have performed onstage with a black DJ: first with Dr. Dre, and then with DJ Hurricane, a bodyguard for Run-DMC who joined the Beastie Boys for their *Licensed to Ill* tour and remained with the group through 1994's *Ill Communication*, after which he left to record a solo album, *Tha Hurra*, showing his skills as a rap vocalist as well as a DJ. Hurricane had previously recorded in side projects with Davy D (aka Davy DMX) and the Afros. His departure from the Beastie Boys was amicable; the three Beastie Boys guest starred on Hurricane's debut album on the song "Four Fly Guys."

After Hurricane left the group, Adam Yauch recruited Mixmaster Mike of the California DJ crew the Invisibl Skratch Piklz for the 1998 album *Hello Nasty*. Mixmaster Mike rounded out the group with two Adams and two Mikes, and was best introduced to Beastie Boys fans on the track "Three MCs and One DJ." *Hello Nasty* marked the return of the Beastie Boys to New York, after living in Los Angeles for nearly a decade and recording three albums there. This move is significant for hip hop, where regional and coastal boundaries are carefully drawn (see Tupac Shakur and Notorious B.I.G. for more background on the East Coast versus West Coast beef of the 1990s). The Beastie Boys are among a select few groups (such as Too $hort and Tha Alkaholiks) to move across the United States and maintain their fan base, and one of the only groups to move back to their roots in midcareer.

Even with their long stint in California, New York is at the heart of the Beastie Boys. It is often erroneously reported that the Beastie Boys grew up in white suburbia. While they may have opened up white suburban listeners to hip hop, taking the torch from Run-DMC, the Beastie Boys show their New York City roots in their lyrics. Ad-Rock reminds the listener, "I'm from Manhattan" on "Hold It Now, Hit It." Adam Yauch traces his lineage back to Ellis Island on the song "Do It," and on "B-Boy Bouillabaisse" Mike D rhymes, "I live in the Village." Growing up in New York City gave the Beastie Boys an eclectic view of culture, musical and otherwise. Their access to the developing hip hop scene allowed the Beastie Boys to create a style of music all their own, blending the styles of Run-DMC, T La Rock, Busy Bee, and other hip hop forerunners with the New York City punk scene that was on the wane as hip hop was on the rise. The Beastie Boys are icons because they have taken hip hop in so many directions while at the same time keeping their music true to the foundations of hip hop culture. Their role in the early days of commercial hip hop was balanced by their musical credibility and their work with artists such as Run-DMC, Public Enemy, Biz Markie, A Tribe Called Quest, and De La Soul.

LICENSED TO ILL

Ad-Rock, Mike D, and MCA grew up in New York City, but *Licensed to Ill* brought rap to the suburbs. Their first MTV video was "She's on It," a song that appeared on their *Rock Hard* EP and on the *Krush Groove* soundtrack in 1985, but it was their second video, 1986's "(You Gotta) Fight for Your Right (To Party)" that would make the Beastie Boys famous. With its electric guitar riff and joking message of middle-class teenage empowerment, "Fight for Your Right" was poised to extend the connections between rap and rock culture that were begun by Run-DMC. With lyrics about not wanting to go to school, being caught smoking, and having porno magazines confiscated by parents, the Beastie Boys tapped into a widening hip hop audience whose experiences were far removed from the crime-ridden New York City streets depicted in songs like Grandmaster Flash and the Furious Five's "The Message." The "Fight for Your Right" video borrowed a jocks-versus-nerds theme from 1980s teen movies, with the Beastie Boys playing the jocks. It opened with parents leaving and urging their two nerdy sons to behave themselves during their absence. The boys plan to invite friends over for soda and pie, hoping no bad people show up. But there are the Beasties, initiating a pie fight, smashing the television with a sledge hammer, pouring Spanish fly in the punch, and setting a copy of *Popular Mechanics* on fire, while someone is reading it. The Beasties brought punk's energy and rock's excess to rap music. Concerts on the *Licensed to Ill* tour featured female dancers in cages, a giant gyrating penis, and a flood of Budweiser that recalled the stage shows of hard rock groups like Motley Crue. Yet the B-Boys also featured stage diving from the world of punk. The "Hold It Now Hit It" music video shows live footage of MCA performing his signature stage dive, the Fosberry Flop.

Licensed to Ill became rap's biggest-selling album, outselling Beastie mentors Run-DMC. With Run-DMC, rap music had entered heavy rotation on MTV, and the Beastie Boys were primed for this same success. Wearing a Volkswagen hood ornament around his neck, Mike D created his own version of Run-DMC's hip hop fashion. Run-DMC built an image from their trademark leather jackets, fedoras, and untied Adidas sneakers; Mike D sparked an international crime spree, causing fans across the globe to steal hood ornaments from Volkswagens. Volkswagen even issued a statement urging kids not to steal their logo and offering to mail them a free ornament upon request.

Vocally, the B-Boys were distinctive as well. Ad-Rock's nasal delivery has been called a distinctively white vocal style, but in the early 1990s he considered collaborating with African American MCs Q-Tip (of A Tribe Called Quest) and JuJu (of the Beatnuts) to form a side group called the Nasal Poets. Ad-Rock's vocal style influenced high-pitched MCs such as Sir Mix-a-Lot, B-Real of Cypress Hill, SonDoobie, and Insane Clown Posse, who would go on to dis the Beastie Boys in their lyrics. With label mates and mentors Run-DMC ahead of them, and producer Rick Rubin connecting rap with rock on "King of Rock," the Beasties took hip hop uptown. They rhymed about renting blue tuxedos for the prom and breaking into classmates' lockers. They set the stage for high school–focused singles to come, like DJ Jazzy Jeff and the Fresh Prince's "Parents Just Don't Understand," De La Soul's "Me Myself and I" video, and Young MC's "Principal's Office," not to mention teen and child rap groups Kriss Kross and Another Bad Creation. A younger market was buying hip hop records, and their material caught the eyes of the kids. The Beastie Boys rhymed about high school, the prom, and dealing with parents, as well as becoming rap stars. They made their music accessible to a new audience. Part of *Licensed to Ill*'s appeal came from a mix of teen-focused subject matter and shock value. The B-Boys rhymed about getting busted for smoking and being told to turn down their loud music, but they also boasted about carrying weapons and smoking angel dust.

The Beastie Boys were managed by hip hop mogul Russell Simmons, the brother of Run from Run-DMC. Simmons would go on to expand his record label to create Def Jam South and to develop HBO's *Def Comedy Jam, Def Poetry Jam*. The Beasties associated closely with Run-DMC. Their track "Slow and Low" was a Run-DMC song given to the Beasties. Run suggested that they flip the drums backward on "Paul Revere." Musically, *Licensed to Ill* was built, like much of Run-DMC's music, largely from hard rock, Led Zeppelin, and AC/DC. The album opens with a sampled drumbeat from Led Zeppelin's "When the Levee Breaks," and features guitar work from Kerry King of the heavy metal group Slayer, who appeared in the video for "No Sleep 'til Brooklyn." Lyrically, they referenced punk songs like the Sex Pistols' "Friggin in the Riggin," rhymed about watching *Columbo*, eating Chef Boyardee, and having more rhymes than Phyllis Diller.

Lyrically, *Licensed to Ill* was a precursor to gangsta rap. There is a lot of debate over where the gangsta subgenre originated, but certain *Licensed to Ill* lyrics, if they don't constitute a gangsta rap album, certainly anticipated the popularity of songs about gun play, drug use, and promiscuity. While N.W.A. popularized the term *gangsta* as well as the musical style and lyrical content that would characterize the West Coast gangsta sound, Ice-T lays claim to inventing the form with his song "Six in the Morning," but Philadelphia's Schoolly D claims he did it first on the East Coast. The Beastie Boys were fans of Schoolly D and were influenced by his style. Mike D is seen wearing a Schoolly D T-shirt in a Ricky Powell photograph, and the B-Boys played a concert in Philadelphia with Schoolly D and Just-Ice. The older, wiser Beastie

Boys may not want credit for their contributions to the development of gangsta rap, but *Licensed* was one of the first albums to promote gun play, drug use, and cartoonish violence to listeners in the mainstream. In fact, N.W.A.'s Eazy-E frequently sampled *Licensed to Ill* on his albums. If the gangsta style is characterized by its macho pose, its depictions of everyday acts of violence, and using women, money, and guns as status symbols, then *Licensed to Ill* is a gangsta rap record. Yet while Eazy-E and N.W.A. claimed to live the criminal lifestyle they depicted in their lyrics, the Beastie Boys have long said that they were writing fictional stories in their lyrics. MCA said in a 2006 interview, "I think most people know it's a goof" (Martens). In the rap era before Vanilla Ice, who was discredited for having falsified his biography so he could claim to be a criminal, many MCs wrote lyrics that lay closer to fantasy than fact. The mix of violent and silly lyrics on *Licensed to Ill* makes listeners question how literally to take the Beastie Boys. They talked about smoking angel dust, sniffing glue, packing .22 automatics, and shooting people at parties, as well as high school pranks like giving people swirlies and breaking into someone's locker to smash his glasses. *Licensed to Ill*'s blend of cartoonish and graphic violence would influence the Beatnuts, Cypress Hill, Redman, and Ill Bill. But it was before C. Delores Tucker, the PMRC, and the "Parental Advisory" stickers. In the Beasties' lyrics, these stories came off as fantasy, even as they rhymed about shooting people and taking hard-core drugs.

Listeners must remember, though, that *Licensed to Ill* was toned down before its release. The version of *Licensed to Ill* that made it to record stores had been changed significantly: The title was originally *Don't Be a Faggot*, and in an era when hip hop was overwhelmingly antidrug, the Beasties' original lyrics had celebrated crack cocaine. Before the album hit shelves, the Beasties removed the line "I smoke my crack" from "Rhymin and Stealin." They removed the track "Scenario," which also included a reference to smoking crack and was later heard in the film *Pump Up the Volume*. The Web site Beastiemania.com reports that after the Beastie Boys parted ways with Def Jam, the label recruited Public Enemy's Chuck D to produce a Beastie Boys album called *The White House*, working from tracks like "Scenario" and "Desperado" that the Boys had recorded but not released. Although the existence of a Chuck D-produced album has never been proven, several of these tracks, in their original forms, have been bootlegged on releases such as *Original Ill*, or uploaded on music-sharing Web sites.

Even with these omissions, *Licensed to Ill* depicted an adolescent male fantasy world, somewhere between punk rock's energy and fraternity films like *Animal House*, somewhere between arena rock's excess and punk's playfulness. Their home video and tour booklet from *Licensed to Ill* celebrates the rock star lifestyle: hotel pranks, trashing rooms, groupies. The video shows them dumping water on sleeping reporters, pouring honey on groupies, and signing breasts with a magic marker. They were known for showcasing a giant inflatable penis onstage. Ad-Rock was arrested in England after a fan accused him of using a baseball bat to hit a beer bottle into the audience. Making an even greater impression on England, the Beastie Boys refused to sign autographs one afternoon, leading the *Daily Mirror* to run the headline "Pop Idols Sneer at Dying Kids." Their antics are documented in the *Licensed to Ill Tour Video* and the *Official Licensed to Ill Tourbook*. This was a lifestyle the Beasties would work hard to live down in their later music. As gangsta rap became hip hop's biggest-selling subgenre, the artists became concerned with being "real," which is to say actually living the lifestyle promoted in lyrics. Yet the Beasties have talked openly about their construction of personas on *Licensed to Ill*. As MCA says in the *Sounds of Science* liner notes, though, with their success they slowly became the characters they played: drunken, prank-playing frat boys. While they would change their personas on *Paul's Boutique*, they would retain some of the elements of *Licensed to Ill*. Ultimately, though, they began a pattern of change and evolution, both in terms of music and persona.

PAUL'S BOUTIQUE

The Beastie Boys split with Def Jam in 1988. Having broken away from their producer Rick Rubin and manager Russell Simmons, as well as the thriving Def Jam label itself, the Beasties found themselves looking for new musical direction. In the three years between the 1986 release of *Licensed to Ill* and their 1989 follow-up, *Paul's Boutique*, the three Beastie Boys explored other artistic outlets. Adam Horovitz moved from New York to Los Angeles and landed a role in the film *Lost Angels* (1989). In this film, as well as 1992's *Roadside Prophets*, in which Horovitz costarred with punk icon John Doe, he played a troubled teen. His bandmates, meanwhile, were playing music with side projects while taking a break from the Beastie Boys after the grueling schedule of the *Licensed to Ill* world tour. MCA recorded music in a side project with Bad Brains' Darryl Jennifer, a friend from the Beasties' punk days. Mike D performed with a group called Flophouse Society.

After Diamond and Yauch joined Horovitz in Los Angeles in 1988, the Beastie Boys signed with Capitol Records and began working on their next album. They sought out LA producers the Dust Brothers, who would produce crossover radio hits for Tone Loc and Young MC. The Dust Brothers created a denser, more sample-laden sound for the Beasties, although it did not translate to crossover hits. The Beastie Boys began rhyming over tracks that the Dust Brothers had intended to stand alone as instrumentals, tracks that were built from a collage of samples rather than the simpler beats and loops employed by Rubin on *Licensed to Ill*. The Beasties were already known for the eclectic mix of pop culture references in their lyrics, and the Dust Brothers brought this same philosophy to their music. *Paul's Boutique*'s mix of sounds ranges from Dolly Parton's "9 to 5" to Johnny Cash's "Folsom Prison Blues," the Ramones, the Beatles, Bob Marley, and the theme from *Pyscho*. This was a different kind of sampling than Rick Rubin had used on *Licensed to Ill*, which was mostly bass lines, drums, and guitar looped to create beats. *Paul's Boutique* brought in more pieces of vocals and wove them into the Beasties' lyrical pastiche of references to 1970s professional basketball, skate culture, punk, Japanese culture, and so on. With its range of samples, *Paul's Boutique* created a cultural mix that the Beastie Boys furthered in their lyrics.

Paul's Boutique is an album that would be very difficult to make now that digital music sampling regulations are more clearly defined. In fact, the release of *Paul's Boutique* was held up because of a lawsuit over a sample on *Licensed to Ill*'s "Hold It Now Hit It." That song sampled the words "Yo, Leroy," and a piece of a drumbeat from Jimmy Castor's 1977 song "The Return of Leroy (Part One)." The Beasties had also been on the other side of a sampling lawsuit, having sued British Airways over the use of their song "Beastie Revolution" from 1983's *Cookie Puss*. This legal battle with Castor, though, would set the stage for future copyright litigation against the Beastie Boys from composer James Newton. In 1991, Singer-songwriter Gilbert O'Sullivan would sue Beastie Boys collaborator Biz Markie for the use of his song "Alone Again (Naturally)" (see sidebar: Sampling Lawsuits).

Sampling Lawsuits
Mickey Hess

In the late eighties and early nineties, the music business faced a series of lawsuits between artists, labels, and publishing companies, all centering on hip hop's invention of digital sampling. Sampling is the process by which hip hop producers extract pieces of existing records and then reassemble them into a new hip hop song. Clearing samples is complicated because the rights to the sheet music and the recording often are held by different entities. Generally speaking, musicians retain the rights to their composition, while record labels assume the rights to the recording. At that time, before there existed a defined legal system of clearing samples, artists such as De La Soul, Biz Markie, and the Beastie Boys were sued by the musicians they sampled.

In 1989, the pop group the Turtles sued De La Soul for sampling sounds from their song "You Showed Me" in De La's "Transmitting Live from Mars." In 1991, artist Biz Markie lost a lawsuit to singer-songwriter Gilbert O'Sullivan after Biz sampled Sullivan's "Alone Again (Naturally)" in his song "Alone Again." Such lawsuits would change the way hip hop artists constructed their music in the studio, and would lead to a new system of sampling clearinghouses, which worked to negotiate song royalties between record companies and to ensure that the original musicians were compensated. Unfortunately, sampling clearinghouses remain fairly inaccessible to hip hop artists who do not record for major record labels.

The Beastie Boys, who sued British Airways in the early 1980s for using sounds from their album *Cookie Puss* in a commercial, have faced sampling lawsuits from Jimmy Castor and, more recently, composer James Newton, who in 2002 sued the B-Boys for not clearing the rights to a sequence of three notes (C–D-flat–C) Newton composed for his song "Chorus." The group had cleared all rights to the recorded music with Newton's record label, ECM, but had not cleared their use of the musical composition, for which Newton still owned the rights. The Beastie Boys argued that their sampling of only three successive notes, originally composed by Newton, on their song "Pass the Mic," did not breach copyright because a sequence so brief (six seconds) does not constitute a musical composition. In a letter posted to their Web site the group argues, "If one could copyright the basic building blocks of music or grammar then there would be no room for making new compositions or books" (www.beastieboys.com). The Beastie Boys extend their print analogy to argue that in digitally manipulating Newton's recorded flute performance to change its tone and duration, they effectively changed the notes Newton composed. Although the Beastie Boys won the lawsuit, they lost their countersuit to recover their legal costs, which they estimated at $100,000.

Further Resources

Hess, Mickey. "Was Foucault a Plagiarist? Hip-Hop Sampling and Academic Citation." *Computers and Composition: An International Journal for Teachers of Writing* 23 (2006): 280–295.

Porcello, Thomas. "The Ethics of Digital Audio Sampling: Engineer's Discourse." *Popular Music* 10:1 (1991): 69–84.

Schloss, Joseph G. *Making Beats: The Art of Sample-Based Hip-Hop*. Middletown, CT: Wesleyan University Press, 2004.

Schumaker, Thomas. "'This Is a Sampling Sport': Digital Sampling, Rap Music, and the Law in Cultural Production." *Media, Culture, and Society* 17:2 (1995): 253–73.

Visually, the cover and liner notes for *Paul's Boutique* are something in themselves. The twelve-inch record folded out to five feet of insert panels including all lyrics from the album. This artistic direction was taken further in the impressionistic music video for the song "Shadrach." Artists worked from film of a Beastie Boys performance and created frame-by-frame oil paintings, which were then animated for the music video. The video for "Lookin Down the Barrel of a Gun" was filmed with a fish-eye lens and an infrared camera, both of which the B-Boys would use in future videos.

With their second hip hop album, the Beasties were already looking forward and backward. They revised lyrics from their punk song "Egg Raid on Mojo" for "Egg Man," a track built around the *Psycho* theme. They used live drums and bass on the record. The album ended with "B-Boy Bouillabaisse," a collection of several short tracks that featured the Beastie Boys' range of styles. While the Dust Brothers' production was groundbreaking, so were the Beastie Boys' rhymes. *Paul's Boutique* is truly Mike D's album. He smoothed out the vocal style he had invented on *Licensed to Ill* and delivered mack rhymes like "I'm so rope they call me Mister Roper."

Today, *Paul's Boutique* is considered a hip hop classic, but its initial sales were disappointing. The album took hip hop music places it hadn't gone before. The release of *Paul's Boutique* the same year as De La Soul's *3 Feet High and Rising* made 1989 a turning point for hip hop. The Beastie Boys have said that De La Soul beat them to the punch by releasing their innovative album in the months before *Paul's Boutique*, but the competition between these groups has been friendly. The B-Boys would later invite De La Soul to perform at their 1996 and 1997 Tibetan Freedom Concerts, and Mike D and Ad-Rock would guest star on De La Soul's "Squat" on their 2003 album *AOI: Bionix*.

CHECK YOUR HEAD

Check Your Head was the first major-label album in which the Beastie Boys took control of their own musical production. Working on their own without Rick Rubin, who engineered *Licensed to Ill*, or the Dust Brothers, who produced *Paul's Boutique*, the B-Boys recorded *Check Your Head* in their own G-Son Studios, and took hip hop in yet another direction as they returned to the live instrumentation of their punk rock origins. Ad-Rock's guitar, MCA's bass (including the stand-up bass), and Mike D's drums feature prominently on *Check Your Head*. The album even concludes with an instrumental track, "In 3's," which combines live instruments with digital sampling. The B-Boys did not turn their backs on traditional hip hop production, but instead merged it with punk, funk, and rock to create a unique new Beastie Boys sound. Certain tracks, including their third single, "Gratitude," didn't sound like hip hop at all. Fuzzed out guitars and distorted vocals (MCA claims that they were just using cheap microphones) brought the Beastie Boys' sound into the alternative rock era. Around this same time, Philadelphia hip hop group the Roots were getting attention for playing instruments. The liner notes made the Beastie Boys' musicianship clear with a photo of the band playing instruments in the studio.

Yet the old-school rhymes of "Pass the Mic," their first single from the album, which maintained the vocal interplay of *Licensed to Ill*, and the hip hop samples (they sampled dialogue from *Wild Style*, one of the first hip hop films) made clear that the Beastie Boys were not leaving hip hop behind. They enhanced their lineup with keyboardist Money Mark Nishita, whom they had originally hired to build cabinets for their recording studio. Mark's work is best heard on "Gratitude." He would remain with the group through their next album, *Ill Communication*, release a solo album on the Beastie Boys'

Grand Royal label, and open for the B-Boys during some dates on their *Hello Nasty* tour in 1998.

Check Your Head was the first Beastie Boys release to bear the label Grand Royal (though it shared the bill with Capitol Records). The name Grand Royal is borrowed from Erick Sermon of EPMD, who called himself "the MC grand royal" on the song "Hostile." The label is one Mike D, Ad-Rock, and MCA started to take control of their own music, as well as release albums from bands that they liked. They started *Grand Royal Magazine*, a tribute to pop culture and a forum for promoting new music acts.

Check Your Head could be called the Beastie Boys' comeback album. While *Paul's Boutique* is considered a hip hop classic, sales had been disappointing, and it had been three years since a Beastie Boys single had hit the radio. In this three years, a lot had changed in hip hop. The biggest difference was Vanilla Ice. The B-Boys had always been readily accepted because they got into the rap game so early, but as hip hop was crossing over to mainstream radio, and with Vanilla Ice outselling black artists like the Beasties did before him, there was a new mistrust of the white artist. The Beastie Boys had been out of the public eye for three years and needed to come back strong. Their first single was "Pass the Mic," but they broke through to alternative music fans with their second single, "So Whatcha Want?"

With the 1992 release of "Smells Like Teen Spirit," Nirvana had given birth to the alternative rock era, bringing a new, punk-influenced style of rock to MTV and the radio. The Beastie Boys were primed to tap into this new market as well. Glen Friedman, famous for his skateboard photography, shot the cover for *Check Your Head*, and the B-Boys further emphasized their connections with skateboard and snowboard culture in lyrics. Adam Yauch became an avid snowboarder, and a snowboarding trip to Asia would ultimately lead him to his interest in Buddhism and the plight of Tibet.

Even with these new interests, the Beastie Boys maintained their connection to old-school hip hop. *Check Your Head*'s first single, "Pass the Mic" contained old-school lyrics like "Rock rock y'all, hip-hop y'all," that recalled the origins of MCs as crowd motivators who helped drive people to the dance floor while the DJ played records. The album featured a song, "The Biz vs. the Nuge," with old-school icon Biz Markie, who began his career beatboxing for Roxanne Shanté and performing with the Juice Crew. Further asserting their connections with hip hop, the B-Boys collaborated with Cypress Hill's B-Real on a remix of "So Whatcha Want?," and Ad-Rock and Mike D collaborated with Milk (formerly of Audio Two) on "Spam," a song from his 1994 album *Never Dated*, released by Rick Rubin's American Recordings.

With the live instrumentation on *Check Your Head*, the Beastie Boys were returning to their roots, but not yet including punk tracks like they would on *Ill Communication*. In between these new albums, they released *Some Old Bullshit*, which combined their early hard-core record *Pollywog Stew* with *Cookie Puss*. In the other direction, they released a compilation of instrumentals, *The In Sound from Way Out*. Were the B-boys moving away from hip hop?

ILL COMMUNICATION

If *Check Your Head* suggested that the Beastie Boys were moving away from their hip hop roots, a listen to 1994's *Ill Communication* would appear to confirm this transition. While the album opens with "Sure Shot," an energetic track driven by a doctored flute sample and peppered with the Beastie Boys' trademark mix of cultural references (lyrics from this song reference professional baseball player Rod Carew, cartoonist Vaughn Bode, and the action film *The Taking of Pelham One Two Three*), the mood shifts quickly to punk on track two, "Tough Guy," and track sixteen, "Heart Attack Man," a mock tribute to Beastie Boys associate and music journalist Bob Mack. Subsequent tracks are devoted to a violin-driven instrumental ("Eugene's Lament"), an instrumental tribute to another friend, hip hop photographer Ricky Powell ("Ricky's Theme"), and Tibetan-inspired songs ("Shambala" and "Bodhisattva Vow"). The album's back cover features the eight people who worked on the album: Ad-Rock, Mike D, and MCA, along with DJ Hurricane, Keyboard Money Mark, producer Mario Caldato Jr., and percussionists Amery "Awol" Smith (who played drums on "Tough Guy" and "Heart Attack Man") and Eric Bobo (a bongo player who would later join Cypress Hill). The influence of this cast of characters on the Beastie Boys' sound was evident. Out of the album's twenty tracks, only nine are hip hop songs.

This formula, however, would not lose the Beastie Boys their fan base. *Ill Communication*'s first single, "Sabotage," although not a hip hop song, was propelled to success by Ad-Rock's screaming rock vocals, Mike D's drums, MCA's powerful bass lines, and a video directed by skateboard filmmaker Spike Jonze, which featured the Beastie Boys as characters in a 1970s police drama. "Sabotage" did employ turntable scratching and samples, but it was by no means a hip hop song. At the same time, "Root Down" serves as a tribute to hip hop's pioneers. "Root Down" samples funk pioneer Jimmy Smith's song of the same title. Mike D's lyrics reference classic New York City hip hop radio shows like Zulu Beats, as well as the classic MC battle between Busy Bee and Kool Moe Dee. The "Root Down" video consists almost entirely of film footage of the 1980s New York hip hop scene: b-boys, graffiti artists, turntablists, and MCs. The success of "Root Down" led the Beastie Boys to release a *Root Down* EP, which featured two remixes of the song and some live tracks, including "Time to Get Ill," from European concerts. On the *Tibetan Freedom Concert* CD, the Beastie Boys included their performance of "Root Down," in which their music is replaced midway through by the classic breakbeat "Apache," taken from the 1960 song "Apache," written by Jerry Lordan, recorded by the Shadows, and made famous in hip hop circles by Sugarhill Gang. In their live performances, the Beastie Boys maintained the tradition of old-school MCs, who would continue rhyming as the DJ changed the record.

Beastie Boys concerts had always been known for their energy. In 1994, they joined Lollapalooza, the annual concert founded by Jane's Addiction singer Perry Farrell, and known to include one or two hip hop acts within a roster of primarily alternative rock groups. The Beastie Boys shared a bill with Green Day, L7, the Breeders, the Boredoms, George Clinton's P-Funk All Stars, Nick Cave, A Tribe Called Quest, and Smashing Pumpkins, who took Nirvana's place after that band backed out shortly before Kurt Cobain's suicide in April 1994.

MCA's Tibetan Freedom Concert, first staged in 1996, borrowed Lollapalooza's mix of bands from different musical genres, yet amplified the range and number of bands included and confined the concert to a three-day affair as opposed to Lollapalooza's summer-long tour. The Tibetan Freedom Concert brought together some of the world's biggest acts to raise awareness of China's occupation of Tibet. The concerts grew out of MCA's conversion to Buddhism. Yauch's personal transformation played out in lyrics as well. *Ill Communication* furthers the Buddhist themes begun by the song "Namaste" on *Check Your Head*. The songs "Shambala" and "Bodhisattva Vow" emphasize the changes in MCA's life, and on "Sure Shot" he offers a "long overdue" apology for the Beasties' treatment of women in their *Licensed to Ill* lyrics (see sidebar: Treatment of Women in Lyrics).

Yet MCA's conversion had not stopped him from indulging in the pranks and humor for which the Beastie Boys were known. He had previously direc-

---

Treatment of Women in Lyrics
Mickey Hess

In the frat-boy humor of their 1986 debut *Licensed to Ill*, the Beastie Boys present women as groupies, celebrate the libido-enhancing attributes of Spanish fly, and, on "Paul Revere," suggest performing sexual acts with a Wiffle ball bat. Twelve years later, at the 1998 Reading Music Festival, a more evolved Beastie Boys requested that British hard dance group the Prodigy not perform their hit single "Smack My Bitch Up," the chorus of which adapts Kool Keith's lyrics from the Ultramagnetic MCs song "Give the Drummer Some."

The Prodigy's music video for "Smack My Bitch Up" caused controversy on MTV, which agreed to play the video only after 10 p.m., and to preface it with a written warning and a spoken statement from MTV veejay Kurt Loder, who justified the video's graphic imagery as artistic. The video, shot from the perspective of one central character, follows that character through bars and strip clubs, where the character gropes female dancers. The video ends with the central character facing a mirror, revealing to the viewer that she is actually a woman.

After the Prodigy refused to cut the song from their set list at the Reading Festival, the Beasties spoke publicly against the single. Although the Prodigy accused them of hypocrisy, the Beastie Boys had attempted to atone for their earlier lyrics on 1994's "Sure Shot," where they call for a "long overdue" end to disrespecting women. On 1998's "Song for the Man," they plead with men to approach women with respect. Since the mid-1990s, the Beastie Boys have often revised their old lyrics in concert, replacing or omitting sexist lyrics from *Licensed to Ill*. Even with these efforts, their public dispute with the Prodigy highlights the trouble the Beasties have had living down their *Licensed to Ill* image.

The Beastie Boys have long demonstrated their dedication to correcting the misogynist images they put forth on *Licensed to Ill*, where songs like "Girls" suggested that women were only useful for washing dishes, cleaning bathrooms, and having sex. They worked to revise this message in the Lollapalooza 1994 tour booklet, where the Beastie Boys urged their male fans to respect their female fans' right to have a good time without being harassed. Speaking about mosh pit etiquette, they reminded fans to keep their hands to themselves and resist the urge to cop a feel when women are crowd surfing. This advice to male concertgoers echoed the riot grrl movement that began in punk rock and alternative rock cultures in the nineties. Ad-rock, who is married to Kathleen Hanna, founder of the riot-grrl movement, has been most vocal of the three Beastie Boys in addressing issues of women's safety at concerts. In his acceptance speech at the 1999 MTV Video Music Awards, Ad-Rock spoke against the sexual assaults that had occurred at Woodstock 1999. He called for musicians to take an active role in protecting their fans and to educate concert promoters and security guards about rape and sexual harassment: "Talk to the promoters and make sure they're doing something about the safety of all the girls and the women that come to our shows."

Further Resource

Morgan, Joan. *When the Chickenheads Come Home to Roost: My Life as a Hip-Hop Feminist.* New York: Simon & Schuster, 1999.

---

ted videos, such as "So What Cha Want," under the name Nathanial Hornblower, and by 1994 he had both constructed a life history for Hornblower and taken to dressing as this alter ego in MTV appearances. Hornblower wore lederhosen and a bright red moustache and claimed to be Adam Yauch's cousin from Switzerland. Famously, Hornblower rushed the stage at the 1994 MTV Music Awards, after the Beastie Boys lost the award for best video to R.E.M.'s "Everybody Hurts." Yauch, dressed as Hornblower, stepped in front of R.E.M. singer Michael Stipe to claim that director Spike Jonze should have won for his Beastie Boys video and, strangely, that Hornblower himself was responsible for the ideas for George Lucas's *Star Wars* movies. Hornblower was escorted from the stage.

Outside the band itself, the three Beastie Boys members were involved in other projects. While Yauch devoted time to directing videos and raising money for Tibet via the Milarepa Fund, Adam Horovitz and Michael Diamond created new outlets as well. Ad-Rock recorded a side project with Beastie Boys percussionist Awol. BS2000, or Beat Science 2000, lies somewhere between hip hop and the hard-core techno sounds of groups like Grand Royal's Atari Teenage Riot, and showcases Ad-Rock's prowess on the EMU SP-12, a classic sampling machine that he used heavily in creating BS2000's two full-length albums. In the years after *Ill Communication* was released, the Grand Royal Records stable of artists was expanding, and Mike D embraced his CEO role much in the way Jay-Z would with Roc-A-Fella a few years later. Grand Royal signed Cibo Matto, Atari Teenage Riot, Butter 08, Ben Lee, and Luscious Jackson, featuring original Beastie Boys drummer Kate Schnellenbach. The label also released a Mike D side project called Big Fat Love, and reissued a record, *Real Men Don't Floss*, from the Young and the Useless, Ad-Rock's pre-Beastie Boys punk band. Looking to the past and the future at once, the Beastie Boys released *Some Old Bullshit*, which compiled their initial punk EPs *Pollywog Stew* and *Cookie Puss*, which were both long out of print. Also, they released *Aglio e Olio*, an EP of new punk songs. These two releases marked, for the most part, the end of the Beastie Boys' return to recording punk music. Only one track, "Remote Control," from their next full-length album, 1998's *Hello Nasty*, would sound even remotely like punk.

HELLO NASTY

In keeping with the theme of looking to both past and future, *Hello Nasty* was at once futuristic and old school. MCA invokes "the family tree of old school hip hop" on "Intergalactic," and on "Unite," Ad-Rock proclaims, "In the next millennium I'll still be old school." The latter song's lyrics play on the famous opening words of Karl Marx and Friedrich Engel's *Communist Manifesto*, yet rather than urging the workers of the world to unite, the B-Boys call out for break dancers, MCs, and DJs to band together. *Hello Nasty*, named for the way a receptionist was known to answer the phone for the Beastie Boys' publicist Nasty Little Man, marked both a return to a truer hip hop sound as well as unprecedented innovations in that sound. Produced primarily by Adam Horovitz, *Hello Nasty* is a beat-focused album. Ad-Rock himself claims to be a "Benihana chef on the SP-12," citing the EMU SP-1200, a classic sampling machine from the 1980s, still favored by many hip hop producers because it combines digital sampling technology with analog filters, giving the music a gritty and unpolished sound less available to producers using the MPC-3000 (a more technologically advanced sampler) or digital production software such as ProTools.

Hello Nasty also marks the addition of Mixmaster Mike to the Beastie Boys lineup. One song, "Three MCs and one DJ," is devoted to introducing this new DJ to listeners and showcasing his unique scratch techniques. The track begins with a message Mixmaster Mike left on Adam Yauch's answering machine, offering his services as a world-class DJ and giving Yauch a listen to his new innovation, "the tweak scratch," which he achieved by hooking his turntables to a wah-wah pedal designed for guitars. DJ Hurricane, who had worked with the B-Boys since *Licensed to Ill*, had departed to record solo albums as an MC. His skills as a DJ had mainly been utilized in concert, and up to that point most of the scratching heard on Beastie Boys albums had been done by one of the two Adams: MCA or Ad-Rock.

As energetic as DJ Hurricane had been in concert, Mixmaster Mike added an entirely new element to the Beastie Boys' stage show. Mike had performed with the DJ Crew Invisbl Skratch Piklz and competed in turntable competitions between DJs, and as a turntablist who had performed without MCs, his style of abruptly switching records or suddenly slowing down or speeding up a beat gave a new feature of improvisation to Beastie Boys concerts. Mixmaster Mike tends to open each song with the original music heard on the album, then switch records for the second and third verses. I saw the Beastie Boys perform on the 1998 *Hello Nasty* tour in St. Louis, Missouri, and it was obvious that Mixmaster Mike was given free reign on stage. In fact, the three Beastie Boys often showed surprise at his choice of record, and even stopped in the middle of performing "The Skills to Pay the Bills" to ask their new DJ to change the record, because it didn't fit with the tempo of the song. Ordinarily, though, Mike D, Ad-Rock, and MCA show remarkable adaptability, working their vocals into new tempos and rhythms to fit with the changes Mixmaster Mike throws at them. When it works, it works brilliantly, and the interplay between MC and DJ recalls early hip hop performances by artists like Grandmaster Flash, when the DJ controlled the music and the MC formatted his or her vocals around the DJ's selection.

The 1998 *Hello Nasty* tour is also significant because it featured A Tribe Called Quest, who called it their farewell concert (although Tribe later reunited to play new shows in 2006). Tribe opened for the Beastie Boys, and then they brought Q-Tip back onstage to perform "Get It Together," a song for which he contributed a guest verse on the *Ill Communication* album. Tip's verse, in fact, is where that album's title came from. The tour was advertised as "Beastie Boys in the Round" because the circular stage slowly rotated throughout the show, so that there was theoretically not a bad seat in the house. Mike D, MCA, and Ad-Rock sported orange jumpsuits and shifted between hip hop songs, instrumentals, and punk songs.

Hello Nasty continued the Beastie Boys' connections with both the old and the new that have made them so adaptable. The Beasties re-emphasized their connections to Native Tongues, with Ad-Rock and Mike D appearing on De La Soul's "Squat." And they looked to new producers. The "Body Movin'" remix by Fatboy Slim was the one they released as a single, rather than the album version. Mike D appeared on *Handsome Boy Modeling School*, a collaboration between producers Prince Paul and Dan the Automator. The B-Boys devoted new songs to correcting their earlier treatment of women in lyrics, a trend that began with "Sure Shot" on *Ill Communication*. In concert, they went back to playing *Licensed to Ill* songs, but often changing lyrics. On "Paul Revere" they changed a suggestive line about a "whiffle ball bat" to "Siamese cat." After *Hello Nasty*, they released *Sounds of Science: The Beastie Boys Anthology*, which featured a picture of the Beastie Boys dressed as old men. They wrote extensive liner notes themselves, telling the history of the songs and offering a behind-the-scenes glimpse at their lives in the studio and on the road. *Hello Nasty* marked the final Tibetan Freedom Concert (in 2001) and the end of the Grand Royal era. The Grand Royal label folded and the magazine stopped production.

TO THE 5 BOROUGHS

The Beastie Boys' 2005 album *To the 5 Boroughs* marked a return to their roots as their first all–hip hop album since *Paul's Boutique*. There were no punk songs, no dub, and no guest stars: just the three Beastie Boys and Mixmaster Mike. They continued the New York focus of *Hello Nasty*, with Ad-Rock, Mike D, and MCA each living back in the city. The album is dedicated to that city, and they offer a tribute to New York on "An Open Letter to NYC," which samples the Dead Boys punk rock classic "Sonic Reducer." *To the 5 Boroughs* is the Beastie Boys' most political recording, with "An Open Letter to NYC" addressing the September 11, 2001, terrorist attacks and other songs containing anti-Bush and antiwar sentiment: "We got a president we didn't elect," MCA rhymes on "Time to Build." Such antiwar material was not new to the Beastie Boys. In the years between *Licensed to Ill* and *Paul's Boutique*, they released a song called "I Want You for Desert Storm," which commented on the first Gulf War. And in conjunction with the 1999 release of *Sounds of Science: The Beastie Boys Anthology*, they released a new single, "Alive," in which Ad-Rock complained about the fact that his tax dollars were being used to build bombs.

With all the political commentary of *To the 5 Boroughs*, the Beastie Boys chose the upbeat "Ch-check It Out" as their first single. This song, through heavy MTV rotation, announced that the Beastie Boys were still here and still relevant. MCA maintains, "No, I didn't retire." The music video featured the Beastie Boys dressed in various costumes: as tourists, as Sir Stewart Wallace, and driving a fanboat through the Everglades. Up-and-coming producer Just Blaze created a remix of the track, for which the B-Boys recorded an alternate video. In keeping with their focus on asserting their continuing relevance and importance to hip hop, Mike D complains that new MCs at Def Jam don't recognize him. He borrows a line from Digital Underground's Shock G to state, "I'm Mike D, the one that put the satin in your panties." In 2005, hip hop was the biggest-selling music in the United States, and the most prominent music videos played on MTV and MTV2. Underground hip hop was making its way into video rotation, introducing viewers to a new breed of MCs and DJs that claimed to stay truer to the roots of old-school hip hop and contrasted with the late 1990s images of champagne parties and diamond necklaces that were so prominent in videos by Bad Boy artists such as P Diddy and Mase. Reaffirming their long-standing commitment to old-school and underground hip hop, the Beastie Boys invited underground MC and Native Tongues affiliate Talib Kweli to join their *To the 5 Boroughs* tour.

Onstage, the Beastie Boys abandoned the orange jumpsuits from their *Hello Nasty* tour and wore clothing similar to their *Licensed to Ill* days: cocked baseball caps, Adidas jumpsuits, and sneakers. Their "Triple Trouble" video, set in Times Square, featured this attire, as did their performance at *The VH1 Hip-Hop Honors*, where they performed "Right Right Now Now" and covered "Sucker M.C.'s" in a tribute to Run-DMC. This performance occurred less than one year after Run-DMC's DJ Jam Master Jay was shot to death in a New York studio. At the end of the song, Ad-Rock said simply, "We love you, Jay," and pointed his microphone at the two remaining members of the group that had worked so closely with the Beastie Boys at the beginning of their career.

THE LEGACY OF THE BEASTIE BOYS

The Beastie Boys have secured their place in hip hop by constantly reinventing the music while at the same time never neglecting the forms on which hip hop music was founded: rhymes, turntables, and beats. They began recording early enough to maintain a connection to old-school hip hop, and their early connections with the Def Jam label and the artists Run-DMC, Public Enemy, and Biz Markie, as well as their later connections with Native Tongues groups A Tribe Called Quest and De La Soul, lend another level to their importance. When MTV awarded the Beastie Boys the coveted Video Vanguard Award, which honors an artist's lifetime contribution to music video innovation, they had Public Enemy's Chuck D present the honor. In hip hop, where artists acknowledge their predecessors and influences in lyrics, the Beastie Boys' name is kept alive. *Licensed to Ill* has remained a commercial dynamo since its 1986 release, but in the late 1990s a rash of hip hop samples solidified the album's place as a classic. Several of these samples came from one song, "The New Style," from *Licensed to Ill*. In 1995 the Pharcyde released the song "Drop," which took its title from the Ad-Rock vocal sample from "The New

Style" that the Pharcyde turned into their song's hook. The "Drop" video was filmed in reverse motion, and two Beastie Boys appeared in the video, with Mike D riding a bicycle backward down the street and Ad-Rock posing for the camera. Dilated Peoples also sampled Ad-Rock's "Mmm ... Drop" and referenced the Beastie Boys in "Another Sound Mission" from their album *20/20*. Tha Alkaholiks use this same sample from "The New Style" on *Firewater* (2006), and Redman recorded a cover of "The New Style" (renaming it "Beet Drop") for his 1998 album *Doc's Da Name*. Redman's cover stripped the original to its final verse (the same verse sampled by Dilated Peoples, Tha Alkaholiks, and the Pharcyde), which Ad-Rock begins by screaming, "Let me clear my throat." DJ Kool borrowed this line for his 1997 single "Let Me Clear My Throat." Ad-Rock's "New Style" verse, via its popularity in samples, has become one of the Beastie Boys' most famous. They even sampled it themselves on "Intergalactic." The popularity of this line and Ad-Rock's recognizable voice solidified the Beastie Boys' position in hip hop circles.

There are further Beastie Boys allusions in many other contemporary hip hop songs, such as Lil' Kim's "Hold It Now," which incorporates music and lyrics from the Beastie Boys' "Paul Revere" and "Hold It Now Hit It," and samples MCA's vocals. Lyrical references to the Beastie Boys extend to Eminem, who mentioned Mike D in lyrics and spoke openly about his admiration for the Beastie Boys. Kid Rock, whose career was given a boost by a spread in the B-Boys' *Grand Royal Magazine*, also spoke openly about their influence and importance to his work. Within the new wave of 1990s white rap and rap-rock acts acknowledging their debts to the Beastie Boys, Insane Clown Posse owed them the greatest debt, as ICP's vocal styles were developed in imitation of Ad-Rock's nasal delivery. Although white groups like Young Black Teenagers and Lordz of Brooklyn had certainly borrowed B-Boy vocal styles before, ICP not only did not acknowledge the influence, but dissed the Beastie Boys in their lyrics: "Fuck the Beastie Boys and fuck the Dalai Lama."

Even with their detractors, the Beastie Boys will always have a place in hip hop history. Their unique and eclectic blend of hip hop and other forms of music, their humor, and their energetic live performances have earned them the respect of hip hop luminaries and fans alike. In 2006, Yauch, under the name of Nathanial Hornblower, produced a film called *Awesome: I ... Shot That!* He handed out fifty Hi-8 and digital video cameras to fans at a 2004 Beastie Boys concert at Madison Square Garden, and compiled the footage into a feature-length film in order to capture the concert experience from the fans; perspective. MCA, Ad-Rock, and Mike D performed in old-school green track suits and baseball caps with their rap names lettered across the front. They performed songs from each of their albums, from *Licensed to Ill* through *To the 5 Boroughs*, and Mixmaster Mike switched LPs and changed the beat at least once per song, prompting the B-Boys to rhyme over a mixture of old-school breakbeats like "Apache" and "900 Number" (aka "Ed Lover's Theme") and contemporary singles such as Jay-Z's "Dirt Off Your

Shoulders" and Fabolous's "Breathe." Darryl "DMC" McDaniels was in the crowd, and Doug E. Fresh joined the Beastie Boys onstage to perform "Time to Get Ill." Even while emphasizing their old-school connections, the Beastie Boys are always looking toward the future.

See Also: Run-DMC, Public Enemy, Eminem, Roxanne Shanté, Native Tongues, Grandmaster Flash

WORKS CITED

Beastie Boys. *Sounds of Science: The Beastie Boys Anthology*. Liner Notes. Grand Royal, 2003.
George, Nelson. *Hip-Hop America*. New York: Penguin, 1999.
Light, Alan. "The Story of Yo!" *Spin Magazine*. September 1998.
Martens, Todd. "Beastie Boys: Dolly Was Robbed at Oscars." ABC News.com. http://abcnews.go.com/Entertainment/wireStory?id=1735883.
McDaniels, Darryl "DMC," and Anita Kunz. "Beastie Boys." *Rolling Stone* 972, 21 April 2005: 84.

FURTHER RESOURCES

Awesome, I . . . Shot That: An Authorized Bootleg. Dir. Nathaniel Hornblower. Perf. Adam Horovitz, Adam Yauch, Michael Diamond. New York: Velocity/Thinkfilm, 2006.
Beastie Boys. *James Newton vs. Beastie Boys*. September 17, 2002. Available http://www.beastieboys.com.
Beastie Mania. www.beastiemania.com.
Beastie Boys DVD Video Anthology. Dir. Evan Bernard and Adam Bernstein. Perf. Adam Horovitz, Adam Yauch, Michael Diamond. Criterion, 2000.
Grand Royal Magazine
Leroy, Dan. *The Beastie Boys' Paul's Boutique*. New York: Continuum, 2006.
Light, Alan. *The Skills to Pay the Bills: The Story of the Beastie Boys*. New York: Three Rivers, 2006.
Tibetan Freedom Concert. www.tibetanfreedomconcert.com.

SELECTED DISCOGRAPHY

Pollywog Stew (EP). Ratcage, 1982.
Cooky Puss (EP). Ratcage, 1983.
Rock Hard (EP). Def Jam, 1984.
Licensed to Ill. Def Jam, 1986.
Paul's Boutique. Capitol, 1989.
Check Your Head. Grand Royal, 1992.
Ill Communication. Grand Royal, 1994.
Hello Nasty. Grand Royal, 1998.
To the 5 Boroughs. Capitol, 2004
Solid Gold Hits. Capitol, 2005.

Courtesy of Photofest.

MC Lyte

Jennifer R. Young

On March 1, 2006, the development of a hip hop exhibit at the National Museum of American History in Washington, DC, was announced in the *New York Times*. This exhibit would be the third nationally recognized effort in preserving hip hop at an institution; the Experience Music Project in Seattle and the Rock and Roll Hall of Fame in Cleveland each had exhibits dedicated to hip hop. As is customary, many pioneers, trailblazers, and overall leaders of hip hop were asked to participate in these exhibits. One might expect Afrika Bambaataa, Grandmaster Flash, Crazy Legs, and Russell Simmons to make the curators' lists. After all, they come from a select pool of innovators. When it comes to recognizing women leaders of the hip hop world, a small group is included almost every time. MC Lyte, a female rapper whose professional career has spanned almost two decades, is one of them.

Lyte's career in hip hop includes roles as a folk scholar, artist, and keeper of the culture. Her writing (and performance) qualifies her as a scholar. Through storytelling and signifying, Lyte conveys messages that do more than rock a party. Her lyrics challenge listeners to think critically. Like other hip hop icons, this rapper uses humor as a storytelling strategy to make broader commentaries on sociological issues that affect urban communities. Her courage as an artist is revealed in the ways she addresses gender, race, health, and spirituality. For instance, Lyte is one of the first rappers to integrate issues regarding HIV and abortion into her lyrical narratives. Other pioneer efforts include her mixed-genre collaborations, philanthropic endeavors, and media appearances, all of which helped to debunk stigmas attached to hip hop culture and rap music in particular.

IN THE BEGINNING

Before becoming MC Lyte, before having enough material for ten albums and additional greatest hits compilations, before being recognized as a trailblazer for male and female MCs, there was a girl maturing into a woman known to the world as Lana Moorer. Born in Queens on October 11, 1971, Lyte spent her youth in Brooklyn, attending Weusi Shule African elementary school in East Flatbush, a junior high school in the same neighborhood, and George W. Wingate high school. In an interview with Michael A. Gonzales, she identified junior high as her initial training ground for writing and performing rhymes. Thanks to family influences, Lyte immersed herself in music from the R&B sounds of Gladys Knight, Al Green, and James Brown and hip hop songs by Funky 4+1 More, the Treacherous Three, and Grandmaster Flash and the Furious Five. Older cousins introduced Lyte to the ways of the culture; between junior high and high school, Lyte become another self-taught MC, ready to work on her signature storytelling style (Gonzales, "Kickin'" 43).

In interviews, Lyte has admitted that she was not always an obedient daughter and diligent student (Gonzales "Kickin'"). However, she witnessed her mother's hard work—bartending at night, taking classes during the day—and that seemed to affect her work ethic to some degree. By high school she had multiple part-time jobs in addition to being a full-time student. Though she and her friends attended clubs and concerts at Latin Quarter and Union Square, Lyte seemed to realize by her teenage years that she would need to work hard to make money.

Lyte did not let her side jobs or schooling distract her from the music. She listened to Mr. Magic's and Red Alert's show, which came on the New York radio station KISS FM. Music videos had just started appearing, and the daily show *Video Music Box*, conveniently scheduled for the 3:30 after-school slot, was another outlet for working MCs and DJs. While the format may have resembled previous shows like *American Bandstand* or *Soul Train*, *Video Music Box* had its own raw appeal with studio interviews, videotaped segments from parties, and the release of rap videos. Some might consider *Video Music Box* a predecessor of the glossier contemporary shows like *Total Request Live* and *106 & Park*. Brooklyn producers (and creators) Ralph

McDaniels and Lionel Martin of *Video Music Box* definitely had the attention of young aspirants like Lyte, who practiced their MC skills daily.

Being exposed to videos by Salt-N-Pepa, Sequence, Sha Rock, Roxanne Shanté, and the Real Roxanne, Lyte was ready to put her own rhymes on tape. Excited and interested in presenting her lyrics in a way that few others had done, she befriended Tony, a fellow Brooklyn dweller who had dreams of contributing to the music from the production end. Thanks to the equipment in his basement—microphone, turntables, and albums—he and Lyte put together her first single, "I Cram to Understand U (Sam)." Soon Lyte would find her own music videos on *Video Music Box*, starting with "Paper Thin" (Gonzales, "Kickin'" 44).

At some point during her high school years, Lyte began using her pseudonym, MC Lyte. While she seemed to have a growing network of friends who could help her lay down tracks, it was ultimately her extended family that assisted in transferring her rhymes from ink on paper to audio on vinyl. She began working with her stepbrother Milk and his brother Gizmo, who performed together as Audio Two. Milk described the advantages of his sister's unique delivery: "Her voice reminded me of MC Shan. She was tough, which was good, because there were no other girls rapping like that" (Gonzales, "Kickin'" 45). Yet it was not just the timbre of Lyte's voice that grabbed people's attention. From this first song "Cram," a saga that reveals a love-torn protagonist whose boyfriend chooses the crack pipe over her love, Lyte's interest in addressing drugs and other serious matters was quite evident.

Milk and Gizmo, known for their trademark song "Top Billin'," helped Lyte pick beats for her rhymes. Audio Two's "Top Billin'" was a rap classic long before the single's official release in 1990 (Lyte would record a live version of "Top Billin'" with Gizmo years later on the album *Seven & Seven*). With the early assistance of her brothers, Lyte also had the financial support of Milk and Gizmo's father, Nat Robinson. An entrepreneur in his own right, Robinson started the First Priority music label to invest in their careers. Becoming a father figure for Lyte, Robinson arranged road trips for the young performers. The artists toured with Heavy D, Kool Moe Dee, Queen Latifah, and Ice-T. Lyte gained professional experience being on the road, behind the microphone, and on the stage in places like the Latin Quarter where she had ventured as a concertgoer with school friends. She found herself part of a growing First Priority family, which included Audio Two and Alliance (headed by King of Chill), people she had spent time creating music with anyway.

No matter the music genre, record labels are known for signing artists of kith and kin. First Priority is no different. Before Lyte recorded her first album, she gained performing experience from being in the public domain with other members of her label family. Similar to jazz musicians allowing guests to sit in on jam sessions, the First Priority artists moved as a unit. Robinson proved his business acumen when he accomplished a feat that no other independent music label of its kind had achieved until then. In 1986 he signed a deal with Atlantic Records, due in part to the foresight of Sylvia Rhone (now CEO of Elektra). Afterward, distribution became less of a challenge and Lyte had a broader stage from which to be heard. With the support of her music label and parent company, Lyte went on to complete four albums, a thirteen-year commitment that turned out to be only one chapter in the rapper's long career.

Labels like First Priority, Tommy Boy, Def Jam, Bad Boy, So So Def, Death Row, and Roc-A-Fella have undergone significant changes, being resold, redistributed, or just plain recycled. Still, one need only listen to the early music of these labels to understand the allegiance between artist and label family. Artists acknowledge their producers, DJs, fellow rap crews, and other collaborators as a way of legitimizing the aesthetic and their roles in it. While some may consider this form of self-aggrandizement to be simply a marketing strategy, these shout-outs are also affirmations, nods to the professional contributors who keep the culture and the music moving.

Regarding her experiences with the First Priority family, Lyte recently said, "I had a great beginning with [them]. It was all about the talent. It was all about what I wanted to put forth in the music. It was all about me staying true to who I really was, and I guess because I had that foundation I was able to set the standard for what was acceptable for me" (Bostick). The label's 2005 release *Basement Flavor* features eleven tracks from its original music family, including Audio Two, MC Lyte, Positive K, L.A. Luv, DJ Soul Shock, See-Que, Alliance, King of Chill, and the Canadian artist Michie Mee (see sidebar: Hip Hop in Canada).

Hip Hop in Canada
Robin Chamberlain

Although hip hop developed much more slowly in Canada than in the United States, it has produced, and continues to produce, some of the most exciting and innovative music in the scene. The first Canadian rap single to break into the Top 40 was Maestro's "Let Your Backbone Slide" in 1989, which is still the best-selling Canadian hip hop single of all time. Along with Maestro, icons of the early era included Devon, Dream Warriors, and Kish. Another icon, Michie Mee, became the first Canadian hip hop artist to sign a deal with an American record label, First Priority. Additionally, Michie Mee was the only hip hop artist to appear on the Canadian pop charts between 1991 and 1998—and then largely because of her collaboration with the hard rock band Reggadeath.

It was not until 1996, however, that Canadian hip hop garnered the momentum it continues to enjoy today. This was the result of several key events, beginning with the creation of the UMAC (Urban Music Association of Canada) to promote Canadian hip hop both domestically and internationally. In 1997, Dubmatique of Montreal became the first hip hop band to make it onto the francophone pop charts. Finally, in 1998, Rascalz, a Vancouver band, recorded "Northern Touch," arguably the most important song in the history of Canadian hip hop. Their album *Cash Crop* won a Juno for the best rap recording that year, but the band refused it because it was presented in the nontelevised portion of the ceremony. In 1999, the award was moved to the main ceremony, in which Rascalz accepted it and performed "Northern Touch" live. This corresponded with unprecedented attention being paid to other Canadian hip hop and trip-hop artists, including Esthero and Choclair. Finally, in 2001, CFXJ (Flow 93.5) became Canada's first urban music station. Many similar stations followed, creating radio venues for Canadian hip hop artists. Artists like K-OS, Swollen Members, and Nelly Furtado emerged as major players in this vibrant new hip hop scene.

These innovations ushered in a new era for Canadian hip hop, marked not only by mainstream successes but also by exciting innovations by independent and experimental artists, including Buck 65 and Sixtoo, both of whom hail from Halifax, Nova Scotia. Both Buck 65 and Sixtoo were a part of the Anticon collective. Although based in Oakland, California, Anticon played an important role in the Canadian hip hop underground by supporting innovative artists like Buck 65. What makes artists like these interesting is their willingness to look outside of the traditional content for hip hop songs, while still maintaining a strong allegiance to the icons they name as influences. Buck 65's more recent albums, for example, increasingly show the influence of jazz, blues, and electronica on his particular brand of hip hop. Sixtoo, meanwhile, showcases a range of talents: While best known for his stellar production skills, he is also an accomplished MC, turntablist, and graffiti artist. While mainstream Canadian hip hop has produced a welter of talented artists, the future of hip hop in Canada lies in its dynamic underground scene.

TEXTUAL STRATEGIES

Storytelling and signifying are the two lyrical strategies that distinguish MC Lyte as a hip hop icon (see sidebar: The Art of Storytelling). First, the particular ways in which Lyte delivers stories are significant. While some of her songs are more lighthearted than others, Lyte generally uses her music as a tool for self-aggrandizement, to warn people to step back. In this she does not differ from many of her peers. However, her use of storytelling makes her music distinctive. Note the basic creative writing formula:

Author → Narrator/Protagonist → Conflict → Crisis → Resolution

As her album credits repeatedly indicate, MC Lyte writes the majority of her rhymes. Her songs that follow story structures all have narrators; some of these narrators even double as protagonists. MC Lyte does this by employing the first person ("I") point of view. Most rappers follow the same

The Art of Storytelling
Jennifer R. Young

Several of MC Lyte's songs present narrative scenarios with conflicts, crises, and resolutions. Her first three albums have numerous cuts that not only tell stories but provide moral endings as well: "I Cram to Understand U (Sam)," "Cappuccino," "Eyes Are the Soul," "Poor Georgie," and "Lola from the Copa." Since early MCs generally used freestyle rhymes rather than structured stories when performing at parties, only a handful of rap artists consistently rhymed in story style before Lyte's debut.

Grandmaster Flash and the Furious Five's "The Message" (1982) set high standards. A song with multiple narratives, "The Message" covers intense situations from poverty and unemployment to violence and drug abuse. The song's convincing list of unlucky circumstances had universal appeal. Run-DMC's songs also illuminated shared experiences with narrative vignettes like "You Be Illin'" and "The Way It Is"; both songs have characters whose silly actions make them seem unintelligent, lessons meant to forewarn the audience. Biz Markie adopted this pattern for himself in "The Vapors" and "Just a Friend," songs that changed his reputation, making him what journalist Michael A. Gonzales called a clever "Hip-Hop harlequin" ("Juice," 106).

Female MCs also experimented with narrative rap. Nikki D's "Daddy's Little Girl" is a cautionary tale about a teenage girl caught in a scenario of unplanned pregnancy. U.T.F.O.'s "Roxanne, Roxanne" takes a different turn, although it does involve the relationships between young men and women. "Roxanne, Roxanne" shows the members of U.T.F.O. touting themselves as plausible catches. Roxanne, the object of their affection, comes off as foolish for not choosing any of them.

Yet Slick Rick serves as the most prominent example of an MC Lyte predecessor who rhymed in story style. He was on the scene years before the production of his first album in 1988. His performance with Doug E. Fresh in "The Show" (1985) only helped his reputation for spitting witty rhymes with his British accent. *The Great Adventures of Slick Rick* appeared the same year that *Lyte as a Rock* was released. "Children's Story" and "Hey Young World" feature bull-headed adolescents with premature demises. Slick Rick's voice serves as the wise narrator, a veritable Dr. Seuss who makes his audience feel smart by not preaching morals to them.

MC Lyte contributed to this new style of rap music, one that had been underutilized. Her aesthetic belongs to a subgenre of rap in which social criticism is the goal and fictitious stories are the methodology. Lyte does what Vernon Reid described as "[translating] experiences we call emotion by expressing inexpressible things" (Goldman 139). Reid, a guitarist with the group Living Colour, a producer, and cofounder of Black Coalition (a group of rock artists who do not confine their songs to those that are funky or soulful), encourages artists to present their music in different mediums, void of marketing tastes. On finding a new context for creativity, Reid explains, "How they're expressed is a function of the context of what's really going on—conflicts, forces in opposition, [and] the amount of resources that are available at a particular time to particular people" (139). Though her songs include an array of characters in desperate situations, MC Lyte uses incidents of desperation to suggest alternative, more successful ways of living one's life.

---

writing principle. They liberally mix their lived experiences with those of others. However, Lyte is distinctive in that her songs tell stories, turning the point of view into that of a main character, one that has full-bodied emotions, pitfalls, and hard decisions. While many artists use the story structure, Lyte is one of the few to use imagery, allusion, metaphor, and subtext in ways that draw greater attention to the verses of the songs rather than the hooks.

Lyte's high-content songs, therefore, are more about the characters and their lessons than they are about the lyrical prowess of the rapper. Take three of her early songs for example: "I Cram to Understand U (Sam)," "Cappuccino," and "Poor Georgie." In "Cram," the narrator struggles for Sam's attention and affection, yet this desire is never realized. Sam's personal cravings conflict with those of the narrator. So even though the song is about the narrator's interactions with Sam, it is also about Sam's tragic flaw. Listeners do not get lost in the angst of the teenage girl; instead, they find out the truth about Sam, a man strung out on crack and unable to put the narrator first. Thus, this song created by a teenage rapper allows listeners to access it on many levels—from the perspective of young love, of drug abuse, and of living in a world where both fight to exist.

Lyte laments her luck in "Cappuccino." The narrator hears about a café that sells the best cappuccino. She goes there to try it, only to discover her bad timing as the police raid the café for its illegal drug trafficking. By a twist of fate, the narrator is shot and enters a dream state. There she reunites with people who have died from drug abuse, car accidents, gun violence, and other foul circumstances. When she regains consciousness, she decides that the drink is not for her. The coffee may serve as a lyrical metaphor: an addiction, even to coffee, can be dangerous.

"Poor Georgie" serves as another example of Lyte's subtle messages. The narrator explains that when she met George he was instantly smitten and wanted to date her. She is drawn to him despite his player status. Soon, the audience gets the conflict. George is in trouble. He is diagnosed with lung and colon cancer. After a series of events, George has a fatal car accident. By the narrator's tone, one cannot be sure whether George's crash was intentional or not. After this crisis, the narrator contemplates the story. In the resolution, Lyte provides the moral: Cherish people every day and make sure they know that you do. Her tales are not vignettes designed to entertain; they are thought-provoking rhymes that arouse audiences to action, not apathy.

Lyte has a way of signifying that gives her a trademark as well. Most, if not all, rappers signify, but few do it as eloquently as Lyte. She roasts both her male and female opponents and triumphs through the ordeal as the survivor. Lyte dedicates at least three songs on each album to proving her credentials. While the song "I Am Woman" is on her debut album (*Lyte as a Rock*, 1988), she does not play the "I'm a girl so love me" card. She appeals to different audiences by integrating universal themes into the music. Most people can relate to the desire to be the best and achieve great success. Songs like "Playgirls Play," "My Time," "Ride Wit Me," "Beyond the Hype," and "I Am the Lyte" convey her competitive nature.

"Cha, Cha, Cha" is an early example of her competing not as a female MC, but as an MC. In this song, she includes the audience as part of her battle strategy. Unlike some of her other songs in which she attacks a rapper or a crew of rappers, this song is a general warning to her competition. Considered an ultimate dis song, Lyte references hip hop and lyricism as if it is a science, a complex skill that few have mastered. The song does not have violent images, yet delivers punishment. The defeat for competitors is in the realization that they are not smart enough to outwit her.

On her early albums, songs like "I Am the Lyte" show her skills and those of DJ K-Rock, her noted DJ on her first few albums. On the live version of "Top Billin'" that she records with Milk D, Lyte positions herself as the ultimate lyricist in tandem with the First Priority family, especially her DJ and Audio Two. She may boast about her abilities, but she does not showboat to stand apart from those who contribute to her success. Lyte's participation in the Roxanne Wars also shows her signifying skills. The first Roxanne battle began in 1984 when the Untouchable Force Organization (U.T.F.O.) recorded "Roxanne, Roxanne." This boy-chases-girl song is about Roxanne, the new, most attractive girl in the neighborhood. The three members of U.T.F.O. share verses in the song while the fictitious Roxanne remains silent. Fortunately, a young teenage lyricist named Lolita Shanté Gooden, aka Roxanne Shanté, responded to U.T.F.O. by recording "Roxanne's Revenge" later that year.

Using the same music track as U.T.F.O.'s "Roxanne, Roxanne," Shanté's single had original lyrics. It is estimated that this young MC from Queensbridge, New York, sold over a quarter of a million copies in the tristate area alone before U.T.F.O. brought a lawsuit against her for copyright infringement (Dennis). If Shanté's song frustrated U.T.F.O., it agitated female MCs even more. After "Roxanne's Revenge," female MCs began creating answer records to take their own shots at U.T.F.O. and to upstage female MC rivals, especially Shanté. In an interview with Sacha Jenkins years later, Shanté reflected on how her song opened the door to mass ridicule: "Every female rapper who came out felt like they had this Shanté thing to prove. If someone didn't know what to make a record about, they would make it about Roxanne Shanté" (26). Sparky D's and the Real Roxanne's songs were only a few in the dozens of recorded Roxanne records. What writers Sacha Jenkins and Reginald Dennis have called "the longest-running series of answer records in the annals of hip-hop" is hard to corroborate, considering that many of the songs are no longer extant. However, both Jenkins (23) and Dennis say that approximately 100 songs were released from different female MCs, all wanting to be the true Roxanne.

Conversely, U.T.F.O. was not the only group engaged in response record battles. Salt-N-Pepa's "The Show Stopper" (1986) was done in response to Slick Rick and Doug E. Fresh's "The Show" (1985). Male rappers singing their own praise served in part as the catalyst for female rap criticism. Starting as one MC outrapping another, the response record trend evolved into something else. The Roxanne Wars signified women wanting to assert their own identities and claim spaces in a world where male MCs had already found creative refuge.

Perhaps MC Lyte's battle with Antoinette (aka the Gangstress) added to the tradition of these wars. Whether this is true or not, Lyte found a unique way of making her response songs more than fallacious appeals. Many rappers fall into the trap of ad hominem attacks, the practice of attacking a person's character as opposed to the content of her argument. Lyte commits this fallacy, but she extends her position by also attacking her opponent's arguments point by point. As she explained to Michael Gonzales, Lyte recorded the song out of respect for Audio Two, whom Antoinette allegedly dissed during a radio interview ("Kickin'" 47). Audio Two's Milk and Gizmo, Gonzales notes, did not want to respond by creating a song that dissed a female MC, but Lyte was willing to do "10% Dis" on her debut album *Lyte as a Rock* in their defense (46). During the hook of the song, a group of hecklers jeer Antoinette in unison, calling her a fake and a beat stealer. MC Lyte attacks in each verse, calling her everything from a liar to a cheat to a thief to a ho. In addition to these insults, Lyte explains why she is the bigger and better MC.

Things unraveled even further when Antoinette recorded "Lights Out" in response. Antoinette denounced MC Lyte from start to finish, calling her a ho, a bitch, part of a wick-wack crew, and hooked on the crack pipe. Similar to the jeering in "10% Dis," Antoinette uses a crowd in "Lights Out." Her crowd chants that Lyte's career, reign, and audience appeal are over. Neither rapper physically retaliated in response to public accusations, but they did attempt to verbally demolish each other's livelihoods. This too speaks to Lyte's class as a rapper. Lyte chose to keep the battles on vinyl despite how ugly things became.

Lyte's 1989 sophomore album *Eyes on This* has another response song for Antoinette called "Shut the Eff Up! (Hoe)." A sample of 1970s R&B singer Millie Jackson starts the song: "I think it's time I start feeling bitchy." Antoinette did not formally respond, but Lyte did become a target of other verbal abuse. In 1992, Roxanne Shanté attacked MC Lyte on "Big Mama." Lyte responded with "Steady F**king" on her fourth album, *Ain't No Other* (1993). Lyte's song samples KRS-One's "Criminal Minded" (1987), in which KRS describes Shanté as being good for nothing but sex. In all of her battle songs, Lyte defends the integrity of MCs by identifying true MCs as those who rap from reservoirs of knowledge. While she does engage in name calling quite a bit, MC Lyte uses rap as more than an outlet for degrading verbal arguments.

WOMANHOOD

One of MC Lyte's biggest contributions to hip hop is her social commentary on the lives of women and men. Just as Salt-N-Pepa and other female MCs had done before her, Lyte expresses her opinions regarding sensuality, sexuality, love, and relationships. The subtle difference is that Lyte's love songs have multiple layers: The songs are usually addressed to women and men; the characters include both genders in romantic situations; and most important, the songs provide deeper understandings of interconnected relationships that allow men to be men and women to be women.

The song "When in Love" works as one of MC Lyte's love anthems. Reminiscent of a piece that Aretha Franklin might have composed, an R&B soprano songstress emphasizes the word *crazy* in the refrain of the song. *Crazy* seems to serve as a euphemism for those who are strung out (or who have been strung out) on love. Washing clothes, picking your lover's nose, letting him or her drive your car, or waiting for your lover to call—these actions suggest the effect love has on people. The song shows regular people doing regular things. Perhaps this is why Lyte has been referred to as a "Hip-Hop Zora Neale Hurston" (Gonzales, "Kickin'" 48). Like Hurston, Lyte celebrates black folk for what they are while revealing the beauty and absurdity of their lives. In the widely read novel *Their Eyes Were Watching God*, readers discover how the protagonist Janie endures many relationships before discovering true self-love and love for another man. Lyte's "When in Love" challenges listeners to redirect their energy, to invest time in themselves and those who truly love them, not simply those who find them attractive.

Her 1993 hit "Ruffneck" may sound crude—with Lyte's voice at its raspiest and the song's content at its grittiest—but it is rather tender. Filled with street imagery and crass behaviors, "Ruffneck" is a piece about respecting brothers for their social and emotional intelligence. The narrator does not applaud men who are law-abiding, polite, and gentle. Instead, she enthusiastically acknowledges men who live and die by the codes of street life. In graphic detail, the narrator announces her desire for a lover who is aggressive in the street, in her company, and in the bedroom. Love exists there, a love for who the man is and who he is not. While some may consider this an anthem for tough guys, it is also an anthem for the women that stay with and put up with the men. Lyte had rapped a gentler version of this theme with Sinead O'Connor in "I Want Your Hands on Me." As Katrina Irving explains, "['Hands'] is an extremely effective political rap, one that stresses the importance both of constructing different modes of subjectivity for women and of an equivalence building" (117). "Ruffneck" has similar qualities in that it empowers the female protagonist to claim affection instead of passively receiving it.

Lyte earned a Grammy nomination for "Ruffneck," which is arguably her grittiest song, stuck between the previous era of socially conscious hits by Queen Latifah and a more sexually liberated era of sexually explicit songs by Lil' Kim. By the time Lyte won a Soul Train Award for "Keep n, Keepin' n" with R&B group Xscape in 1996 (Lyte's second gold single), Queen Latifah had earned a gold album for *Black Reign* and Da Brat's *Funkdafied* album had gone platinum, the first solo female rapper to do so. Lyte's "Cold Rock a Party" in collaboration with producer Sean Combs earned her another gold single in 1997. The Bad Boy record label had approximately a half-dozen gold singles that year, not including the platinum albums or other collaborations.

Lyte had to contend with a rap world that was becoming much more obscene and graphic. Somehow, she managed to keep love, loyalty, and commitment as central themes in her love songs. She did this without making the songs too sensitive. Cuts from her more recent albums—"U Got It," "Where Home Is," "Maybe I Deserve," and "It's All Yours"—have their own sultry style of conveying the importance of love. She continues to work toward positive public images of black women and men. She once reflected on her career and position as a role model for others: "I think I speak for generations of women who aren't afraid to take responsibility. [Those] who identify with strength and courage and independence. And hopefully I've sparked a whole lot of women to be able to speak for themselves and stand for what it is they believe in" (Gonzales, "Kickin'" 49). Her music videos convey these interests in promoting intelligent, respectful images of women. From her first video "Paper Thin," where she is fully clothed in a sweatsuit, turtle neck, jacket, and boots, Lyte seemed more concerned with the delivery of her art than any ill modification of her body.

MUSIC VIDEOS

The music video for "Paper Thin" starts with two red Volkswagen Jettas pulling up to a subway station. Lyte jumps out of one car and yells to her crew that she wants to take the subway. One of her friends escorts her. As soon as they get on a crowded train car, Lyte spots a guy engaged in intimate conversation with two women. From the way she looks at him, it seems that she is dating the guy. The audience can infer her disappointment. The intercom beeps. The doors close. The train moves, and Lyte begins rapping:

"When you say you love me, it doesn't matter." The subway train serves as Lyte's stage; the riders are her audience. A man with a guitar, another with an oversized portable radio, and a third with a mini-set of drums accompany her as she hurls lyrical insults at the guy who is caught in the act.

Like other videos in the late 1980s, Lyte's use of the subway station and the actual train suggest her affection for the environment from which she came. There is nothing glossy about the video set, which is indeed a subway station. Dirty stairs and subway platforms, graffiti walls, haggard subway riders, coated windows, and unpolished stainless steel poles all add texture to the video. However, the video is part of the natural elements of the underground, not the other way around. The use of subway trains in early rap videos should not be overlooked. More than just a low-budget decision, video directors who had some, if not a lot of, input from rap artists tapped into a train metaphor whose meaning may have changed, but whose aesthetic traditions stayed intact. Twentieth-century rap videos were not the first to use trains. Black visual artists from the Reconstruction period forward have used trains as an artistic symbol of change. Visual artist Romare Bearden (1911-1988), for instance, is known for incorporating locomotives into his paintings, watercolors, collages, and murals. The train is said to impart several meanings: the migration patterns of African Americans moving from south to north, the upward mobility of an oppressed people, and the overall promise of a better future. The video "Paper Thin" is postmodern in the way that it contributes to hip hop culture, where subways indicate the music's origins (even borough specific), the audience's originality, the art's potency, and the rapper's resolve despite limited resources and bleak surroundings.

"Cappuccino" is another one of Lyte's videos in which movement through the urban streets is essential to the storyline and video plot. The video follows the song pretty closely, taking viewers to the café, to heaven, to Lyte waking up in her bed from a bad dream (even in bed, she arises in a business suit), and then back to the café. A black man in a white suit with dark sunglasses seems to represent an angel of sorts, especially since he appears and dissolves just as quickly. This angel stays with the protagonist through many of the scenes. In the end when she refuses the cappuccino and accepts the pink flower from the angel (who looks remarkably like KRS-One), viewers are left to discern the moral choice of coffee or no coffee, drugs or no drugs. Lyte drives off at the end of the video in a black luxury convertible with a red leather interior. She yells, "Leave them drugs alone!" The camera pans out to show the late-day sunlight hitting the brick stone buildings. Like "Paper Thin," this video has many visual elements that suggest homage to the culture. Hip hop itself is likened to a funny valentine, one with unconventional beauty but undeniable appeal.

"Everyday" is a lighthearted video that shows a different side of MC Lyte. In the song, a man romantically involved with Lyte cleans the house, the pool, and the grounds, all in anticipation of his woman's homecoming. These shots are intercut with segments of Lyte eating out, driving around, playing tennis, and enjoying the spa with her girlfriends. "I demand my respect," the words in Lyte's song play as the camera cuts to the man placing flowers in a vase by the floor-to-ceiling kitchen windows. By the end of the video, the guy is happy to see Lyte even though he is visibly exhausted from putting the house back together. While he may have enjoyed being in the house alone while Lyte was away, he had no intention of letting her see the place in such dishevelment. Clearly, the gender roles are reversed here, a common theme in Lyte's videos.

Usually wearing gold hoop earrings and modest gold chains, Lyte remains fully dressed in her videos. She is either in jerseys and jeans, sweatsuits, or tastefully fitted business suits. Her appearance is reiterated with her video characterizations. These roles usually portray her in powerful positions. Lyte's videos are a rarity in a time when the trend is to show scantily clad, hypersexualized women dancing lasciviously for the entertainment of the viewer, who is generally expected to be male, horny, and heterosexual. Even when the video's singer and protagonist is a woman, objectifying images far outweigh empowering ones.

Lyte works against such sexist debauchery in her videos. In "I Go On" she raps behind a business desk as if the viewer is a business client. In "Ruffneck" the women are the gazers behind the camera, scrutinizing the men and comparing notes with each other in a loft apartment and on the rooftop of a building. In "Stop, Look, & Listen" a simulated live concert shows Lyte and her all-male musicians and dancers in suits. The dancers do the suggestive routines. Lyte sticks to the music. In "Cold Rock a Party" the same holds true. Lyte raps. The impromptu party in the elevator continues and she stays tastefully engaged in the fun. The highest degree of dancing occurs in "When in Love." Between vignettes that follow the song's verses, Lyte and others are shown wearing brightly colored sport clothes. Their performances combine modern dance and hip hop moves. Dance was being popularized through videos, movies, and television shows. Recall the fly girl dance routines during the opening credits of *In Living Colour*, *The Arsenio Hall Show*, and *Living Single*, as well as sorority and fraternity steppers on *A Different World*.

MC Lyte conveys her most empowering images in "Stop, Look, & Listen" and "Lyte as a Rock." At the start of "Stop, Look, & Listen," viewers see Lyte deplaning and riding off in a limousine. Her promotional managers review the itinerary with her during the ride to the concert hall: She has a public service announcement to do for the Children's Defense Fund; her appearance on *Arsenio Hall* will air that night; she has to complete interviews with *Newsweek* magazine and *Rolling Stone* in the week to come. No sooner do they get to the concert space than the camera cuts to an anxious crowd who chant, "We want Lyte!" She has not even begun to perform yet, and already the images suggest her autonomy, popularity, and professional demands. In contrast to other videos where women are dancing as extras or walking down the street as moving props, Lyte is in control of her situation and body image, thereby altering audience reception.

"Lyte as a Rock" is a highly intellectual music video. It starts with words in white letters scrolling up a black screen, like the prologue to *Star Wars* (1977). The video's words read, in part: "Lyte is Here—No One / Can Stop Me!!!" The video then begins. A young girl holding a little black baby doll entertains herself by observing several skits that it seems she is imagining. The first skit shows Lyte dressed like a cave woman. Perhaps the suggestion is that the rapper's influence spans centuries, not just decades. The second skit shows Lyte dressed as an Egyptian queen. There are pyramids, fire pits, servants to fan her as she raps, male escorts to carry her away, and females to adore (or hate) her. The video then transitions to the third skit where Lyte is likened to a powerful Mafia-like boss, suit, hat, and sneering thugs to match. As she raps, she intimidates the opposing mob leader, who is also a woman.

The last two skits are educational. In the fourth, the camera cuts to a poster of Malcolm X holding a gun and looking out a window. The words "By Any Means Necessary" are written in bold black letters. Viewers see Lyte and her crew wearing fatigues. She is in a red T-shirt and wears a leather medallion that has an imprint of the African continent. At first it appears as though Lyte is in prison behind bars, yet as her rhyme continues, viewers realize that she is locking up the competition. Once again, she remains in control and in the lead. The last skit shows a group of young people in a mock classroom setting. The chalkboard has two words: "Metaphor" and "Simile." Two men are explaining how Lyte's name qualifies as examples of both terms on the chalkboard. Then everyone gets up and grooves. The camera pans away until the little girl in the beginning of the video returns. She waves goodbye to all of her imaginary friends. One may infer that Lyte understands the critical positioning of hip hop culture and rap music in particular. The young girl may signify the promise of things to come. The historical images suggest the legacy upon which hip hop stands. Lyte positions herself as the current torch bearer, conscious of her political role as lyricist.

Robin Roberts references Queen Latifah and Monie Love's video "Ladies First" as the most politically charged video, especially for women. "Ladies First" has pictures of Madame C. J. Walker (millionaire cosmetic manufacturer); Sojourner Truth (famous public speaker for abolition and women's rights, self-educated despite being enslaved); Angela Davis (writer, educator, and activist, especially against the oppression of women); Winnie Mandela (politician and key proponent of the African National Congress during Nelson Mandela's imprisonment); Harriet Tubman (escaped slave who helped hundreds of others escape through a dozen return trips on the Underground Railroad); and Cicely Tyson (seasoned actress who once played Tubman in *A Woman Called Moses*). Roberts applauds Queen Latifah for working with her producers and colleagues to create positive images that legitimize her as an agent.

Lyte falls into this same category of positive interpretation. Like Queen Latifah, Lyte subverts traditional methods of presentation and makes herself look successful, smart, and sophisticated, void of gyrations and dimwitted expressions. Her references to Malcolm X suggest knowledge of both activism and pacifism. Malcolm X's orations repeatedly focused on autonomy and community independence. Lyte repeats this theme in several of her songs. Strong men and women contribute to a stronger society. Her songs and videos reflect such a notion.

COMMUNITY HEALTH

Just as Lyte is conscious of the ways in which she portrays herself, her music reflects an intense interest in community survival. MC Lyte's songs praise urban communities, especially the New York borough in which she spent most of her adolescence. On her first single, "Cram," she mentions a roller disco near Empire Boulevard—the place where her protagonist meets the fictitious Sam. It isn't that Brooklyn defines her, but it seems to have a strong influence in informing her worldview. "Kickin' 4 Brooklyn" and "Brooklyn" are entire songs dedicated to the borough. Lyte sends shout-outs, accompanied by K-Rock's scratches and clap beats.

She shows her familial connections not just to her kin and her record label, but also to her community. Others like Big Daddy Kane, Busta Rhymes, and Biggie Smalls claim Brooklyn as their native turf. This practice of allegiance holds true for national and international rappers—Ice Cube (Los Angeles), KRS-One (South Bronx), Master P (New Orleans), Three 6 Mafia (Memphis), Common (Chicago), Lauryn Hill (South Orange), TI (Atlanta), IAM (Marseille, France), and Prophets of Da City (Cape Town, South Africa), to name a few. Lyte participates in the tradition of naming and claiming her space. Since "Kickin' 4 Brooklyn" on her debut album, Lyte has included references to Brooklyn in at least one song on each of her albums that followed.

One might mislabel Lyte as a standard rapper who repeatedly announces her hometown affiliation. However, Lyte does more than name drop; she uses Brooklyn as the setting for many of her lyrical stories. This tradition is reminiscent of previous black literary writers who used national and international locations to explain the plight of black and Latino protagonists, situations that seemed to have pan-African relevance, a common shared experience despite world boundaries. Just as Harlem, Senegal, Guinea, Spain, Italy, Russia, and other areas inspired writer Langston Hughes, or France gave James Baldwin new perspective, or Eatonville, Florida, revealed anthropological secrets to Zora Neale Hurston, and Chicago, Illinois, served as the muse for Gwendolyn Brooks, MC Lyte remains true to the rousing world of Brooklyn.

Lyte recognizes that people enliven spaces. Urban neighborhoods are her backdrops, canvases filled with colorful settings in which her characters roam. How different is Lyte's artwork from the murals done by Romare Bearden or the films directed by Spike Lee? Lyricists like Lyte strive to make stories as riveting and visual as other art forms. People, with all of their triumphs and tragedies, become her artwork. Songs like "Lola from the Copa," in which a young woman contracts HIV after a one-night stand, show the characters' frustration, isolation, and ill-fated situations. "Drug Lord Superstar," "Two Seater," and "King of Rock" are other songs with similar antidrugs, antidisease, and antiviolence themes. Lyte uses narrators and characters to disagree with the drug lifestyle. To be cool is to ride with her, and to ride with Lyte's alter egos is not to do drugs.

"Eyes Are the Soul," from her *Act Like You Know* album, has similar caveats about personal health issues. All three verses provide different montages. The first verse describes a man infected by HIV from sharing drug needles and having unprotected sex. A controversial and almost unspeakable subject for 1991, this song predates the Grammy Award-winning song "Waterfalls" by TLC (1995), which promotes a similar message. Verse two of "Eyes" highlights a nineteen-year-old who goes from crack to outer space, thinking he can do things that he cannot do. From accidentally killing his mother to robbing grocery stores, he does not know fantasy from reality. Verse three describes a young girl who must choose between having a baby or an abortion. "Eyes" is arranged with jazz instrumentals. The trumpets and percussion add the contrast of chaotic coolness; a smoky layer masks the tragedies.

The communities in some of Lyte's songs are in grave danger; the causes and effects, she suggests, threaten youth. While some may think Lyte focuses on the crime-ridden, drug-infested, and health-deprived areas of urban life, she is actually doing the opposite. Her music suggests that people do both positive and negative things. There is no monolithic group in the urban environment, or any other place for that matter. Furthermore, one may infer Lyte's insistence that no young person is beyond guidance and support. Aside from the bad influences, Lyte shows her affection for her community, ever careful to note that some are not representatives of all.

Lyte's songs are not morbid nor are the themes focused on guns, violence, and desperation. On the contrary, her music is legendary because it shows the flip side, the side where people, contrary to popular belief, do not want to live in hectic, unsafe, and unclean environments. Lyte's commitment to community is evident through her verses. Characters like Sam from "Cram" or George from "Poor Georgie" or those in "Eyes Are the Soul" may be called sour apples, yet Lyte is not one to discard those who have made major missteps. Her narrators suggest partial blame should go to the toxic environments from which the characters come. She brings light to the forgotten, the abused, the isolated, and the marginalized. It is as if she is saying, "I love my people—all of my people—not just the sane, healthy, and safe ones." Her narrators show compassion for everyone, especially the ones in the most troubled situations. Her groundbreaking songs arm listeners with new tools for moral discernment.

In addition to helping community through her songs, Lyte has been involved in campaigns like Rock the Vote and antiviolence initiatives since the start of her career. When it was clear that violent incidents were beginning to plague neighborhood hip hop parties, concerts, and clubs, Lyte joined forces with KRS-One and others in the Stop the Violence Movement. KRS-One's 1989 "Self-Destruction" single and music video had themes that coincided with Lyte's lyrical messages. Artists donated their time to participate in the event, and proceeds from the single were donated to the National Urban League. Often referred to as a compilation of rap all-stars, the track included Public Enemy, Red Alert, Daddy O, Heavy D, KRS-One, Miss Melodie, LL Cool J, Lyte, and others (allhiphop.com). This assembly of artists resembled the "We Are the World" song and video event of 1985. "We Are the World," an effort to raise funds for medical research in Africa, involved music artists from many genres, especially the cowriters of the song, Michael Jackson and Lionel Richie, and the producer Quincy Jones.

However, hip hop artists were not a part of that event. Still, KRS-One and other hip hop leaders made their own public statement. By assembling as positive-minded artists attacking violence in urban communities across the nation, they made their own landmark moment. Lyte's involvement with "Self-Destruction" showed her early philanthropic inclinations, something she continues to fulfill.

People should consider Lyte a hip hop icon for the ways in which she mentors the next generation. Several projects help her achieve this end. She is cofounder of the Let Your Light Shine Youth Foundation, along with Yolanda Whitaker (YoYo). As stated on their official Web site, "the LYLSYF focuses on education, academic acceleration, and extracurricular activities." Their mission statement also includes the objective to raise charity and scholarship funds for Los Angeles youth.

Lyte recently self-published *Just My Take*. In her 2005 interview with Octavia Bostick of www.allhiphop.com, Lyte described the book as words of inspiration for younger audiences and discussed the challenges of self-publishing. Lyte joins other female MCs who turned to writing books, namely Queen Latifah (*Ladies First: Revelations of a Strong Woman*) and Sister Souljah (*Coldest Winter Ever* and *No Disrespect*). Lyte also continues to be an active contributor in the "Take Back the Music" initiative, a call to action that addresses "the visual and lyrical depiction of black women in Hip-hop videos and culture" (Johnson). She took part in the campaign's first town hall meeting in February 2005, cohosted by Spelman College and *Essence Magazine*. Months later, she served as one of the Berklee College of Music contest submission reviewers (along with other recording artists, DJs, and faculty members). Lyte discussed her responsibility as a woman in the music industry. In "Said: MC Lyte," an interview with Joan Morgan, Lyte challenged people to be responsible for each other: "You have to teach a younger generation of women about self-respect and self-esteem. They can separate themselves from what they see and hear on television and radio. And they have to see enough variety in the types of portrayals of women to know they have a choice."

From Lyte's first album onward, several of her songs have dealt with difficult issues. Her contribution to "Self-Destruction" affirmed the work she was already doing through her music for others. She used the power of the pen to fight battles against not only MCs but also grave issues like poverty, disease, drugs, violence, unemployment, and injustice that plague urban communities. Lyte plays a significant role in hip hop since her work mainly adheres to critical issues rather than superficial or divisive topics that threaten unity and communal responsibility.

SPIRITUALITY

MC Lyte's music does not often refer to her spiritual beliefs. Death is a consistent subject, but her music rarely reflects the rapper's position on the life hereafter. Yet "Better Place" (*Seven & Seven*), "God Said Lyte" (*Da Undaground Heat*), and "Fabalous" (*The Shit I Never Dropped*) are three examples of her songs that do deal with spirituality and mortality. The narrator in "Better Place" delivers consolation for those grieving for the departure of their loved ones. "Better Place" works for listeners in a variety of situations. Whether the listener has lost a mother, brother, best friend, baby, significant other, or some other loved one, the narrator assures the listener that brighter days are ahead. Written in second person, the narrator calls out to the audience, creating intimacy by challenging them to share the same space. All three verses describe death as if the person has just passed away. Immediacy is the goal. It is as though the narrator is talking to someone in the first stage of grief, when despair and confusion are at their heaviest. Heaven and God are mentioned in this song, relating the sadness of death to the happiness of life beyond earth. Once again, MC Lyte's focus stays on the living. She encourages the listener to hold on through devastating times.

Most of "God Said Lyte" is an exercise in self-aggrandizement. Lyte recounts some of her lines from other songs where she boasts of her excellent lyrical skills versus the horrendous ones of her opponents. At the same time, Lyte uses the metaphor of her name here (see sidebar: Rap Names). Relating herself to the beginning of God's creation, she tells the listener that she is blessed with the skills to rip up the microphone. Her song

Rap Names
Jennifer R. Young

Rap music follows the African oral tradition of signifyin(g), which includes the practice of using old word combinations (or in the case of music, previously recorded songs) to create new meanings that either compliment or critique a situation in an indirect way. In *The Signifying Monkey* (1988), Henry Louis Gates explains the connections between African American folktales and the pan-African Yoruba Esu-Elegbara, rhetorical strategies that inherently influence vernacular discourse in the African American tradition. Gena D. Caponi's *Signifyin(g), Sanctifyin', & Slam Dunking* (1999) extends Gates's claim, identifying the tropes in rap music that serve as metaphor for new social commentary on age-old issues.

Very much in this tradition of signifying, MC Lyte is a metaphorical rap name complete with a new spelling of the word. The standard definition of light refers to illumination or the levity of an object. MC Lyte uses several of its idiomatic expressions. She brings light to unfathomable situations; she asserts codes of ethics in her narratives by encouraging people to walk in the light; and she serves her competition with lyrical stompings. She calls out her name in many of her songs, using it as a conduit for affirming, calling, boasting, and roasting.

In "I Am the Lyte" she boasts of her rhyming capabilities, calling herself "Me the L the Y the T the E the me." Lyte's love song "Keep on Keepin' On" also shows the MC spelling her name to remind others of her self-worth. Songs like "God Said Lyte" and "Brooklyn" from one of her later albums, *Da Undaground Heat*, continue to suggest that her rap name is part of her lyrical prowess.

On the other hand, there are rappers like Erick Sermon, Will Smith (who has abandoned his rap name the Fresh Prince), Tupac Shakur (spelled 2Pac on some albums), Missy Elliot, Kanye West, Keith Murray, Mike Jones, and Obie Trice, who do not use rap pseudonyms. Still, these MCs find ways to engage in signifyin'. For instance, both Obie Trice's "Rap Name" (2004) and his remix featuring Keith Murray convey the same message: "Real name, no gimmicks." His lack of a nickname gives him license to roast those who have them. Obie Trice uses his real name to signify on his opponents, suggesting that he is real, and his lyrics are real, no fiction necessary.

Lyte's name is an assertion of her identity, her claiming a voice and space for herself and for others, like youth of the hip hop movement, who feel subjugated and marginalized by larger society.

---

is reminiscent of Prince's "My Name Is Prince" from his 1992 album *Love Symbol* where he talks about God creating him and making him an unforgettable musician. MC Lyte and Prince make brave moves. Not only do they position themselves as black people at the time of creation, but they also suggest their direct connection with God as human prototypes. While many have claimed to be descendants of Eve, few female artists and even fewer female rappers have actually likened themselves to Eve. "God Said Lyte" is full of bravado, and the verses are not even the song's boldest statement.

MC Lyte raps over R&B singer Jaheim's song in "Fabalous" [sic]. Jaheim's song of the same name was part of his 2002 album *Still Ghetto*. (His version is spelled "Fabulous.") Her lyrics are as uplifting as the children's chorus. The song is about black people (especially children) believing in themselves despite what others think about their speech, dress, skin color, hair, or other attributes and actions. In essence, she sends the same message that Jaheim does: It is not a negative thing to be black. Similar in theme to Nina Simone and Weldon Irvin Jr.'s original 1969 song "To Be Young, Gifted, and Black," "Fabalous" is a song with high expectations. Jaheim and MC Lyte want kids to see themselves as gifts to the world, geniuses waiting to discover their own unique ways to contribute to society. This is spirit-guided even if MC Lyte does not claim it as such. She encourages her listeners to look within themselves for what's beautiful and right.

On every one of Lyte's albums, there is some reference to self-worth, mortality, heaven, or hell. From the underground world in "Cha, Cha, Cha" (*Eyes on This*) to despair and redemption in "Eyes Are the Soul" (*Act Like You Know*) to the insanity of substance abuse in "Druglord Superstar" (*Bad as I Wanna B*) and "King of Rock" (*Seven & Seven*), Lyte's music is profound. One could infer that the rapper is unapologetic about addressing the ugly monsters in the room, those beasts that rob people of their freedom and obliterate their joy. If for no other reason, this rapper should be recognized for her music that often separates foul actions from otherwise beautiful people.

PIONEER MOVES

A woman in touch with her spirit, her womanhood, and her place in the community, Lyte has enjoyed a lot of firsts in her career. Her collaboration with Irish singer Sinead O'Connor was an innovative move for 1988. At that time, rappers were mostly collaborating with each other inside the genre. Categorized as an alternative rock singer, O'Connor could have tainted Lyte's image as a rapper with a tough exterior. Their music video even came off as more vulnerable and touching, a tribute to love and happiness. Katrina Irving says, "O'Connor's contribution to this rap record does not appropriate a threatening black sound and make it 'safe.' Instead, a dialogue is set up between the two women, each communicating in her own way" (118). With a few exceptions like Run-DMC and Aerosmith's "Walk This Way" (1986), rappers did not start appearing on singles with artists from other genres until the 1990s. In the spirit of "Ladies First" by Queen Latifah and Monie Love or "Sisters Are Doing It for Themselves" by Aretha Franklin and Annie Lennox, Lyte made a refreshing single that extended the art form, all while celebrating sisterhood. Since then, Lyte has collaborated with dozens of artists from Missy Elliot, LL Cool J, and Will Smith to Chuck D, Jamie Foxx, Giovanni Salah, and Moby.

Collaborations are important to the genre in that they expose more audiences from different ethnicities, nationalities, and socioeconomic groups to rap music. Lyte's ability to maintain professional relationships with artists from different genres speaks to her versatility as well. Her work on movie soundtracks like *Deliver Us from Eva*, *Wild, Wild West*, and *Sunset Park* shows her ability to work in a medium that complements visual storytelling. Contributing music to movie projects seems like a natural progression for this rapper who is used to the storytelling aesthetic. Lyte has further experimented by working on a Bob Marley track. Her interest in combining reggae and rap is not original, yet it does show her reverence for another artist that moved a local Caribbean sound to the international stage.

Her import CD from the England-based Tuff Gong label was released in 2000. It features her rhymes over the Bob Marley track "Jammin'." She has four versions of "Jammin'" (the original, Island remix, Ghetto Youth remix, and the Olav Basoski remix). The original "Jammin'" remix can also be found on *Chant Down Babylon*, a tribute album to Marley. This project seemed to be a logical step on the vertical ladder for Lyte. Rap music had been pervasive for decades, but Lyte's "Jammin'" singles propelled her music into the international arena. In 2000 only a handful of American rappers were active in international music markets if one does not count international superstars such as Lauryn Hill or Sean Combs. Lyte's pioneer move to create this import CD suggests her foresight about the music industry and her capabilities to keep the music going. With "Jammin'," Lyte helps sustain American rap in an international market.

Regarding more international exposure, Lyte had the honor of being the first female rapper to perform at Carnegie Hall in 1990. One of the most significant venues for classical and popular music, Carnegie Hall has hosted musicians on its world-renowned stage since 1890. Lyte also became the first rapper to take on another international venue: the USO (United Service Organizations) for the American military. Lyte toured in July 1997 to Italy, Greece, Sicily, and Sardinia to perform for sailors, marines, and their families. Ellen Brody, executive director of entertainment at the USO, said, "the troops and their families loved her so much—we had to ask her back" ("USO"). Lyte embarked on a second tour when she traveled to Germany in November 1998 to entertain American service members stationed there. The rapper noted, "It's wonderful to have been invited back once again. We hope to give the troops an experience that's fun, motivating, uplifting, and different from their everyday routine" ("USO"). Since Lyte's tours, other popular rappers like

Master P, Lil' Romeo, and Lil' Mo have volunteered, but as with other hip hop milestones, MC Lyte was the first.

LYTE'S IMPACT AND LEGACY

Flourishing in artistic activities, Lyte continues to reinvent herself without compromising her integrity. In addition to writing, performing, and producing songs, she is an entrepreneur, educator, and philanthropist. She co-owns the Shaitel Boutique in San Fernando Valley, California; she hosts a weekend Sirius Satellite radio show on HOT JAMZ; and she has several voice-over commercial credits including Nike, McDonald's, Pepsi, and Wherehouse Music. She is even the animated voice for Tia, one of the dolls in the Mattel Diva Starz collection. As a seasoned television personality, Lyte has served as the backstage host for VH1's *Hip-Hop Honors* several years in a row. During the 2005 ceremony, she interviewed predecessors like Salt, Spinderella, Pepa, Big Daddy Kane, and Russell Simmons.

In addition to television appearances as herself, she has over a dozen credits on her acting resumé. She joins other artists who transitioned successfully from performing on concert stages to studio sets. Lyte has appeared in numerous television shows—including guest appearances on *For Your Love, Strong Medicine*, and *The District*, as well as a cast role on *Half and Half*—and several films, including *Civil Brand, Burn Hollywood Burn*, and the critically acclaimed independent film *Train Ride*. Still, her passion for music, which she has had since her teen days in Brooklyn, has not faded. In 2006 she released "Wonder Years," produced by DJ Premier, as the first single off her next album *Back to Lyte*. Lyte's talent for responding to the sign of the times is evident. As advertised on her official Web site, her latest album will have musical guests from her days with First Priority as well as artists that she has met along her journey.

Through the years, Lyte has changed record companies, updated her musical style, traveled the world, and created entrepreneurial and philanthropic projects. More noticeably, she has traded her Pumas for pumps. She no longer creates girl characters who weep over clowns named Sam; MC Lyte's music and other endeavors have an integrity that demands respect for herself, her audience, and the ever-maturing movement that is hip hop.

See also: Queen Latifah, Roxanne Shanté, Lil' Kim, Salt-N-Pepa

WORKS CITED

Bostick, Octavia. "MC Lyte: Poetic Justice." Allhiphop.com, Features Section. August 2005. www.allhiphop.com.

Caponi, Gena Dagel. *Signifyin(g), Sanctifyin´, & Slam Dunking: A Reader in African American Expressive Culture*. Boston: University of Massachusetts Press, 1999.

Dennis, Reginald C. "Record Notes." *Street Jams: Hip-Hop from the Top, Part II.* Rhino Records, 1992.

Gates, Henry Louis, Jr. *The Signifying Monkey: A Theory of Afro-American Literary Criticism.* New York: Oxford University Press, 1988.

Goldman, Vivien. "Explorers." *The Black Chord. Visions of the Groove: Connections Between Afrobeats, Rhythm & Blues, Hip-Hop and More.* Photography by David Corio, Text by Vivien Goldman. New York: Universe Publishing, 1999. 139-173.

Gonzales, Michael A. "The Juice Crew: Beyond the Boogie Down." *The Vibe History of Hip-Hop.* Ed. Alan Light. New York: Three Rivers Press, 1999. 101-109.

Gonzales, Michael A. "Kickin' 4 Brooklyn." *Hip-Hop Divas.* New York: Three Rivers Press, 2001. 42-49.

Irving, Katrina. "'I Want Your Hands on Me': Building Equivalences Through Rap Music." *Popular Music* 12.2 (May 1993): 105-121.

Jackson, Michael, et al. "We Are the World" Video Event. USA for Africa. Thorn EMI Video. Burbank, California. 1985.

Jenkins, Sacha. "We Used to Do It Out in the Park." *Vibe Hip-Hop Divas.* New York: Three Rivers Press, 2001. 22-29.

Johnson, A. J. "Spelman College and Essence Magazine Co-host Take Back the Music Town Hall Meeting." Office of Public Relations at Spelman College. February 2005. www.spelman.edu.

MC Lyte. "About the Organization." Let Your Light Shine Youth Foundation. 2005. 1 April 2006. http://www.letyourlightshineyouthfoundation.com.

MC Lyte. *Just My Take.* The Shaitel Boutique. 1 April 2006. http://www.mc-lyte.com.

Morgan, Joan. "Said: MC Lyte." Take Back the Music Web site. Essence Communications, 2006. http://www.essence.com/essence/takebackthemusic/said_mclyte.html.

Roberts, Robin. "Ladies First: Queen Latifah's Afrocentric Feminist Music Video." *African American Review* 28.2 (summer 1994): 245-257.

FURTHER RESOURCES

KRS-One. *Criminal Minded.* Sugar Hill Records, 1987.

KRS-One. *Ruminations.* New York: Welcome Rain Publishers, 2003.

Malone, Bonz. "Microphone Fiends: Eric B. and Rakim/Slick Rick." *The Vibe History of Hip-Hop.* Ed. Alan Light. New York: Three Rivers Press, 1999. 94-96.

MC Lyte. "12 Music Videos Feat. MC Lyte." MTV Overdrive. 1 April 2006. http://www.mtv.com/music/artist/mc_lyte/artist.jhtml#/music/artist/mc_lyte/artist.jhtml.

Pough, Gwendolyn. "I Bring Wreck to Those Who Disrespect Me Like a Dame: Women, Rap, and the Rhetoric of Wreck." *Check It While I Wreck It: Black Womanhood, Hip-Hop Culture, and the Public Sphere.* Boston: Northeastern University Press, 2004. 75-102.

Schloss, Joseph G. *Making Beats: The Art of Sample-Based Hip-Hop.* Wesleyan University Press, 2004.

"USO to Bring MC Lyte to the Troops in Germany." USO Media Room. 15 April 2006. http://uso.mediaroom.com/index.php?s=press_releases&item=55.

SELECTED DISCOGRAPHY

Lyte as a Rock. First Priority Records, 1988.
Eyes on This. First Priority Records, 1989.
Act Like You Know. First Priority Records, 1991.
Ain't No Other. First Priority Records, 1993.
Bad as I Wanna B. East West Records, 1996.
Seven & Seven. East West Records, 1998.
Jammin. Import CD, Tuff Gong (England), 2000.
The Very Best of MC Lyte. Elektra Entertainment and Rhino Entertainment, 2001.
Da Undaground Heat, Vol. 1. iMusic, 2003.
The Shit I Never Dropped. Unda Ground Kings, 2003.
Back to the Future. Company unknown, 2006.

© Waring Abbott/Alamy.

Eric B. & Rakim

Shawn Bernardo

Eric B. & Rakim are the J. D. Salingers of hip hop. Like Salinger, the author of *The Catcher in the Rye* who famously retreated from the public eye and stopped releasing books at the height of his career, Rakim Allah has long maintained a self-imposed exile from the calcium light of the media, routinely shading himself from being misquoted and misrepresented by the press. And while Eric B. may have acted as de facto ambassador for the act, his gruffness and aphoristic style of communication has frequently left reviewers, critics, and biographers feeling a bit shortchanged. After the group broke up in 1992, Eric B. & Rakim retreated to the company of good friends and family, and their relative anonymity, reclusive propensities, and reticent natures cloaked their work in an alluring cloud of mystique that only served to bolster their cult stardom and iconic standing.

From the beginning, Rakim's style was that of a collagist rather than a storyteller. To Rakim, an MC was defined by his innate ability to collocate words from every facet of human life—from the real mean streets of New York to the metaphysical highways of the mind—into a lexical mosaic of verbs, nouns, and adjectives. He eschewed hip hop's conventional narrative structures for a mixed bag of topics and themes refracted through a prism of metaphors and similes. There is rarely a story, a tale, or a fable to be heard on Eric B. & Rakim's earlier works. "My Melody" could just as accurately have been titled "My Medley," what with Rakim's casual but steady assortment of abstract boastings and Sucker MC disses. The R is an abstractionist. He rhymes for the sake of rhyming. Eric B.'s sonically abstruse productions lend themselves naturally to Rakim's conceptual rhymes.

In the mid to late 1980s, there was nothing in the sonicscape of rap more abstract than the grimy boom-bap of an Eric B. production. To produce their hit "Follow the Leader," Eric B. mixed a volatile cocktail of breakneck drums from Baby Huey's "Listen to Me," horns from Coke Escovedo's "I Wouldn't Change a Thing," and an earth-rumbling bass line. Bob James's oft-sampled "Nautilus" finishes off the mix with its jazz-funk sound. With an instrumental beat of this caliber on tape rotation, Rakim would literally stare at his speakers for hours, attempting to give lyrical form to this abstractness. He was a blind artist painting rhymes on an invisible canvas, as he was wont to say. And the beats themselves could evoke a montage of visuals for the R: the darker and more frenetic a beat, the fiercer and more furious the concepts he would spin. With all of this in mind, "Follow the Leader" has Rakim stepping into the gale with malice to deliver what rightfully earned him his MC crown: skills defined. Roughly one minute into the cut, the listener is skyrocketed upward and outward, millions of miles into the cosmos, where stargazing is experienced at the speed of light. Sooner than the retina can adjust to the sun, the planets, and the interstellar medium rapidly receding from view and to the eclipse that follows, the R suddenly appears in the void like a star exploding forth from a vacuum. And that's only the first verse.

Eric B. kept the music fully equalized at the conceptual level with "Let the Rhythm Hit 'Em." He renders Rufus Thomas's "Do the Funky Penguin," the Commodores' "Assembly Line," and Bob James's "Nautilus"/"Night on Bald Mountain," all but rhythmically and melodically unrecognizable as Rakim takes his characteristic rap-as-weaponry metaphor and stretches it seamlessly over the track spanning an entire verse. The human mouth has been metaphorically compared to weapons since biblical times (Rev. 1:16, 19:15). But no poet has explored the metaphor more assiduously than Rakim.

Like an age-old prophet, he wages war against the enemies of Rah with his words. Rakim's mouthpiece is a gun, his tongue the trigger mechanism, his lyrics the ammunition. Though Rakim never personally calls out potential challengers to his throne by their actual names, one can be sure that each lyrical bullet has the ever-generic Sucker MC moniker inscribed upon its shell. And like a lyrical marksman with MCs locked in the crosshairs, he hits each one squarely with the rhythm. With bulletproof rhymes like these, Rakim is the original Teflon MC.

Rakim could shift his metaphorical focus from weapons of the hand to the apperceptive powers of the mind, his metaphors becoming increasingly intricate while remaining altogether long-playing. "In the Ghetto" takes the listener on a socio-religious journey of Dostoyevskian proportions, traveling through the visual cortex via Rakim's all-seeing, panoptic third eye. Here is a potential thesis on the Five-Percenter mythos and the locomotion of thought (see sidebar: Five-Percenter Terminology and Hip Hop Slang).

Five-Percenter Terminology and Hip Hop Slang
Shawn Bernardo

Many phrases from hip hop slang are derived from the Nation of Islam, and specifically from the NOI's Five Percenters (aka the Nation of Gods and Earths), a splinter group founded by Clarence 13X in 1963. Wu-Tang Clan, Eric B. & Rakim, Busta Rhymes, and many other groups employ Five Percenter terminology in their rhymes, as well as its numerology. The Five Percent Nation was founded on numerology. Its followers believe that there has always been a great divide between the inhabitants of planet Earth: eighty-five percent suffer from an ignorance of self and the world in which they live; ten percent benefit from a partial knowledge of truth and use it to exploit and control the eighty-five percent, and five percent possess the full wisdom of self-divinity and seek to liberate the eighty-five percent. Five Percenters memorize and recite the Infinity Lessons, which further explain these concepts of ignorance versus knowledge of self and which present black men as gods and black women as earths.

Rakim is one rapper who used the microphone to call the hip hop faithful to Islam. Rakim infused his raps with references to the Five Percent Nation. His language was freshly dipped in the terminology of the Five Percenters' Supreme Mathematics and Supreme Alphabet. As a servant and messenger of the Supreme Being, Rakim regarded Islam as the foundation stone of life and set out to teach the world who was the sole controller of the universe: Ruler, Allah, Kingdom, Islam, Master. Before acknowledging the nation of MCs that he influenced, it is worth lifting the stylus from the record to note his Pythagorean penchant for numerology. Rakim has always entertained an ongoing fascination with numeral 7 and its Five Percent associations with the mathematical perfection of his Lord and Creator. The seventh letter of the alphabet is G, which in Five Percenter thinking is understood to signify God and, by extension, the black man.

Rakim has a tattoo of the number 7 encircled by the words "RAKIM ALLAH" on his left bicep. The R was the first god of rap. He also identified himself as hip hop agent 007: William Michael Griffin, the god-MC born with three seven-letter words in his name. Rakim would make countless references to sevens throughout his rap career, from *Paid in Full* to *The 18th Letter*. Both albums were released in the seventh year of a decade, 1987 and 1997 respectively, and Rakim's seventh studio project and forthcoming LP *The Seventh Seal* is set for release in 2007. Ever since Rakim Allah put Islam in the mix, well over seventy underground and mainstream acts have raised their mics eastward. A notable seven are Lakim Shabazz, Digable Planets, Poor Righteous Teachers, Brand Nubian, Kam, and Brother Ali.

Further Resources

Miyakawa, Felicia M. *Five Percenter Rap: God Hop's Music, Message, and Black Muslim Mission.* Bloomington: Indiana University Press, 2005.

Alas, the musical parchment upon which Rakim's verse is laid is a reel of heavy-gauge sandpaper that hisses, crackles, and pops because of a worn-out drum break from Bill Withers's "Kissin' My Love." Eric B. is nonetheless able to redeem the cut through a prodigious use of 24-Carat Black's "Ghetto: Misfortunes Wealth" to create a drifting, quietly dreamy ambience for Rakim's most introspective opus to date. He transports the listener backward in time to the physiological instant of his inception, the ignition of life itself and his coming to being in mental existence as a thought. Rewinding the clockwork of his mind further still, Rakim rides his ancestral thoughtways through millennia in space and theological time to the primordial world of the original man and a race divided. This journey comes full circle with a vision-stirring trip to the sacred cities of Mecca and Medina in present-day Hijaz and ends in South Africa, where his train of thought reaches its final destination with a visit with his blood kindred in the throes of apartheid. These heady abstractions can only come from the mind of a consummate rap poet.

Rakim did not wholly limit himself to abstract poetics. On later Eric B. & Rakim albums, abstractions solidify into extended metaphors and afterward trompe l'oeil representations and appraisals of inner-city life. Periodically the R would descend from his transcendental perch to survey the prosaic world below. He whistled the familiar melodies of everyday life, its simpler pleasures and pains. A solitary verse from "Paid in Full" allows a glimpse into the realistic, street-based raps that would later come from Rakim. Eric B created a backdrop for Rakim's words, composing a track that samples Dennis Edwards's "Don't Look Any Further" and B-Side and Fab 5 Freddy's

"Change le Beat." Along with sampling sounds from these well-known songs, Eric B stitches in a drumbeat and tops off the track with a then-obscure flute riff that he sampled from the Soul Searchers' "Ashley's Roachclip." This musical montage sets the stage for Rakim to tell his autobiographical story of a hoodlum made good. He waxes nostalgic about forsaking a life of criminality and criminal-mindedness—the cut is replete with a veristic description of a robbery in progress with Kid Wizard quick on the draw—for the promise of getting paid as a bona fide rap artist. Rakim's portrayal of real-life situations and their environs is accomplished with an almost Proustian attention to narrative detail as he takes the time to highlight the startled, apprehensive smile of a man being robbed for what he has and the lint-lined pocket of a man who has not.

The eye of Rah is at its most perceptive when focused on his preeminence in concert. Performing live onstage is the métier of any MC and it is peculiar that the Mic Controller was not known for his stage-scorching pyrotechnics. He was first and foremost an author of rhyme flows. The R would pen raps in the dark on spotlighted pieces of paper. During recording sessions like the early, formative ones with Marley Marl, he would also write spontaneous verse, hastily scribing cheat sheets that would be brought into the mic booth for recitation. He would recount the process of bringing a verse to life in "Move the Crowd." Listening to an instrumental track of tediously programmed drums and synthy interpolations from James Brown's "Don't Tell It" and the J.B.'s "Hot Pants Road" and contemplating how to properly set his audience in motion, Rakim is drawn closer and closer to a lone stereo speaker until he is hit with a lyrical epiphany: Words symphonize into rhymes by the aural gravity of the very track to which he is rapping. Thus inspired, Rakim's raps write themselves, in a manner of speaking. In scores of Eric B. & Rakim joints, references would continue to be made to the ingenuity of songwriting and to the musical scaffolding that both supported and inspired Rakim's verse.

While Rakim is often described by eyewitnesses as a tad stage-shy, a simple keyword search of Eric B. & Rakim's complete lyrical anthology reveals that three words were invoked more than any other single piece of language: *microphone*, *rhymes*, and *crowd*. Rakim would take a novelistic approach to the contextualization of these words in a panoply of onstage anthems: "Move the Crowd," "I Know You Got Soul," "Put Your Hands Together," and so on. Listening to these cuts in tandem, one is provided with a broadly detailed impression of what it is genuinely like for MCs to put their skill set to the test on the ultimate proving ground—the stage. Rakim welcomes the listener into the gray corners of his mind, from which rhymes are formulated, then to the white-hot spotlight of center stage, where Eric B. & Rakim prepare to perform before a sold-out crowd. Rakim expands on this theme in "I Know You Got Soul" and telescopes in on the action. A marvel of lyrical stagecraft, no rapper makes an entrance like the R. The stage is a void. A microphone stands idle. Rakim resists a vaudevillian rush to the footlights.

He consciously allows the less skillful rhyme sayers to have first crack at treading the boards, whereupon they act as a prefatory foil to Rakim's much-anticipated appearance on the mic. In good time, Eric B. lets the record go and in heavy syncopation drum kicks from Funkadelic's "You'll Like It Too" slam like anvils from the rafters over a slap-happy guitar riff from Bobby Byrd's "I Know You Got Soul." Without warning, Rakim descends to deliver his soulful refrain. His stagemanship whips the crowd into a frenzy. Some fans nearly break their wrists from clapping so hard while others dislocate their jaws from lip-synching. Rakim even goes so far as to proclaim that he is the unmoving mover of crowds in "Put Your Hands Together."

RAKIM

No rapper has influenced hip hop more profoundly than Rakim. This rap architect and master builder of rhymes was born William Michael Griffin, Jr., on January 28, 1968, in suburban Wyandanch, Long Island (known as Crime Dance, Strong Island, to the initiated). His mom, Cynthia Griffin, was a civil servant for the State of New York and his father, William Sr., a hard-working family man, an auto mechanic, and an airplane maintenance supervisor with American Airlines. Rakim's parents met in Newark, New Jersey, at the Highway Inn, a nightclub where jazz great Sarah Vaughan was headlining. Music was a rich, participatory custom of the household; a mix of classical, jazz, rock, soul, and disco lilted through every room. Mother Griffin was an aficionada of opera divas and jazz vocalists. She once sang the blue notes on a Brooklyn-based radio station, but her career as a singer was abruptly cut short by her marriage and the birth of her children.

Rakim was a pet nephew of 1950s R&B legend Ruth Brown, whose sultry chart-burners helped establish Atlantic Records as an industry powerhouse. The Queen Mother of the Blues acted as a kind of surrogate parent, minding the boy now and again and sometimes taking him to see her perform her by-then retrospective concerts. It was Brown who first exposed Rakim to the music business. She continually expressed an appreciation for Rakim's lyrical aptitude and rhythmic faculties, and he would later rely on her to keep him grounded and focused as he grew musically. As a boy, Rakim aspired to become a professional saxophonist. He picked up the tenor sax in the fourth grade, but preferring a deeper sound, he soon switched to the baritone sax and participated in statewide music competitions. Later years found him playing the drums, an avocation he retained throughout his life and career.

But the turntable, the newest and most innovatively adaptive musical apparatus, was Rakim's true love. Cutting and scratching became his principle forte under the name Kid Wizard. The turntablist DJ Maniac, a friend of Rakim's older brother, occasionally brought DJ equipment over to the house and let the Kid practice his wizardry as the DJ's apprentice. Scratching with DJ Maniac and listening to the mixtapes that his brother Stevie played in his boombox first set Rakim on the expressway to rap. As hip hop gained popularity in New York City, Rakim was swept up in the movement and became an avid devotee of the four elements of the urban vernacular arts: DJing, MCing, break dancing, and graffiti. He was reportedly the one and only graffiti artist in all of Crime Dance, throwing up his ineffaceable tag on Suffolk county walls and even bombing his own quarters with a spray-painted depiction of Sir Nose D'Voidoffunk from the cosmonautical funk group Parliament. Rakim also trained himself in b-boying, from pop-locking to backspinning to street styling. And he also experimented with the vocal-percussive techniques of beatboxing, often called the fifth element of hip hop. But the real ether of interest for Rah was becoming an MC. He scribbled rhymes on notebook paper while his classmates were adding and subtracting fractions and decimals.

Rakim cultivated his penchant for rhyming and developed a distinctive style of vocal delivery under the tutelage and mentorship of DJ Maniac. He spent hours deconstructing the songs of his favorite rap groups: Fantastic Five, Furious Five, Cold Crush Brothers, Treacherous Three, and Force MCs. And when it came to his own style of rapping, Rakim was most concerned that his listeners perceive him as a boy of letters, an educated MC who was capable of lacing his own lyrics with a proficient utilization of the English language, particularly in regard to diction, syntax, and creative expression. His linguistic bent and inspiration came from a confluence of old-school wordsmiths and raconteurs: Grandmaster Melle Mel, Grandmaster Caz, and Kool Moe Dee. Refusing to bite any one particular style, the R set out to be a trendsetter with originality, versatility, and innovation.

Rakim was too young to be recruited by any of the neighborhood MC crews, and he was therefore unable to make anything of his newfound rap alias, Love Kid Wiz. But as he matured in years, Rakim stepped from behind the turntables to be in front of the microphone, rapping for DJ Maniac and other resident DJs like Teddy Tuff and Cool Breeze. He was introduced to the Love Brothers crew, with whom he would perform at outdoor and indoor jam parties both above and below ground, battling older MCs for respect and defending his own fledgling title in parks, backyards, gymnasiums, and basements. Once knighted by his peers as a true MC, he participated in his first major hip hop venue: an MC contest and rap convention hosted by the Original Human Beatbox, Doug E. Fresh, and produced by Mike and Dave Records of Crash Crew fame. That night at Harriet Tubman School in New York City, Biz Markie, the Clown Prince of Rap, made the music with his mouth while Rakim rhymed a cappella and moved his first crowd. MCing became commonplace for the R and kids soon forgot his previous adventures on the wheels of steel.

ERIC B.

It is Eric B. who will be long remembered as a DJ and shortly forgotten as an MC (see sidebar: Crooked Fingers). Born in 1965 in the heart of East

Crooked Fingers
Shawn Bernardo

Eric B. scratched his way into the history books as a *produttore universale*, a DJ skilled in all aspects of beat production. From the crate to the needle, he defined the modern producer. Both Eric B. and Rakim dug deep into their family music plots, dirtying their fingertips looking for the perfect beat and the Holy Grail of vinyl. What set Eric B. apart from previous producers was his sudden and decisive step away from routinely sampling popular R&B hits to searching for that lost and forgotten James Brown & Co. groove in rows upon stacks of proto-funk vinyl. He approached each LP with the ear of a minimalist—one that worked in a reductive tradition like Ad Reinhardt and Barnett Newman, Run-DMC and LL Cool J—and like a chandler he was adept at melting waxen platters down to their essential loop-friendly ostinatos and recasting them anew in those flickery, stripped-down melodies and atonal rhythms that comprise an Eric B. production like "I Ain't No Joke" or "I Know You Got Soul." He put it down hard on the SP-1200 sampler and the Roland TR-808 drum machine, the meat and potatoes of hip hop musical production past, and demonstrated to subsequent producers that they could utilize the same equipment to bang out fresher beats by tapping into atypical sample sources from different genres of music and manipulating them in new and innovative ways. But the real innovation that Eric B. brought to the tables was his Illadelph-rooted technique of cross-fader transforming and his early contribution to the art of turntablism: "Chinese Arithmetic." As a matter of course, this theme-based remix of a retranslated *mélodie orientale* has been derided by fans and critics as substandard filler—like all of his scratch-and-cut old-school DJ showcase blends: "Eric B Is on the Cut," "Eric B. Never Scared," "Eric B. Made My Day"—an adhesive digression from the verbal mathematics being steadily formulated by the R on flanking tracks. Yet the composition itself is literally built by Eric B. from scratch as he handles the turntable like an instrument throughout the track, manipulating aphonetical sounds and sound effects with nary a Rakim vocal snippet, perchance the only MC the DJ ever effectively put in the mix. While this nonfigurative style of DJing was later popularized by new-school turntablist virtuosi like the wave-twisting DJ Q-Bert and the Invisbl Skratch Piklz, the thematics would be expanded upon by audiographers like D-Styles, DJ Shadow, and RJD2. There was a time when DJs stood in front and to the side of their MC counterparts, and it is a facile thing to play past Eric B. and his skillfulness as a producer when he forever stands behind Rakim, one of the greatest MCs to ever nominate his DJ for president.

Elmhurst, Queens, to a Department of Water Resources workman and an eighth grade middle school teacher, Louis Eric Barrier was every bit as musically inclined as his counterpart. As a boy he played trumpet and guitar but traded them in for the turntable while a student at W.C. Bryant High School in Long Island City. As a teenager he performed at local clubs and roller rinks and by 1985 his quick-mix virtuosity was such that he was able to secure a job as a mobile roadshow DJ for New York City's 107.5 WBLS-FM. The station was home to Mr. Magic and his famed *Rap Attack* radio show featuring the Magellan of sampling, Marley Marl, as in-house DJ. Eric B. and Marley Marl were all-purpose roommates in Queensbridge, 12th Street Apartment 2E, where the superproducer operated a makeshift studio and ran his newly founded Cold Chillin' label out of the livingroom of his sister's apartment.

During that time, the R had made a trip to DJ Maniac's studio to immortalize himself on cassette, a ninety-minute megablast of Rakim's latest hits, that he originally intended to floss with on his future college campus. Included in this songbook of old rhymes and recycled verses was a raw and uncut version of "My Melody," which was first conceived on a miniature Casio keyboard. Eric B. met Rakim in the context of this very recording through the auspices of Alvin Toney, a mutual acquaintance and future record executive. With one play-through a partnership was formed: Eric B. & Rakim, established 1985. Initially Rakim had reservations about entering into any contractual commitment as he still considered himself college bound. He had also recently discovered the Five Percent Nation and devoted much time to the understanding of his divine Asiatic pedigree and studying the supreme mathematical sciences of the secularized Islamic sect. But after adapting the name Rakim Allah, he felt somehow destined to be the first deity of rap capable of subliminally spreading degrees of knowledge across the world as "The God" (see sidebar: Islam and Hip Hop).

Islam and Hip Hop
Aine McGlynn

There are two "proto-Islamic heritages that feed contemporary rap" (Allen 165). The first is the Nation of Islam, whose secular leader Louis Farrakhan speaks on behalf of the late prophet Elijah Muhammad. NOI philosophy is rooted in Elijah Muhammad's apocalyptic vision of the world, wherein black people will eventually defeat their devilish white masters in a great celestial battle. Before the battle takes place, though, NOI maintained that as many black people as possible need to be converted and therefore saved. The second derivation of Islam that hip hop draws on is the Five Percent Nation. Five Percent referred to the percentage of the population that was actually enlightened. The other ninety-five percent were either blindly ignorant or actively engaged in keeping the black population down. This splinter group of the NOI was formed by Clarence 13X, a disgruntled member of the NOI who left that group in 1963 and sought to form a more loosely bound collective of young members of the Harlem community. Clarence 13X elucidated the "Supreme Alphabet" as well as the "Supreme Mathematics." In the Alphabet, each letter stands for a word: A for Allah, B for Be or Born, G for God, and so on. In the Mathematics, 1 equals knowledge, 2 equals wisdom, 3 equals understanding, and so forth.

The Nation of Islam and its Five Percent offshoot both gained a great deal of currency in the hip hop community. It created order out of a chaotic society governed by racist and hegemonic authorities that excluded them entirely, they believed, because of their race. A philosophy that proclaimed that all black men were kings was empowering in the face of American nationalism that continually relegated its black population to the margins. That both conscious and gangster rap groups took on the core tenets of the Nation of Islam demonstrated the contradictory ways each style of rap imagined the improvement of the black community. For the former, the individual subsumed himself in the collective struggle, while for the latter, an aggressive individualism would ensure the black man's rise to power (Allen 172). The Zulu Nation and the Nation of Islam share some similarities. The Infinity Lessons that formed the core of Zulu Nation philosophy were formatted in the same question-and-answer style, while their content "drew on the Black Muslim's evocation of a glorious, original African past" (Chang 106). Both nations also share a belief in life beyond this planet. They both cite the American government's denial of UFOs as a prime example of the type of obfuscation that governments enact upon their populations in order to control them.

The Nation of Islam, largely because of the charisma and unwavering Afrocentrism of its leader, Louis Farrakhan, was a persuasive doctrine for young black men to grasp hold of in the late eighties and early nineties. References to NOI, the Five Percenters, and Farrakhan pop up throughout the Native Tongues' recording careers. *Beats, Rhyme and Life* in particular, recorded after Q-Tip's conversion to Islam, demonstrates the clean living principles that come along with adopting Islamic or proto-Islamic beliefs. Wu-Tang Clan, Busta Rhymes, Brand Nubian, and Rakim are all artists who maintain NOI political stances in their rap.

Works Cited

Allen Jr., Ernest. "Message Rap." *Droppin Science: Critical Essays on Rap Music and Hip-Hop culture*. Ed. William Eric Perkins. Philadelphia: Temple University Press, 1996. 163-185.

Chang, Jeff. *Can't Stop Won't Stop: A History of the Hip-Hop Generation*. New York: St. Martin's Press, 2005. 7-85.

Both Eric. B. and Rakim's parents thought rap to be a silly and impractical fad that would never pay the rent. Eric B. was nevertheless able to sufficiently persuade their parents to let the two hit the studio to get paid in full. Through an unwritten agreement, Rakim would be compensated monetarily for his efforts but opted to be represented only as a special guest on all branding and promotional hype (hence the "Eric B. featuring Rakim" designation printed on the group's first twelve-inch singles), thereby giving him an opportunity to bounce out of the venture at will. Purportedly this arrangement caused some misperceptions as some first-time listeners believed Eric B. to be the MC and Rakim the DJ. Even more confusingly, the twosome was nearly known as Eric. B & Freddie Foxxx. When Eric B. was taking applications for MCs, Foxxx, aka Bumpy Knuckles, was hired for the position but failed to show up for work on his first day of recording at Marley Marl's studio. As designated rapper, Rakim stepped up to the mic and recorded "My Melody" and "Eric B. Is President," the first-ever Eric B. & Rakim singles released in the spring of 1986 on Robert Hill's Harlem-based indie label, Zakia Records.

Much dispute exists about who in fact was the mastermind behind these tracks and correspondingly the whole of Eric B. & Rakim's production catalogue. Discrepancies abound throughout the engineering credits; the atomic beatsmith Large Professor, breakologist DJ Mark the 45 King, and the late and unsung Paul C have laid their claims, and even Rakim himself has lately claimed to have self-produced the bulk of his repertoire. Although this hip hop whodunit is of course beyond the scope of this biography, an investigation should doubtless begin with Eric B.'s unsuccessful debut as one of the first MC-producers to come solo on his own 95th Street Recordings label (*Eric B.*, 1995).

All sources agree that Marley Marl can be credited with arranging and layering "My Melody." He was assisted by his cousin and Queensbridge champion, MC Shan, who was in the studio when the tracks were recorded pro bono. Both attempted to hype Rakim in the booth, not recognizing that a new über-sedate style of rapping was being birthed right before their ears. The R may have paid them no mind because his eyes were fixed upon the pages of his notebook, wherefrom he recited lyrics into the mic that he had conceived ad libitum only hours before. Musically speaking, both "My Melody" and "Eric B. Is President" were entirely orchestrated by Marley Marl at his workstation; witness the identical drum kit that he used contemporaneously on MC Shan's "The Bridge." And while both singles were in no way mixed down, the roughness of their fluttering vocal distortions and dub-generated feedback elicited a gritty cacophony of sound that the hip hop street embraced.

PAID IN FULL

The Awesome Two (Special K & Teddy Ted) were the first to broadcast Eric B. & Rakim's inaugural single, "Eric B. Is President," on 105.9 WHBI-FM, and though it barely peaked commercially on Billboard's Top R&B Singles charts, it was celebrated by partygoers as the most danceable track of the year. Rakim first heard his song live on the radio from the cracked window of a parked car. He later recalled that it was at this moment that he knew the hand of Allah was fixed squarely upon Eric B. & Rakim. He made the decision then and there to enter the rap game as a professional player. What had begun as a part-time hobby would flourish into a full-time career spanning seventeen singles and four albums, three of which would be certified gold by the RIAA: *Paid in Full*, *Follow the Leader*, and *Let the Rhythm Hit 'Em*.

Eric B. & Rakim's career played out on fast forward. With the local success of the first singles, the group was snapped up by 4th & Broadway in the spring of 1987 to create their seminal flagship LP, *Paid in Full*. While the album itself promptly earned a spot on Billboard's Top Black Albums chart and the group a standing on their annual Top Black Artists list, each new Eric B. & Rakim single was a *prêt-à-écouter* classic, and "Paid in Full," "I Ain't No Joke," and "I Know You Got Soul" would all be listed on Billboard's Top Hip-Hop Singles charts. "Paid in Full" was a club hit at home and a discothèque sensation abroad compliments of a remix by Coldcut titled "Seven Minutes of Madness," the first commercially successful one of its kind. To Eric B.'s extreme dissatisfaction—he referred to the remix as "girly disco"—the experimental DJ team triaged "Paid in Full" and merged it with the strident microtones of Israeli mezzo soprano Ofra Haza's "Im Nin Alu." The remixed cut was soon featured on the soundtrack of the LA gangbang-land flick, *Colors*. The enigmatic electronic group M/A/R/R/S would also utilize Haza's vocals and a Rakim quotable in their house-adapted acoustical collage, "Pump Up the Volume," a one-off single that was heralded as the first sample-based number one smash in the UK.

The release of "I Know You Got Soul" would prove more controversial as Eric B. & Rakim's sampling of James Brown sideman Bobby Byrd's "I Know You Got Soul" resulted in swift legal action against the group for pirating material without permission or due compensation. The protracted lawsuit was one of the first highly profiled copyright infringement cases of a musician seeking statutory damages from another musician for reappropriating a prior recording into a new (and admittedly more soulful) composition. Despite all repercussions, Eric B. & Rakim would continue to raid the legacy cache of James Brown and Co. In doing so they started the godfather rap vogue; groups like the Jungle Brothers, Ultramagnetic MC's, and Kool G Rap & DJ Polo began sampling the rhythm section of the J.B.s. On "Talkin' All That Jazz," the original sampling advocate Daddy-O of Stetsasonic would point out that doing so was mutually beneficial to both the sampler and samplee, as it revived the careers (and bank accounts) of outmoded and pensioned-off musicians, predominantly the Godfather of Soul. Brown would later respond to these rappers on a sample-based song of his own called "I'm Real," where he alludes to Eric B. & Rakim's "I Know You Got Soul" and personally calls out the God, reminding him that James Brown invented soul.

Keeping pace with the ensuing successes of *Paid in Full*, Eric B. & Rakim were sprinting with Marley Marl and his illustrious Juice Crew, booking gigs through their manager Tyrone "Fly Ty" Williams and performing their re-souled rap arias in some of New York's most respected hip hop venues such as Latin Quarter, Union Square, and the Roxy, where ecstatic fans tossed rolled-up dollar bills on stage to pay their entertainers to the fullest. Positive reaction to the group was such that stewardship of their business portfolio was swiftly turned over to Rush Management and up-and-coming rap moguls Lyor Cohen and Russell Simmons. The latter was introduced to the group by Rakim's brother Ronnie, who played the keyboard for Rap's first mainstream artist, Kurtis Blow, a Rush client. Over 750,000 units moved and Eric B. & Rakim would consolidate their marketability by shopping their sophomore album to MCA for a 1 million-dollar long-term recording contract, a first-time anomaly in the rap industry and a half million more than Island would offer the group to stay with their 4th & Broadway imprint. This meteoric rise to fame and fortune struck Eric B. & Rakim completely unprepared. Though Eric B. seemed at ease mobbing a ghostly Rolls-Royce Silver Shadow with Gucci interior and Rakim a white-on-white Mercedes-Benz with a landau top by Louis Vuitton, a $15,000 sound system, and a custom Euro-plate on his front bumper that read BENZINO, the R also found himself standing in line for a century-old brownstone mansion. Paid to the fullest, Eric B. & Rakim geared up to lead their listeners into the age of modern rap with *Follow the Leader*, their second album.

FOLLOW THE LEADER

As the *New York Times* reported that rap music and hip hop culture were hijacking mainstream America in the late 1980s, fans telephoned their favorite radio stations and hit the request line for the next single from Eric B. & Rakim. The R heard the call and blessed his followers with "Microphone Fiend," a verse to end all verses. His delivery is a ticking clock of intensity as he confronts a serial addiction to dopeness and spits his autobiography over sixty-nine consecutive bars of pure, unadulterated heat. This cut cinched Rakim's status as the greatest of all time among his contemporaries. Other singles followed suit: "The R," a lecture on rapping, and "Follow the Leader," an event horizon that defined the stock in trade of the rap soloist. The latter single was nominated one of Melody Maker's singles of the year for 1988 and would gain a peak position on the Billboard's Top Hip-Hop Singles chart.

A dozen or so singles off the previous and subsequent Eric B. & Rakim albums were translated into videos. And "Follow the Leader," the first rap video epic and period piece of the new televised world of hip hop, would premiere on the pilot episode of *Yo! MTV Raps* in 1988. Throughout Eric B.

& Rakim's video productions, the R took on myriad personas: imam, dictator, politician, racketeer, businessman, soldier, celebrity, playboy, baller, fugitive, and rap star. Eric B. was contented playing the background and standing sentinel as DJ and hip hop strongman. Aside from two-toned FILA tracksuits, throwback hoodies, and an endless wardrobe of leather and suede gear, Eric B. & Rakim were most often filmed rocking their aureate trunk jewelry, custom designed by Jacob the Jeweler (diamond setter to the rap stars), and those ghetto-fabulous, faux-Gucci leather getups that were tailor-made by twenty-four-hour-a-day Harlem couturier Dapper Dan's, who was incidentally the go-to spot for the group's designer upholstery. As they matured as artists and men, later videos and photo shoots presented the two modeling Italian sport coats, Coogie sweaters, and Nehru-collared shirts.

Eric B. & Rakim could also reinvent themselves on the pop/R&B catwalk. Their hip-pop crossover duet with label mate Jody Watley, "Friends," initially slated for Will Smith, catapulted Eric B. & Rakim into Top 10 rankings for the first and last time on both Billboard Pop and R&B singles charts during an era when rap music received less than modest radio play. With a respectful Kangol tip to Chaka Khan and Melle Mel and their Grammy winner "I Feel for You," the success of the Eric B. & Rakim and Jody Watley team-up, as well as Rakim's duet with English vocalist Mica Paris on her *Contribution* LP in 1990, would make permanent the now-formulaic pop/R&B singer X featuring rapper X prerequisite for a Billboard chart-topper. Eric B. & Rakim would never again touch the mainstream. Nonetheless they would come close with their amatory "What's on Your Mind" track for the *House Party 2* soundtrack.

The group also recorded two jingles for the malt liquor St. Ides, "Real Men's Drink" and "Get Some," that were aired with some frequency on major R&B stations until the 8.2% alcohol by volume malt liquor became embroiled in controversy and their advertising banned from the radio. Even more contentious was Rakim's open endorsement of the "Crooked I." As a devout Muslim, he was obliged to abstain from all things alcoholic and his community responded reproachfully to his willful and dubious associations with Pabst Brewing Company. His response to the criticism was dismissive and unapologetic, and Rakim Allah would later elevate himself from the cooler to the top shelf as the new hip hop face of Hennessy.

Eric B. and Rakim took a surprising two-year breather at the top of their game, precisely when they had gained a wider audience and appeal on both sides of the railway. Rakim stepped away from the studio to mourn the deaths of his father and good friend Paul C. McKasty, the white whiz kid music engineer who was in the process of teaching him how to freak the SP-1200 for Eric B. & Rakim's upcoming *Let the Rhythm Hit 'Em* LP. Paul C. was murdered in his sleep by unknown assailants for unknown reasons and Rakim honored his memory by placing his senior snapshot next to a photo of

Rakim's father on the back of the album cover. Meanwhile, Eric B. founded Lynn Starr Productions and Mega Starr Management, working with artists like Freddie Foxxx on *Freddie Foxxx Is Here* and Kool G. Rap on *Wanted: Dead or Alive.*

With the R's sudden and prolonged disappearing act, would-be haters alleged that he was doing time in Rikers Island for slanging crack cocaine, a rumor as tabloid worthy as the unfateful rivalry between Rakim and Big Daddy Kane. The R had opened fire on the smooth but raw-edged MC in a demo for "Let the Rhythm Hit 'Em," the eventual leadoff single for Eric B. & Rakim's third album, but mics were holstered when Kane heard the track via Eric B.'s brother and called Rakim to wave the white rag. Both rappers agreed not to battle and the lyrics in question were withdrawn. Notwithstanding, an unreleased Eric B. & Rakim demo titled "Hypnotic" does appear to contain a snipe at Kane and, if accurate, it is the only extant example of Rakim personally calling out another rapper for battle on tape. Rakim would later allege that a kind of ultimate rapping pay-per-view was in the works where the two MCs would face off before a televised audience for upwards of $50,000, but the proposal got scrapped at some point during the planning stages.

LET THE RHYTHM HIT 'EM

Eric B. & Rakim's hiatus proved far too long an absence from the rap game. Stylistically, Eric B. had revved up his production tempo, and Rakim responded by accelerating his rapping speed and downshifting to new lyrical themes. Critics, fans, and even the group's manager, Amanda Scheer-Demme, grumbled that Eric B.'s beats stalled out behind Rakim's flow on *Let the Rhythm Hit 'Em*. Still, the album was one of *Spin* magazine's top picks for 1990 and earned the group a handsome five mics from *The Source*, that magazine's highest rating.

Eric B. & Rakim released several singles ("Let the Rhythm Hit 'Em," "Mahogany," and "In the Ghetto") before they finally brought the sun down on their empire with "Don't Sweat the Technique" and the most knocking of swan songs, "Juice (Know the Ledge)." Released in May 1990, *Let the Rhythm Hit 'Em* was the group's final album. At this juncture in their career, both artists wanted to release solo albums as their last recordings under their MCA contract and planned to later reunite as a collective on another label. The final straw for the group was Eric B.'s refusal to sign a release for Rakim, an incident that would land the rapper in court battling his ex-partner and ex-label for half a decade. With animosity in the air, Eric B. & Rakim broke up in 1992. They were last seen together in the Big Willie-styled "Don't Sweat the Technique" video and as cameo characters along with Big Daddy Kane, Kid Frost, Doctor Dre, and Ed Lover in Mario Van Peebles's black spaghetti western, *Gunmen*. Despite these final appearances together, Eric B. & Rakim had left the building.

Naturally, the R had plans to take off on his first solo mission. Over the next few years he would team up with a motley squadron of emerging rap producers, opening his laboratory door to Buckwild, Salaam Remi, and Pete Rock, among others. MCA would eventually release Rakim's first twelve-inch solo, "Heat It Up," a rough-hewn jazz binge that appeared on the 1994 soundtrack for *Gunmen*. This was immediately followed by "Murderer (Jeep Version)," remixed by Sly Dunbar, a peppy R&B-tinged revise of Barrington Levy's dance hall reggae triumph. Both songs went largely unnoticed by the hip hop establishment, as did the later "Shades of Black," a somber piece of social militancy that was specifically composed for *Pump Ya Fist (Hip Hop Inspired by the Black Panthers)*, a soundtrack to Mario van Peebles's 1995 movie, *Panther*.

Meanwhile, Eric B. received an even worse reaction to his premier single, "I Can't Let You," a love ballad. Image-wise, Eric B. was the absolute antithesis of LL Cool J (Ladies Love Cool James), who established a market for hip hop love songs with "I Need Love" in 1984; the ladies apparently did not love cool B. enough to establish his reputation as a soloist on the charts. The last the world would hear from Eric Barrier would be an unfounded Internet report of his being shot and killed on August 28, 2005, in a barbershop in Camden, New Jersey. While he went on to pursue an executive position with Street Life/All American Records, Eric B. faded into rap legend, hip hop lore, and obscurity. Rakim was at least able to keep the R brand current and on the periphery of the multimillion-dollar urban entertainment market with his singles and a memorable guest appearance on the 1995 final episode of *Yo! MTV Raps*; DJ Scribble juggled an instrumental of EPMD's "It's My Thing" as a pole-positioned Rakim gave shots to his new record label, the Last Platoon, and freestyled alongside KRS-One, Erick Sermon, Chubb Rock, and MC Serch. These sporadic recordings and appearances, however, did not return Rakim to his former status as rap god.

RAKIM'S RETURN

Rakim's relative absence and unpopularity in the rap game was but a small thing to a giant as he returned to reclaim his throne in 1997 under new management from his longtime associate and hypeman, Bill Blass. To hip hop aficionados, no revival album has been as hotly anticipated as *The 18th Letter*, a full clip of fourteen songs and three remixes released by Universal Records. The label also released a double CD set containing *The Book of Life*, which included a compendium of Rakim's greatest hits during a time when Eric B. & Rakim were riding the Soul Train with Don Cornelius;

"I Know You Got Soul" was taped in 1987 and "What's on Your Mind" and "Don't Sweat the Technique" in 1992.

For old-school rap fans, the R was the self-prophesied holy redeemer of hip hop, a messianic figure predestined to usher in a renaissance of rap music and a rebirth of the skillworthy MC. Standing atop Mount Sinai in a windswept robe like Black Moses, the R premiered himself to the world in a phantasmagoric *Clash of the Titans* meets Fellini's *Satyricon* video exclusive: "Guess Who's Back." The album reached Number One on the U.S. rap charts, yet while critics and fans reacted amicably to a recrudescent Rakim Allah, *The 18th Letter* was ultimately judged against Rakim's earlier work with Eric B. & Rakim. During their golden age, Eric B. & Rakim signified the wisdom of actual street knowledge long before N.W.A. co-opted the phrase for Compton. Rakim had envisioned his comeback album as a kind of panacea that would resurrect, heal, and elevate the once intelligently wise and spiritually enlightened mindfulness of golden-age hip hop. After all, it is on *The 18th Letter* that the R asks the mysterious age-old question: "Who is God?" While he hoped to be eternalized as the first and last conscious MC who introduced spirituality into the rap game, he also wanted his lyrical codification of the streets to be part of his living legacy. Yet rough-and-tumble jewels like "The Saga Begins" from Pete Rock and "New York (Ya Out There)" from DJ Premier were lost among mismatched tracks and incompatible producers. Nevertheless, in their first-ever collaboration, Premier and Rakim deliver a sure-shot contender for best hip hop comeback song: "It's Been a Long Time." It was on this cut that Rakim first publicly affirmed that he was no longer down with Eric B. While the R remained lyrically on point throughout his first solo album (he had updated and modernized his narration to include an array of new technological and theological innovations), thematically the album most often found its creator revisiting the ghosts of hip hop past like Just-Ice in "Going Way Back." Even though *The 18th Letter/The Book of Life* sold 648,000+ copies, most have been laid to rest in the markdown bins of the used CD store.

The late 1990s would witness the fall of the house that Rakim built, mic by mic and stage by stage. It is difficult to pinpoint the pivotal moment when Rakim began his gradual descent from status as a rap idol. He hooked up with alternative remixologist Danny Saber to record "Take the Train," which was featured in the children's film *Rugrats: The Movie*, and lent his vocals to Art of Noise for a soundtrack album to a film about the life of French composer Claude Debussy that was never made. Neither track registered the slightest blip on the hip hop radar screen. Nevertheless, Rakim's 1999 donation of his Dapper Dan jacket (as featured on the *Follow the Leader* LP) to Roots, Rhymes & Rage, the first major exhibition on hip hop culture at the Rock and Roll Hall of Fame, and a guest appearance with infamous Mobb Deep on their video single for the *Hoodlum* soundtrack, which earned Rakim *The Source*'s Hip-Hop Quotable of the Month, kept his reputation from flatlining.

Later that same year, Rakim premiered his final full-length LP on Universal Records: *The Master*. Apparently lessons were not learned from the programmatic failings of his first solo CD, as he involved himself with yet another cadre of mismatched producers. Granting that his flow was still masterful, *The Master* seemed more like a jerry-built compilation than a cohesive concept album. And with the new badass arrivistes Sean "Puffy" Combs and Jay-Z reigning over the airwaves with all of the pomp and ghettiquette associated with chasing the Benjamins and living the life of the rich and infamous, Universal Records wanted a more radio-friendly crossover album to market to the cheap-suited heads ever aspiring to be part of the hip-pop beau monde. Rakim thus dedicated this predictable, chorus-overdriven omnibus to the Jigga-set and returned under the guise of a shot-calling papi chulo with a snifter full of artless club bangers. His appearance as a denimed-down roughneck in the video single for the album, DJ Premier's "When I Be on the Mic," is a brief moment of redemption that recalls the halcyon, "I Ain't No Joke" days of Rakim in his MC prime. Still, one slice of butter out of a baker's dozen worth of songs does not an album make. And already cynical fans had to come to terms with the dispiriting reality that Rakim was no longer capable of lyrically reinventing the mic.

The R had unwittingly transitioned himself from microphone soloist to microphone collaborationist, involving himself in a surfeit of Marvel-styled team-ups with his contemporaries. On the hip hop front, he partnered with Rahzel on "It's a Must," Gang Starr and WC on "The Militia II," Canibus on "I'll Buss 'Em U Punish 'Em," G. Dep and Kool G. Rap on "I Am," and Japanese producers in residence Nigo and Muro on "Once Upon a Rhyme in Japan"; a partnership was renewed between Rakim and Art of Noise on "(New York London Paris) Spleen" and with Jody Watley on "Off the Hook"; and a first-time reggae venture was embarked upon with Steven Marley on a remix of Bob Marley's immortal ghetto lament, "Concrete Jungle." Increasingly relying on the éclat of other producers, rappers, and singers, it seemed ever more apparent that Rakim could no longer handle the whole weight of MCing on the solo slab.

Yet just as the clock struck Y2K, the hip hop world braced for an all-time collaboration of collaborations, one that would rock the new American century: Rakim Allah and Dr. Dre together on an album felicitously titled *Oh My God*. In the previous year, *Blaze* magazine had listed the rapper as number one of the fifty greatest MCs in the history of rap, and listed at number one of the ten greatest producers was Dr. Dre, the so-called inventor and master guardian of the G-Funk soundscape. In interviews, the first producer to hold the Source Awards (and subsequently the Grammy Awards) title Producer of the Year promised fans that supper rappin' would meet super producin' on the best rap record Dre ever produced—'nuff said.

As a portent of the album to come, Aftermath Entertainment raised the curtain on Rakim in the hip-pop mainstream with a henna-laced single mixed and arranged by DJ Quick that featured R&B vixen Truth Hurts and an unwitting Lata Mangeshkar, who would later sue Interscope Records/Universal Music Group (Aftermath's parent companies) in 2002 for the wanton disrespect of her religion, disregard for her culture, and unsanctioned use of her song, "Thoda Resham Lagta Hai." With the music video rotating dizzily on MTV and BET and the track itself burning up the Billboard Hot R&B/Hip-Hop singles charts and the Billboard Hot 100, anticipation for *Oh My God* ran high. Standing shoulder to shoulder with the new-school pharaohs of the millennial rap kingdom, Rakim appeared on Eminem's *8 Mile* soundtrack and guest-starred on Jay-Z's "The Watcher 2," lending him increasing exposure and commercial credibility. In spite of these great expectations, the one album that could possibly have bridged the age-old East Coast–West Coast schism would never leave the mix room at Encore Studios and Studio B at Chalice Studios. On July 16, 2003, *Oh My God* was pronounced DOA in an official statement posted on Rakim.AftermathMusic.com: "The Mic God Rakim has left the Aftermath Camp."

The official word was issued by Zach Katz, the new manager and marketing hotshot behind Rakim who had transformed the R into a retail powerhouse brand for Hennessy and later Reebok in their Lyrical Classic shoe campaign. After Katz relinquished his managerial role and cited the obligatory "creative differences" as the principle reason for *Oh My God*'s abortive launch, Rakim boarded a flight and left the City of Angels behind for the Salingerian seclusion of suburban Connecticut. He was characteristically tight-lipped about the matter and would reiterate this nonexplanation in random interviews for three long and relatively unproductive years, during which time he reentered the hip hop limelight on but a few occasions: to model urban wear for Sean John's Be Legendary promotion, to spit a cappellas of old standards on Russell Simmons's Def Poetry Jam, to record the relatively unheard-of "Streets of New York"—an import-only, mixtape-bound bonus track featuring Nas and Alicia Keys that marked the first occurrence of the God and his Son blessing the mic in unison—and to appear micless and playing the background in Missy Elliot's "Cop That Disc" video with Timbaland interpolating a farcical cook-up of Eric B. & Rakim's "I Know You Got Soul."

The R would eventually clear the air in 2006 about how, musically, *Oh My God* was to feature a West Coast production style that was uninspiring to an MC raised on the raucous sample-based productions of Marley Marl, who had always been Rakim's ideal producer. Rakim much preferred a choice selection of beats that were submitted to Aftermath by DJ Premier, but Premier's tracks were rejected by the Aftermath staff. Dre himself would claim that many of these beats never reached his desk, and it was rumored that he actually spent minimal time in the studio with Rakim.

It was perhaps unclear from the start if Dr. Dre really envisioned *Oh My God* as a salute to neo-gangsterism with Rakim picking the guns back up to celebrate the already overexamined living of hood life. To ensure the album was infused with a new and gratuitously marketable strain of thuggish vim and vigor, Rakim claimed that his pen was guided from on high by Dre and Aftermath staff who pressured him to sling ink on the gangsta tip. And if the ayatollah-orchestrated "A Cold Feeling," a track tentatively approved by Dre and originally destined to be on his soundtrack for *The Wash*, is any indication of the direction the album was to head lyrically, somebody definitely touched the soldier in Rakim. A chronic-puffing, corner-clocking, cash-snatching, pistol-packing, drive-by-shooting Rakim conducts himself like an honorary member of G-Unit, showing and proving how to live and never die in New York. While the style is evocative of "Juice (Know the Ledge)" hopped up on phencyclidine, Rakim's steelo was never born to roll. Hence each blustering verse sounds scripted, uncharacteristically hard and knuckle bare. While he maintained mad respect for Dre, it was never Rakim's intention to sensationalize the often crime-stricken neighborhoods that both supported and inspired his craft for the sake of entertainment.

First and last, Rakim was a socially conscious brother, an epigrammatist whose lyrical mode was that of a poet, a philosopher, an anthropologist, an occultist and, above all, an MC. It was the imponderable sensibilities of the intelligent mind articulated skillfully and not the hair-trigger sensitivities of an ignorant body given to villainy that Rakim wished to inspire his listeners to emulate. It must be noted that the only extant track positively attributable to Dr. Dre himself is "After You Die," a leaked-out demo featuring a pensive Rakim contemplating the hereafter; the theme is itself an intriguing one as the Eternalist may have been able to slip some imponderables into the mix after all. What life will be and where you go after you die is all too indeterminate, but one thing is certain: The haunting vocals from the hook (seemingly purred by Eartha Kitt) would later find themselves reincarnated by Dre and Aftermath on Busta Rhymes' recent "Legend of the Fall-offs." The relationship between Rakim and Dre was anything but sanctified. And Rakim would later jibe that had he known that *Oh My God* would wither and die on the Aftermath vine and his talents would be directed elsewhere.

THE LEGACY OF ERIC B. & RAKIM

Rakim Allah is hip hop. The view from behind his microphone was one of a crowd moved by the integrity he brought to the stage. Kool Herc, the founding father of hip hop, said that Rakim set the tone for what hip hop is today. Yet it would take over a decade for the print and broadcast establishment to recognize Rakim's contributions to the rap idiom. After *Blaze* magazine knighted Rakim with Greatest of All Time status in 1998, *The Source* became the first periodical to confer five mic recognition upon his achievement as a collective, further awarding Eric B. & Rakim a spot on the Top 115 Artists from 1988-2003. To coincide with this fanfare, 4th & Broadway rereleased *Paid in Full* as a two-disc "Platinum Edition." And as hip hop geared up to hit its thirty-year mark, one album was routinely singled out for high honors and special distinction more than any other in the history of rap discography. The critics were in unanimous agreement: Eric B. & Rakim's *Paid in Full* (along with *Follow the Leader*) was duly listed in the upper echelons of *The Source*'s 100 Best Rap Albums of All Time, *Rolling Stone*'s 50 Coolest Records and 500 Greatest Albums of All Time, *Spin*'s Top 100 Albums of the Last 20 Years and 100 Top Alternative Albums, and *Vibe* magazine's 100 Essential Albums of the 20th Century and 51 Albums Representing a Generation, a Sound, and a Movement. *Ego Trip*'s Book of Rap Lists listed the album (along with *Follow the Leader* and *Let the Rhythm Hit 'Em*) among Hip-Hop's 25 Greatest Albums by Year. Most recently, *Entertainment Weekly* named *Paid in Full* as the Greatest Rap Album, MTV selected it as the single Greatest Hip-Hop Album of All Time and ranked Rakim in the top ten of the Greatest Hip-Hop MCs of All Time; VH1 would follow suit by adding Eric B. & Rakim to the list of 50 Greatest Hip-Hop Artists and bestowing hip hop honors upon Rakim in 2006. But still no hip hop lifetime achievement award for Eric B. & Rakim.

The legacy of *Paid in Full* lives on to the present day as the R inaugurated his third comeback with a gala performance of "Paid in Full" at the B. B. King Blues Club & Grill in New York. After a jam-packed crowd of aged, lip-synching b-boys and rap notables thrust lighters, and cell phones, and electronic organizers into the air to commemorate the recent passing of Mrs. Griffin and the love and brilliance that she inspired, Rakim gave an enthusiastic shout-out to Eric B. and dedicated the song to his former producer. During the show he announced that he would release a new solo album titled *The Seventh Seal*, on his brand-new independent label, Ra Records. The release date was originally set for summer 2006, but Rakim later postponed this date, telling fans that the album would hit stores in Spring 2007. Rakim promised that *The Seventh Seal* would showcase last and for all the lyrical fire and ice that made him the Microphonist. The album itself will literally be of apocalyptic proportions as Rakim responds to the recent spate of inauspicious events afflicting the world today: the geopolitical havoc wrought by global warming and the melting of the polar ice caps, the terrorist attacks of 9/11, the invasion of Iraq and the War on Terror, the Indian Ocean earthquake and tsunami, and Hurricane Katrina. *The Seventh Seal* is set to be produced by the original East Coast Dream Team: Large Professor, Pete Rock, and DJ Premier.

Eric B. & Rakim patented a style of rap that would launch a thousand MCs on a quest to become the new dons and mafiosos of hip hop. Rakim's flow has long been canonized, his lyrics plagiarized, and his status coveted since he first passed through the door with Eric B. and his melodies. While many rappers acknowledge a debt to Rakim and his vocal, lyrical, and thematical innovations, only an elect one has been skilled enough to be recognized by the emperor of rap as a lyricist worthy of his court: Nasty Nas, the illmatic MC who was hailed by critics as the second coming of the God. As "God's Son," Nas ultimately paid tribute to his namesake and mentor on "U.B.R. (Unauthorized Biography of Rakim)" and would appear on MTV2's "The Life and Rhymes of ... Nas" to cover one of Eric B. & Rakim's greatest hits, "Paid in Full."

Rakim Allah set the platinum standard for what it really meant to be an MC, a crowd-moving master of ceremonies. For the R, MCing was a vocation strictly reserved for those with a cast-iron will and an imperturbable seriousness of mind. He thought of the microphone as a lethal weapon, and when operated correctly it could shatter the image and reputation of rival MCs. Eric B. & Rakim were not gangsta rappers—the mid-1980s had original gangsta rappers like Schoolly D and Ice-T on their respective East and West Coasts—but Rakim was the first smooth criminal of rap, a lyrical assassin par excellence. Rakim's rhymes hearken back to the legendary battles in the early days of rap, when skills were tested and reputations were made and unmade by the word manifested in rhyme. Rakim's earliest influences would include a laundry list of elite warriors that held it down on the front lines of battle-rhyming royals, most notably Grandmaster Melle Mel, Grandmaster Caz, and Kool Moe Dee. For years MC crews like the Furious Five, the Cold Crush Brothers, and the Treacherous Three had battled for supremacy on the city streets and in the public parks of New York City. As an initiate in this tradition of verbal fisticuffs, Rakim was all but duty-bound to harass and murder his nemeses on the other side of the mic.

Rakim's style is distinguished by his baritone vocal delivery and its sexy, velveteen smoothness. The self-proclaimed Microphonist is methodical as he monotonically delivers verse after slow-pitched verse in deliberate, uninflected intonations. Not since Shawn Brown and his eponymous twelve inches of novelty, "Rappin' Duke," hit the airwaves in 1984 had rhymes been delivered at such a slow and even-toned velocity. Shortly after Rakim began releasing records, the collective voice of hip hop all but lowered an octave in pitch and scale; listen to King Sun's "Hey Love," LL Cool J's "The Boomin' System," and DJ Jazzy Jeff and the Fresh Prince's "Summertime" for examples of Rakim's influence. Rakim's wolf-in-the-night vocal delivery always left his rivals guessing whether he would pounce or just growl idly in the darkness. Nary a stammer nor a stutter would prevent him from hunting down his prey, the ever-elusive Sucker MC. In an effort to stay one mic ahead of the crowd, he would quicken the rate of his delivery. Never at a loss for words, Rakim's hastened cadence allowed him to pack more verbiage and, by extension, subject matter between each and every four-bar section of his verse. And still, his staccato delivery was nothing less than glacial in its icy coolness, every verse inflected with fistfuls of flavor.

With a predilection for battling, the R brought a quiet ferocity to rap. Many MCs have said that one of the most difficult feats to pull off on the mic is to be equally laid back and charismatic, and only Rakim could sound coldly inactive and hotly reactive at one and the same rhyme. "I Ain't No Joke" is a testament to Rakim's chilled-out, no-nonsense attitude toward rapping. He held up the album title as a catchphrase signifying his prowess on the microphone. Amid a pile-driving Roland TR-808 drum interpolation of Dexter Wansel's "Theme from the Planets" and brassy, sky-scraping blasts from Fred Wesley and the JBs' "Pass the Peas" riff scratched briskly over and above the drummed break, Rakim remains calm. He describes himself meditating on the cut like a forensic audiologist, nonchalantly explaining how his vocal stylings are impervious to impersonation. MCs like the notorious 7/21 who would try in vain to replicate Rakim's style are casually warned that their actions can and will invite serious injury and even death. None but Rakim can lead the unversed through hellfire and back à la Virgil and emerge scatheless and unsmiling without a bead of perspiration. Rakim is no comedian—and "I Ain't No Joke" would become the stylistic blueprint for what was to come vocally from the R.

At the time, Rakim's stolid composure was at polar opposites with the chest-pounding, two-fisted vociferations of hard-core rappers like Run-DMC and LL Cool J, whose in-your-face lyricism took on the subtlety of a riot-control megaphone. The Gospel of Rakim spoke for itself, and it would be preached in a mellifluous cadence and most regularly without exclamations. When Eric B. & Rakim released their genre-defining twelve-inch, "My Melody" backed with "Eric B. Is President," raising hell at 33-1/3 rpm had suddenly and precipitously become démodé.

Yet for all the restraint Rakim brought to the mic, there was an aggressive underlying structure to his raps. He was the first MC to derive a formula for what is universally known today as *flow*: the rhythmic verbalization of a complex calculus of rhyme. Rakim has long been considered the inventor of compound rhyming, the internalized patterning of single- and multisyllabic words. Throughout the pre-Rakimian era (circa 1978–1985), rhyme couplets were most regularly used as idioms with terminal rhyming words anchored to the end of line phrasings like osmium bookends. This straightforward and inelaborate style of rapping was championed by MCs like Kurtis Blow and Melle Mel, as well as crews like Whodini and the Fat Boys. And with the establishment of flowing as the new lingua franca of the rapping world, Rakim single-handedly founded the new school of rap and kick-started the Golden Age of hip hop (circa 1986–1994). In recent times, the obstreperous Eminem was singled out by Rakim as the new millennial master of flow.

The old-school guard had dropped larger-than-life verses, each one seemingly improvised for the hyperkinetic movement of arm-throwing, hand-waving hip hop crowds. While rappers have always preformulated their raps in some manner, rap music has deep roots in oral traditions and past MCs would pepper their raps with a vast repertory of stock phrases ("Yes, yes, y'all") that lent the vocalization of their lyrics a live, spontaneous feel—particularly when battles were fought in person, grill-to-grill. In razor-sharp contrast, Rakim was more of an offstage composer than an onstage improvisor, and as such he took copious amounts of time to set his rhymes down in ink and stone. Before he even picked up his Paper Mate, the song was envisioned in its entirety—the thematic structure and narrative direction—and Rakim most typically wrote his raps from ending to beginning so as to squeeze every last word and idea into his verses. The rhythmic directions of his raps were plotted on paper with the skill and accuracy of a cartographer. As an exercise in linguistics, he would sometimes select sixteen or twenty-four of the illest words surrounding his concept and build his rap around this vocabulary. To ensure that his rhyming patterns were always sure-footed, Rakim devised a kind of metrical templating system whereby the pages of his jotter were split into three equally spaced columns sectioned off by drawing two parallel lines down each sheet of paper. Rakim appliquéd each individual section with a paisley-like filigree of vowel-chimes and like-sounding words that were simultaneously cross-stitched across all three sections to form an interpenetrating unity of periodic and continuously compounded rhymes. When he christened his second album *Follow the Leader*, the R was not merely inducing his listeners to follow the yarns he spun on the mic—the rhymes themselves were meant to be followed. No MC before Rakim invested as much time and energy into the stylistic mechanics of rapping. He elevated rap from an improvisational activity to a compositional art. In other words, he prepared himself for battle.

Rakim at once invented and mastered the science of the written rap. His invention was anything but elementary. It was a scientific formulation and a codification of the rap laws of rhyme. To grasp Rakim's formula ($R = MC^2$), one must briefly consider his love and understanding of jazz music and his willful translation of its improvisational melodies and rhythms into vocal sonorities. Pianists like Thelonious Monk and saxophonists like John Coltrane would have a profound impact on the R. Monk's angular, discordant variations on Asian-derived keyboard phrasing and notation, as showcased in his "Japanese Folk Song," and his challenge to conventional Amerocentric chordal structures held particular resonance for Rakim. He studied the many ideological expressions of jazz—its technical intricacies of timing and patterns—and readapted the music's serpentine phrasings to fit his brave new scheme of rhyming. Rakim's rhymes respectively and characteristically meander on, around, and off Eric B.'s sonic backdrops like jazz musicians' instrumentation (see sidebar: Hip Hop and Jazz).

To the same degree that a classically trained musician lays down note symbols on a staff to indicate pitch and timing, Rakim took the trouble to syncopate his rhyme patterning with an almost compulsive precision. His rhymes connect internally and externally like the intricate and well-fitting pieces of a jigsaw puzzle. His inner metronome keeps every word quantified and is seldom if ever off the beat. Throughout his career as an MC, Rakim associated his rhythmic twists and turns with everything from the aerosolled

Hip Hop and Jazz
Robin Chamberlain

Both jazz and hip hop are more than musical genres: Both are cultural phenomena arising from, and giving voice to, the struggles of African Americans. In addition to being unique musical styles, both incorporate fashion, aesthetics, dance, speech, and graphic representations in communicating the experience of disenfranchised African Americans. It should not be surprising, then, that these two genres have found many points of intersection, giving birth to a new and unique musical form, jazz rap, that continues to evolve as artists from both jazz and hip hop backgrounds produce new and increasingly experimental albums. Originating in the 1980s, jazz rap is often characterized by Afrocentric lyrics that address a wide range of sociopolitical issues. It is also a genre that thrives on experimentation (as do both jazz and hip hop), and, as such, is one of the genres in which the most exciting alternative hip hop has been, and continues to be, produced.

Jazz rap emerged as a distinct genre with the 1988 release of Gang Starr's "Words I Manifest" and Stetsasonic's "Talkin' All That Jazz." These were soon followed by influential offerings from De La Soul, Jungle Brothers, and A Tribe Called Quest. In 1992, jazz legend Miles Davis's posthumous final album, *Doo-Bop*, was released, and drew new interest to the genre by its use of hip hop beats and collaborations with MC Easy Mo Bee. Other notable artists combining jazz and hip hop include Nas, the Roots, and MC Soweto Kinch. In 1996, DJ Shadow (aka Josh Davis) pushed the boundaries of the genre even further with his critically acclaimed album *Endtroducing . . .* , which incorporated not only hip hop and jazz but also rock, soul, funk, and ambient. Since then, jazz rap has become a forum for hip hop artists to explore the boundaries and meaning of the genre, as well as for a more eclectic listening audience to take interest in hip hop as a genre that is, both musically and politically, inherently progressive and malleable.

---

schematics of graffiti art to the geometric designs and arabesque motifs of Persian rugs. The internal architecture of a Rakim joint is something to aurally behold and his lyricism is best appreciated by peeping "I Know You Got Soul" and "Follow the Leader" without the advantage of musical accompaniment. Once heard a cappella, listeners will truly understand why Sucker MCs would die to get the formula of the R.

See also: Nas, Roxanne Shanté, Dr. Dre and Snoop Dogg

FURTHER RESOURCES

The Art of 16 Bars: Get Ya' Bars Up. Dir. Peter Spirer. Image Entertainment. 2005.
Canibus. "Lyrics of Fury: The Sequel." *The Source: The Magazine of Hip-Hop Music, Culture and Politics* (February 1998): 150-153.

Coleman, Brian. "Rakim Told Me." *Wax Poetics* (Summer 2005): 68-74.
Frederick, Brendan. "Rakim: That's Me (Part I)." *XXL Mag: Hip-Hop on a Higher Level* (22 March, 2006). 27 July, 2006. http://xxlmag.com/online/?p=625.
Frederick, Brendan. "Rakim: That's Me (Part II)." *XXL Mag: Hip-Hop on a Higher Level* (22 March, 2006). 27 July, 2006. http://xxlmag.com/online/?p=629.
"Hip-Hop Icon Series: Rakim." *Half Time: Walking the Fine Line Between Insanity and Genius* (6 July 2006). August 2006. http://halftimeonline.com/hip-hop-icon-series/rakim-2.
"Hip-Hop Icon Series: Rakim Pt2." *Half Time: Walking the Fine Line Between Insanity and Genius* (1 August 2006). August 2006. http://halftimeonline.com/hip-hop-icon-series/rakim-pt-2.
Kearse, Abbie. "Rakim's Back." MTV Music. August 2006. http://www.mtv.com/bands/archive/r/rakimfeature/index.jhtml.
Malone, Bonz. "Microphone Fiends: Eric B. and Rakim/Slick Rick. *The Vibe History of Hip-Hop*. Ed. Alan Light. New York: Three Rivers Press, 1999. 94-99.
Marriott, Robert. "Allah's on Me." *And It Don't Stop: The Best American Hip-Hop Journalism of the Last 25 Years*. Ed. Raquel Cepeda. New York: Faber and Faber, 2004. 187-201.
The MC: Why We Do It. Dir. Peter Spirer. Image Entertainment. 2005.
Ndlovu, Dumisani. "Rakim: Long Live the King." *Music Monitor* (March 1998). August 2006. http://www.penduluminc.com/MM/March/Rakim.html.
Neal, Mark Anthony. "... And Bless the Mic for the Gods: Rakim Allah." *Pop Matters* (19 November 2003). 27 July 2006. http://www.popmatters.com/music/features/031119-rakim.shtml.
Ogg, Alex. "Marley Marl." *Rock's Backpages Library* (1999). 27 July 2006. http://www.rocksbackpages.com/article_with_login.html?ArticleID=7500.
"Rakim: Tha Return of tha Mic God (Part I)." *Tha Formula: World's Best Source for That Ol Boom Bap*.27 July 2006. http://www.thaformula.com/rakim_-_tha_return_of_tha_mic_god_-_part_1.htm.
"Rakim: Tha Return of tha Mic God (Part II)." *Tha Formula: World's Best Source for That Ol Boom Bap*. 27 July 2006. http://www.thaformula.com/rakim_-_tha_return_of_tha_mic_god.htm.
Ro, Ronin. "The Professional." *Rap Pages* (January 1998): 64-68, 110.
"Status Ain't Hood Interviews Rakim." *Village Voice* (6 June 2006). August 2006. http://www.villagevoice.com/blogs/statusainthood/archives/2006/06/status_aint_hoo_13.php.
Sutter, Joe. "Pay Dirt." *Record Mirror*. 28 November, 1987. 40-41.

SELECTED DISCOGRAPHY

Eric B. & Rakim

"My Melody" (12-inch). Zakia Records, 1986.
"Eric B. Is President." (12-inch). Zakia Records, 1986.
Paid in Full. 4th & Broadway, 1987.
"Paid in Full" (12-inch). 4th & Broadway, 1987.
"Paid in Full—the Coldcut Remix." (12-inch). 4th & Broadway, 1987.
"I Ain't No Joke" (12-inch). 4th & Broadway, 1987.

Eric B. & Rakim

"I Know You Got Soul" (12-inch). includes a cappella. 4th & Broadway, 1987.
The Mixpak Elpee (EP). 4th & Broadway, 1987.
Follow the Leader. Universal Records, 1988.
"Follow the Leader" including a cappella. (12-inch). Universal Records, 1988.
"Microphone Fiend" (12-inch). Universal Records, 1988.
Let the Rhythm Hit 'Em. MCA Records, 1990.
"In the Ghetto" (12-inch). MCA Records, 1990.
"Juice (Know the Ledge)" (12-inch). MCA Records, 1992.
Paid in Full—The Platinum Edition. Island Records, 1998.
20th Century Masters—The Millennium Collection: The Best of Eric B. & Rakim. Hip-O Records, 2001.

Rakim

The Book of Life. Universal Records, 1997.
"It's Been a Long Time" (12-inch). Universal Records, 1997.
"New York (Ya Out There?)" (12-inch). Universal Records, 1997.
"The Saga Begins" (12-inch). Includes a cappella. Universal Records, 1997.
"When I B on the Mic" (12-inch). Universal Records, 1999.

Courtesy of Photofest.

Public Enemy

George Ciccariello-Maher

In hip hop history, no group is more emblematic of the purely political than Public Enemy. The group serves as a lens through which to survey the history of rap, past and present, sketch its broad strokes, chart its highs and lows, and above all map its relation to the political mainstream of the United States. What may come as a surprise given the legendary status the group enjoys is the relatively apolitical nature of Public Enemy's early work, the result of having to work without a blueprint to craft a new genre of explicitly political rap.

Their rise from the relative obscurity of Long Island to massive popularity and political controversy in the early 1990s, and their return to a degree of obscurity thereafter, tells us much about the history of hip hop and particularly about the fate of the specific political project that Public Enemy would come to promote through their music.

EARLY YEARS: FROM THE 'VELT TO SPECTRUM CITY

Chuck D was born Carlton Douglas Ridenour on August 1, 1960, in Flushing, Queens, to a radical family. He moved as a young child to Queensbridge, later home to such artists as Marley Marl's Juice Crew, Nas, and Mobb Deep, before settling at the age of eleven in Roosevelt, Long Island (later to be affectionately called "the 'Velt," Strong Island). Relocating to Roosevelt would prove crucial to Chuck D's development, as he recalls the surprisingly large black population and a well-organized community, as well as the proximity to such institutions of higher learning as Hofstra and Adelphi Universities, which offered radical summer courses for young blacks taught by Black Panthers and members of the Nation of Islam, among others. Although they had yet to meet, two other future members of the broader Public Enemy circle—Professor Griff and Hank Shocklee—also attended the same summer programs, and it was Chuck D's inspiring experience there that would influence him, after graduating in 1979 from Roosevelt High, to enroll at Adelphi.

Shortly after beginning his studies at Adelphi, Chuck D waited in line at a party for a chance to rap on the mic, and was approached afterward by Harlem-born Hank Shocklee. Born James Henry Boxley III, Shocklee was a founder of the well-known DJ outfit Spectrum City, which despite its popularity conspicuously lacked MCs to hype the crowd. Shocklee invited Chuck to join the crew, which would later evolve into the legendary production crew the Bomb Squad, consisting of Hank's brother Keith Shocklee, Bill Stephney, Carl Ryder (Chuck D's producer alias), and Eric "Vietnam" Sadler, who would collectively provide the notorious sonic backing for Public Enemy.

Hank and Keith Shocklee were born to a family whose savvy united the musical and the electronic: a crucial combination during the early years of hip hop, and especially prophetic for future Bomb Squad members. Hank's musical influences were drawn from across the spectrum, and he recalls that during his formative years, rock would win out over the funk and jazz to which he had been exposed as a child. His attachment to the raw energy, drive, and overt delivery of 1970s rock would foreshadow the music Hank would mastermind in later years. But funk would make a comeback. After hearing a neighbor plug turntables into a local band's PA system, Hank remembers how amplification gave funk an entirely new energy. Shocklee would go on to produce an intricate fusion of these two elements—electrified rock and amplified funk—the two most fundamental ingredients of what would become the Bomb Squad sound.

It was from this very same amplification technique that the Spectrum Sound System was born. Originally billed as a "radio station," Hank and Keith would basically drag their speakers and mismatched turntables around to play impromptu shows by plugging the tables into the microphone jacks on the speakers. During the next few years, Spectrum would engage in a variety of DJing activities—spinning records as diverse as disco, rock, and Kraftwerk at venues as diverse as parties and wedding receptions—as well as recording and selling mixtapes and hyping new hip hop. Chuck D describes Hank's genius during these early years as simultaneously technological and acoustic—a reflection of his early influences—and Hank elaborates on this by noting that despite the power of his sound system during those early Spectrum years, balance was the key, setting him apart from legends like Kool Herc: "I would make sure that my crossover frequencies—I would make sure that my bass, everything, was working in tune with each other, and I made sure that I covered the entire frequency spectrum" (Lapeyre 123). Spectrum was a fitting name for the operation.

It was during the course of his work with Spectrum that Chuck D would become acquainted with Hank's brother Keith Shocklee, and after seeking out contacts at Adelphi's radio station WBAU, he would also connect with Bill Stephney, whose Monday night show eventually came to be closely associated with Spectrum and immensely popular among Strong Islanders. The *Spectrum Show* on WBAU appeared around the same time that their work at parties was on the decline as lack of profitability had resulted in the closure of several key venues, and the Spectrum crew turned the production talents of the embryonic Bomb Squad toward the direct recording of new and previously unheard artists for exclusive play on WBAU. It was during the course of one such recording session that Chuck D would be introduced to another central member of P.E.: Flavor Flav, born William Jonathan Drayton Jr. on March 16, 1959, in Roosevelt. Flav was trained as a classical pianist and had attended a different high school than Chuck D before also enrolling at Adelphi. Shortly after meeting Chuck, then program director Stephney gave Flav his own show right before Spectrum, under the moniker MC DJ Flavor.

During these years, Chuck D considered himself more of an MC than a rapper, but the temptation to make records was ever present, and he soon came to recognize the need to record, especially if he wanted to break into the rap scene from the relative obscurity of Long Island. And Hank Shocklee's encouragement didn't hurt, either: Hank would listen to the entire line of amateur rappers who lined up for the mic at Spectrum parties, before realizing that Chuck's brief interventions as an MC—in a booming baritone borrowed from sports announcer Marv Albert—were more compelling than any of the rappers. It would take nearly a year for Hank to convince the introverted Chuck D—a description bearing little relation to his later front man persona—to start rapping. After Chuck had released a couple of records with the dual aim of demonstrating his skills and hyping the *Spectrum Show*—including the underground 1984 hit "Check Out the Radio," released as a B side to "Lies"—Flav told Chuck that another local rapper wanted to battle him. Since the two were working together for Chuck's father at the time, they rehearsed a response together, and in the end Chuck invited Flavor Flav to join him on what would be their first joint recording. The track would bear a prophetic name, originally meant to express Chuck's surprise at being targeted for a battle: "Public Enemy No. 1."

THE BOMB SQUAD'S SONIC BOOM

It was during the course of these early recording experiments that the classic Bomb Squad sound would emerge in embryonic form. At one point, Hank approached Larry Smith and Russell Simmons to produce beats for Spectrum, hoping to recreate what he perceived to be the best aspects of the Run-DMC and Kurtis Blow sound. What it was that Hank appreciated about Smith and Simmons's production sheds some light on where the early Spectrum sound was coming from: They were musicians, but unlike most musicians they kept it minimal. This frustration with musicians that drove Hank's vision of rap production would become central to the Public Enemy sound, but only through a certain degree of productive tension with the Bomb Squad's own musician: Eric "Vietnam" Sadler.

Sadler entered the picture because Smith and Simmons declined to produce Spectrum. Hank had moved his equipment into the same Hempstead studio shared by Sadler, and since Sadler was the most approachable musician around from a hip hop perspective, Hank asked him to fill out the sought-after Kurtis Blow sound. Vietnam declined at first, but after a year of meager income as a musician, he agreed to work with the Spectrum crew, and his first contribution came on the 1984 "Check Out the Radio" single. This was only the beginning, and it was in the context of what some perceived as a lukewarm response to that single that Hank and Eric would begin to reformulate their sound. Vietnam was the only one who knew how to use the drum machines and samplers, so this reformulation consisted of Hank and Chuck describing the sounds they wanted and Sadler attempting to recreate them electronically.

And Sadler also had to be disabused of some bad habits, specifically, a too affectionate relation to Prince and the eighties sound more generally. The vaccine was the 808. The Roland TR-808 drum machine, released in late 1980 and immediately considered by many to be an inferior machine, had an infamously artificial sound, but its biggest selling points were a relatively low price and a classic kick drum sound. It was largely as a result of this kick drum, and the artists like Public Enemy who venerated it, that the popularity of the 808 would skyrocket later in the 1980s, well after Roland had ceased production of the early device. Hank told Eric Sadler, "*This* is your fuckin' God. This is in *every fuckin' record*. If you don't do anything in life, you put this shit in there, and it's a fuckin' smash" (Lapeyre 128). Through Eric with his 808 and Hank with an increasingly massive collection of samples, the Bomb Squad sound began a slow and often painful process of development and refinement, a process that spanned three years and two albums.

In 1985, the *Spectrum Show* on WBAU came to an end, as its participants felt that it had reached a limit, and specifically that it wasn't paying off financially. Chuck was also being actively courted by Rick Rubin at the upstart label Def Jam, which had already signed Original Concept, the Beastie Boys, and LL Cool J. Spectrum continued to do live gigs, and it was around this time that Chuck was reintroduced to another crucial member of what would become Public Enemy: Professor Griff, born Richard Griffin on the same day as Chuck D. The two had known one another in Roosevelt during their younger years, but after joining the army and learning martial arts Griff returned to Roosevelt to found the local black security organization Unity Force, which had provided security for the 'Velt's hip hop scene, often working at Spectrum shows.

Chuck and Hank finally consented to a deal with Def Jam in June 1986—what they would later deem "the great surrender"—inspired largely by the commercial success of Run-DMC and the feeling that the mainstream rap game needed some conscious players in (Chuck D 82-83). Even then, however, Chuck only envisioned himself as operating behind the scenes as a manager, but after some pressure from Rubin, he agreed to be front man for the newly renamed Public Enemy. Despite label pressure to remain a solo rapper, Chuck D immediately began to assemble a crew in the mold of Grandmaster Flash's Furious Five. He first approached Flavor (with significant resistance from Rubin) and then Spectrum DJ Mellow D, whom Chuck D immediately granted the less-than-mellow title "Terminator X." Griff was next, whose Unity Force was immediately recast as Security of the First World (S1W), which according to Chuck D's vision represented a rejection of the alleged third world status of blacks.

While the lineup had been formalized, and while the moniker Public Enemy had finally been selected (at the suggestion of Hank Shocklee), it is worth bearing in mind that the name still referred to Chuck D's original resistance to battle rapping. Moreover, while Terminator X and S1W had been incorporated into the group, this was still initially for aesthetic reasons, backed up by a hazy political agenda. Indeed, Chuck D recalls that the political significance of the name Public Enemy came only after it had been chosen, but this isn't to say that they were apolitical. Bill Stephney suggests that part of the reason the group adopted the name Public Enemy was their growing realization—in the aftermath of the 1986 Howard Beach incident, the 1983 killing of graffiti artist Michael Stewart by New York transit cops, and Bernhard Goetz's 1984 shooting of four unarmed black teens on the subway—that "the Black male is definitely the public enemy," a recognition which formed the basis of the group's later radicalization (Chang 247).

BUM RUSHING THE SHOW, A YEAR LATE

Chuck D locates the official emergence of Public Enemy between two micro-eras within the history of rap. First came the old-school period epitomized by Grandmaster Flash, Kurtis Blow, and Afrika Bambaataa, which was followed by a second period—between 1984 and 1986—dominated by LL Cool J, Run-DMC, and others. But in 1987 the rap game changed again, ushering in a third era, as Rakim and KRS-One broke the preexisting lyrical mold. This vocal innovation, epitomized by Rakim's intricate and jazz-inspired rhyming, broke with the regular and simplistic meter, flow, and emphasis of earlier rap, which remained rooted in the Jamaican tradition of toasting. Chuck recalls that *Yo! Bum Rush the Show* was made in the outmoded 1986 style, and this simplistic meter and flow would remain visible on tracks like "Timebomb."

The reason for the outmoded character of the album was the slow production schedule of Def Jam, then distributed by major label Columbia, as Chuck D recalls that "major record companies move big-time, but they move like dinosaurs" (Chuck D 86). By the time the single "Public Enemy No. 1" was released in February 1987, its original incarnation was nearly two years old, and the rerecorded version had existed for more than six months. The album was made in the 1986 style because it was made in 1986, but not released until 1987. Learning their lesson from this, Public Enemy's next hit single was not reserved for their follow-up album. Instead, going over the head of Russell Simmons, they released "Rebel Without a Pause" as the B side for *Bum Rush*'s "You're Gonna Get Yours." "Rebel" was recorded in a week and released less than two weeks later, which meant that the first track from Public Enemy's second album was released less than two months after their first record finally saw the light of day. This did the trick: "Rebel Without a Pause" blew up, and this was the break that Public Enemy needed.

What characterized this early sound that had become so outdated by 1987 can be gauged by taking a closer look at the stylistic differences that characterized *Yo! Bum Rush the Show* and the 1988 release *It Takes a Nation of Millions to Hold Us Back*, for which P.E. is best remembered, and for which the "Rebel Without a Pause" B side served as a prelude. The earlier album showed a less than fully matured Bomb Squad, which combined with the influence of Rick Rubin to give a much more minimalist sound, more evocative of LL Cool J and the Beastie Boys than the heavily layered Bomb Squad sound that would emerge a year later. The early *Bum Rush* sound emerged from the chaotic process by which Eric Sadler sought to translate Hank Shocklee and Chuck D's demands into music, and this process of translation was not limited to the internal dynamics of the Bomb Squad, as Sadler would often find it necessary to translate these unsystematic demands for oblivious sound engineers, some of whom flatly refused to participate in the Bomb Squad's unorthodox production techniques.

Neither process was painless, but it was precisely this discomfort that would make the Public Enemy sound so profoundly inimitable, as this external tension reflected an aesthetic conflict inside the Bomb Squad. This tension often revolved around the opposition between Hank's desire for "offness" and Eric's tendency to seek "musical resolution": While Hank was raising and lowering levels to create imperfection and prevent sterility, adding "frequencies that push and pull against each other," Eric would be doing the opposite in an effort to smooth out the track. Hank even recalls looping at two and a quarter bars in order to disrupt the track's closure by creating an infinite-sounding loop, a technique most conspicuous on tracks like the "Mind Terrorist" interlude. The clash between the two was not balanced, however, since Hank was still the boss, the brain, and the "rugged rebelness that goes in when something *sounds* like 'I don't give a fuck'" won out over the closed circle of resolution (Lapeyre 128). "Music's worst nightmare," as Hank so often described it, defeated the musician.

At the time that *Bum Rush* was constructed, this production process had yet to fully develop, and one clear difference that distinguishes the album is the prevalence of recorded music, which Chuck D recalls as having constituted more than half of the album. Eric would even play live drums before overlaying them with a complicated and never-repeating drum pattern. After the basic elements of the track were laid down, Chuck would then formulate his contribution, before the Bomb Squad tweaked the sound and added samples and scratching. Since Terminator X was still more of a party DJ, Johnny "Juice" Rosado was enlisted to add the complicated cutting and scratching, and it is often argued that Rosado never got enough credit for his contribution. Moreover, few recognize that much of the scratching was done by Chuck himself after the other DJs had gone home for the night. The DJs were also enlisted in Hank's quest for offness, as he recalls that "Rightstarter," his favorite track on the album, sounded too good, too clean in its original incarnation, so he took out the kick drum and had Rosado scratch it back in. But this was all the final step: The Bomb Squad would map it out, Chuck would add his vocals, and then Flavor and Terminator X would come in and perform their largely preconceived parts.

Like the Bomb Squad sound, Chuck D's rhyming was also in transition, booming loudly but not erasing entirely an earlier party MC mentality. While political themes such as references to South African apartheid and the Black Panthers gain mention on "Timebomb," these were backgrounded to the sort of battle rapping and playful boasting that played more prominent roles on tracks such as "Public Enemy No. 1" and "You're Gonna Get Yours." Flavor Flav's contribution, moreover, differs considerably from his later-developed persona. While the interplay of "the treble" (Flav) and "the bass" (Chuck) was beginning to develop, we also see a serious side to Flav on "Too Much Posse," and the heavy filtering of the album's vocals further diminishes the contrast between the vocalists (see sidebar: Hype Men).

Hype Men
George Ciccariello-Maher

While the role of the hype man is clearly visible in such early figures as Cowboy and Creole of Grandmaster Flash and the Furious Five (Kool Moe Dee specifically credits the latter), Flavor Flav's most significant impact on hip hop was undoubtedly his popularization of this role. A hype man is a figure who plays a central but supporting role within a group, making his or her own interventions, generally aimed at hyping up the crowd while also drawing attention to the words of the MC.

Although Chuck D recalls modeling Public Enemy explicitly after Run-DMC, the differentiation of roles would be much more pronounced in P.E., as Chuck and Flav perfected the interaction of the serious preacher-rapper with a comical hype man. Other notable hype men include Proof of D12 (who played Eminem's onstage hype man for many of his world tours), Freaky Tah of the Lost Boyz, and Bushwick Bill of the Geto Boys. Since the late 1990s, some producers, including notables like Puff Daddy, Lil Jon, and Jermaine Dupri, have transitioned from a hype man role to become rappers and stars in their own right.

Public Enemy was invited, in the aftermath of the release of *Bum Rush*, to join the Beastie Boys on tour, the beginning of which coincided with the release of "Rebel Without a Pause" in April 1987. The group was then invited to join headliners LL Cool J and Eric B. & Rakim on an infamous European tour toward the end of 1987, during which LL was booed off stage and Eric B. & Rakim got sick of the food and tour conditions and left. Public Enemy, however, was extremely well received, and much of their international popularity can be attributed to this early breakout opportunity.

IT TAKES A MILLION SAMPLES

Public Enemy dropped the epic *It Takes a Nation of Millions to Hold Us Back* in April 1988 to much critical acclaim, before joining Run-DMC on yet another European tour at the end of the same year. Given the swift and radical transformation that the group had undergone since the production of *Bum Rush the Show*, it is perhaps of little surprise that the success of *Nation of Millions* (considered one of the most influential albums of all time by VH1, *Spin*, and *Rolling Stone*) has condemned P.E.'s first release to an undeserved oblivion. It would be the combined maturity of Bomb Squad production and Chuck's political vision that would make *Nation of Millions* literally the centerpiece, and indeed the turning point, in the history of Public Enemy.

"Rebel Without a Pause" ushered in this era of Public Enemy's perfection, or to put it more accurately, their imperfection. "Rebel" was recorded with an early Mirage sampler, which could only capture three-second samples, resulting in a split-second delay between sample and track. This sort of imperfection was music to Hank Shocklee's ears. Moreover, it was on "Rebel" that Terminator X's potential began to appear. After hearing the initial track, Hank was disappointed by the muddy sound of the scratching, so he asked the engineer to "pull off the bottom" of the track. This did the trick: "the whole shit popped out like crazy, and it was my favorite piece.... I thought that was probably the most brilliant piece of scratchwork on a record, ever" (Lapeyre 134). While Chuck was still adding some "ol' fucked-up shit ... at three in the morning" and DJ Juice contributed some "fast cutting," Terminator X's role was now more befitting of his image.

"Rebel" was released well before the rest of *Nation of Millions* was even recorded, but before heading back to the studio, the Bomb Squad would make a slightly unexpected detour. Hank realized in 1987 that Slick Rick—already a legend from such hits as 1985's "La-Di-Da-Di" and "The Show"—was still on the back burner at Def Jam and had not yet recorded an album. It was the Bomb Squad running the machines that produced the 1988 *The Great Adventures of Slick Rick*, and once we recall Eric Sadler's role in the Bomb Squad—often muted but central nonetheless—we can begin to feel Hank behind the scenes, letting Eric's musical side flourish in the extended bass solo on "Teenage Love."

Back in the studio later that year to back up "Rebel" with a full follow-up album, the Bomb Squad had reached its peak. As Eric Sadler recalls, "*Nation* was the only album that the so-called Bomb Squad worked on as a whole together" (Lapeyre 135). The process was intensive, all the more so since the album was completed in less than a month. The process was the following: The Bomb Squad would come up with a basic idea, a basic beat in the preproduction stage. Once in the studio, the first step was to see what Chuck had come up with lyrically, to lay the lyrics down, and then to take a new perspective—invoking a sort of hip hop cubism—on what the finished project should look like. As "Vietnam" Sadler explains, the next step was the crucial ingredient to the new formula: "Then Hank and Keith would come in. It's like, a'ight, now we're gonna fuck this up ... basically, they'd take it apart and then we would slap it back together and I would just put stuff in place" (Lapeyre 134). The final ingredients, as with the first album, would be the scratching by Juice and Terminator and Flavor Flav's vocal contributions, but it was in the all-too-crucial "fucking it up" stage that the Bomb Squad would develop a trademark sampling style.

A crucial ingredient in what Hank Shocklee describes as "music's worst nightmare" was the heavy layering of equally heavy samples. In *Nation of Millions*, the predominant source would be James Brown—whose importance Hank Shocklee attributes to a "jungle grit," an "ability to tap into deep

African rhythms" and "create a frenzy"—and who found himself featured on exactly half of the tracks on the album. These samples were drawn from five classic tracks (Allen 72). Indeed, the break from Brown's "Funky Drummer"—one of the most heavily sampled songs of all time—was included on three tracks (and would later find its way onto "Fight the Power"). Later, some would attribute the decline of the Bomb Squad in part to new legal requirements for clearing samples, which rendered the use of material from legends like James Brown too costly an endeavor, a problem the group anticipated on "Caught, Can We Get a Witness?"

This prevalence of sampling was in itself a significant departure from *Bum Rush*, on which the sparse musical samples were generally looped and pushed into the background (as with the Neville Brothers sample on "Timebomb" or the JB's on "Public Enemy No. 1"). This was a result of the second shift engendered by KRS-One and Eric B. & Rakim's 1987 interventions. Chuck D recalls that it was the latter's "I Know You Got Soul" that "flipped it for good," a track which is often considered unique for the isolation of a James Brown sample, and which some claim single-handedly kicked off the era of "godfather rap" (Chuck D 86). Moreover, Chuck also cites KRS-One's "South Bronx" as another transitional track, and it was on the latter that Public Enemy's own transition would be explicitly modeled: "We started ['Rebel Without a Pause'] the same way that KRS's 'South Bronx' started off with the 'Get Up Off of That Thing' by James Brown" (Chuck D 91). James Brown was a crucial ingredient to the new Bomb Squad sound—"James Brown is the main course. Other samples are the flavoring"—and in this Public Enemy was in many ways a product of the times (Allen 72).

But the uniqueness of the Bomb Squad's new sound consisted of more than an increased sample density: The character of the flavoring was vital. These samples were to make up part of a complex tapestry of sounds, alongside the random sounds, sirens, and rock guitars featured on *Bum Rush*. In a recent interview, Bomb Squad guru Hank Shocklee recalls, "I just wanted to take the sampling and OD [overdose] on it. You know, I wanted to use it so much that you didn't know what anything was and where things was coming from" (Welte). Soul samples were deeply enmeshed with heavy metal samples—Slayer's "Angel of Death" appears on "She Watch Channel Zero?!"—as well as a myriad of other unidentifiable sounds. The Bomb Squad would even record themselves simultaneously playing a chaotic array of sounds in the studio, before listening to the playback and lifting out a sample that had struck just the right combination of frequencies. Such techniques created a collage effect that has been described as a "wall of noise" or "sonic wall" within which Chuck D's fuller and by now less filtered baritone pounds the listener into submission like "the voice of God in a storm," in the words of Hank Shocklee (Warrell).

The contrast between *Bum Rush* and *Nation of Millions* goes beyond the merely aesthetic, as the latter would mark the emergence of Public Enemy's trademark brand of political critique: As production was revolutionized, so too was P.E.'s politics. It was this element more than even the album's innovative production that made it a landmark for a generation of fans and which marked the emergence of the first wave of truly political rap. The album turns to more political sampling: Jesse Jackson is summoned to begin "Rebel Without a Pause," and the ostensible interlude "Show Em Whatcha Got" references an entire lineage of black radicals, from Marcus Garvey to Steve Biko, Rosa Parks to Martin Luther King, and of course Nelson Mandela.

These samples provide the background for a new Chuck D, one rarely glimpsed on *Bum Rush*, who lays out the group's dual political heritage, from the Black Panthers to the Nation of Islam (especially on "Party for Your Right to Fight"), as well as the spirit of revolt embodied by Nat Turner. Further, Chuck D repeatedly claims federal complicity in the deaths of Malcolm X and Martin Luther King, dismisses mainstream television as brainwashing, and issues stinging critiques of Oliver North, J. Edgar Hoover, and Margaret Thatcher, as well as the prison-military complex, for which he coins the memorable term "anti-nigger machine." These various strands of political critique come together in the video for "Night of the Living Baseheads," which rap critic and historian Tricia Rose sees as a "visual, symbolic, and conceptual tour de force," embodying the essence of Public Enemy and "the tension between postmodern ruptures and the continuities of oppression" (115). Public Enemy had finally earned the self-imposed title of "prophets of rage."

Moreover, Chuck goes out of his way on *Nation of Millions* to defend NOI leader Louis Farrakhan and then presidential candidate Jesse Jackson, both of whom had recently come under attack for anti-Semitism (see sidebar: Anti-Semitism in Rap). This defense of Farrakhan and Jackson would prove prophetic of the rage of others as well, and Public Enemy would soon find themselves embroiled in their own controversy over anti-Semitism, one that would irrevocably transform both the internal dynamics of the group and its public reception.

Anti-Semitism in Rap
George Ciccariello-Maher

Currents within hip hop often mirror broader trends within the black community, and the sometimes-justified accusation of anti-Semitism often leveled against rap is no exception. This is often due to the fact that incidents of alleged anti-Semitism often have the same sources in both. For example, the controversy that engulfed and in many ways destroyed Public Enemy cannot be understood without reference to the similar controversies surrounding Jesse Jackson and Louis Farrakhan, and without grasping certain tenets of black thought, most specifically those of black Muslims.

Often, accusations of anti-Semitism involve broader disagreements about history, the present situation in the Middle East, and the relation between the two: Many in the black community have long maintained a clear sympathy with the Arab cause (as a result of both ethnic and religious ties) and have moreover challenged the singularity of the Jewish Holocaust by drawing attention to earlier experiences of colonialism and the black holocaust of American slavery. In 1994, a report by Fairness and Accuracy in Reporting made note of the double standard to which rappers are held, especially on questions of anti-Semitism, pointing out that during the Public Enemy controversy, similarly offensive comments by the lead singer of Guns N' Roses were largely ignored.

Even the conscious rapper Mos Def courted controversy by referring to a "tall Israeli" who's "runnin' this rap shit" on his 2004 track "The Rape Over." Mos Def insists that the line was a direct reference to current Warner Brothers CEO and former CEO of Island/Def Jam Lyor Cohen, whose parents were Israeli immigrants, and that hence the statement was not anti-Semitic. Regardless, the line was eventually removed from the album's second pressing under pressure from executives, ostensibly due to difficulties clearing samples. More recently, at the 2005 Hip-Hop Summit Action Network, rap mogul Russell Simmons reacted angrily to demands by the Anti-Defamation League that rappers publicly renounce the Nation of Islam, citing the organization's long history of defending the black community.

THE INFAMOUS GRIFF

At a meeting in 1988, up-and-coming film director Spike Lee asked Chuck D to write an anthem for his next project, *Do the Right Thing*. Through Lee, moreover, Chuck came into contact with the head of Motown, which had recently been acquired by MCA, and he, Hank Shocklee, and Bill Stephney were offered their own subsidiary record label under MCA. Chuck promised to deliver the track for Lee upon returning from the Run-DMC tour, and it was on a series of flights criss-crossing Europe and Japan that he would return to an old Isley Brothers favorite and pen the lyrics for P.E.'s most influential track of all time: "Fight the Power." Chuck recalls being surprised at the prominence that "Fight the Power" was given in *Do the Right Thing*, at the fact that the song and the film essentially merged into one, and this prominence certainly contributed to P.E.'s newfound stardom.

Chuck found inspiration for the track by reflecting on the disparity between the "heroes" of black and white culture, and this spurred him to write the infamous third verse of the song, which denounces Elvis Presley and John Wayne as racists, before summing the issue up with the observation that, "most of my heroes don't appear on no stamps." The song opens with one of the few of these heroes to actually make it onto a stamp, Martin Luther King, and production on the track epitomized the classic Bomb Squad sound: "begin [ning] with a pow, crashing like a fist against the senses" as "alarms sound and basses thump as a groovy yet caustic guitar riff moves over staccato rhythms.... You don't know whether to dance or stand at attention" (Warrell).

Do the Right Thing opened at the end of June 1989 and catapulted Public Enemy into the spotlight. But they were headed to the spotlight regardless, due to a now-infamous interview that Public Enemy's "Minister of Information" Professor Griff had given only a month earlier. Griff had made some mention on BET of a connection between "Jews" and "jewelry," and *Washington Times* reporter David Mills wanted to discuss the comments with the rest of the group. Chuck was busy with other interviews, and so made the decision—unfortunate in retrospect—to have Griff deal with Mills himself. The interview didn't go well, as Griff told Chuck afterward. Griff repeated the claims about jewelry, and cited the fact that the head of the De Beers mining dynasty is Jewish. Mills was even more bothered and scheduled a follow-up meeting. Chuck wasn't feeling conciliatory and again decided to skip out on the meeting to handle other business.

In this second interview, Mills spoke at length with other S1Ws and members of the P.E. entourage. Neglecting the fact that it was the very premise rather than historical detail that reproduced the circular logic of anti-Semitism, they attempted to provide historical substantiation for Griff's claims by citing among other things the heavily discredited (and NOI-published) book *The Secret Relationship Between Blacks and Jews*. As the story goes, this meeting was going reasonably well until Griff himself appeared, demanding the tape from his original interview to ensure that he wouldn't be misquoted. This provoked an altercation with Mills, who became angry and left, publishing his story as is in the *Times*. The original story was then commented upon in late June by the *Village Voice*, and the two articles would produce an unprecedented backlash against the group. It is worth mentioning that Chuck D recalls that Mills later regretted having published the article immediately without doing more research into the matter first, and that he subsequently offered an apology to Griff himself.

Chuck takes most of the responsibility for the controversy, identifying a series of moments in which he could have intervened but chose not to: He could have intervened in either of the Griff interviews, and above all he could have intervened in the brewing controversy rather than waiting for it to disappear. Instead, the fight was brought to him, not from critics, but from the industry and even from some friends: "They couldn't fuck with us directly, so what they did was to go after everybody around us.... They were fucking with Russell at Def Jam, messing with the MCA [label] negotiations, and fucking with Spike Lee" (Chuck D 228). The issue "festered into a mushroom cloud by the end of June," the same time that *Do the Right Thing* appeared, and Chuck realized that something needed to be done. But his final mistake was the press conference he organized, in which he read a prepared statement that had been approved by Stephney and Def Jam publicist Bill Adler without consulting Griff or the other S1Ws, which declared that Griff was no longer with the group.

THE BOMB SQUAD, DEFUSED

Chuck's reflections on the uproar would be committed to vinyl later that year when the group recorded the controversial "Welcome to the Terrordome" in October 1989, the second track (after "Fight the Power") for their third album, *Fear of a Black Planet*, which would appear the following spring. This track, Hank Shocklee recalls, came out of a track released in the same year by Brooklyn-based Full Force titled "Ain't My Type of Hype," and this explains why the track was produced prior to the remainder of *Fear of a Black Planet*. Hank recalls hearing the Full Force track for the first time while driving, and becoming so excited that he needed to stop: "It was like, 'Yo this is crazy! But they didn't finish it!' ... I turned around, went back to our studio: 'I'm gon' put this shit together.' I took what they did, added some extra stuff, changed it around: 'Terrordome'" (Lapeyre 135).

The Bomb Squad would then spend a couple of months producing albums for other acts—including Bell Biv DeVoe's *Poison*, which sold more than 4 million copies, as well as Ice Cube's epic solo debut *AmeriKKKa's Most Wanted*, which topped rap charts and remains among the most influential rap albums of all time—before returning to the studio for Public Enemy's equally epic third album. As Chuck D recalls, the team had effectively produced three number-one albums in a span of only fourteen weeks, between January and March 1990. But this was no longer the same Bomb Squad that it had been only a year earlier.

By the time P.E. got into the studio to put together *Fear of a Black Planet*, irreparable rifts had emerged within the organization, mostly as a result of the Griff controversy and Chuck D's reaction to it. Sadler recalls that the split was between Hank Shocklee and Bill Stephney on the one hand, and Chuck D and Keith Shocklee on the other, and that the latter pair began to work on *Fear of a Black Planet* while the others were still putting together Bell Biv DeVoe. Upon hearing some of what Keith and Chuck had come up with, Sadler remembers becoming depressed and deciding to help out on the album. In the end, even with Sadler's intervention, the absence of the mastermind, the brain, proved too difficult to overcome. *Fear of a Black Planet* remains a classic and the most commercially successful of Public Enemy's albums, but its status would be driven largely by the unforgettable impact of "Fight the Power," as well as the album's lead single, "Welcome to the Terrordome," both of which can be seen as leftovers from Public Enemy's prior era, in which Hank Shocklee fully controlled the reins of production and masterminded the intricate combination of elements that had constituted the Bomb Squad sound. In the end, the album lacked all the pieces.

And the recent Griff controversy didn't help the situation. In the year that had passed, the outcry had died down a bit, but we can be sure that Public Enemy's critics were prepared to resume the attack if necessary. The release of the

"Terrordome" single, in the words of one reviewer, "catapulted Public Enemy into the unenviable position of being the most scrutinized group in pop music," and critics would go over *Fear*'s lyrics with a fine-toothed comb (Watrous). But the group's detractors only needed to look as far as the lead single, and "Welcome to the Terrordome," which was written as a response to the Griff controversy, soon generated a controversy of its own. In a discussion of the attacks leveled against the group for anti-Semitism, Chuck D concludes with the line, "Still they got me like Jesus." To speak of crucifixion at the hands of the press is of course commonplace—and according to Chuck, this is all that was meant—but when the attacks are coming from Jewish organizations, doing so inevitably runs the risk of echoing the historical claim of Jewish complicity in the crucifixion.

There is little doubt that the rift introduced by the Griff controversy was a determining factor in the effective dissolution of the Bomb Squad and the consequent decline of Public Enemy as a significant force in rap. Hank Shocklee, putting a positive spin on the situation, nevertheless insists that the group had accomplished its purpose and reached its limits as a creative project. This belief was additionally influenced by the impending deal by which the remaining members of the Bomb Squad would be offered a deal by MCA to found SOUL Records. The original production team was to have consisted of Hank and Keith Shocklee, Bill Stephney, Chuck D, and Eric Sadler, but with tangible disappointment, Eric recalls the moment at which Hank essentially dismissed him and Keith, moving forward with Stephney and Chuck.

Hank's justification for this gesture lies in the claim that Public Enemy had gotten too big too quickly and that it would self-destruct if he didn't intervene to preemptively dissolve the group. Regardless of whether or not this was the case, Keith and Eric decided to leave the picture for their own reasons, and after Chuck backed out to take the heat off the SOUL deal in the aftermath and reignition of the Griff controversy, the Bomb Squad era had been definitively ended. While Public Enemy has continued to make music since then, and indeed up to the present day, it had already lost one of its central ingredients by 1990. After that point, the group would require a total renovation, a task all the more difficult in the face of a hostile media keen on highlighting the slightest political impropriety or artistic shortcoming.

PUBLIC ENEMY STRIKES BLACK?

This renovation would go on display in late 1991, with the release of *Apocalypse '91 ... The Enemy Strikes Black*. The response from critics was positive but muted, with many sensing in the music the growing dissension within the group as well as a certain repetitiveness of political themes. As a result of the breakdown of the Bomb Squad, the latter was elevated on *Apocalypse* to executive production status, whereas in practice the beats were made by Bomb Squad disciples Gary G-Wiz and the Imperial Grand Ministers of Funk. What made a bigger difference, according to Hank Shocklee, was Chuck D's occupation of the position of sonic mastermind: Chuck, according to Hank, is not a musical genius, and his control over the process since *Apocalypse* has led to a lower quality sound on the more recent records.

Politically, however, some consider *Apocalypse* to be more on point than ever, having moved beyond the "integrationist sentimentalizing" of *Fear of a Black Planet* (Henderson 328). While the sound had changed, tracks like "Can't Truss It" and "Shut Em Down" still bring the message, and both are backed up by black-and-white videos that compare capitalism to slavery, celebrate past resistance, and exhort future rebellion. The album also contains the classic "By the Time I Get to Arizona," an attack on Evan Mecham, the former governor of that state, who had created a political furor by refusing to observe Martin Luther King Day in Arizona. The P.E. video depicts armed S1Ws storming the governor's offices and closes with Mecham's car exploding.

Despite this, from the perspective of public reception *Apocalypse* marked the beginning of a slow decline. It is always a risky endeavor to privilege one moment of an artist's work over another, but it is equally undeniable that Public Enemy's status as icons of hip hop derives almost exclusively from their first four albums. After the disintegration of the Bomb Squad, the group would release a series of albums whose critical reception went from lukewarm to downright awful, but not always justifiably so. The 1992 album *Greatest Misses* got the new production team to rework and remix old classics, with mixed results, as well as to lay down a few tracks in the new, more laid-back mold, but was almost universally snubbed by critics and the public.

The group mounted a comeback on the 1994 *Muse Sick-N-Hour Mess Age*, a savage attack on the nascent gangsta era that, despite some excellent tracks, was uniformly dismissed by music critics, notoriously receiving two stars in *Rolling Stone*. Many have sought to explain the album's reception more through the context that received it than its inherent qualities: The gangsta era was in full swing, having yet to be turned toward more positive ends and fused with political projects. Two years later, we would see Chuck D's solo effort, *Autobiography of Mistachuck*, an album that moved as far as one might think possible away from the classic Bomb Squad sound. More soulful and funk-oriented—musician Eric Sadler returned to the production team, this time without the overbearing gaze of Hank Shocklee, and Isaac Hayes was invited to do a guest spot—the album was conceived as a direct answer to those critics who dismissed his relevance in the new era of rap. Most ignored the album, and even sympathetic reviews observed a certain repetitiveness in Chuck's subject matter.

In the late nineties, Spike Lee once again enlisted Public Enemy to back up a film, this time the basketball drama whose name the album would share: *He Got Game*. Released in 1998, the album would be greeted by a significantly more hospitable atmosphere than had been the case just a few years earlier. The album also constituted something of a reunion, seeing the return of Griff (after solo work), Terminator X (after a serious motorcycle accident), Flav (after a number of run-ins with the law), and the original Bomb Squad lineup, although given the laid-back melodies and clean beats, one ultimately wonders who was playing the perennially crucial role of production mastermind. Critical reviews showed a marked recovery (*Rolling Stone*'s assessment recovered to a still-modest three and a half stars), and the group scored a minor hit with the Buffalo Springfield-inspired title cut.

He Got Game would be the group's last album on Def Jam. After posting the industrial remix album *Bring the Noise 2000* on the group's Web site for free downloading in support of MP3 technology, Chuck D was forced by distributor Polygram to remove it. On December 9, 1998, he posted the following on his "Terrordome" column on the Public Enemy Web site: "The execs, lawyers and accountants who lately have made most of the money in the music biz, are now running scared from the technology that evens out the creative field and makes artists harder to pimp." His final word was less than conciliatory, expressing a deep-seated grudge against the entire industry: "Let 'em all die.... I'm glad to be a contributor to the bomb." The group also posted an MP3 version of "Swindler's Lust," an antiexploitation and antiindustry rant whose title some have interpreted as anti-Semitic. Not surprisingly, Public Enemy would be released from their Def Jam contract shortly thereafter.

From then on, Chuck would be a spokesperson for file-sharing technology, and their next album, *There's a Poison Goin On,* would be released entirely as MP3s. Public Enemy was out of the industry, but whether this was a blessing or a curse is hard to say. After a couple of remix and compilation albums, Public Enemy put out two more full albums. In 2005 we saw the release of *New Whirl Odor*, with DJ Lord replacing Terminator X, and while the sound was strong, few were able to look past Flavor Flav's appearances on a series of reality shows, from *The Surreal Life* to *Strange Love* and finally *Flavor of Love.* Unfortunately, Chuck D's own forays into the public arena as a television and radio host on Air America have been all but entirely eclipsed by his partner's exploits (see sidebar: Grills).

In 2005, Chuck D ran into a self-described disciple of his, revolutionary Bay Area rapper Paris (most famous for his 1992 "Bush Killa"), who offered to collaborate on the next P.E. album. To Paris's surprise, Chuck asked him to write and produce the entire album, and to release it on his own Guerrilla Funk Records. The album, released under the title *Rebirth of a Nation* in early 2006, is an attempt to escape the rut that Public Enemy had fallen into, and it does so by simultaneously looking forward and backward. Explicitly framed as a throwback album, *Rebirth* contains a multitude of references and samples that draw the listener back to the classic Public Enemy of *Nation of Millions*. But the album also propels the group forward into the post-gangsta

Grills

George Ciccariello-Maher

Flavor Flav popularized wearing gold, silver, platinum, or diamond-studded teeth, now called grills, as part of his hip hop attire. Flav once remarked that he would never wear platinum teeth, but this didn't prevent his sporting of gold teeth from catching on. Since the late 1990s, grills have exploded in popularity, largely driven by their prominence among Dirty South, Crunk, and Houston's Chopped and Screwed rappers, and are known variously as fronts, plates, golds, and pullouts. As a result of their popularity and expense, grills have become one of rap's premiere status symbols.

Specifically, grill artists-turned-rappers such as Houston's Paul Wall have consistently made grills a central reference point in their lyrics. Appearing on Kanye West's 2006 single "Drive Slow," Wall raps: "I open up my mouth and sunlight illuminates the dark." Moreover, in 2005 Wall collaborated with Nelly, Jermaine Dupri, Ali, and Gipp (who claims he orignated the style) on "Let Me See Your Grill," a track dedicated entirely to flashy mouthwear. In music videos, these artists flashed their grills for the camera. Paul Wall's Web site devoted to his Houston-based grill-fitting business features a number of grills that can be ordered, ranging in price from $65 to $1,800 per row.

The mainstream popularity of grills is evident from the fact that artists as diverse as Kelis, Hulk Hogan's daughter Brooke, Korn, and Marilyn Manson have appeared in public with the flashy mouthwear. Recently, there has been a certain degree of backlash against the popularity of grills, as they were singled out to be banned by some Texas school districts in 2006, giving rise to claims that such a specific targeting of grills was a racist gesture.

---

era—no doubt largely due to Paris's influence—through collaborations with former NWA member MC Ren as well as post-gangsta revolutionaries dead prez, Kam, and Immortal Technique. After a few aborted Public Enemy comeback attempts, Paris's influence may help kickstart a proper "rebirth."

REVOLUTIONARY, NOT GANGSTA

The decline of Public Enemy, while sparked largely by the implosion of the Bomb Squad, reflects a broader shift that had been taking place in rap ever since the rise of gangsta rap in the early 1990s. Public Enemy essentially created political hip hop and pioneered a revolutionary vision, and as that vision was increasingly interrogated by later artists, Chuck D would turn his attention to attacking those he saw as responsible for undermining Public Enemy's political project and harming the black community in the process.

We will conclude by discussing the broader legacy of Public Enemy's politicized rap and some critiques leveled against it.

In the early 1990s, Public Enemy's nascent genre of political hip hop came to be steadily undermined by a new wave of rap: "By 1991 the rules and rulers of hip-hop were changing, with biting black nationalist commentary and an Afrocentric worldview giving way to sexual hedonism and the glamorization of violence. Public Enemy failed to react" (Dyson 167). But they did react, especially on the 1994 *Muse Sick*, where Chuck D devotes significant lyrical venom to attacking the rise of gangsta, especially on tracks like "Give It Up" and "So Whatcha Gone Do Now?" Dyson rightly worries that such interventions reflect a Public Enemy that refused to change and come to terms with its own abandonment by hip hop fans (see sidebar: Stop the Violence).

More worrying still are the strange bedfellows that accompany a critique of the gangsta genre, including "reactionary elements of the black bourgeoisie and white conservatives" (Dyson 170). While Chuck D explicitly denies any common cause with the white conservatives who demonized rap music during the 1990s, the charge of sympathy with conservative blacks may be harder to shake. This is because Chuck D goes on the offensive against those who would criticize Reverend Calvin Butts or C. Delores Tucker, who he argues were only targeting the companies distributing rap, not the artists themselves. But in their quest, Butts and Tucker teamed up with precisely those white archconservatives—like William Bennett and Bob Dole—that Chuck D would

Stop the Violence
Mickey Hess

Gangsta rap was born out of the street gang culture of the 1980s. Artists like Schoolly D, the Geto Boys, N.W.A., and Ice-T brought gang imagery into their music through stories of gunplay, drug dealing, and avoiding the police. The 1989 Stop the Violence movement and the 1990 single "We're All in the Same Gang" were efforts to use hip hop music to promote an antigang message. The Stop the Violence All Stars consisted of rap artists KRS-One, Just-Ice, Doug E. Fresh, Kool Moe Dee, MC Lyte, Public Enemy, Heavy D, and Stetsasonic, who collaborated to produce a track, "Self Destruction," that urged young black men to stop turning their guns on each other. Similarly, King Tee, J.J. Fad, Michel'le, Body and Soul, Above the Law, N.W.A., Tone Loc, Digital Underground, Young MC, Oaktown's 3-5-7, and MC Hammer collaborated to form the West Coast Rap All-Stars and to record the song, "We're All in the Same Gang," which promoted a message of unity in the face of recent gang standoffs, particularly between LA factions of the Bloods and Crips. These songs raised awareness of gang issues but of course did not end gang violence. N.W.A., in fact, continued to tell stories of gang violence in their songs, even after recording this antigang message.

attack, and their method was nothing less than a Senate subcommittee, a reactionary arm of the U.S. government. In the end, Chuck even went so far as to blame the victim by claiming that it is gangsta rappers themselves who are responsible for the censoring and limiting of rap.

What Public Enemy, and Chuck D more specifically, seemed to neglect was the crucial reality reflected in the rise of gangsta, a reality that exceeded the financial incentives recognized by Chuck. Rather, one could interpret the rise of gangsta rap as in part a critique of the shortcomings of the early political rap epitomized by Public Enemy. "L.A. gangsta rappers are frequent critics of black nationalists," Robin D. G. Kelley argues, and the same could be said of "ghettocentric" culture more generally, a culture wary of all abstract political statements that run the risk of "obscur[ing] the daily battles poor black folk have to wage in contemporary America" (212). Gangsta rap seeks to make up for this deficiency by providing a series of perspectival first-person narratives that illustrate the reality of life as a young black male in a country where they can only be viewed—as Public Enemy's name reflects—as a threat.

Perhaps more damningly, Errol Henderson questions even Public Enemy's revolutionary credentials. He highlights the potential, especially in early P.E., to foster little more than a "myth of action" or "politics as theater" that "promotes proclamation over demonstration," and which was revealed when Chuck caved to public and industry pressure during the course of the Griff controversy (328-329). Moreover, Henderson argues that it was more organizationally rooted cultural nationalists like X-Clan that pushed Public Enemy to move beyond the lukewarm politics of *Fear of a Black Planet* and on to a more radical nationalism on *Apocalypse*.

P.E.'S IMPACT AND LEGACY IN THE POST-GANGSTA ERA

Michael Eric Dyson argues that "Public Enemy is, hands down, the most influential and important group in the history of hip-hop" (165). However, given the fact that Public Enemy pioneered early political rap and given the group's close ties to the genre, we might not be so content with a sanguine account of the group's massive influence. This is because the decline of Public Enemy, their earlier influence notwithstanding, tells us a great deal about the potential and limitations of political rap more generally, or at least those forms of political rap that fit the aesthetic and didactic molds crafted by this seminal group.

In terms of influence on a younger generation of rappers—political or otherwise—it would be difficult to overstate the importance of Public Enemy, and this legacy spans the political, aesthetic, and technological realms. By pioneering and essentially inventing a style of straightforwardly political hip hop, P.E. were a direct influence and a necessary precondition for much of what followed: Few political rappers who followed could deny that their work had been influenced by Public Enemy. Beyond the purely political, moreover, Public Enemy's explicit disciples span from the early gangsta rap of N.W.A. to the more mainstream Busta Rhymes, the underground stylings of El-P and the Def Jux label, and even slam poet Saul Williams.

Aesthetically, the list is at least as long, if not longer. The erratic layering and sampling of the Bomb Squad would be deemed postmodern by critics and would inspire a generation of rappers. Moreover, Public Enemy's very sonic compositions would make their sound more available and accessible to artists outside the genre, and this would appear explicitly in the 1991 collaboration with thrash metal band Anthrax on a remix of "Bring the Noise" (see sidebar: Hip Hop and Metal). This collaboration would almost single-handedly spawn the "rap metal" genre, with which Chuck D would later reconnect on a 1996

Hip Hop and Metal
Robin Chamberlain

The relationship between metal and hip hop has always been tenuous, as evidenced by the multiplicity of names that have been used to describe music that includes elements of both genres. These labels include rapcore, rap-rock, rap-metal, and nu metal (a term that includes, but is not limited to, metal with hip hop elements). Rather than being defined by a distinctive sound, the many intersections of hip hop and metal are best characterized by their openness to fusion and a willingness to address contentious political issues. In both sound and content, rap-metal tends to be aggressive and confrontational. This is only one of the reasons that rap-metal is a genre viewed with suspicion by many fans and artists of both metal and hip hop. Another key reason for the uneasy relationship between rap-metal and hip hop is that rap-metal has been, and continues to be, largely the domain of white musicians. Despite these tensions, rapcore's continued success since its genesis in the mid-1980s anchors it within the history and development of hip hop.

The forefathers of rapcore include such popular groups as Beastie Boys, Run-DMC, and Public Enemy, all of whom used elements of rock and metal in their music. The Beastie Boys featured Slayer guitarist Kerry King on "No Sleep 'til Brooklyn" and Public Enemy collaborated with the thrash group Anthrax to record a metal version of their hit "Bring the Noise." The first group that can clearly be defined as rapcore, though, is Urban Dance Squad, a little-known Dutch group whose contributions to musical history include inspiring the hugely popular band Rage Against the Machine. The metal band Body Count, fronted by rapper Ice-T, managed to bring together fans of both rap and rock, and are remembered for the controversy they created with their song "Cop Killer." Despite, or perhaps because of, the conflicted relationship between metal and hip hop, not to mention between hip hop and rapcore or metal and rapcore, these genres continue to be mutually influential, both intentionally and through attempts to both define and transcend generic categories.

collaboration with Rage Against the Machine—yet another group claiming to have been influenced by P.E.—which covered "Black Steel in the Hour of Chaos."

Technologically, Public Enemy was always at the forefront of developments, even to the detriment of their careers. From sampling technology to a fidelity to MP3 technology that ended their distribution deal, their radicalism was as much technological as it was political. Currently, Public Enemy composes their work electronically and transmits it back and forth by e-mail, and Hank Shocklee is engaged in projects that aim to push the limits of electronic music.

However, to fully grasp the importance of Public Enemy, we must situate their influence within the broader history of hip hop. While all attempts to periodize are necessarily problematic, it is useful to consider the development of political rap in terms of three historical stages, as suggested earlier. The first wave is represented by rappers like Public Enemy and KRS-One, who from the late 1980s explicitly endorsed radical political transformation through programmatic statements in the form of music, thereby contributing massively to the political development of the post–civil rights generation.

However, this early political rap would come under severe critique as early as 1990, with the expanding popularity of gangsta rap, a first-person narrative of the effects of Reaganomics, the crack cocaine epidemic, and the resulting militarization of black communities. Gangsta was critical of the preachy nature of early political rap as well as its tendency to emphasize foreign politics at the expense of conditions in domestic ghettos. Such neglect would often emerge from the black middle classes and often contained idealist arguments such as the so-called culture of poverty, which ignore structural economic conditions and racism, focusing instead on criticizing and criminalizing the behavior of lower-class blacks.

Post-gangsta political hip hop (see sidebar: Post-Gangsta Political Hip Hop) is a dialectical synthesis of the radical political impetus of early rap and the more materialistic and ghettocentric focus of gangsta, allowing for a more

---

Post-Gangsta Political Hip Hop
George Ciccariello-Maher

While one can find traces of the synthesis in earlier artists (and even on Boogie Down Productions' *Criminal Minded*, prior to KRS-One's turn to more explicitly political rap), the third stage in the political development of hip hop emerged fully with the increasing popularity of rappers like Black Star's Mos Def and Talib Kweli, Nas, the Roots, Paris, and Common in the late 1990s. However, the highest development of post-gangsta political rap can be found in groups like the Coup and dead prez and is most explicitly enunciated by the latter.

Dead prez expresses the character of post-gangsta political rap best when, on the track "I'm a African" from their first album, *Let's Get Free* (2000), they claim that their music creates a space between the street-gang-themed gangsta rap of N.W.A. and the black militant politics of of Public Enemy. This song continues with an explicit endorsement of the gangsta critique of preachy rap, in which they transform Stetsasonic's classic Afrocentric anthem "Free South Africa," which in its original version falls into a culture of poverty argument by claiming that Africans and African-Americans both need help: "them with their government, us with mentality." To correct this error, dead prez replaces the original list of African nations with diasporic communities: "Puerto Rico, Haiti, and J.A., New York and Cali, F.L.A."

This post-gangsta mentality is deepened throughout the course of the two mixtapes released in 2002 and 2003 under the moniker "dpz," which prepared the ground for the album whose title can be interpreted as best summing up the post-gangsta synthesis: *Revolutionary but Gangsta* (2004). On these mixtapes, revolutionary black nationalism is fused with gangsta culture: The acronym RBG is derived from the colors of the Garveyite flag and O.G. (original gangsta) becomes "original Garvey." Moreover, gangstas are equated with freedom fighters, complementing a redefinition of gangs themselves: "dedicated, ready to bleed for what they believe." This post-gangsta fusion appears most clearly on a collaboration with the Coup titled "Get Up," in which warring street gangs such as the Crips and Bloods are urged to unite against the true enemy, the government: "it's one team: get up and let's ride." This is the political program of the post-gangsta era.

sophisticated approach to black politics that avoids the twin dangers of the preachy "culture of poverty" argument and the inward-oriented nihilism of an uncritically gangsta approach. It is from this recognition that we can understand the historical importance of Public Enemy, as well as those who have charted a political course beyond the parameters of the early political rap that Public Enemy invented. Even for their radical critics in the black community, Public Enemy still represents the fundamental starting point and reference point for any attempt to construct a revolutionary hip hop. That is to say, even in the negative gesture of critique Public Enemy exerts a positive influence on the further development of rap.

There is a certain degree to which the critiques of Public Enemy voiced earlier come together: The nationalist critique of a merely "mythical" action and the gangsta critique of the mythologization of some nationalisms are but the flip side of the same coin. Rappers of the post-gangsta era are forced to tread the political line that runs between the two by recognizing the crucial observations provided by gangsta rap while tethering these observations to a resolutely political project. If we have reason for optimism about the future of Public Enemy—the continuing impact of their icon status—it lies with their recent collaborations with some central members of the post-gangsta generation of political rappers. Public Enemy forges into the post-gangsta era on *Rebirth of a Nation*, maintaining their politics but also building the necessary ties to a younger generation of artists to whom the recasting of the post-gangsta political genre will fall.

See also: Beastie Boys, Run-DMC, Ice Cube

WORKS CITED

Allen, Joe. "Academic Archive, Volume XII: The Soul of Hank Shocklee." *Wax Poetics* 17 (June–July 2006): 70-72.

Chang, Jeff. *Can't Stop Won't Stop: A History of the Hip-Hop Generation*. New York: St. Martin's Press, 2005. 223-297.

Chuck D, with Yusuf Jah. *Fight the Power: Rap, Race, and Reality*. New York: Delacorte Press, 1997.

Dyson, Michael Eric. *Between God and Gangsta Rap: Bearing Witness to Black Culture*. New York: Oxford University Press, 1996. 157-186.

Henderson, Errol A. "Black Nationalism and Rap Music." *Journal of Black Studies* 26.3 (1996): 308-339.

Kelley, Robin D. G. "Kickin' Reality, Kickin' Ballistics: 'Gangsta Rap' and Postindustrial Los Angeles." In *Race Rebels: Culture, Politics, and the Black Working Class*. New York: Free Press, 1996. 183-228.

Lapeyre, Jason. "Louder than a Bomb: An Oral History of the Bomb Squad, Public Enemy's Production Machine." *Wax Poetics* 17 (June–July 2006): 118-136.

Rose, Tricia. *Black Noise: Rap Music and Black Culture in Contemporary America*. Hanover, NH: Wesleyan University Press, 1994. 99-145.

Warrell, Laura K. "Fight the Power." *Salon.com*. 3 June 2002.

Watrous, Peter. "Public Enemy Makes Waves—and Compelling Music." *New York Times*. 20 April 1990.

Welte, Jim. "Hank Shocklee: Louder Than a Bomb." *Mp3.com*. 20 April 2006. http://www.mp3.com/news/stories/4195.html.

FURTHER RESOURCES

McLeod, Kembrew. "How Copyright Law Changed Hip Hop: An Interview with Public Enemy's Chuck D and Hank Shocklee." *Stay Free! Magazine* 20 (November 2002). http://www.stayfreemagazine.org/archives/20/public_enemy.html.

Public Enemy. *It Takes a Nation: The First London Invasion Tour, 1987*. [DVD] Music Video Distributors, 2005.

Public Enemy Web site. http://www.publicenemy.com.

Serwer, Jesse. "Bomb the Suburbs: Adelphi University Radio Station WBAU Put Strong Island on the Map." *Wax Poetics* 17 (June–July 2006). 61-66.

Courtesy of Photofest.

Salt-N-Pepa

Athena Elafros

In a business in which music careers are made and broken overnight, the fourteen-year career of the group Salt-N-Pepa is worth analyzing and celebrating. From their humble beginnings as telephone representatives for Sears, through surviving two different DJs, several record companies, a difficult separation from their longtime manager, and five albums, the trio of Cheryl "Salt" Renee James, Sandra "Pepa" Denton, and Deidre "DJ Spinderella" Roper have proven that they are indeed strong and independent women.

And their careers as members of Salt-N-Pepa are ones that many female artists and fans can relate to, as the group faced many challenges being one of the first all-female rap crews (see sidebar: Women and DJ Culture).

The success and longevity of Salt-N-Pepa proved that rap music was not solely for men, since these women, along with many other women before and after them, were responsible for carving out a space for female MCs and DJs in the rap business. In fact, they achieved their success by making rap music

---

Women and DJ Culture
Athena Elafros

DJing is an artistic form that played a central role in the formation of the hip hop movement, a youth movement in the South Bronx that began around the mid-1970s and consisted of four key elements: break dancers, MCs (who would eventually become what we know as rappers), DJs, and graffiti artists. Rappers and rap music are the most successful of the art forms to emerge from hip hop culture. Although there are very few female DJs with record contracts in rap music, there is a very strong tradition of female DJing in the hip hop movement. Long before Deidre "Spinderella" Roper was bringing us such classics as "Spinderella's Not a Fella (But a Girl DJ)," there were pioneers in the movement by the names of DJ Jazzy Joyce and DJ Wanda Dee.

Originally from the Bronx, DJ Jazzy Joyce began deejaying in 1981 when she was only eleven years old. By 1986 she was the DJ on Sweet Tee's seminal rap, "It's My Beat." Currently, Joyce and DJ Cocoa Chanelle broadcast a radio show called *Ladies Night* on New York City's HOT 97 FM.

DJ Wanda Dee began to DJ as a member of Afrika Bambaataa's Zulu Nation. She was the first female DJ to be featured in the 1984 Harry Belafonte movie *Beat Street*, which resulted in a European tour and a record deal. Eventually Wanda Dee became a recording and songwriting artist, and she has cowritten numerous multiplatinum hits. She was also one of the first solo female rap artists to release two consecutive platinum singles—"The Goddess" and "To the Bone" in 1989. Her career continued to flourish as she became, and still is, the lead vocalist of the multiplatinum British techno group called the KLF.

Despite this long tradition, female DJs are still outnumbered by male DJs. This may be because female DJs are paid much less than male DJs, they are more severely critiqued in their musical choices, and they do not become producers as easily as some of their male counterparts. Yet the numbers of female DJs seem to be increasing, since the aforementioned trailblazers have been followed by a slew of successful female DJs such as DJ Belinda Becker (of Buddha Bar fame), Brooklyn veteran Cocoa Chanelle, Japanese-born DJ Kaori Ueta (whose manager is Funkmaster Flex), and Manhattan-based DJ Beverly Bond, among others. As the number of female DJs continues to rise, these DJs can continue to challenge and change the male-dominated arena of DJing and production from the inside.

from a woman's point of view—a point of view with appeal to a population that had been craving such an outlet. By focusing on messages of female self-empowerment and positive female sexuality, and placing women's issues in the forefront, the group garnered a strong female following. Even when Salt-N-Pepa were not in full creative control of their musical careers, due to the strict command of their manager, Ernst "Hurby Luv Bug" Azor, they could still be heralded as an example of women who succeeded in the rap industry.

Furthermore, with their catchy R&B-inspired rap songs, many of their albums reached gold and platinum status, thereby expanding the audience of rap music and crossing over into the pop music charts. Thus, the members of Salt-N-Pepa were female pioneers in the rap business, and they should be remembered as one of the first thriving all-female rap acts to succeed in the business. Through their immense popularity they were able to challenge racist assumptions about rap music in general, and as one of the first accomplished all-female rap groups, they were also able to challenge sexist assumptions about female rappers in particular. Most important, building upon the inroads made by Roxanne Shanté and others, they carved a space for female MCs in rap music, and they promoted woman-centered messages in their music, such as their emphases on the themes of female sexuality and independence.

FEMALE RAPPERS IN THE 1980S

By the time Salt-N-Pepa entered the rap game in 1985, it had been six years since Sugarhill Gang released the worldwide hit "Rapper's Delight." Yet, despite the success of rap music on independent labels such as Sugar Hill Records, Tommy Boy Records, Def Jam, and the like, major labels were still hesitant to offer record deals to rap artists. This was because of the commonly held belief at the time that rap music was a passing fad. Similar to the fleeting success of hypercolor shirts, snap bracelets, and other novelties of the eighties, rap music had been unfairly pegged as a musical form that lacked any staying power. The situation was even more difficult for a female MC, let alone an all-female rap crew like Salt-N-Pepa.

The female rap artists of the time were extremely aware of how hard it was to enter the music industry. They had to challenge not only the biases against racially oppressed groups and working-class art but also the male biases and double standards that were applied exclusively to female artists (Guevara 80). One of the most prominent female MCs of the time, Roxanne Shanté, noted in an interview in 1985 with Nancy Guevara that "men say that women are only good for cooking, cleaning and making babies. That's changing." And she was adamant that her music was about moving women "out of the kitchen and into the streets" (Guevara 57). In other words, Roxanne Shanté views rap music as a vehicle through which women are moving out of the private sphere and into the public realm.

Salt-N-Pepa was one of the first all-female rap acts to use rap music as a way to gain presence in the public sphere. They were one of the first rap acts that provided black women with a voice in the rap industry. This is one of the key reasons why Salt-N-Pepa hold a prominent place in rap music, since they were one of the first successful all-female rap groups, and they were one of the first groups to cross over into the mainstream music industry. Thus, the success of Salt-N-Pepa not only confirmed that rap music was an art form and indeed a legitimate variety of music, thereby challenging racist assumptions about rap artists, they also proved that female rappers were just as successful, if not more successful than male rappers, thereby challenging sexist assumptions about female rap artists.

In accomplishing these tasks, Salt-N-Pepa was one of the first female rap groups to bring women's issues to the forefront in rap music. They challenged the male hegemony of rap music by participating and succeeding in what was increasingly being perceived as a masculine music genre. As is often the case, perception and reality may conflict. For although rap music was increasingly being viewed as being synonymous with black masculinity, numerous women were involved in the early years of rap music.

For example, between 1978 and 1986, over sixty records were released that featured female MCs and DJs, as well as the first female human beatbox on wax by the name of K Love (Veran, "Women on Wax," 16-18). Thus, the success of Salt-N-Pepa was a result of numerous female rappers who came before them, whose stories play an important role in the formative herstory of hip hop. Groups such as the Mercedes Ladies, the first all-female MC and DJ crew who formed in 1977, and West Philadelphia's Lady B, who signed a record deal with T.E.C. Records and released "To the Beat Y'all" in 1980, and South Carolina's Sequence, a female singing and rapping trio that consisted of Blondie, Cheryl the Pearl, and Angie B. (now known as Angie Stone), who laid some of the groundwork necessary for more women to enter the rap music industry. As already noted, the influence of Roxanne Shanté cannot be underestimated, since Salt-N-Pepa's entry into the music business was a result of an answer rap directed at Doug E. Fresh and Slick Rick's "The Show." The answer record, pioneered by Roxanne Shanté in 1984, is still a popular means by which women rappers are able to gain entry into the realm of rap music. Los Angeles native Yolanda Whitaker, also known as Yo-Yo, a protégé of Ice Cube, entered the rap scene as part of a choreographed answer rap, like Roxanne Shanté and Salt-N-Pepa had before her, on a track from Ice Cube's 1990 release, *AmeriKKKa's Most Wanted*. The song was titled "It's a Man's World" and her response to this song was responsible for launching her music career. N.W.A. was often criticized for its depictions of women in lyrics, but Ice Cube was not the only former N.W.A. member to bring female rappers into the scene. In fact, it was Eazy-E and his Ruthless Records label that introduced J.J. Fad, a female rap trio consisting of three girls from Compton by the names of MCJ.B., Baby-D, and Sassy C. With Dr. Dre producing the album, this group was the first female rap ensemble to sell a million records through their 1988 platinum album, *Supersonic*.

It is important to discuss these female rap pioneers, since so many of their accomplishments are often omitted from the history of hip hop. Despite the evidence of women playing an active role in the formative years of the movement, much of the writing on rap music has a tendency to focus solely on the roles of male rappers. Therefore, focusing on the importance of Salt-N-Pepa as one of the first all-female rap crews and one of the first rap acts to cross over into the mainstream, we are able to understand how they paved the way for other female rap artists, and rap music in general, to gain greater acceptance on the pop charts. Since their music was fun and danceable yet also conscious of women's issues, the trio connected with both male and female audiences alike by providing just the right mix of sex appeal with a critical edge, and they specifically connected with their female audience by focusing on issues that mattered to women by providing a female point of view through their lyrics. From self-empowerment to sexuality and feminist critique on the one hand and having fun, dancing, and partying on the other, the music of Salt-N-Pepa had something to offer to everyone.

THE EARLY YEARS (1985–1986)

The members of Salt-N-Pepa include Cheryl "Salt" Renee James, Sandra "Pepa" Denton, and Deidre "DJ Spinderella" Roper (who replaced Salt-N-Pepa's original DJ, Pamela Latoya Greene, sometimes called "The Original Spinderella"). Salt-N-Pepa come from the Queens and Brooklyn boroughs of New York City. Cheryl grew up in Queens with her parents, elder brother, and younger sister. Her childhood was the most difficult of the group, with her father drinking and her brother eventually being sentenced to a juvenile facility. Sandi also grew up in Queens in a middle-class nuclear family consisting of seven sisters and one brother. Born in Jamaica, her fairly affluent West Indian family moved to Queens while she was a child. Her family was well-educated—one of her sisters is now a lawyer, another sibling is a geologist, and a few of the others own businesses. Deidre, the last member to join the group, grew up in Brooklyn as part of a family of five sisters and brothers. All the members of her family were musical, and by the age of eight she was a dancer in the East New York Theatrical Workshop. A key influence in her musical career was her father, who, during the disco era, had painted their living room black and red and had equipped it with a turntable and lighted ball.

Cheryl and Sandi met at Queensborough Community College while taking classes in nursing. The two were the unlikeliest of friends, with Cheryl being very reserved and introverted and Sandi being very loud and extroverted. It was Cheryl who assisted Sandi in finding a part-time job at Sears' College

Point, New York, branch. The two friends were employed as Sears telephone service representatives, selling maintenance agreements for Kenmore appliances. It was there that Cheryl and Sandi met Ernst "Hurby Luv Bug" Azor (who would eventually become their manager and Cheryl's boyfriend). Ernst was also working as a part-time sales rep at Sears, and he convinced Cheryl and Sandi to help him with a school recording project he was working on, as he was a student in the Center for Media Arts in Manhattan. The end result was the 1985 recording of "The Show Stopper," which was an answer rap, also known as a response, to the Doug E. Fresh and Slick Rick song "The Show." It was perhaps the immense popularity of "The Show" that made it an excellent target for an answer rap and a great way to launch a career in the rap music business. Capitalizing on the immense success of another Queens native, Roxanne Shanté, and her 1984 answer rap "Roxanne's Revenge," Ernst saw "The Show Stopper" as an excellent opportunity for Salt-N-Pepa to successfully enter the rap scene. So, once the track was completed, he contacted his friend Marlon "Marley Marl" Williams.

Marley Marl had been the producer and engineer of Roxanne Shanté's first musical release, and Ernst convinced him to play Salt-N-Pepa's "The Show Stopper" for some people he knew at Pop Art Records. From there, the track was released as a record single and reached number 46 on the *Billboard* R&B singles chart. 1985 proved fruitful for numerous female MCs like Sparky D (one of the MCs who replied to Roxanne Shanté's answer rap against the rap group U.T.F.O.), who procured the first commercial endorsement for a rapper when she appeared in a Mountain Dew radio ad; K Love, who was the first female human beatbox to be recorded on wax; and Shaunie Dee, who became the first female rapper to take part in the 1985 New Music Seminar's MC Battle for World Supremacy against the infamous Kool Keith ("Hip-Hop Herstory" 170-171).

That same year, based on the success of "The Show Stopper," Cheryl, Sandi, and Ernst earned a contract with the independent label Next Plateau Records. During their early years, the group had not gone by the name of Salt-N-Pepa; rather, they called themselves Super Nature. It was only once they signed with Next Plateau Records that their name changed, as did the dynamics of the group. Next Plateau released Salt-N-Pepa's first album, *Hot, Cool & Vicious*, in 1986, and the album earned them a Grammy nomination.

HOT, COOL & VICIOUS

Hot, Cool & Vicious (1986) featured Salt-N-Pepa's successful single, "The Show Stopper," among other classic tracks. One of the seminal songs from this album is "Tramp," where Salt-N-Pepa flip the script, or turn the tables on their male counterparts by using the word *tramp* to describe aggressive men who hit on women in nightclubs. They resignify or change the meaning of *tramp*, which generally refers solely to loose or sexually promiscuous women, by using it against men. Thus they reclaim a derogatory word that is normally used against women by expanding its definition to include men. In essence, they offer a critique of the double standard for men and women in terms of sexuality. The group poses this question to their audience: Why are men allowed to sleep with whomever they choose, yet women are labeled as tramps for the same behavior? In order to remedy the situation for women, they stigmatize male promiscuity by defining promiscuous men as tramps, therefore undermining the degrading woman-as-tramp image (Rose 118). Many female rappers have since adopted this type of redefinition. For example, in Yo Yo's 1992 release, *Black Pearl*, she has a song called "Hoes" that resignifies the term *ho* so that it applies to men as well as women. Just as Salt-N-Pepa did with "Tramp," Yo Yo takes a term that is most often used against women and challenges the double standard of sexuality by expanding it to include men.

Salt-N-Pepa achieved some success with "Tramp" and other songs, but it was not until the release of a remix of "Push It" in 1988 that the group gained much notoriety. Originally recorded as a joke and the B side of "Tramp," this track launched their careers and was one of the first rap songs ever to receive a Grammy nomination. "Push It" differs greatly from "Tramp" in that it is possible to interpret the message of this song in more than one way. The first reading may suggest that unlike the pro-woman message of "Tramp," the lyrics of "Push It," which are few and far between, are not particularly emancipating. With the group asking men to pump "it" hard like the music that is playing, this song is a far cry from calling men tramps. It may be interpreted as merely reinforcing the all-too-familiar stereotype of women as sexual objects who exist only to pleasure men. But the song may also be seen as portraying women as the subjects of their own sexuality. They are not waiting for a man to make the first move—they are telling him to do so. However, to this day the trio contends that "Push It" is not about sex but about dancing and pushing it on the dance floor. Regardless of the exact meaning of the song, what is central in each interpretation is that it focuses specifically on the black female body with an emphasis on physicality and enjoyment.

Comparing and contrasting "The Show Stopper" and "Push It" exposes two of the recurrent issues in Salt-N-Pepa's music. Salt-N-Pepa's reaction to these issues offers a feminine correction to the masculine biases of rap music, provides an empowering message to all women about their bodies, and is one of the primary reasons why Salt-N-Pepa are rap icons (see sidebar: "Feminism in Rap Music"). The first recurring theme deals with male-centered ways of thinking, which are picked apart and criticized by Salt-N-Pepa when they challenge the double standards between men and women—not only in the rap music business but in society in general. The second recurring theme is black female sexuality, which at the time was not commonly considered as the

Feminism in Rap Music
Athena Elafros

The label *feminist* has proven to be a difficult type of self-identification for many black female rappers. As Tricia Rose notes, it is sometimes seen to apply to members of a white middle-class women's social movement, and as such, it is an identifier which many black women have a difficult time connecting with, and many black female rappers try to distance themselves from.

Intersections of race, gender, and class make it difficult for black female rappers to engage in cross-racial sisterhood, especially if that sisterhood exists at the expense of black women's racial identity (Rose 127). This is not to say that black female rappers do not critique and challenge the misogyny and sexist discourses of their male counterparts. As the work of Salt-N-Pepa, Queen Latifah, Yo Yo, MC Lyte, and others illustrates, a central aim of black female rappers is to challenge sexism within rap music and to provide a space for the voices of women rappers.

Some of the seminal songs from these early female rappers include Queen Latifah's "Ladies First," which offered an Afrocentric and pro-woman message critiquing sexism in the rap music industry; MC Lyte's "Paper Thin," which is a "scathing rap about male dishonesty/infidelity" (Rose 119); and Yo Yo's "The IBWC" (Intelligent Black Women's Coalition), in which she succinctly tells men that if they are not "with her" on the same footing and do not treat her with the respect that she deserves, then they are "behind her," since they are not her equal. What is central about all these songs is that sexism is being challenged in both the public realm (rap music industry) and the private sphere (relationships).

More recently, one of the most important and decisive attacks on misogyny in rap music has come from a female lyricist named Sarah Jones. Signifying on the seminal Black Arts Movement song, "The Revolution Will Not Be Televised" by Gil Scott Heron, Jones's rendition of this track has the chorus "Your revolution will not happen between these thighs." In this song, titled "Your Revolution," she acts as lyricist and DJ Vadim is the DJ, and she critiques Shaggy, LL Cool J, Foxy Brown, and many others whom she feels contribute to the proliferation of degrading images of black womanhood which hurt the self-image of many black women. It should be noted that by extending her critique of misogyny to a female artist (Foxy Brown), she is drawing attention to the fact that not all black female rappers challenge the sexist portrayals of black women, since some of them are deeply implicated in the production of such negative images. She is also critiquing the hypercommodified materialism of certain strains of rap music, while at the same time providing an alternative to this commodification.

Now, whether Queen Latifah, MC Lyte, Yo Yo, or Sarah Jones adopt or reject the label of feminist seems somewhat unimportant. What is very important, however, is that in their actions these women are providing a critique of misogyny from a woman's point of view.

Work Cited

Rose, Tricia. "Never Trust a Big Butt and a Smile." *Camera Obscura* 23 (1991): 109-131.

image of North American beauty among many Americans. In many of their songs, Salt-N-Pepa depict the black female body as beautiful—a message that reinforces a positive body image for all women that also challenges stereotypical and racist beauty ideals.

These two songs also touch upon the complicated and contested matter of the representation of female sexuality in rap music and the controversial terrain between self-empowerment and exploitation. One of the questions often raised about this issue is whether images of female sexuality empower women or exploit them. As we have already seen from the various interpretations of "Push It," this matter is much more complicated than a simple dichotomy of exploitation versus empowerment.

RISE TO STARDOM (1987–1991)

In May 1987, Ernst held auditions in his garage to find a new DJ because Salt-N-Pepa's original DJ, Pamela Latoya Greene, was leaving the group to get married. Thus Deidre "DJ Spinderella" Roper became the third member of Salt-N-Pepa, although Cheryl and Sandi had to convince Deidre's parents to allow her to become part of the group.

With Deidre in the new lineup, Salt-N-Pepa released a new album on Next Plateau Records in 1988 called *A Salt with a Deadly Pepa*. Although it did not do as well as their debut album, it nonetheless certified gold. In the liner notes are excerpts from a *Spin* magazine interview by Jessica Bendinger and Harry "The Hip Hop Activist and Media Assassin" Allen. In the interview Cheryl and Sandi recall the hard times they went through when they first started out, including all the shows they played in the middle of the night in school cafeterias in New York. With the success of their past album under their belts, the trio no longer had to worry about performing in such small venues, since they were now able to fill larger auditoriums. Yet these comments in their liner notes serve as a reminder of how far rap music had come from the start of the group's career only been three years previously, and the fact that Salt-N-Pepa was paving the way for female artists for years to come.

One of the key tracks from this album is Salt-N-Pepa's rap duet with the band E.U, "Shake Your Thang." Salt-N-Pepa offers a verbal display of black women's sexual resistance (Rose 124). This song serves as a confirmation and assertion that black female bodies and black female sexuality are beautiful. Salt-N-Pepa sing about the freedom of dancing and enjoying your body, and specifically of showing no shame in this enjoyment since it is your body and you are able to do with it as you please. In the song, they also specifically emphasize their butts—better known as "thangs"—which they can shake in whichever way they feel. This could be seen as a way of challenging the beauty bias that renders the black female body sexually unattractive (Rose 125). Once again, Salt-N-Pepa support a positive body image for black women while simultaneously expressing their own sexuality.

However, it is important to remember that in these early stages of their careers, Ernst was the group's manager and producer and he also exercised very strict control over both the sound and the image of the group. In terms of sound, Ernst produced most of the songs on the first few albums, although the trio claim that they provided many lyrics for earlier albums, for which they never received production credits. In terms of image, Ernst would dictate what the girls would wear and whom they would associate with, thus controlling most aspects of their lives. This was accomplished through his management company, Idol Makers, through which he oversaw the careers of Salt-N-Pepa and Kid 'N Play, among others.

Kid 'N Play was a hip hop duo consisting of Christopher "Kid" Reid and Christopher "Play" Martin, who had also met Ernst by working at Sears as sales representatives. Originally known as Fresh Force in 1985, they changed their name in 1987 and released the track "Last Night," which was a cheesy tale of an unfortunate double date. It was also around this time that they teamed up with Ernst, who would eventually release the duo's debut album, *2 Hype* (1988), which featured wholesome parent-friendly raps. As with Salt-N-Pepa, Ernst exercised a certain degree of creative control over the music and image of Kid 'N Play.

So what degree of control or agency did Salt-N-Pepa have over their creative product? More important, does the question of agency even matter? Does the message of empowerment and sexual resistance in the song "Shake Your Thang" change if Ernst was responsible for the lyrics, concept, and music video? Or is it more important to examine the ways in which audiences respond to the music, thus reducing the original intent of the artist to secondary importance?

To complicate matters further, what had also changed in this brief time span since the inception of the group was that Cheryl and Ernst had become lovers. This placed a great deal of strain on the group since Sandi felt that she was not able to be critical of Ernst. She also felt that Cheryl supported Ernst more than she supported Sandi. Cheryl and Ernst became one of rap music's first famous couples, and together they helped place rap music on the charts.

However, all was not as glorious as it seemed. Ernst was constantly cheating on Cheryl. For a long time it was not apparent, but eventually Cheryl came to realize what was happening. In an effort to stop the cheating, Cheryl proposed marriage to Ernst, who responded that he did not want to get married. After this turning point in the relationship, the couple had a series of breakups and reconciliations that led to a permanent split in 1989. The final album in which Ernst played a primary and controlling role was released in 1990, *Blacks' Magic*. This was also the last album to be released on Next Plateau Records.

The eventual departure of Ernst from the group would be significant, in that it would allow Salt-N-Pepa, or more specifically Cheryl, an opportunity to play an increased role in the creative process and production of their music. Also, the split with Ernst would also allow them to get better recording contracts, since much of the money they had made thus far was being pocketed by Ernst and his recording company.

BLACKS' MAGIC

Beginning in the late 1980s and continuing well into the early 1990s, a different strain of rap music emerged on the hip hop scene. It had gained steam around 1987 with the release of Public Enemy's *Yo! Bum Rush the Show* (Def Jam), which featured the influential track "Rightstarter (Message to a Black Man)." The cover of the album featured members of the group in black berets and black bomber jackets. They were a visual representation of the Black Panthers, and their song lyrics featured Nation of Islam teachings. Public Enemy's follow-up album in 1988, *It Takes a Nation of Millions to Hold Us Back* (Def Jam), was more politicized than their first album and even more influential in its scope.

Some very important female MCs also emerged during this period. One year prior to the release of *Blacks' Magic* in 1989, Queen Latifah had released her debut album, *All Hail the Queen* (Tommy Boy). In full military regalia and African headdress, Queen Latifah's image on her album cover was a physical incarnation of the symbol for Mother Africa. Her music was woman-centered and Afrocentric, and along with Public Enemy and other artists during this era, a specific strain of Afrocentric nationalism in hip hop began to rise. Given these developments, it is not surprising that *Blacks' Magic* had a more Afrocentric message. Although Salt-N-Pepa were not part of this new strain of hip hop, songs such as "Negro Wit' an Ego" show the influences of this strain of rap on their musical sound. Other than this apparent change in their image and sound, the release of *Blacks' Magic* marked another turning point in the career of the group, especially in terms of creative control of their music.

By 1990 the group was thriving, with *Blacks' Magic* attaining platinum and selling more than 1 million copies. The album was so successful that it stayed on the charts for two solid years. Yet, despite these successes, the trio were unhappy with the record deal they had made when they first started out.

Years before, the group had signed a deal with Next Plateau Records that had paid Idol Makers, Ernst's production company, a reported $5 million for production costs. This money was divided, with half going to Ernst and the other half going to the group to be divided three ways. For the trio, this was a very unfair distribution of the finances, since Salt-N-Pepa insist that they had written tracks on previous albums for which they had never received any monetary rewards. Some of these problems were addressed on *Blacks' Magic*. Cheryl received production credits for five of the fourteen tracks on the album, and three of those five tracks were produced solely by her. In addition, Deidre produced a track, and all of the members of the group contributed lyrics. The most successful track from the album was the Top 20 *Billboard* hit "Let's Talk About Sex," which skyrocketed their careers even further.

This song was significant because it was released during a time when the threat of HIV and AIDS were being broadcast on media networks across the country. The early 1990s was also a time of intensive education on the subject of sexually transmitted diseases and this song played a key role in educating young people about the dangers of unprotected sex. The song was so popular that it was eventually rewritten and rerecorded by the group as "Let's Talk About AIDS." Acts like T.L.C. followed in the footsteps of the successful trio by making explicit references to safe sex practices on their debut album released in 1992, *Ooooooooh... On the T.L.C. Tip* (LaFace Records). During this period in their careers, T.L.C. wore multicolored unwrapped condoms on their clothing in their music videos and onstage. In 1994 they recorded a song about drug use and AIDS called "Waterfalls" on their album *CrazySexyCool* (LaFace Records). Thus, Salt-N-Pepa were partially responsible in popularizing safe sex practices in popular music during the early 1990s, and they made talking about sex and sexually transmitted diseases such as AIDS socially acceptable.

Another seminal track from the *Blacks' Magic* album was "Expressions," written and produced solely by Cheryl, which also garnered the title of Top Rap Single of the year by *Billboard* magazine. Due to the immense success of Madonna's *Like a Prayer* (1989, Sire/Warner), which had been released one year prior, and a hit single from that album titled "Express Yourself," songs about female self-expression proved to be very popular and profitable. Whether or not the trio was taking advantage of this trend is debatable. What is certain is that this track uncovers a third theme in the music of Salt-N-Pepa: female independence and equality with men.

"Expressions" espouses female self-expression and its message is that women are just as capable as men of being in command of their lives. The song also makes it very clear that men do not have the right to tell women what to do, since women are able to be independent and in control of any situation. Given the struggle Salt-N-Pepa were going through in terms of the creative control of their music, there is a very important subtext in this song in relation to their own personal struggles over being in charge of their musical careers. For Cheryl, this struggle was even more personal, given that she and Ernst had recently ended their tumultuous relationship, and she was starting to remove herself from the control and abuse that relationship entailed.

THE END OF *BLACKS' MAGIC* (1993–1997)

After the release of *Blacks' Magic*, the process of separating from Ernst, finding another label, and making another record took roughly three years, but they eventually entered into a new distribution deal with London Records U.S. In the deal, their former label, Next Plateau Records, gave London Records Salt-N-Pepa's entire catalogue through a licensing agreement. It was also during this time that the trio renegotiated their contract with Ernst. Ernst originally owned 100 percent of the royalties received in Salt-N-Pepa's name, but his ownership was reduced to 50 percent. However, he was still entitled to one third of all the income that they made, including any royalties from new albums, regardless of whether he played a role in their creation. Unfortunately, conflicts over creative control between male managers and their female clients occur fairly regularly in the rap music industry (see sidebar: Female Rappers with Male Producers).

Despite the conflicts over creative control, *Very Necessary* (1993) proved to be the most successful of all their releases. The album was divided between Ernst on the one hand and Salt-N-Pepa on the other, with both sides ultimately creating hit tracks. In addition, the ladies of Salt-N-Pepa were responsible for the concept of the video for the hit song "Shoop." Instead of the usual scantily clad women, Salt-N-Pepa provided some eye candy for their female fans by shooting the video almost entirely with men.

Notwithstanding the immense success of *Very Necessary*, their final album, *Brand New* (1997), took several years to release due to the fact that

---

Female Rappers with Male Producers
Athena Elafros

From Roxanne Shanté and Marlon "Marley Marl" Williams to Salt-N-Pepa and Ernst "Hurby Luv Bug" Azor, to Yo Yo and Ice Cube, to Queen Latifah and Mark the 45 King, many female rappers have entered the rap game through ties to male producers who were already part of the scene.

Due to the overwhelming majority of male producers in the business, this gendered dynamic of entry should not be surprising, as it is mirrored in other musical forms as well. Although some women rappers are operating and founding their own record companies, many still believe that is easier for women to make it if they are connected to a male producer. As Lil' Kim notes in a 1999 article by Elena Oumano, in *Billboard* magazine, "It's happening less, but the ones who come in on their own have it harder as opposed to me coming in with Biggie [Smalls, aka the Notorious B.I.G.]."

However, although female artists have entered the rap game through ties with male rappers, many of them, such as Salt-N-Pepa, Yo Yo, and Missy Elliot, eventually gained creative control of their musical product. As more women gain creative control, it should become easier for women rappers to enter the scene through ties with female producers, such as Missy Elliot, thereby challenging the notion that women rappers need male producers in order to succeed.

Work Cited

Oumano, Elena. "Girlz Power." *Billboard* 111.23 (1999): pars 38. 12 March 2006. http://proquest.umi.com/pqdweb?did=42043944&sid=1&Fmt=4&clientId=14119&RQT=309&VName=PQD.

---

conceptually and musically it was very different from their past albums. Eventually, however, the group secured a deal with three recording companies, Red Ant Entertainment, Island Black Music, and London Records. Due to personal changes among the members of the group, as well as lackluster sales, this was to be the final album released by the trio.

VERY NECESSARY

In the three years between the release of *Blacks' Magic* and their fourth album, Cheryl and Deidre gave birth to children. Sandi had been the first to have a child, her son Tyran, in 1989. He was followed in 1991 by Cheryl's daughter, Corin, and eventually by Deidre's daughter, Christenese, in 1992. Some other important changes also occurred during this time, such as certain members of the group, primarily Cheryl, becoming more religious in their outlook. It was these sorts of lifestyle changes that would eventually lead the group to disband in a few years' time.

However, 1993 was a very successful year for the group, and after a three-year hiatus to spend time with their families—and after the successful separation from their former label and the partial separation from their manager—Salt-N-Pepa came back to the business stronger than ever and released the most successful album of their careers. *Very Necessary* would eventually go five times platinum. Also, due to its immense success and record sales, the group had once again crossed over into the pop charts. Ernst was still the executive producer on most of the songs, although Cheryl, Sandi, and Deidre were involved in every stage of the album from songwriting to production.

Unlike past albums where Ernst held the majority of creative control, this album was divided between Ernst and Salt-N-Pepa. Ernst created the hit song "Whatta Man" featuring En Vogue, which reached number three on the U.S. charts, and the hit song created by Salt-N-Pepa was "Shoop," which reached number four on the U.S. charts. The writing credits for the rest of the songs were heavily contested. It was also this album that won Salt-N-Pepa a Grammy for Best Rap Performance in 1995 for "None of Your Business," one of the tracks produced by Ernst.

However, although this album had more input from the trio than any of the past albums, the themes did not stray much from their previous releases. "Shoop," which was coproduced by Mark Sparks, Cheryl, and Sandi was definitely written from a woman's point of view. The trio once again flips the script on their male counterparts, since the video and the lyrics turn men into sex objects. Instead of showcasing scantily clad women in their music video, the trio has a group of scantily clad men. Thus the sexual desires of women are at the forefront, and the song centers on the trio's weakness—men.

Female sexuality is at center stage. The male gaze is captured and replaced by the female gaze. The song celebrates women's sexuality and at the same time places the needs of women first. This was a refreshing change in a time period where blunts, bitches, and booze had become the norm in rap music. Indeed, with the ascendance of gangsta rap and the start of the G-funk era in 1992, after the release of Dr. Dre's *The Chronic* (Death Row/Interscope) and Snoop Doggy Dogg's 1993 debut album, *Doggystyle* (Death Row), songs by women, about women, from a pro-woman perspective were very important. These albums were more significant than earlier misogynist releases by N.W.A., 2 Live Crew, and the Geto Boys because their songs and videos were reaching a much wider audience, due to the heavy rotation of their music videos on MTV in the United States and Much Music in Canada. Though the themes in the raps of Dr. Dre and Snoop Dogg were not significantly different from those of their precursors, or in the case of Dr. Dre one of the rap groups he had founded, what had changed was the scope and breadth of their fan base due to technological advances and an increased likelihood of actually receiving airplay.

Also, the ascendance and immense influence of gangsta rap, which may be traced back to Philadelphia's Schoolly D, the West Coast influences of South Central LA's Ice-T and Compton's N.W.A., influenced not only the themes but the reception of rap music. More specifically, the themes of authenticity in rap music were inextricably linked to one's connection with the streets, economic hardship, and black masculinity. "Keeping it real," a sense of staying close to one's roots and being true to oneself, now became synonymous with "keeping it gangsta." The immense success of Salt-N-Pepa and their crossover into the popular music charts resulted in some critics viewing their music as inauthentic (see sidebar: Are Female Rappers "Authentic?").

Although the trio did not change their sound to reflect the growing influence of gangsta rap, their image, as presented on the album cover of *Very Necessary*, was significantly different. While *A Salt with a Deadly Pepa* (1988) showed the group wearing tight-fitting black and red leather outfits and *Blacks' Magic* (1990) had them drawn as cartoon figures reading a bedtime story in their nightgowns, *Very Necessary* (1993) had them on the cover

Are Female Rappers "Authentic"?
Athena Elafros

Since the formative years of the hip hop movement, female rappers have had a difficult time claiming authenticity in their music. At first, this may have been a result of sexist assumptions about women's roles being in the home and not on the streets rapping, which may have resulted in fewer women being involved in the seminal years of the hip hop movement.

For example, Roxanne Shanté, a member of the Juice Crew, which consisted of Marley Marl, Big Daddy Kane, Biz Markie, Kool G. Rap, MC Shan, Craig G., T.J. Swan, and Masta Ace, was reminded of her proper place in the rap scene during one of the most famous beefs, or lyrical feuds, in rap history. The beef all began when MC Shan of the Juice Crew released "The Bridge," wherein he proclaimed that Queensbridge was the real home of hip hop. When it was released on vinyl in 1986, KRS-One of Boogie Down Productions released "The South Bronx" (B-boy, 1986) and "The Bridge Is Over" (B-boy, 1987) (Jenkins 23-27). It was on "The Bridge Is Over" that KRS-One claimed that Roxanne Shanté was only good for one thing—providing sexual pleasure for men. In a single lyric, her career as a hip hop artist and her authenticity as a rapper were reduced to nothing more than a sexual appendage to male rappers.

This does not mean that women were not involved in the movement, but over the years there has been an active erasure and marginalization of the roles of women rappers in its formative years. For example, groups such as the Mercedes Ladies, the first all-female MC and DJ crew who formed in 1977, and West Philadelphia's Lady B, who signed a record deal with T.E.C. Records and released "To the Beat Y'all" in 1980, and South Carolina's Sequence, a female singing and rapping trio, laid some of the groundwork necessary for more women to enter the rap music industry, although many of these artists do not receive the credit they deserve.

This combination of sexism and the diminishment of the roles of women rappers have resulted in hip hop authenticity becoming synonymous with black masculinity. Women rappers were further disenfranchised with the emergence of misogynist strains of gangsta rap in the late 1980s, which resulted in authenticity also becoming equated with sexism. These forms of sexism, erasure, and redefinition of authenticity have made it very difficult for women rappers to break into a very male-dominated music genre.

Yet debates over authenticity in rap music have been occurring since the inception of the genre, and women have actively tried to redefine authenticity in more pro-woman ways. Whether it is through challenging misogyny or rewriting the *her*story of the genre, women always have and always will provide feminine correctives to male-centered conceptions of what it means to be an authentic rapper.

Work Cited

Jenkins, Sacha. "Roxanne Shanté: We Used to Do It Out in the Park." *Vibe Hip-Hop Divas*. New York: Three Rivers Press, 2001. 20-29.

in jeans and plaid jackets. It would appear that with their increased creative control, the group may have wanted an album cover that portrayed them in their everyday clothing instead of being represented as sex objects. Perhaps they wanted to symbolize powerful womanhood by reclaiming a male uniform, as they had reclaimed sexist male terminology in the past, as a decisive critique of the rap industry. Or perhaps they wanted to show that women were sexy in jeans and jackets. Or maybe the plaid jackets were merely a result of the aforementioned influences of gangsta rap, as well as the grunge and alternative rock movements, on the fashion trends of the time. The resurgence of the plaid shirt, at first seen as a symbol of gang affiliation, then as a symbol for dispossessed Generation X teenagers, was eventually incorporated as a unisex fashion for men and women.

Overall, this release marked some very necessary changes in the group. The trio changed record labels and management, as well as their look, and they kept making money. Yet there were more changes to come. Only two years after signing with London Records, they signed a new contract in 1995 with MCA Music Entertainment. Unfortunately, their back catalogue remained with London Records, but the new contract did serve to establish Salt-N-Pepa's record label, Jireh Records, which allowed the group to sign four acts to their label each year for four years.

Following in the footsteps of Salt-N-Pepa, many female rappers have since established their own record labels in an effort to have greater control over their careers. Some of the most popular and successful of these female-run record labels include Lil' Kim's Queen Bee Records and Missy Elliot's Gold Mind Label. Missy Elliot not only has her own label, she also writes and produces most of her songs.

It was in order to gain this sort of independence that the group left London Records. Salt-N-Pepa wanted a long-term commitment from an established record label, which was very difficult for female rap artists to find. However, given the fact that Salt-N-Pepa had been in the business for over a decade, they felt entitled to some security. So, after several years with their MCA contract and no albums released, Salt-N-Pepa and their new manager, Darryll Brooks, went looking for another label to buy out their contract with MCA. The end result was that Salt-N-Pepa's fifth and final album, *Brand New* (1997), was worked and released through three record companies.

Thus, it would appear that Salt-N-Pepa had finally achieved a level of success that allowed them complete creative control over their recording careers and musical product and also provided them with the somewhat fleeting opportunity to form their own record label. Although gaining their independence was a long and difficult process, the trio persevered and eventually found a new manager and several new labels through which they would release their final album.

BRAND NEW

The group officially signed with Red Ant Entertainment in 1997. Unfortunately, Red Ant lacked distribution rights, so the label approached London Records for a distribution contract. Island Black Music, a division of London Records and Island Records, entered the deal because their sales and promotion staff were shared between London Records and Island Black Music.

Ernst was not involved in any aspect of this album, although he nonetheless collected one third of the royalties. The title is very revealing because, for Cheryl and Sandi, this album was a brand new start for their careers, now that they finally possessed full creative control of their music and image. The album took a year to make, and most of it was written and produced by Cheryl and Sandi in Cheryl's basement. In fact, nine of the thirteen songs were cowritten and coproduced by Cheryl.

Brand New was the final album with new material to be released by Salt-N-Pepa. Lyrically it was also the most politically conscious and empowering of their albums. Musically, the breadth and scope of the album was eclectic, ranging from the gospel song "Hold On," which featured Kirk Franklin, to "Imagine," featuring rock vocalist Sheryl Crow. The album certainly expanded their musical repertoire. There were also plenty of songs that continued the Salt-N-Pepa tradition of female self-empowerment, such as "Do Me Right" and "The Clock Is Tickin'."

"Do Me Right" lets women know that if their man is not treating them right, they should leave him. The song urges women to place their needs first, and if their needs are not being met they should find a new relationship. Instead of condoning fun and one-night stands, the trio, all with families of their own, focus on a more serious message for their female fans.

Following this more serious trend in their lyrics is the track "The Clock Is Tickin'." This song is directed primarily at women, yet it is also directed at men. It deals with the somber issue of abuse, both verbal and physical, and it urges women to leave abusive relationships, both for their own sake and the sake of any children they may have. The song also has a message for men in that it suggests men leave superficial relationships when their female partners are only interested in their money.

Other songs maintained the Salt-N-Pepa tradition of promoting assertive black female sexuality. Specifically, "Gitty Up" and "Boy Toy" (written and produced by Sandi) are playful songs that place women in control of their sexuality.

From these very diverse track selections, we can also see that a division was becoming more apparent in the group. Although Cheryl and Sandi had always had very different personalities, these differences were becoming more pronounced in terms of the direction each of them wanted to take with their creative product. Whereas Cheryl was more interested in focusing on uplifting gospel types of songs, Sandi wanted to uphold Salt-N-Pepa's image of fun and playful female sexuality. Such irreconcilable differences eventually led the group to disband.

Furthermore, despite the trio's combined efforts, this album was the least successful of their releases. In comparison to *Very Necessary*, which went five times platinum, *Brand New* only reached gold. Perhaps the breadth of the album was too eclectic and their fans could no longer relate to the songs. Or maybe it had less to do with Salt-N-Pepa and more to do with changes in the rap music industry and consumer taste.

As noted earlier, the influence of gangsta rap on the hip hop landscape in the mid-1990s cannot be underestimated. In conjunction with a slew of male gangsta rappers, there also emerged a contingent of female rappers who were much edgier and more sexually explicit than the women rappers before them. Although they were undoubtedly influenced by the works of Salt-N-Pepa, these new ladies of rap took representations of female rappers in a whole new direction.

Two of the most influential of these hard-core female rappers were Lil' Kim, who was associated with the Junior M.A.F.I.A., and Foxy Brown, who was associated with the Firm. With the release of Lil' Kim's debut album *Hard Core* (1996) and Foxy Brown's *Ill Na Na* (1997), there was a new brand of self-assertive and very explicit female sexuality on the market. Their lyrics were raunchier, sexier, and more overt than Salt-N-Pepa's ever were. With explicitly sexual, as opposed to playful, lyrics, hypersexualized imagery in their music videos, and provocative descriptions of sex in their raps, Lil' Kim and Foxy Brown took female rap artists in a new direction by moving beyond the suggestive lyrics of tracks such as Salt-N-Pepa's "Push It," and toward much more explicit lyrics, such as Lil' Kim's "Big Momma Thang" from *Hard Core*, and Foxy Brown's "Ill Na Na" from her album *Ill Na Na*. This may be why Salt-N-Pepa could not or, more realistically, did not want to compete with them.

Nonetheless, although Salt-N-Pepa did not lyrically compete with these up-and-coming divas, their music and that of other female rap pioneers nevertheless influenced them. As Rob Marriott notes, Lil' Kim followed in the footsteps of female rappers before her, such as Salt-N-Pepa on "I'll Take Your Man," Roxanne Shanté on "Have a Nice Day," and MC Lyte on "Stop, Look and Listen," by struggling to define herself outside of the confines of a male-centered gaze (138). Foxy Brown explicitly credits Roxanne Shanté as one of her idols, and she notes that Shanté is "a pioneer for the type of shit I'm doing. I swear by her" (quoted in D. Smith 122).

ON THEIR OWN (1999 AND AFTER)

After the release of *Brand New*, Cheryl told Sandi and Deidre that she did not want to do any more albums with the group operating the way it was. Cheryl was now interested in working solely on inspirational and gospel music, since during the course of her musical career she had undergone a very significant spiritual journey on which she became a born-again Christian. Unfortunately, her change in outlook was not shared by Sandi, and the three went their separate ways after a final tour in 1999. Salt-N-Pepa officially disbanded in 2002, after the release of a greatest hits album in 2000, *The Best of Salt-N-Pepa*.

After their final tour in 1999, Cheryl married her longtime partner and father of her two children, Gavin Wray, in 2000. Working with Wray, who was an up-and-coming producer, she wanted to pursue a career in gospel rap music, so they began working on her debut solo album, *Salt of the Earth [Matthew 5:13]*. Unfortunately, this album would not come to fruition. In 2005, Salt's homepage, www.saltunrapped.com, announced her plans to release a new solo album, *Salt Unrapped*, but it has yet to be released. Her homepage describes the album's genre as "urban inspirational."

Sandi married Treach of Naughty by Nature, a rap group originally from East Orange, New Jersey, and the group consisted of Anthony "Treach" Criss, Vinnie Brown, and Keir "Kay-Gee" Gist. Brown and Gist were originally in a group called New Style, but they changed their name once they joined forces with Criss. With their name change and with help from fellow New Jersey native Queen Latifah, who is one of the few female rappers to successfully introduce a male rap act into the business, Naughty by Nature released their self-titled debut album in 1991. The track from this album for which they are most often remembered is the pop-rap radio hit "O.P.P.," which has the double meaning of "Other People's Property" as well as "Other People's Pussy." Sandi had met Treach in 1991 in Daytona Beach while shooting *MTV's Spring Break*. The couple divorced a year after they were married, but they share custody of their daughter, Egypt. More recently, Sandi was part of *The Surreal Life*'s season five cast (2005). Deidre is now an online music personality for the Los Angeles radio station KKBT 100.3 The Beat, where she hosts *The Spin Cycle* with DJ Mo' Dav.

THE LEGACY OF SALT-N-PEPA

On September 22, 2005, Salt-N-Pepa reunited for the first time in six years and performed "Whatta Man" with En Vogue on VH1's *Hip-Hop Honors* program. In an interview for the VH1 program, Cheryl succinctly summarized the career and legacy of Salt-N-Pepa when she stated that "we've always been about being powerful as females and demanding our respect and wanting to be heard." During the program, Salt-N-Pepa was honored as a hip hop legend, along with other greats such as LL Cool J, Grandmaster Flash and the Furious Five, Ice-T, Notorious B.I.G., Big Daddy Kane, and the cast of *Boyz N the Hood*. Salt-N-Pepa was the only female rap group to be honored during the program.

According to the *VH1 Hip-Hop Honors* Web site, Salt-N-Pepa was honored on the program because they brought "a woman's perspective to the testosterone realm of hip hop" since they were not "afraid of talking about sex, advocating contraception, or telling a man exactly what to do when it came to the wild thing." The legacy of Salt-N-Pepa nonetheless lives on in the music of the female rappers who came after them. From Queen Latifah to Yo Yo, T.L.C., Lil' Kim, Foxy Brown, Missy Elliott, and others, the centrality of rapping from a female point of view lives on.

The female point of view for Salt-N-Pepa often involved the themes of self-empowerment and female sexuality, which are present in the music of their successors. For example, on tracks such as Queen Latifah's "U.N.I.T.Y." and Yo Yo's "Sisterland," the themes of self-love and solidarity among women are emphasized. In terms of female sexuality, although the "hard-core" sexuality of Lil' Kim and Foxy Brown is much more pronounced than the playful and suggestive sexuality of Salt-N-Pepa, what is of central importance is that female sexuality is openly discussed in the lyrics of female rappers, thereby providing an outlet and space for women to discuss issues related to women's health, desires, and sexuality. Finally, female rappers such as Missy Elliott and Lil' Kim have been able to build upon the inroads made by Salt-N-Pepa in terms of creative control, and they have successfully created their own record companies.

Thus, the influence and legacy of Salt-N-Pepa for present-day female rappers is most pronounced in terms of the focus on rapping from a female point of view, the emphasis on the subject matter of women's issues such as self-empowerment and sexuality, and the increased gains in terms of creative control of the musical product. Although each of the aforementioned female artists have taken rap music in different directions, they all owe a small part of their success to the pioneers and rap icons that are Salt-N-Pepa—one of the first and most successful all-female rap acts of all time.

See also: Missy-Elliot, Queen Latifah, MC Lyte, Lil' Kim, Roxanne Shanté

WORKS CITED

Guevara, Nancy. "Women Writin' Rappin' Breakin'." *Droppin' Science: Critical Essays on Rap Music and Hip-Hop Culture*. Ed. William Eric Perkins. Philadelphia: Temple University, 1996. 49-62.
"Hip-Hop Herstory. Vibe Timeline: 28 Years of Women in Hip-Hop." *Vibe Hip-Hop Divas*. New York: Three Rivers Press, 2001. 164-195.

Marriott, Rob. "What Price Queen Bee?" *Vibe Hip-Hop Divas*. New York: Three Rivers Press, 2001. 130-139.

Reynolds, J. R. "Salt-N-Pepa's 'Necessary' Changes." *Billboard* 105.51 (1993): 18-19. 10 July 2006. http://proquest.umi.com.libaccess.lib.mcmaster.ca/pqdlink?index=0&did=1550477&SrchMode=1&sid=1&Fmt=6&VInst=PROD&VType=PQD&RQT=309&VName=PQD&TS=1152550188&clientId=22605.

Rose, Tricia. "Never Trust a Big Butt and a Smile." *Camera Obscura* 23 (1991): 109-131.

Salt Unwrapped. 1995. 12 March 2006. http://www.saltunrapped.com/.

Smith, Danyel. "She Got Game." *Vibe Hip-Hop Divas*. New York: Three Rivers Press, 2001. 120-129.

Veran, Cristina. "First Ladies: Fly Women Who Rocked the Mic in the 70s and 80s." *Vibe Hip-Hop Divas*. New York: Three Rivers Press, 2001. 4-15.

Veran, Cristina. "Women on Wax." *Vibe Hip-Hop Divas*. New York: Three Rivers Press, 2001. 16-19.

VH1 Hip Hop Honors. 2005. 12 July 2006. http://www.vh1.com/shows/events/hip_hop_honors/2005/.

FURTHER RESOURCES

Allen, Harry. "Salt-N-Pepa: The Queens from Queens." *Vibe Hip-Hop Divas*. New York: Three Rivers Press, 2001. 30-39.

Cain, Joy Duckett. "The Growing Pains of Salt-N-Pepa." *Essence* 25.6 (1994): pars. 46. 10 March 2006. http://search.epnet.com/login.aspx?direct=true&db=rch&an=9410114298.

Cepeda, Raquel. "Ladies First Female DJs Got a Foot Through the Door, Ain't Goin' Nowhere." *Village Voice* 18–24 July 2001. pars 17. 18 March 2006. http://www.villagevoice.com/news/0129,cepeda,26472,1.html.

Cheney, Charlise L. *Brothers Gonna Work It Out: Sexual Politics in the Golden Age of Rap Nationalism*. New York: New York University Press, 2005.

Dunn, Jancee. "The Spice of Life." *Rolling Stone* 685 (1994): pars. 31. 10 March 2006. http://search.epnet.com/login.aspx?direct=true&db=rch&an=9406167906.

Erlewine, Stephen Thomas. "Salt-N-Pepa Biography." *VH1.com*. pars. 5. 16 Feb 2006. http://www.vh1.com/artists/az/salt_n_pepa/bio.jhtml.

Forman, Murray. "'Movin' Closer to an Independent Funk': Black Feminist Theory, Standpoint, and Women in Rap." *Women's Studies* 23 (1994): 35-55.

Forman, Murray and Mark Anthony Neal, eds. *That's the Joint! The Hip Hop Studies Reader*. New York: Routledge, 2004.

Gonzales, Michael A. "Yo-Yo: Not for Play." *Vibe Hip-HopDivas*. New York: Three Rivers Press, 2001. 62-69.

Gregory, Deborah. "Salt-N-Pepa." *Essence* 29.1 (1998): pars. 5. 10 March 2006. http://search.epnet.com/login.aspx?direct=true&db=rch&an=551302.

Keyes, Cheryl. *Rap Music and Street Consciousness*. Urbana and Chicago: University of Illinois Press, 2004.

Kim, Serena. "Discography." *Vibe Hip-Hop Divas*. New York: Three Rivers Press, 2001. 201-205.

"KKBT." *Wikipedia: The Free Encyclopedia.* 18 February 2006. http://en.wikipedia.org/wiki/KKBT.

Kool Keith Biography. 2003. 8 July 2006. http://www.koolkeith.co.uk/bio.htm.

McLeod, Kembrew. "Salt-N-Pepa." *The St. James Encyclopedia of Pop Culture*: pars 6. 3 Feb. 2006. http://www.looksmarthiphop.com/p/articles/mi_g1epc/is_bio/ai_2419201067.

Moore, Trudy S. "Salt-N-Pepa: Hottest Female Rap Trio Talks About Men, Music and Motherhood." *Jet* (1994): 18 pars. 3 Feb. 2006. http://www.findarticles.com/p/articles/mi_m1355/is_n18_v86/ai_15779690.

Mundy, Chris and Peggy Sirota. "Mamas Got a Brand New Bag." *Rolling Stone* 771 (1997): 107 pars. 10 March 2006. http://search.epnet.com/login.aspx?direct=true&db=rch&an=9710025045.

Pough, Gwendolyn D. *Check It While I Wreck It: Black Womanhood, Hip Hop Culture and the Public Sphere.* Boston: Northeastern University Press, 2004.

Reynolds, J. R. "Salt-N-Pepa Form Jireh Records." *Billboard* 107.43 (1995): 12, 107. 10 March 2006. http://search.epnet.com/login.aspx?direct=true&db=rch&an=9512073734.

"Salt-N-Pepa: Ladies First." *VH1: Hip-Hop Honors.* 12 March 2006. http://www.vh1.com/shows/events/hip_hop_honors/2005/editorial.jhtml?name=saltnpepa.

"Salt-N-Pepa Talk About Things Men Need to Be Taught." *Jet* 93.2 (1997): 21 pars. 10 March 2006. http://search.epnet.com/login.aspx?direct=true&db=rch&an=9712050565.

Shapiro, Peter. "Kid 'N Play." *The Rough Guide to Hip Hop.* London: Penguin Books, 2005. 206.

Shapiro, Peter. "Naughty by Nature." *The Rough Guide to Hip Hop.* London: Penguin Books, 2005. 273-274.

Shejay. 2004. 12 March 2006. http://www.shejay.net/.

Shuler, Deadra. "Wanda Dee: The Goddess Is Here and What a G.E.R.L. She Is." *GBN (Global Black News)*: 11 pars. 7 November 2003. 18 March 2006. http://www.globalblacknews.com/Shuler4.html.

Smith, Shawnee. "Red Ant's Salt-N-Pepa Gets 3-Label Campaign." *Billboard* 109.41 (1997): pars. 28. 10 March 2006. http://search.epnet.com/login.aspx?direct=true&db=rch&an=9710142146.

Take Back the Music Campaign. 2005. 12 March 2006. http://www.essence.com/essence/takebackthemusic/about.html.

Veran, Cristina. "Jazzy Joyce." *Vibe Hip-Hop Divas.* New York: Three Rivers Press, 2001. 168.

Veran, Cristina. "J.J. Fad." *Vibe Hip-Hop Divas.* New York: Three Rivers Press, 2001. 172.

"Wanda Dee Vocalist for the KLF." *ABC (Australian Broadcasting Corporation)*: 18 pars. 17 July 2004. 18 March 2006. http://www.abc.net.au/rage/guest/2004/klf.htm.

SELECTED DISCOGRAPHY

Hot, Cool & Vicious. Next Plateau, 1986.
A Salt with a Deadly Pepa. Next Plateau, 1988.

A Blitz of Salt-N-Pepa Hits: The Hits Remixed. London, 1989.
Blacks' Magic. Next Plateau, 1990.
Very Necessary. Next Plateau/London, 1993.
Brand New. Polygram, 1997.
The Best of Salt-N-Pepa. WEA International, 2000.

Courtesy of Photofest.

Queen Latifah

Faiza Hirji

Although she is currently devoting most of her time to a flourishing film career, Queen Latifah will perhaps always be best known for her role in the world of hip hop. Bursting onto the music scene in the late 1980s, Queen Latifah made a name for herself in a number of respects. A talented young rapper, Latifah released songs brimming with a sense of confidence and black female empowerment. She was not the first female rapper and some would argue that she is hardly the greatest, but her success is notable for a number of reasons. Independent, business-savvy, and fiercely proud of her gender, her race, and her roots, Latifah brought a new sense of positivity to rap and became a role model almost instantly (see sidebar: Overcoming the Stereotypes: Women in Hip Hop).

Overcoming the Stereotypes: Women in Hip Hop
Faiza Hirji

When Queen Latifah first appeared on the musical scene, she was still a mere teenager, but her appearance spoke of maturity and authority. Full-figured, dressed in Afrocentric-tinged clothing that ranged from military uniforms to tracksuits, Latifah was almost immediately categorized as an earth mother type. Less visible factors likely played a role: the title Queen, the self-sufficiency employed in managing her career, and the lyrics that spoke of women's importance as mothers and caretakers of society.

While Latifah has occasionally expressed discontent with this image, it has not been easy to discard, despite her acquisition of longer hair, makeup, and glamorous clothing. Women in music often occupy certain set roles. In particular, the world of hip hop has not been open to a large number of different interpretations of women's personalities. Even if Latifah had possessed the physical characteristics to occupy the kind of sexy vamp role played by young rappers such as Foxy Brown and Lil' Kim, she was firm from the beginning of her career that she had no intention of doing so. She has spoken out about the portrayal of young women as "hos" in music videos, expressing disappointment with the rappers who choose to surround themselves with such images and with those young women who lack sufficient self-respect to reject such positions. As she once noted in a CNN interview, "Just because some rappers choose to sell sex—I'm a big woman and I'm not going to embarrass myself by pulling my gut out. I can be sexy and sensual in my own way.... besides, I think big chicks rule" (Mayo 56).

Big chicks may rule, but they are also frequently labeled as mammies, as in the type made famous by Hattie McDaniel in *Gone with the Wind*. While Latifah's caretaker-style roles in *Bringing Down the House* and *Chicago* are more racy than Scarlett's mammy or *Gimme a Break*'s Nell, they are also tinged with a hint of the sexualized black woman. However, for the most part, she has avoided being pigeonholed in any of the media categories so often assigned to black women, such as those of "chickenheads"—women who are easily persuaded to perform sexual acts, particularly oral sex—criminals, or young single mothers, although her tough-talking characters do recall some of those intimidating black mothers who have ruled both the small and big screens, from Patti LaBelle on *A Different World* to those protective mothers who block progress in inspirational films such as *Lean on Me* and *Coach Carter*. However, the strength of her character and her body has also meant that she has sometimes been characterized as someone who does not fit into heterosexual norms; while the movie *Set It Off* provided a rare Latifah turn as a black woman involved in a passionate relationship, the relationship was one with another woman. Latifah may command too much respect to fear being labeled a chickenhead or a ho, but like so many other black women, she has also had to function within the limitations of a form that only recognizes certain kinds of women.

Work Cited

Mayo, Kierna. "The Last Good Witch." *Vibe Books: Hip Hop Divas*. New York: Three Rivers Press, 2001. 52-61.

Queen Latifah established an Afrocentric, positive approach, offering words of praise and encouragement for black women while avoiding criticism of black men. As comfortable as she was within a circle of male friends, Latifah was clear in her belief that women needed to hear a positive message. Well aware of the consequences of living in an environment that denigrated black women, Latifah drew on her knowledge of black history and her own pride in her people to craft songs that would inspire her sisters to be their best. Two songs on this theme helped establish her place as an icon: "Ladies First," a duet with Monie Love from Latifah's 1989 debut album, *All Hail the Queen*, and "U.N.I.T.Y," a Grammy-winning classic from 1993's *Black Reign*.

The subject matter of her music distinguished Latifah from other hip hop artists, but so did the fact that she lived as she rapped. An around-the-way girl who seemed most comfortable in track suits, Latifah avoided the materialism and emphasis on appearance that came to define the hip hop industry. Filming her first videos and appearing in public wearing outfits she had cobbled together as cheaply as possible, this Queen was one who opted for comfort first—not only in terms of her clothes, but in terms of herself (see sidebar: True to Their Roots: Afrocentric Fashion). MTV had never seen anything like her, and neither had most fans. While other major female stars reacted to media attention and record company pressure by slimming and stripping down, Latifah remained at peace with her shape and her persona, helping to set the stage for the success of later stars such as Missy Elliott. Even later in her career, when she began to appear in movies and in public wearing more feminine, sophisticated ensembles, Latifah did not follow through with the strict diets or training regimens adopted by so many of her counterparts. The result? Ironically, the woman who became a powerful role model for young women by refusing to conform to societal standards of beauty and slenderness was rewarded with a contract to serve as a Cover Girl spokesmodel.

Ironies such as these seem to say it all: Latifah's life represents a series of paradoxes, yet there are definite, consistent truths. Even when she seems to stray from her roots—putting movies before music, adopting a softer, jazzy

True to Their Roots: Afrocentric Fashion
Faiza Hirji

Queen Latifah has left behind many of the Afrocentric themes found in her earlier music as well as the clothing that characterized those years. Fashion has often been an important part of rap, supporting verbal messages through appearance. As a member of Native Tongues, the collective endorsing peaceful activism, equality, and pride in their African roots, Latifah adopted many of the same fashions and interests of fellow members such as A Tribe Called Quest, X Clan, De La Soul, and Jungle Brothers.

Leaving aside her sincere interest in the African diaspora and African history, Latifah also had a more practical reason for cultivating an Afrocentric look when she first arrived on the scene: It was cheap. This was important for a fledgling rapper, and for one who agreed with her Native Tongues brethren that it was necessary to move away from the materialism and conspicuous consumption that characterized many hip hop artists. Latifah and her partners rejected the flashy gold jewelry and supposedly ghetto-appropriate attire that was becoming popular, choosing instead to wear clothes similar to those favored by the Black Power movement. Kente cloth and dashikis were popular, as well as the black, green, gold, and red that evoked a number of African flags, and some rappers added dreadlocks or Afros rather than cultivating a straight-haired, quasi-European look.

The Afrocentric look was particularly pronounced in X Clan, known for militant activism. They could frequently be seen in dashikis and kofi hats. Although Jungle Brothers and A Tribe Called Quest were less overt in their Afrocentric fashion than X Clan, they did utilize African colors and motifs on their early albums, a trend that eventually faded away.

Latifah, generally casual and relaxed in her attire, nonetheless became a type of fashion icon in her own way during her Afrocentric period, even making an appearance at a 1991 Todd Oldham show wearing a very regal kufi, described by Wilbekin as "an African crown that looks like a tube of fabric on your head" (280). This look became her trademark in her early videos and appearances, projecting not only her connections to Africa but the royal lineage of African women. This image defined the cover of her early albums, disappearing only with the release of 1998's *Order in the Court*.

De La Soul also carved out a niche for themselves with a style that seemed to be both Afrocentric and hippie at the same time, including items such as brightly colored shirts, tie-dye, baggy pants, and medallions. Eventually De La Soul, however, like Latifah, moved away from that image, crafting a new style of music and a less African-inspired mode of dress.

While stars such as Latifah have changed styles, and Native Tongues has dissolved, Afrocentrism is hardly a thing of the past. Stars such as Erykah Badu, for instance, carry on the tradition proudly, sporting an appearance different from that made famous by Queen Latifah but still with some African distinctiveness, including head coverings and loose dresses. The look has changed but the principle lives on.

Work Cited

Wilbekin, Emil. "Great Aspirations: Hip Hop and Fashion Dress for Excess and Success." *The Vibe History of Hip Hop*. Ed. Alan Light. London: Plexus, 1999. 277-283.

---

vocal style, trading in the track suits and runners for haute couture—Latifah continues to retain her independence, her control, and her desire to blaze trails in unexplored territory. Perhaps one of her most pioneering qualities is her business sense, a rare trait in an industry where starstruck teenagers are so excited to receive recording contracts that they often surrender control of their music. It is even rarer for a woman in a business where men dominate; many successful female singers have therefore achieved status by linking themselves to a male partner, platonic or otherwise. Surrounded by men that she loved, and turning over her business affairs to one particularly reliable male friend, Latifah never lost sight of who she was in any relationship.

Latifah presented herself with professionalism, even in the midst of tragedy, and maintained control over her image and her rights. Unlike some of her contemporaries, she did not allow herself to be sucked into the vortex of the music industry, even when Tommy Boy passed on the opportunity to renew her initial contract and she had to move over to Motown. Along with her insistence on investing her money wisely, Latifah has resisted the temptations of excessive consumerism. While she is perhaps one of the most successful hip hop artists of all time, she has not displayed her wealth with the same enthusiasm as many of her contemporaries, who flaunt diamonds and gold in their videos as a symbol of having made it to the top. She has had her run-ins with the law, but these are minor in comparison to the legal battles, not to mention physical battles, that dog some of her fellow rappers.

Strong, independent, and personable, Latifah dealt with hip hop's short shelf life by moving outside of its boundaries. The firsts that she piled up in her music—the feminist power of "Ladies First," the gold status of *Black Reign*, the formation of her own company, Flavor Unit—were merely a prelude to the barriers she broke down in a career as an actress and all-around performer. She has built a rich body of film work, distinguished by stellar appearances in *Set It Off*, the award-winning *Chicago*, and *Bringing Down the House*, allowing her to move beyond the cliché of the singer who wants to be a movie star. Having demonstrated her range, Queen Latifah can now settle comfortably into a role as someone who is famous for a variety of accomplishments. Singer, actress, soul sister, celebrity spokesmodel—Latifah's range and determination combine to make her an indisputable hip hop icon. Even though her most recent work does not always demonstrate her rapping roots, the story of Latifah's life is that of a woman whose queenly stature owes a great deal—if not everything—to hip hop and to her own overflowing confidence. She may be better known now as a movie star, among other things, but the fact is that there could not have been a Queen without hip hop, and without the Queen, hip hop would have been denied one of its rare female pioneers. Queen Latifah has distanced herself from the rap world, becoming part of hip hop's storied past more than its present or future, although she continues to make music in a softer, gentler vein. However, her legacy lives on in the inspiration she provides at a number of levels: as an entrepreneur who has enjoyed a long and diverse career, as a woman who is unafraid to stake her claim to success, and as a rapper who spoke out about inequality and injustice when those words most needed to be said. Her moves into the mainstream have had the rather paradoxical effect of promoting some of the same notions she once eschewed, as contemporary female rappers embark with enthusiasm on acting careers, sometimes with little regard to the quality of the roles or the depth of their own talent, in order to make money and to maximize the benefits of a career that might not last. Despite the efforts Latifah made early in her career to instill pride and respect in hip hop gender relations, there are still negative references to women in rap songs and videos, and a new breed of female rappers who seem to embrace the oversexualized images that Latifah spoke against. Many women in hip hop, however, continue to cite Latifah as a role model, one who has carried on the legacy of the early female rappers and added to it.

ALL HAIL THE QUEEN — THE EARLY YEARS

The woman who would be queen of hip hop was born Dana Elaine Owens in Newark, New Jersey, on March 18, 1970. Queen Latifah helped place New Jersey on the hip hop map. A neglected outpost at a time when most of the success stories seemed to be coming out of New York City, New Jersey has always been home to Latifah, and her music was one of the biggest hip hop stories ever to emerge from there, even though New Jersey can also lay claim to bringing up stars such as Ice-T, Lauryn Hill, Redman, and Naughty by Nature.

While she was slow in arriving—so slow that labor had to be induced after ten months—that was the last time Dana would be caught dawdling. Unlike many other female rap pioneers, she enjoyed the stability and support of a close-knit and loving family, investing her with the confidence to pursue whatever she desired. Her mother, Rita, a high school teacher, was a particularly strong influence and source of encouragement, instilling ambition in the two young children she raised essentially alone after separating from her husband, Lancelot.

Rita and Lancelot Owens separated in 1978, leaving Dana and her brother Lancelot Jr., better known as Winki, in the custody of Rita, who moved the family to less affluent surroundings as she worked to support her children. Lancelot, a Vietnam veteran and former police officer who was battling an addiction to drugs, was unable to help consistently and became a less central figure in Dana's life, but nonetheless she has noted the many ways in which her father remained a positive force. Like Rita, Lancelot was raised among strong women and saw no reason why Dana should be less empowered than her brother. He attempted to provide both children with equally sharp instincts for survival and encouraged Dana's eagerness to accompany her brother in his athletic pursuits. Thus, despite teasing from neighborhood children who referred to her as a tomboy, Dana developed a diverse set of interests, from karate, basketball, and baseball to dance and music lessons. She also learned how to tolerate teasing and to combat it with cool self-possession, informing her young critics that she was entitled to her athleticism.

By the age of eight, Dana had already decided that she would benefit from a name change, spurred by the fact that many of her friends and relatives were adopting Muslim names. With the help of her cousin, Dana chose Latifah. She felt that its meaning—beautiful and sensitive—was entirely apt. Although she was so evidently strong and athletic, and had developed a tough exterior to handle any challenges that came her way, her inner, gentle self was best described by the name Latifah. Latifah, then, was not only a rap persona but a name that arose originally out of a desire to create a clear and self-defined identity.

Ever versatile, Latifah demonstrated her Renaissance qualities early, playing basketball for her high school's state championship-winning team, starring as Dorothy in the school production of *The Wiz*, and in her spare time, rapping—independently and within a group called Ladies Fresh. She was immersed in the music scene in other ways, visiting New York City clubs to see the famous and the up-and-coming. Surreptitious visits to the Latin Quarter with her friends provided her with an impeccable background in hip hop, as she took in shows featuring performers ranging from Grandmaster Flash to the Beastie Boys to MC Lyte. However, as interested as she was in music, it was not initially her ambition to forge a career in that field. Instead, bearing in mind her mother's emphasis on education, Latifah stayed in school, considering the possibility of becoming a journalist or a lawyer.

Ironically, it was actually Rita Owens who provided Latifah with the introduction that would further stoke her interest in rap music. As the person responsible for social activities at Irvington High School, Rita met Mark the 45 King when she needed a DJ for a school party. The subsequent introduction to the 45 King marked a turning point in Latifah's life, as she began spending much of her spare time with him and his friends, experimenting with music and testing out her own rapping skills. While her early attempts were, by her own admission, less than stellar, her interest was sparked, and when some of her friends formed a group Latifah was part of it, labeling herself Princess of the Posse.

It was the inspiration provided by a couple other princesses, however, that really gave Latifah the impetus for a rapping career. On her visits to the Latin Quarter and to clubs and house parties in Brooklyn, the Bronx, and Harlem, she rarely saw female rappers, and the ones she did see were sometimes difficult to identify with for a young woman who felt most at ease in athletic clothing. Two women would change that for her in a single night. A performance by Sweet T and Jazzy Joyce resonated with Latifah, who saw them as female rappers who were talented and successful, and who had maintained their own casual look. With this in mind, she began to consider the possibility that rap, rather than detracting from her career goals, could enhance them, offering her another means of communicating with an audience.

At that point, however, Latifah needed to have an audience before she could consider the best mode of communication. As would be the case throughout most of her career, her friends, like her family members, believed in and supported her efforts. A longtime friend insisted that she accept a loan—which he himself could ill afford—in order to cut a demo. Buoyed by his support, Latifah followed instructions, collaborating with Mark the 45 King on a record for "Princess of the Posse" and "Wrath of My Madness," in which she made reference both to the 45 King and Ramsey while injecting a reggae sound that few others were using at the time in their rapping. "Princess of the Posse" went on to become her first single to garner radio play, appearing in the summer of 1987. That same demo put her on the path to a recording career, as the 45 King passed it on to Fab 5 Freddy of *Yo! MTV Raps*, who then passed it on to Monica Lynch at Tommy Boy Records. Lynch was interested enough to offer Latifah a contract, and after that there was no looking back.

It was around this time that Latifah adopted the Queen moniker, a natural step in the midst of a wave of Afrocentric consciousness that acknowledged African history, the dignity of a people oppressed by slavery, and the nationalism and pride of leaders such as Malcolm X. On "Princess of the Posse" and "Wrath of My Madness," the only name she provided was Latifah. It was only later, when Tommy Boy offered her a contract and her lawyer wanted to know what name she would employ professionally that Latifah decided to use something more elaborate. Out of respect for those African queens, such as Nefertiti and Numidia, who occupied a strong, nurturing role as the foremothers of an ancient civilization, she chose the name Queen Latifah.

QUEEN ON THE SCENE—THE LATIFAH BREAKTHROUGH

In 1989, Queen Latifah, still a teenager, captured the rap world's attention with her debut album, *All Hail the Queen*, released by Tommy Boy and produced by Mark the 45 King. As she had foreseen, the kind of communication she learned at the Borough of Manhattan Community College, where she studied for a year and a half, did not have quite the impact of her rhyming skills. *All Hail the Queen* included a number of landmark songs, but the one that engraved Latifah's image in the public consciousness as a female rapper who was serious about her message was the single "Ladies First," a duet with the young British rapper Monie Love.

Born Simone Wilson in the same year as Dana Owens, Monie Love did not reach the same heights of popularity as Latifah. Nonetheless, Love was one of a very small number of British rappers who achieved some kind of name recognition in the United States, and her contribution to "Ladies First," using a very different rapping and personal style than Latifah, was both significant and memorable. Her own work, best exemplified by catchy singles such as "Monie in the Middle" and "It's a Shame (My Sister)," featured the same kind of strength and warmth directed toward women that made "Ladies First" a standout. "Ladies First" would be one of the signature songs of Love's career, which she has kept on the musical path by establishing herself as a radio deejay. As for Latifah, the choice of Love as a partner on "Ladies First" was especially significant in that her heritage as a British woman of Afro-Caribbean ancestry demonstrated the song's universality and reach.

With Latifah presenting a powerful image in the accompanying video, dressed in different types of African clothing that alternately depicted her as earth mother and military general, Love's honeyed lyrics and Latifah's tough talk offered a powerful and uplifting tribute to black history and black women. The two teenagers rapped together, supported by other female vocalists, while the background featured one significant black woman after another, going back in time and all over the African diaspora. From Angela Davis to Sojourner Truth, from the United States to South Africa, powerful images of black solidarity and struggle lit up the screen. "Ladies First" made it clear that the young Latifah expected to be taken seriously, and that she would be different from other youthful female rappers who burst onto the scene with more provocative or less substantial songs. The Afrocentrism of that song and video was one defining feature of the Queen's early work, and of the work of her closest compatriots.

Latifah's early work carried extra credibility because of her association with highly respected artists, most of whom had a commitment to promoting pride in their African roots and culture. Afrika Bambaataa, in particular, was a major influence and companion. Viewed by many as the father of hip hop following his transition from street gang member to singer, Bambaataa drew youth of different races and identities into his Zulu Nation, urging them to find positive energy in dance and song. The Zulu Nation was only one of many groups and coalitions that could be found in the world of hip hop, but it was one whose message never lost its relevance to Latifah.

Emerging at a time when negative images of African Americans, especially women, could be found everywhere, "Ladies First" reminded listeners and viewers that there was a lot more to members of the African diaspora than the negative images that made it onto the news. It also offered an image of African American women in hip hop that was far different from the scantily clad young women who are criticized even now for their willingness to expose themselves to denigration in rap videos. Covered up and taking care of business, Queen Latifah and Monie Love made it clear they would by no means be relegated to the background as supporting actors.

Another defining feature was her refusal to engage in the infighting that had driven—and to some extent still drives—the careers of other female rap stars, such as Roxanne Shanté, the Real Roxanne, and MC Lyte in earlier days, and Lil' Kim and Foxy Brown in more recent ones. The so-called dis records, stinging personal criticisms aimed both at male critics and at other women, which helped Shanté and the Real Roxanne establish themselves professionally, gained a great deal of fame for both, but also meant that female rap stars suffered from a profound sense of alienation. Engaged in insulting one another on vinyl, Shanté, the Real Roxanne, and MC Lyte were only three of the best-known early rappers who were unable to build a sense of community or unity, instead feeding their own fears and insecurities.

This was not, of course, the only barrier such rappers faced. They were not only female, a drawback in the world of hip hop all by itself, but they were young and often vulnerable. Many came from broken homes or poor backgrounds; for some, it became increasingly difficult to pursue an education; most lacked positive role models. It was common for these rappers to be exploited by managers and promoters once they did land recording contracts, and in the desire to succeed and live up to the expectations of their record companies, it is perhaps not surprising that these young women attempted to attract attention any way they could. Given the many obstacles these women faced, the surprise is not that many of them had short careers; the real surprise is how long some of them lasted. Although Latifah would go on to have a longer and more stable career, she owed those pioneers a debt for breaking down some of the first barriers.

As inspiring as the female rap pioneers might have been for Latifah in some sense, the pattern of hurling insults at her contemporaries was not one she intended to follow. From the beginning, in keeping with her association with an Afrocentric movement grounded in principles of pride and positivity, Latifah decided that she was going to carve a different niche for herself. Her message of empowerment was intended for all black women, competitors or not, and was relatively easy to embrace at a mainstream level because of her avoidance of profanity or perceived negativity. It was this message that set Queen Latifah apart, making her one of the few women to attain iconic status in the masculine world of hip hop. Her cultural significance far outstripped her commercial success.

Commercially and culturally, Latifah helped begin a tradition that continues today in the rap world. Whereas the earliest rap successes came out of New York City, a place that influenced Latifah and others, New Jersey was barely on the map in musical terms in the late 1980s. Latifah would hardly be the last major artist with New Jersey roots to explode onto the scene, but she was certainly one of the first. Although some of her albums were subject to a spottier reception than *All Hail the Queen*, she had already begun the process of making her name—and that name belonged to a young woman whose roots were unapologetically Jersey. Even when the demands of her acting career compelled her to begin splitting time between California and New Jersey, Latifah has proudly proclaimed that her true home remains the one of her childhood.

All Hail the Queen sold a million copies globally and achieved Top 10 placement on R&B lists, carried not only by the strength of "Ladies First" but by other notable songs such as the fun-loving "Come into My House," which invites listeners into her queendom and nation, and "Mama Gave Birth to the Soul Children," a duet with De La Soul that makes oblique reference to the Zulu Nation and the family ties it contained. The rasta-infused "Wrath of My Madness"—which spoke of Latifah's talent, confidence, and friends, but also of her belief in black unity—and the self-affirming "Princess of the Posse," those first songs that captured Tommy Boy's attention, were also on the album. Songs such as "The Evil That Men Do," with KRS-One making references to apartheid and political neglect, further demonstrated her interest in social and political issues affecting the African American community. "The Evil That Men Do" addressed the numerous challenges faced by black women on welfare, from the indifference of those who could make a difference to the threat of drugs and the lack of housing. The hard-hitting nature of the lyrics on songs such as "Ladies First" and "The Evil That Men Do" inspired other community-minded rappers, including the far more controversial Sister Souljah (Keyes 268). *Nature of a Sista'*, her 1991 follow-up, was considered by some to be less substantial, and Tommy Boy's response was to decline the opportunity to renew Latifah's contract when it expired, despite the fact that singles such as "Latifah's Had It up 2 Here" performed well. The defiant tone of that song, in which Latifah addressed criticism and rumor by asserting her command of any situation, seemed an appropriate prelude to her break with the record label that launched her career. Some have suggested that Tommy Boy grew wary of dealing with Latifah because of her preference for running the show her way and including an unexpected level of variety in the songs on her albums. Regardless of the reason, the outcome seemed to be positive for Latifah, who went on to create a hit album for Motown.

Queen Latifah was not the first female rapper to have widespread popularity. Others such as Salt-N-Pepa were also making waves, but again, Latifah's ability to carve out a niche for herself saved her from unfair comparisons. While Salt-N-Pepa attracted occasional fire for being, in the eyes of some, too mainstream and too popular, Latifah's early work carried extra credibility for its associations with, among others, Afrika Bambaataa, the trailblazing rapper whose Zulu Nation collective included, in addition to

Latifah, De La Soul, A Tribe Called Quest, and the Jungle Brothers. These members, in addition to Monie Love, were also members of the Native Tongues Posse, which came to be regarded by some as a family with Afrika Bambaataa and Queen Latifah at its head. An American whose mother came from Barbados, Afrika Bambaataa was always conscious of the need to spread a message not only within North America but across the diaspora, a message that resisted racism and encouraged investment in the future. Musically, these rappers all created fresh and innovative work at some point, but their other common ground lay in a shared belief that rap was not simply an entertainment vehicle—it was, as Latifah had hoped from the first, a way of raising consciousness without falling into the trap of promoting violence, consumerism, and misogyny.

Native Tongues was a strong and creative force while it lasted, and for some time many of its members experienced considerable success. A Tribe Called Quest and Queen Latifah did very well commercially, but they were perhaps not the members with the most intense investment in Afrocentricism. Afrika Bambaataa worked hard to maintain everyone's commitment, but as time went on, the members drifted apart. There was no major rift or pivotal incident, merely a sense that each person or group was growing into an individual career, separate from the collective. Eventually the Jungle Brothers would go on to release an album in 1993—following some reported interference from Bambaataa, who tried to influence the record's sound—that clearly showed how far they had moved from strictly Afrocentric themes, while De La Soul released an album the same year that made oblique and negative references to the dissolution of the Native Tongues. They retracted those on a subsequent album, but by that time, Native Tongues was no longer the force it had been, and even if it was, Latifah had moved on to her own projects and to different themes. Unlike some female rappers who could not sustain their careers without the support of a male crew, Latifah benefited from her association with Native Tongues but maintained her momentum after the group's meltdown.

Latifah was also different from her female colleagues in one other, significant respect. Unlike young stars such as Shanté or Salt-N-Pepa, Latifah maintained creative and financial control as early and as often as possible. Realizing early on that she needed someone to collect from promoters, Latifah assigned a reliable friend and kept close track of what was happening. Younger stars who arrived earlier on the scene, such as Shanté, often struggled to collect what they were owed. Youth was not the only factor—some of those rappers lacked a sufficient base of supportive advisors who would manage their funds honestly and fairly, while personal stresses and the distraction of being on the road, pushed from venue to venue, also sapped some of the energy needed to inquire closely about their affairs. A number of female rappers, such as Salt of Salt-N-Pepa, also fell into the trap of surrendering their management to lovers, only to realize later what complications could ensue. Blazing a trail for equally strong and smart successors such as Missy Elliott—who refers to Latifah as a friend and role model—Latifah managed her own business affairs or delegated them to trusted members of her family, such as her mother, or to longtime friend Shakim Compere, who had been a former student of Rita's and eventually became one of Latifah's closest companions. Always quick to recognize financial implications, she was careful to trademark the Queen Latifah name as well.

Demonstrating her fearlessness in the face of opposition, she moved over to Motown when Tommy Boy lost interest after *Nature of a Sista'*. The jump to Motown meant leaving behind some of her longtime allies, including the 45 King, whose skills were not considered essential by Motown, but it didn't mean that Latifah gave up all of her creative control or her interest in working with friends. In the 1990s, Latifah established her own record label and management company, Flavor Unit, which referred to a posse of New York and New Jersey rappers such as Chill Rob G, Storm P, and Apache. Among the acts she discovered and managed for Flavor Unit was Naughty by Nature, whose hugely successful debut album featured Latifah as executive producer, rapping on the song "Wickedest Man Alive." Naughty by Nature returned some of Latifah's favors, acknowledging her in their songs and acting as producers on *Nature of a Sista'*. Although Naughty by Nature made its name with the lighthearted "O.P.P.," many of their other songs were powerful anthems for black pride and progress in the face of indignity and injustice. Much of their work resonated with the same themes as those favored by Native Tongues, and several of their records included some mention of Native Tongues and Zulu Nation, including their Grammy-winning 1995 album, *Poverty's Paradise*. Flavor Unit's roster would eventually include artists such as Outkast, Next, and LL Cool J, and some of the artists loaned their talents on one another's albums. Once again, Latifah's mother, always a powerful force in her life, assumed an important role at Flavor Unit, serving as its vice president, while Shakim Compere served as Latifah's business partner in Flavor Unit and other ventures.

While Queen Latifah has refused to describe herself as a feminist, she does espouse clearly feminist ideals, promoting female strength wherever possible. When describing the motivation behind songs such as "Ladies First," Latifah has noted the level of distress and puzzlement she experienced when she realized that the sexism in hip hop was becoming more acceptable to female rappers as well as male ones. Female rappers began embracing negative labels for themselves and other women, a development that Latifah observed critically. Rather than attacking the men of hip hop, Latifah's response was to nurture the self-esteem of her female compatriots. If she could build up their consciousness, she felt, then empowerment and respect would follow. Given her investment in a sense of sisterhood, it was no surprise that she was a participant in a 1991 concert called Sisters in the Name of Rap, a nationally televised hip hop event featuring thirteen female rappers, including

Salt-N-Pepa, MC Lyte, Nefertiti, Yo Yo, and Shanté. Despite the fact that the Queen's image has changed substantially over the years, from tough-talking Afrocentric rapper to glamorous jazz-singing actress, Latifah's dedication to social activism seems consistent. Her pride in her culture and her gender made her a natural, articulate spokeswoman at events organized to support charitable efforts or social activism.

Although "Ladies First" remains, perhaps, the defining song of the Queen's career, a close second would have to be "U.N.I.T.Y.," the Grammy-winning call to arms that condemned the misogyny for which hip hop is so often criticized. Preaching love for black men and black women alike, the song also let both know in no uncertain terms that disrespect and name calling are unacceptable. Offering tough solutions for men who treat women as sexual objects or who take out their frustrations on them, "U.N.I.T.Y." reminded black women to keep their pride and self-respect in the most difficult of situations. Moreover, it returned to some of the themes that were so important in "Ladies First," emphasizing again the unity needed within the African American community and the power such unity provides. Aside from the Grammy for Rap Solo Performance, "U.N.I.T.Y." also garnered an NAACP Image Award and a Soul Train Music Award in 1994. "U.N.I.T.Y." was the standout single on Latifah's 1993 *Black Reign* album, a darker and more diverse collection of songs than that found on *All Hail the Queen*, which highlighted social problems but also preached optimism and positivity. *Black Reign*, written during a difficult period in Latifah's life, reflects some of her moodiness, although the strength of "U.N.I.T.Y." clearly indicates that her tough, enduring spirit has prevailed through everything.

Order in the Court, her 1998 follow-up album, featured an attention-grabbing cover, with spikes of fire erupting from Latifah's head, but this implied anger is not in major evidence on the record itself. *Order in the Court* did not feature any songs that made the same strong social waves as "Ladies First" or "U.N.I.T.Y.," instead offering a lighter R&B sound and duets with artists such as Faith Evans. Sales for *Order in the Court* were moderately good, buoyed by popular singles such as "Bananas," an increasingly rare rap track in which the Queen once again served notice that she wanted respect and reminded competitors that she was in a class of her own, and "Paper," featuring Pras Michel and Jaz-A-Belle and sampling "I Heard It Through the Grapevine." A song that garnered less attention was "Black on Black Love," where Latifah demonstrates that she still has something to say about the social ills affecting her people, and about the lack of unity among them. "Paper," which raps, in part, about the difficulties of the music business and criticizes MCs who might be trying to interfere in her friendships and imitate her success, is yet another venue where Queen Latifah is frank about the sacrifices needed to succeed. Perhaps it is not surprising, then, that *Order in the Court* represents what could be her last complete album of original rap songs. Released at a time when her television and film career was heating up,

Order in the Court did not enjoy as much critical success as her earlier work, which may reflect the fact that she was beginning a slow drift away from a full-time musical career. The more mellow musical sounds, featuring less rapping, may also have served as a predictor of Latifah's eventual move toward experimenting with jazz.

Her final original album to date under the Queen Latifah name, *She's a Queen: A Collection of Hits*, released by Universal in 2002, received tepid critical attention, although it did feature some of her early major songs. In between those major releases, Latifah has also loaned her talents to a number of soundtracks, including *Living Out Loud*, *Bringing Down the House*, *Chicago*, *Set It Off*, *New Jersey Drive*, *Sunset Park*, *Nothing to Lose*, *The Associate*, *White Men Can't Jump*, and *New Jack City*. She has also been included in a number of collections, including *Queen Latifah and the Original Flavor Unit*, a 1996 collection featuring longtime collaborators such as Lakim Shabazz, Lord Alibaski, and Apache. Her most recent album taps into the world of jazz she explored in films such as *Living Out Loud*, and is titled simply *The Dana Owens Album*. Although jazz may seem a world apart from *Black Reign* or *All Hail the Queen*, critics were favorably impressed by her range on the *Living Out Loud* soundtrack, and more than one noted that the Latifah tracks were perhaps the best on the entire album. Small wonder, then, that she followed up by delivering a complete album dedicated to jazz. The departure from her early work is marked not only by the difference in sound, but by the messages contained. That is to say, there are no real messages from the Queen on *The Dana Owens Albums*, which is a collection of covers, many of which are considered quite good—particularly the wistful "Lush Life"—but none of which deliver the forceful rhymes and frank talk of her rap albums. Although Queen Latifah still performs rap songs in concert, there are few signs that she plans to reposition herself at some point as an original and fearless contributor to the world of rap.

THE HIGHS AND LOWS

If Queen Latifah has changed in terms of her professional focus and musical style, her personal life has been marked forever by one particular transformation. While Latifah's family continues to provide a strong support base in a number of respects, the loss of one family member was a devastating blow. At first, 1992 started out as one of the best years of her life, marked by a Top 10 single, "Latifah's Had It up 2 Here," a Grammy nomination, and a bit part in *Jungle Fever*. However, in March, a tragedy transformed that year into one of unimaginable sadness. Latifah's brother Winki was killed in an accident, riding a motorcycle that she had purchased for him as a birthday gift. The death was unexpected and the grief so sharp that Latifah struggled with depression and confusion for some time after, using alcohol and marijuana in an unsuccessful attempt to cope. Only two years apart in age, Latifah and Winki had been close friends as well as siblings, and in many ways he was the man in her life. Her father was an important figure, but his presence was inconsistent. Battling his own demons and lurching from one affair to another, he fathered other children whose existence had taken Latifah and Winki by surprise. Eventually the two learned that they had two half-sisters, Michelle and Kelly, and a half-brother, Angelo. The man who had raised Latifah to be self-sufficient, strong, and confident also proved to be a man who was unfaithful and who concealed the results of his affairs. While Latifah managed to maintain a relationship with her father, she did experience a sense of betrayal that affected not only her faith in her father, but her faith in other men as well.

It was, in part, the example of her father, who struggled constantly with a cocaine addiction, that helped Latifah realize that drugs were not helping her deal with the pain of loss. She decided to seek solace in her music, since she was already contractually obligated to Motown and since work appeared to be therapeutic. On *Black Reign*, the first album by a female rapper to attain gold status, Latifah was able to discuss her grief and pay tribute to her brother. Released in 1993, the album mentioned Winki in the song "Black Hand Side," but the key song was "Winki's Theme," which allowed Latifah to express her belief that her brother was watching over her and also spoke to her faith in God despite her confusion over what had taken place, as well as her insistence that she would have to continue being herself. The effect was so positive that she suggested the inclusion of a song mentioning Winki might be a trademark on each of her future albums.

Although questions about her sexual orientation have dogged her for years, particularly following her convincing portrayal of the lesbian Cleo in the movie *Set It Off*, Latifah's personal life has rarely occupied the popular press in the same way as that of fellow rappers. Her reputation has been mainly impeccable, resulting in a considerable shock for the public when she was pulled over by the police in 1996 for possession of marijuana and a handgun. That brush with the law was followed by another in 2002 when she was pulled over for driving while intoxicated, but while her public may have been disappointed and surprised, Latifah has always been candid about her drug use. Despite eschewing prolonged use or experimentation with the hardest drugs, the rapper went so far as to list the drugs she has tried in her 1999 autobiography.

While Queen Latifah has never attracted the more piercing and strongly critical attention commanded by audacious counterparts such as Lil' Kim or Foxy Brown, her increasing commercialism and attempts at entering the mainstream have drawn criticism. The Afrocentrism and social commentary that guided her earlier efforts appear to have given way to a desire to be more accessible and more diverse. Although her music is no longer the key component of her career, her most recent collections are far from the fierce battle cries found in "Ladies First" and "U.N.I.T.Y." In fact, her decision to release her 2004 collection of jazz and soul songs, *The Dana Owens Album*, under her given name seems to signal a greater desire than ever to leave behind the Queen Latifah persona. Interestingly, however, the album cover does feature Queen Latifah's name despite the contrast with the title.

CELLULOID CELEBRITY: THE RAPPER GOES HOLLYWOOD

However, that persona has enjoyed considerable success inside and outside the world of music. Queen Latifah's early decision to enter the world of acting is hardly unique in the world of hip hop, where pragmatic rappers, particularly female ones, have concluded that a movie or television career may be a boon if the notoriously competitive world of hip hop forces an early end to musical prospects. Latifah's success, however, has few peers. With her cameo role in Spike Lee's 1991 hit *Jungle Fever*, she made a strong foray into territory that no other rappers had entered decisively at that point, following it up swiftly with appearances in *House Party 2* and *The Fresh Prince of Bel-Air*, both vehicles for other rappers—Kid 'N Play in the first case and Will Smith in the second.

With her starring role as Khadijah on the Fox situation comedy *Living Single*, she followed in Smith's footsteps as a rapper starring in a successful situation comedy (see sidebar: Keep 'Em Laughing: Hip Hop and Sitcoms). *Living Single* ran from 1993 to 1997, but before that, Latifah appeared as a straight-talking record executive opposite young rising stars Omar Epps and

---

Keep 'Em Laughing: Hip Hop and Sitcoms
Faiza Hirji

Although the rapper-as-actor scenario has now reached the status of near-cliché, it was still quite unusual when Queen Latifah was selected to headline *Living Single*, a situation comedy revolving around a group of close, very different friends. *Living Single* debuted in 1993, and LL Cool J's *In the House* debuted in 1995, following on the early nineties success of the show that helped blaze the trail for rappers in sitcoms: Will Smith's *The Fresh Prince of Bel-Air*. Latifah made guest appearances on *Fresh Prince* before her own foray into television stardom.

The Fresh Prince of Bel-Air, which can still be found in reruns, had a long and successful run from 1990 to 1996, increasing Will Smith's profile both as an actor and as a rapper. *Fresh Prince*, a lighthearted comedy about the cultural clash between an affluent Los Angeles family and their mischievous West Philadephia-raised nephew, paved the way for a long career. However, Smith's position at the beginning of *Fresh Prince* was quite different from that of LL Cool J or Queen Latifah. In many ways, he had no street credibility to lose as he assumed the role of the goofy Will. His musical success had begun even before Latifah's, but from a very different platform. His biggest songs, such as "Girls Ain't Nothing but Trouble" and "Parents Just Don't Understand" were inoffensive, humorous, and completely apolitical.

The stakes were a bit higher for LL and the Queen. It was the latter who landed a sitcom first, although both rappers had been testing out their acting skills with small film roles. *Living Single* featured Queen Latifah as a magazine editor whose interactions with her three girlfriends and male neighbors formed the basis of the show. Running 1993-1998 on Fox, the show only seemed to make Latifah more popular, but it also marked a period when music appeared to give way to a focus on acting.

LL Cool J, otherwise known as James Todd Smith, enjoyed a popularity similar to Latifah's as early as 1984, when he joined forces with the newly emerging Def Jam. His work, ranging from funky to romantic to hard-hitting, was perhaps bolder and more controversial than Will Smith's, but it was still classified by some as mediocre and unoriginal. Nonetheless, LL racked up sales for records, endorsements, and merchandise, and like Queen Latifah, he always demonstrated solid business sense, trademarking LL Cool J (Ladies Love Cool James) and maintaining a presence in different forms of media and marketing. *In the House*, which debuted in 1995 on NBC, was his attempt to master yet another medium. The show, also starring Debbie Allen as the head of the family renting from LL's character, a former football player, was not hugely successful in the ratings, but the support of upstart network UPN kept it on the air until 1999.

UPN has continued to provide a home to hip hop artists in sitcoms, featuring Brandy's *Moesha* (1996-2001) and Eve's self-titled show (2003–present), but few situation comedies featuring rappers have managed to come close to the resounding success that was *Fresh Prince*, just as very few rappers have attained the kind of acting resume that Will Smith and Queen Latifah have accumulated during their careers.

Tupac Shakur in the gritty urban drama *Juice*. Although her role was relatively small, it offered a sly nod to music insiders: Playing an industry veteran faced with a bevy of aspiring DJs, Latifah's character dresses down one such DJ in no uncertain terms before conceding that Epps's character, the Harlem-based Q, may have some promise despite having only local experience playing for his friends. Having been discovered by a female executive while still a teenager embedded in a New Jersey crew, the Queen may have been enjoying a laugh and some nostalgia in this scene, as well as a subsequent one where Q impresses the audience in his first major audition, a contest hosted by Latifah and featuring an appearance by Fab 5 Freddy, who also contributed to Latifah's big break.

Whether or not the parallels to Latifah's industry experience were intended in *Juice*, her next move took her away from movies set in the world of hip hop as she accepted a role in the Michael Keaton film *My Life*. However, this was followed three years later by the notable role as Cleo in *Set It Off* alongside Vivica A. Fox, Jada Pinkett Smith, and Kimberly Elise. While Latifah also contributed the song "Name Callin'" to the soundtrack, the real object of attention during that movie was the sexy and explicit scene between Cleo and her female lover, spurring inquiry regarding what was acting and what was natural. *Set It Off* brought in a Black Film Award for the Acapulco Film Festival in the category of Best Actress, as well as nominations for an Image Award and an Independent Spirit Award.

In 1997, Latifah had a small part in the movie *Hoodlum*, set in 1930s Harlem and starring Laurence Fishburne, Cicely Tyson, Tim Roth, Vanessa L. Williams, and Loretta Devine. Following *Living Single*'s run, she made a return to the movies. She didn't quite hit the ground running with the poorly received *Sphere*, a science-fiction film based on the Michael Crichton novel, but she followed that up with the very different—and more nuanced—feature *Living Out Loud*, in which she played a jazz singer who befriends the lead characters played by Holly Hunter and Danny DeVito. Following *Living Out Loud*, for which she received positive reviews and an Image Award nomination, she reunited with Cicely Tyson in the television miniseries *Mama Flora's Family*, based on Alex Haley's novelized account of his mother's life. In 1999, she teamed up with another black powerhouse in Denzel Washington, playing nurse to his paralyzed detective in the crime thriller *The Bone Collector*.

She had a far smaller role in *Bringing Out the Dead*, also in 1999, which coincided with yet another watershed moment—the launch of her daytime talk show, *The Queen Latifah Show*, which ran in syndication until 2001. Given her air of easy confidence, approachability, and humor, she was a natural choice to head a talk show, despite the fact that the market appeared to be glutted at that time with such shows. Also, 2001 was a busy year in general on the television front—she made appearances on *Spin City*, followed up the next year with a supporting role in the television drama *Living with the Dead*. A small part as herself in the Disney film *The Country Bears* was followed by an Image Award–nominated role as the best friend of Sanaa Lathan's lead character Sidney in the hip hop love story *Brown Sugar*.

That same year, Latifah snagged what has thus far been one of her most significant roles: the part of the corrupt jailhouse warden in *Chicago*, the award-winning musical that generated Oscar, Golden Globe, and Screen Actors Guild nominations for Latifah in the category of Best Supporting Actress, as well as a BET award and a Black Reel Award. Other nominations came from the Teen Choice Awards, the MTV Movie Awards, and the British Academy of Film and Television Arts Awards. The Academy Award for Best Supporting Actress ultimately went to Latifah's costar, Catherine Zeta-Jones, but the nomination and Latifah's performance provided confirmation of what some critics had been saying all along: Latifah was in Hollywood to stay, and she deserved her spot. It was perhaps only appropriate that this affirmation should come in a musical, a form rarely embraced by present-day Hollywood and yet one that the audience seemed to welcome. *Chicago* was not without its critics, however; although Latifah was compelling in her role, the idea of the bawdy, dishonest, and manipulative Mama Morton was one that seemed to play on a number of stereotypes about black women, especially when Mama flaunted her natural assets in a sexy number.

Bringing Down the House, in which Latifah starred alongside Steve Martin while producing as well, attracted some of the same criticism. Playing a wrongly convicted inmate who ingratiates herself into Steve Martin's life in order to secure his legal services, Latifah's character alternately parodies every stereotype of poor black people in the United States and then demonstrates her ability to appear polished and sophisticated when required. This performance, which seemed to highlight both the character's and Latifah's chameleon-like qualities, snagged her an Image Award for Outstanding Actress in a Motion Picture. At the same time, however, while many viewers were pleased to see Latifah in such a high-profile role, others questioned her success in satirizing stereotypes rather than reinforcing them. As Allison Samuels noted in a *Newsweek* article, the theme of the black woman teaching an uptight white man to get in touch with his emotions—in part by grasping her breasts, at one point—is hardly new, and seemed to fit neatly into a genre of comedies that produce laughs by mining ethnic stereotypes. In the same article, however, acclaimed director John Singleton and rapper Snoop Dogg both agreed that work is so scarce for black actors that they cannot always afford to reject such subject matter. As a producer, however, Latifah seemed comfortable with the overall moral of *Bringing Down the House*, which she saw as a sly reminder that people are not always what they seem, a message reinforced rather absurdly in the satire *Scary Movie 3*, where Latifah had a small role. Certainly Latifah has not fit neatly into any category that might have been designated for her—unlike other rappers who have made a career out of appearing in stories about hip hop or urban life, she has managed to cover a vast spectrum of projects in her acting.

Rapping is never far from her heart, however, as demonstrated in *Barbershop 2: Back in Business*, where a typically tough Latifah character puts her rhyming skills up against the male competition in an impromptu battle of wills. Although it did not match the success of the original and Latifah's role seemed peripheral at times, *Barbershop 2* was still enough of a crowd pleaser to snag a BET Comedy Award for Latifah. Following work on television projects such as *Eve* and *The Fairly OddParents*, Latifah turned her attention to writing, devising the story for *The Cookout* with friends Shakim Compere and Darryl "Latee" French. Latifah also acted as executive producer for that film and appeared in a supporting role, but those efforts proved mainly futile as *The Cookout* debuted to cool reviews. A lead appearance in *Taxi* opposite Jimmy Fallon proved no better, but Latifah's star turn in *Beauty Shop*, the *Barbershop* spinoff, was a considerable improvement, earning her nominations from the BET Comedy Awards, the Image Awards, and the Teen Choice Awards.

Demonstrating her versatility yet again, Latifah added a role as Auntie Em in *The Muppets' Wizard of Oz*, followed by another leading role in *Last Holiday*, a remake of a 1950 Alec Guinness movie. The story of a shy woman who must cast aside her considerable inhibitions if she wants to enjoy what she believes are her final days, *Last Holiday* paired Latifah with another rap icon, LL Cool J.

With the same determination she has applied to her musical career, Latifah continues to build on her rich body of screen work, refusing to be stalled by the misses sprinkled among the hits. Latifah rarely surrenders to typecasting or the lure of the consistently ordinary. Her *Ice Age 2* work is joined by the film *Stranger Than Fiction*, a surreal comedy starring Will Ferrell. Thus Latifah's film interests remain versatile, and she ensures that she has several avenues open for success. Continuing to demonstrate a good eye for strong talent, Latifah and Compere recently signed an agreement to comanage Oscar-nominated actor Terrence Howard through their Flavor Unit Entertainment agency. Even at a young age, Latifah seemed to recognize that she would need to develop the talent of others, rather than relying simply on the promise of her own career. Managing others and producing films have allowed her to expand the potential for success. At the same time, her attempts to be all things to all people can result in more mediocre movies than notably good ones. In general, she remains one of the most successful rappers to move into film, bearing in mind how difficult the transition has been for many of her peers. Although she has only made a handful of truly notable films, that still sets her apart, and has contributed to the fact that she is now viewed as an actress as much as a musician.

Interestingly, Latifah is also viewed, to a lesser extent, as a model, appearing in magazines and elsewhere as a spokesperson for Cover Girl. Latifah is not Cover Girl's first musician-cum-actress-cum-model, or its first black spokesperson—Brandy and Tyra Banks have also modeled Cover Girl products. The real surprise lies in the fact that Latifah is not a typical model on a number of levels. In contrast to the days preceding her career, when her first sight of Salt-N-Pepa failed to inspire her because the rappers were more sexy than the down-to-earth Latifah, Queen Latifah is now frequently packaged as an elegant, well-dressed, meticulously made-up woman. The young rapper in cobbled-together Afrocentric ensembles or, alternately, casual athletic gear, appears to have been subsumed into a glossier version. That version, however, still does not conform to Hollywood standards of thinness or beauty, and Queen Latifah has been adamant in stating that she would never attempt to diet her way down to the kind of slimness embraced by many other women, including most of the African American women who succeed in hip hop or in acting. She advocates a healthy and active lifestyle, but reminds women that model-like body types cannot be realistically achieved by most.

Despite suggestions that she did undergo a breast reduction, Queen Latifah remains visibly heavier than her counterparts, which makes her contract as a Cover Girl model even more remarkable. Previous contracts have been awarded to those who do appear to fit into the Hollywood mold, such as the thin and light-skinned Halle Berry or the aforementioned Brandy. As with Latifah's move away from rap and toward a smoother, more mainstream sound, it is difficult to know if this transformation also marks a departure from her determination to be accepted on her own terms, or a reaffirmation that she can be a role model for other women who do not quite fit the mold.

AT THE TOP OF HER GAME? MAPPING THE LATIFAH LEGACY

While she has certainly left behind many of her early trademarks—the short haircut, wearing the colors of the African National Congress, her queen's crown, the military or sporty gear—it is difficult to say if this means Latifah has lost her political or social consciousness. When comparing the regal stance of the young woman on the cover of *All Hail the Queen*—head swathed, next to a black, red, and green symbol that evokes Africa—to the elegant, pinstripe-clad woman with silky straight hair on the cover of *The Dana Owens Album*, it is equally possible to speculate that this is a performer who has merely grown up and now presents a more mature face, or that Latifah has now entered more fully into a glossy corporate system that requires her to tone down any rough edges. Her recent hints that she might contemplate a political career suggest that she may be finding new ways to get across the social messages that she once delivered through forceful raps and in-your-face performances.

Although she seems to have left behind many of her early ambitions to rap about misogyny and self-respect in a way that would empower women and African Americans, she remains a trailblazer in other, unanticipated ways. The Latifah story is still being written—in 2006, she has shown no sign of slowing down, voicing a character in the animated sequel, *Ice Age 2: The Meltdown* and working on a 2007 film production of *Hairspray*. Her filmography continues to grow and she keeps her hand in the musical scene, reminding her fans of both her versatility and her tirelessness. Her own star on the Hollywood Walk of Fame—the first ever awarded to a female hip hop artist—provides further confirmation of the distinctive nature of her accomplishments. While some of her fellow rappers—male and female—have wilted under the pressures of a merciless industry, Latifah has put together a model for success that lasts. She makes no apologies for her mistakes or for her apparent moves away from the rap world, and in fact, she may have no need to do so. Lorraine Ali, offering a generally favorable review of *The Dana Owens Album*, points out how great a shift Latifah has made away from the world of hip hop, noting that it's unlikely that many of today's rappers devote much consideration to her current musical projects: "Too many years have passed and they know her as an icon and an actor, not as a rapper. That's likely fine with Latifah. She is, after all, the Queen of Reinvention" (59).

As the Queen of Reinvention, Latifah has still managed to highlight music in her career, but the music she has performed most recently is softer, far less political, and arguably less original. The Princess of the Posse who once collaborated with Jungle Brothers, Naughty by Nature, and De La Soul went back on tour in 2005, this time with fellow Grammy winners Jill Scott and Erykah Badu. As the three main personalities behind the Sugar Water Festival, Latifah, Scott, and Badu have provided a showcase for black, mainly female vocalists that they hope will make an annual appearance for some time to come. Given Badu's own status as a talented, creative singer who tackles political and social issues as she sees fit, as well as her moves in and around an Afrocentric aesthetic, it is certainly interesting to see Latifah collaborating with her at this stage of their careers. Badu's musical sound and life story have been markedly different from Latifah's, but it may be that artists such as Badu, not just rappers such as Missy Elliott, provide the best evidence that Latifah's legacy is meaningful and yielding fruit for the future.

In the meantime, Latifah continues to sing, to act, to host awards shows, and to foster a kind of omnipresent image in various forms of media. It is difficult to evaluate whether she has managed to fulfill the definition of success she provided in 2002, before the string of movies that came to define her more as actor than rapper: Speaking to Rhonda Baraka and Gail Mitchell on the subject of women in rap, she explained her philosophy by saying that any "female rapper who comes with her own style, stays true to what she does, understands the work that's involved and stays with the right people will be around 10 years from now. But you won't be on top all the time. If you can accept that, you'll be all right" (101). In rap terms, of course, it is impossible to see Latifah as currently on top, a position she seems to accept as she moves toward a softer, more mainstream sound. It does not seem to faze her successors either, many of whom are also working on building diversity into their own careers. The young hard-core rapper Trina, in the same article, commented on the inspiration provided by MC Lyte, Salt-N-Pepa, and Latifah as women who have been successful at different levels and in different settings, a success she has attempted to mimic through her own work in rap, film, and other forms of entrepreneurship (Baraka and Mitchell). Similarly, Eve, one of the most successful young rappers in recent times, has indicated that she thinks female up-and-comers must acknowledge and respect the dues paid by predecessors such as Lyte and Latifah.

The central paradox of Latifah's career is one that can be seen with other rappers as well. Hailed as an icon, worshipped as hip hop royalty, imitated by her successors, Latifah's status as a rapper is both unassailable and frozen in the past. She still has talent, and plenty of it, both dramatic and musical, but she has chosen to use her talents differently than she once did. If she has inspired young women significantly, it seems to be primarily by showing them how to conduct themselves with confidence, to diversify in order to avoid a narrowly focused and unnecessarily short career, and to create strong and meaningful relationships with male and female colleagues alike. The result is a new generation of tough, savvy young female rappers, many of them concentrating on the potential for crossing over into mainstream celebrity. If they demonstrate self-sufficiency, perhaps Latifah's example deserves some of the credit. At the same time, however, Latifah's marketing legacy sometimes seems to overshadow her musical legacy. Her early hits will always be remembered for their frankness, their sincerity, and the impeccability of their timing, as Latifah's pro-woman rhymes dropped into an industry where gender relations were so troubled. However, as Latifah has moved away from lyrics that promoted strength, honesty, and pride for both men and women, few successors have picked up the gauntlet. Hip hop is still a venue where too many women are marginalized, and the rapper who once spoke out against this with such passion now seems to have adopted a new coping strategy: walking away and onto other roads. Regardless of this fact, Latifah remains an iconic figure in the industry, one who helped mentor other young female rappers, to pave the way for hip hop's entry into other fields, and one whose longevity, determination, and versatility still mark her as true hip hop royalty.

See also: Lil' Kim, MC Lyte, Salt-N-Pepa, Roxanne Shanté, Native Tongues, Missy Elliott

WORKS CITED

Ali, Lorraine. "God Save the Queen." *Newsweek* 4 October 2004: 59.
Baraka, Rhonda and Mitchell, Gail. "Lady Rappers: Wider Acceptance, Big Ideas and an Expansive Entrepreneurial Spirit Animate Top Female MCs." *Billboard* 7 December 2002: 101.
Keyes, Cheryl L. "Empowering Self, Making Choices, Creating Spaces: Black Female Identity via Rap Music Performance." *That's the Joint! The Hip-Hop Studies Reader*. Eds. Murray Forman and Mark Anthony Neal. London: Verso, 1994. 265-276.
Samuels, Allison. "Minstrels in Baggy Jeans?" *Newsweek* 5 May 2003: 62.

FURTHER RESOURCES

Lipsitz, George. *Dangerous Crossroads: Popular Music, Postmodernism and the Politics of Place*. London: Verso, 1994.
Mayo, Kierna. "The Last Good Witch." *Vibe Books: Hip Hop Divas*. New York: Three Rivers Press, 2001. 52-61.
Owens, Dana and Karen Hunter. *Ladies First: Revelations of a Strong Woman*. Foreword by Rita Owens. New York: William Morrow, 1999.
Quinones, Ben. "Sista Act." *LA Weekly* 5 August 2005: 100.
Roberts, Robin. "'Ladies First': Queen Latifah's Afrocentric Feminist Music." *African American Review* 28:2 (1994): 245-257.

Wilbekin, Emil. "Great Aspirations: Hip Hop and Fashion Dress for Excess and Success." *The Vibe History of Hip Hop*. Ed. Alan Light. London: Plexus, 1999. 277-283.

SELECTED DISCOGRAPHY

"Come into My House." *All Hail the Queen*. Tommy Boy, 1989.
"Ladies First." Duet with Monie Love. *All Hail the Queen*. Tommy Boy, 1989.
"Mama Gave Birth to the Soul Children." Duet with De La Soul. *All Hail the Queen*. Tommy Boy, 1989.
"Latifah's Had It up 2 Here." *Nature of a Sista'*. Tommy Boy, 1991.
"U.N.I.T.Y." *Black Reign*. Motown, 1993.
"Winki's Theme." *Black Reign*. Motown, 1993.
"Paper." *Order in the Court*. Motown, 1998.
"Goin' Out of My Head." *Living Out Loud*. RCA, 1998.
"Lush Life." *Living Out Loud*. RCA, 1998.

FILMOGRAPHY

Bringing Down the House. Dir. Adam Shankman. Touchstone Home Entertainment, 2003.
Chicago. Dir. Rob Marshall. Miramax, 2003.
Juice. Dir. Ernest R. Dickerson. Island World, 1992.
Last Holiday. Dir. Wayne Wang. Paramount Pictures, 2006.
Set It Off. Dir. F. Gary Gray. New Line Cinema, 1996.

© Orlando Garcia/Getty Image.

The Geto Boys

Jason D. Haugen

The Geto Boys would rather be hated for what we are than loved for what we are not.

Bushwick Bill

Emerging primarily from the West Coast in the mid to late 1980s, one of the most influential and oft-maligned movements of hip hop and rap music was what came to be known as hard-core or gangsta rap. Although originally associated with such California-based rappers as Ice-T and N.W.A., few would argue that not many artists took this genre to a level as extreme as the Geto Boys, the first major rap group to emerge from Houston, Texas. Considered among the hardest of the hard-core gangsta rappers, the Geto Boys attained iconic status through their intermingling of themes of acute mental psychosis with the standard gangsta images of urban street life, where the violence concomitant with the hustling lifestyle is so vividly portrayed in the narratives penned by gangsta rappers (see sidebar: *Hustle and Flow*).

Hustle and Flow
Jason D. Haugen

Perhaps the most significant rap-related film to cross into the mainstream to date is 2005's *Hustle and Flow*, an independently financed film written and directed by Craig Brewer. This film focuses on DJay, a down-and-out pimp and drug peddler played by Terrence Howard, who struggles to break free of his lowly life through creating rap music. Unlike many representations of the pimp persona that have appeared before, the character of DJay is not portrayed in a glamorous way. Rather, he is a conflicted man who hustles because he feels like he has to, on the one hand, but who also shows compassion toward the women for whom he feels a great deal of responsibility.

Facing a midlife crisis of personal and artistic identity, DJay views the upcoming return of an acquaintance-turned-rap superstar (Skinny Black, played by Ludacris) as his last chance to make it, if he can come up with some way not only to produce a worthy sample of original music to present, but also to get Skinny Black to actually listen to it.

The film highlights the obstacles DJay must face in pursuing his dream, from being too poor to afford adequate equipment to being too unknown for successful artists and radio stations to take him seriously. Along the way, we are given a glimpse into the darker side of Memphis street life, as we are exposed to DJay's relationships with women, whom he both exploits and depends on: the pregnant Shug (Taraji P. Henson), the extremely negative Lexus (Paula Jai Parker), and Nola (Taryn Manning), the girl who has to turn tricks in order to finance DJay's recordings. Also emphasized in the film is the collaborative nature of the process of producing rap songs, as DJay works on his lyrics and vocal delivery while his friends Key (Anthony Anderson) and Shelby (DJ Qualls) take on the technical tasks of actually coming up with the music and recording DJay's songs.

Hustle and Flow features original rap songs written by local Memphis underground rapper Al Kapone, as well as the Three 6 Mafia. It was critically acclaimed and nominated for many awards, and won the Audience Award at the Sundance Film Festival. Terrence Howard was nominated for an Academy Award for Best Actor for his performance of DJay, although that award was ultimately presented to Philip Seymour Hoffman for his portrayal of the title character in *Capote*. Three 6 Mafia became the first rap group to ever win an Academy Award for Best Achievement in Music Written for Motion Pictures (Original Song) for "It's Hard Out Here for a Pimp" and was also the first rap group to actually perform at the ceremony.

Being the godfathers of the Houston rap scene, the Geto Boys were not only the forerunners of the recent explosion of Texas hip hop, they were also the first major rap figures to emerge out of what would later be a dominating force in rap music and hip hop much more generally: the Dirty South or the Third Coast. Thus, the influence of the Geto Boys was huge not only to the local scene in Houston but also across the South, and their style would inspire many artists who would later rise out of scenes in New Orleans, Atlanta, Memphis, and elsewhere (see sidebar: The Memphis Rap Scene).

Of course, the fame of the Geto Boys was not limited to hip hop insiders. The invocation of their name still recalls their notoriety in American pop culture at large in their earlier days. The response to their eponymous breakthrough album in 1990 was one of such shock and dismay that not only did

---

The Memphis Rap Scene
Jason D. Haugen

Memphis, Tennessee, is rightfully known as a historical hotbed of American music. Not only was it a major hub of early rock 'n' roll (spawning such legendary artists as Elvis Presley, Roy Orbison, Jerry Lee Lewis, and Carl Perkins), but it was also an influential source of legends of country music (Johnny Cash), the blues (Muddy Waters, Howlin' Wolf, and B.B. King), soul (Otis Redding, Aretha Franklin, Sam Cooke, and Booker T. and the MG's), and funk (Isaac Hayes).

More recently, however, Memphis has served as home to a vibrant hip hop community, being one of the major centers of Southern rap. Although some artists like Eightball and MJG have been influential throughout the South since the early 1990s, the explosion of the Dirty South into national consciousness in the late 1990s brought various Memphis artists to national attention. Memphis rappers have been heavily influenced by the crunk movement, featured on the dance floors of clubs throughout the South.

Eightball and MJG, the first major rap artists to emerge from Memphis, formed Suave House Records in 1993, in order to distribute their own records and those of such other artists as Tela and Crime Boss. They are acknowledged as major early influences of the style of rap that would later be associated with the Dirty South and have maintained a successful career since those early days.

Of late, the best-known Memphis-based group is the Three 6 Mafia. They began life as the Triple 6 Mafia, a hard-core underground rap group; their name alludes to the biblical "Number of the Beast." Over the years many lineup changes have occurred, but the stable members have been Juicy J and DJ Paul. Other members have included the rappers Crunchy Black, Koopsta Knicca, Lord Infamous, La' Chat, and Juicy's older brother, Project Pat. While garnering a large underground following over the years, the group eventually crossed into mainstream success with their Sony Records album *Most Known Unknown* in 2005. They will probably be best remembered as the first rap group to win an Academy Award for Best Achievement in Music Written for Motion Pictures (Original Song). "Hard Out Here for a Pimp" was written for the soundtrack to the movie *Hustle and Flow*, a film that depicts a struggling young pimp trying to garner success in the Memphis rap music scene. Three 6 Mafia won their Oscar in 2006, beating out their more mainstream fellow Tennessee native Dolly Parton for the honor.

---

the group's major label (Geffen, who at that time was the distributor of Rick Rubin's Def American label) refuse to distribute it, the original CD manufacturer refused even to print copies of it. Although the controversy over *The Geto Boys* occurred in the wake of the furor over the sexually explicit lyrics of the 2 Live Crew, the addition of the Geto Boys' uniquely explicit brand of violence to the already turbulent brew of attitude, sex, and "foul" language inherent to rap music went way over the line for many. As Greg Baker pointed out, the popular perception of rap music at the dawn of the 1990s was that 2 Live Crew was "too nasty," N.W.A. was "too dangerous," and the Geto Boys were "too nasty *and* too dangerous" (60, emphasis mine).

In a genre that is intrinsically (and intentionally) controversial, the emergence of the Geto Boys as the most controversial of a lot that included such notable figures as N.W.A. (also including the solo work of Eazy-E, Ice Cube, and Dr. Dre), Ice-T, and myriad others would itself make them icons for pushing the boundaries of what was deemed possible to express through music.

THE EARLY DAYS: FROM INAUSPICIOUS BEGINNINGS TO OVERNIGHT NOTORIETY

The story of the Geto Boys begins with the Ghetto Boys. The prescriptive English spelling of their name is not the only thing unrecognizable about the initial incarnation of the group of rap performers assembled by visionary Houston businessman James "Lil' J" Smith, who set out to create, manage, and promote a rap group that would focus on issues that were relevant to his own friends and personal experience. Established in 1986, the original lineup of Ghetto Boys consisted of Prince Johnny C, the Slim Jukebox, DJ Ready Red, and, much more marginal in the earlier days than he would eventually grow to be, Bushwick Bill. They released their first album, *Making Trouble*, in 1988. This record met with little acclaim (and not much higher record sales), and has been dismissed as little more than a Run-DMC ripoff, with the Ghetto Boys utilizing the Run-DMC musical model of two MCs and an old-school mixing and scratching DJ, throwing in a dancing dwarf as their only truly novel contribution. The album cover alone shows not a small amount of stylistic homage to those New York City rap pioneers, with the

Ghetto Boys wearing black top hats and gold chains in the classic Run-DMC style. What is contained within the album itself has not been the subject of very much discussion in light of what would come shortly after.

When Prince Johnny C and the Slim Jukebox left the group to pursue other career paths, Lil' J was forced to replace them. In stepped Mr. Scarface (originally billed as DJ Akshen, Brad Jordan) and Willie D (Willie James Dennis). Although different versions of the replacement story have been told, and different people have taken credit for the breakout success that was soon to follow, this new lineup (minus DJ Ready Red, who would depart the group after the second album) very quickly established itself as the classic lineup of Geto Boys. Who were these little-known rappers that would come together to create such a potent force as a group?

Bushwick Bill was born with the name Richard Shaw in Jamaica, although he was raised in the Flatbush district of Brooklyn. His induction into the music business was not as a rapper, but as a break dancer. He moved to Houston with his family in 1987 and joined up with the Rap-A-Lot crew as Little Billy, the dancer for the original incarnation of the Ghetto Boys. Willie D would eventually write some lyrics for Bushwick (including his eventual breakout song, "Size Ain't Shit") to see if he could rap, and when he proved that he could, he became a full-fledged member of the group. He would eventually develop his own smooth-flow style and become one of the more recognizable voices and characters in gangsta rap.

Scarface (Brad Jordan) grew up in the South Acres neighborhood in southern Houston. He seems to have had a relatively troubled childhood, with several trips to mental hospitals for what was regarded as unpredictable behavior, and it has been reported that he made a suicide attempt at age fourteen. He is also reputed to have spent some time dealing drugs on the streets of Houston. However, the young kid who would develop into a rap music legend had always had diverse musical tastes, and before becoming a rapper he played lead guitar and sang for a rock band in Houston. By the time he met up with Lil' J and joined the Geto Boys, he had already recorded a single, "Big Time," at age sixteen under the name DJ Akshen. He would eventually adopt the moniker (Mr.) Scarface after recording the song of the same title, which was based on the cocaine-dealing Cuban refugee mob boss character Tony Montana, played by Al Pacino in the 1983 film *Scarface*, which itself became a classic source of samples for many rap groups. It must be pointed out that the original Ghetto Boys might be considered the first rap group of many to utilize this particular cultural source for samples to use in their music—they had previously tapped it for the track "Balls and My Word" on *Making Trouble*. This film, with its focus on the violent lifestyle of an underworld gangster, naturally lends itself to appropriation by rap artists who want to perpetuate similar identities for themselves in the songs that they perform.

Of the three members of the classic lineup of Geto Boys, it was Willie D alone that had already established himself with a solo album (*Controversy*,

1989) before he joined the group. The reestablished Geto Boys recorded some of Willie D's solo songs as a group (e.g., "Do It Like a G.O.," "Bald Headed Hoes"), and it was Willie D who was given the credit for penning most of the tracks on their breakthrough album, *Grip It! On That Other Level*, including such classic Geto Boys songs as "Trigga Happy Nigga" and "Mind of a Lunatic." From the get-go, Willie D was outspoken with an extremely hard edge. With DJ Ready Red behind the mixes, this new lineup respelled their name as the *Geto* Boys and recorded *Grip It! On That Other Level* in 1990. This original recording gained the positive attention of legendary music producer Rick Rubin, of the Def American music label, who was sufficiently impressed with the material to sign the band and then rerecord, reproduce, or simply repackage ten of the twelve songs from *Grip It!*, along with a few new songs, for the self-titled album *The Geto Boys*. It was still 1990, and this revised album brought the Geto Boys into the national spotlight, stirring up controversy before it was even released—indeed, before it was even printed. Because of the controversial nature of the lyrical content, Geffen refused to distribute *The Geto Boys*. The Def American label was able to work out a distribution deal with WEA (owned by Time Warner). By 1991, however, when the Geto Boys recorded their follow-up album, *We Can't Be Stopped*, even WEA backed out and Def American had to move on to yet another distributor, Priority Records.

Although most of the lyrical material was identical to that which had already been produced by the local, independently owned Rap-A-Lot label (in the form of *Grip It! On That Other Level*), the controversy sparked by their attempts at getting national distribution with the major labels is what propelled the Geto Boys into the national spotlight. They would go on to record several more albums with various lineup changes (and others with the classic lineup back intact), but *The Geto Boys* and *We Can't Be Stopped* in particular set the tone for the way that the Geto Boys would go down in history, and it was by means of the public perception created in these records that the iconic status of the Geto Boys was solidified for posterity.

THE MAJOR THEMES OF THE GETO BOYS' MUSIC

What was the fuss all about?

The name Geto Boys has become synonymous with extreme gangsta rap, and the group has been accused of promoting everything from rape to murder, with cannibalism and necrophilia even rearing their heads in various songs (e.g., "Mind of a Lunatic," "Chuckie").

While some cynics have contended that the extreme approach of the Geto Boys was deliberately engineered to stir up controversy and record sales, the band themselves steadfastly maintained that they were simply painting portraits of the reality that they had experienced by means of the lyrics that they chose to record in their songs. Although the songs and albums that they have recorded over the years include a good deal of topical diversity, there are several thematic threads that hold together the Geto Boys' oeuvre.

At the heart of the Geto Boys' songs are primarily tales of urban street life, and particularly of urban "gangsta" life. In some sense, the Geto Boys portray themselves as modern urban outlaws. As with most gangsta rap as a genre, the Geto Boys' narratives emphasize drug dealing and other "gangstafied" images, and all of these tales require a certain level of authenticity to be taken seriously by the audience. One thing that is not in doubt is that these Geto Boys had the street credibility that is so necessary for performers within this particular genre. Before joining the group, Scarface is said to have dealt drugs in his youth, and Willie D had served prison time for an armed robbery. Mid-nineties Geto Boy Big Mike (Mike Barnett) later served a prison term after his gig with the group, and both Scarface and Bushwick Bill have sustained serious injuries during various scuffles outside the studio (and, no doubt, outside the law).

While participating in a genre that takes the gangsta lifestyle as its fundamental backdrop, the Geto Boys are especially noted for the extremity and explicitness of the violence and sex in their narratives. They have also often been regarded as particularly misogynistic in a genre already derided as intrinsically misogynistic.

Beyond the usual gangsta clichés, however, the narratives of the Geto Boys have often centered on the telling of "horror stories," which were usually detailed fictional narratives involving rape, torture, and murder, but placed in the context of the rough inner-city environments with which the rappers themselves had been associated. Although the Geto Boys are not typically considered as overtly political as some other groups like Public Enemy or N.W.A., they certainly do deliver commentary on various political issues. It could be argued that any discussion of the inner-city reality portrayed in gangsta rap is inherently political, but some of the Geto Boys' songs address even more macro-social issues.

Beyond taking gangsta rap "to the next level," perhaps the most notable aspect of the thematic ground covered by the Geto Boys was overtly psychological in nature, the introspective lyrics of many of their songs covering everything from psychotic breakdown ("Mind Playing Tricks on Me") to suicidal tendencies (e.g., "I Just Wanna Die," "Mind Playing Tricks on Me"). The suicidal impulse permeates a fair number of Geto Boys songs, which is remarkable considering that the Geto Boys were some of the foremost proponents of a genre that places so much emphasis on individual strength, and braggadocio, and swagger. All empirical evidence suggests that this was not just a gimmick. One example is Scarface's suicide attempt as a teenager. However, the most (in)famous eruption of the suicide urge occurred in real life for Bushwick Bill, in a scene immortalized in the cover art for the album *We Can't Be Stopped*. While it is not exactly clear what transpired that night, most versions of the story involve a heavily intoxicated Bushwick coaxing his girlfriend to shoot him, possibly while threatening her infant son. The bullet wound in his face led to the loss of Bushwick's right eye, and a photograph of Scarface and Willie D escorting him through the hospital appears on the album cover. This singular image also vaults the Geto Boys into a pantheon of artists that are associated with unforgettable images, one which transcends the narrow genre of hip hop or rap music, fitting into American pop iconography much more generally.

Since all of the themes mentioned above emerge from the rendition of lyrics in particular narrative contexts, it is helpful to consider in more detail some of the most notable specific songs that the Geto Boys produced that address each of these themes.

The Gangsta Lifestyle

One of the Geto Boys' first songs to become known nationally was the 1989 single "Do It Like a G.O.," which brought the gangsta ethos directly into the studio and almost instantiated what might have been the first label-on-label rivalries in rap music. Among other things, this song called out the heads of East Coast and West Coast music labels for ignoring black-owned independent labels like Rap-A-Lot. In this song, the Geto Boys called on other rap musicians to not "sell out" to the white-owned, corporate music industry, which they saw as being in the habit of ignoring raw, streetwise groups such as themselves. The song closes with a skit featuring a phone call supposedly from an executive representing a white corporate label dismissing smaller, independent and black-owned labels, saying that black businessmen would never be able to get themselves together in any significant way. Lil' J asserts otherwise, and he assures the caller that he is willing to "go to war" if that is what is required.

Other songs give narrative recountings of what life is like in the ghetto and highlight what the Geto Boys (and many others like them) think they have to do in order to survive in such a hostile environment. In one particularly descriptive song, "Straight Gangstaism," Big Mike details observing older gangstas from his neighborhood from when he was a small child. He talks about how he used to study and emulate their styles, and how he admired everything from their cars to their nicknames to the way they stood and wore their hats. He reports that he himself is maintaining the same lifestyle that he had marveled at as a boy, and that with the respect and admiration he has gained from others from maintaining this lifestyle he sees no reason to leave it behind. Thus he promises to always be "straight 'g.'" In the next verse, the local cachet of the gangsta image is brought home even more strongly, when the narrator talks about how he used to emulate his own grandfather and how he himself is now only "doing shit like grandpa in every way." Although it is acknowledged that this lifestyle might lead to prison, this is the environment and lifestyle that is familiar, and it will not be abandoned. (That prison is framed as a possibility but not an inevitability is different from the even more pessimistic vision of fellow Houston rapper E.S.G., who, in one chorus, exhorts to his friends "in the grave" and "in the pen," "I'll see you when I get in").

Like other gangsta rap artists before and after (e.g., N.W.A. and Ice-T), the Geto Boys also address the issue of perceived persecution by white law enforcement, particularly in the wake of the notorious video of the beating of Rodney King. "Crooked Officer" is a very direct indictment of law enforcement, particularly of "brainwashed" black police officers. In one verse, Bushwick states that he's not "going out" like Rodney King but would instead grab his gun and come out blasting. They state in no uncertain terms that they and others like them have been persecuted for too long, and they express the desire to put the crooked officers into their coffins. According to their lyrics, the fear of the police permeates all age levels, as does the desire for reprisal. In "Straight Gangstaism," Big Mike talks about playing "Cops and Robbers" when he was a child, when nobody wanted to play the part of the cops because doing so was guaranteed "to get yo' ass kicked."

One particularly poignant portrait of life in the ghetto is delivered in the song "Six Feet Deep," which discusses the aftereffects of gang violence. Here the Geto Boys highlight the grief expressed by mothers who lose their sons and friends who lose their homeboys. They reflect on the senselessness of the death of their friends, how life is going to be without them, and also upon their own mortality and, specifically, their own vulnerability to inner-city violence, which subsequently leads to a need for them to carry their own weapons for self-defense. This tale of ghetto life and loss followed Ice Cube's "Dead Homiez" but foreshadows such later songs as "The Crossroads," Bone Thugs-N-Harmony's eulogy for the late Eazy-E, and Puff Daddy's "I'll Be Missing You," in memory of the Notorious B.I.G.

Tales of Horror

While many songs by the Geto Boys can be considered violent, the violence is usually portrayed in the context of stories of hard inner-city lives that are themselves often punctuated by sudden violence. Some of the group's songs, however, forego the lessons learnable from those contexts and head straight for what may be regarded as pure horror stories, in the tradition of the classic slasher films well known from the cinematic genre.

A prototypical example is "Chuckie," from the album *We Can't Be Stopped*, which makes an obvious allusion to a film of this very nature—the first in a series of movies released under the name *Child's Play*. In these films, a psychopathic (human) killer is able to transfer his soul into a red-headed talking doll named Chuckie. From his new soul-shell he begins a rampage, attempting especially to murder the child that had tried to befriend the Chuckie doll. In the Geto Boys' song, Bushwick Bill raps from the perspective of a psychotic child killer. He describes the murder and dismemberment of several victims, and he exhorts the audience, when they find the victims, to just tell the authorities that "Chuckie did it." Bushwick brags that he would win any murder competition, and that for him murder comes very easily—it is nothing but "child's play." The song opens, closes, and is otherwise infused with audio samples of Chuckie from the movie (e.g., "Hi, I'm Chuckie. Wanna play?"), and other horror movies are alluded to throught the narrative (e.g., *Friday the 13th* and *Night of the Living Dead*).

Bushwick's invocation of Chuckie as a figure of horror to emulate in this particular song is notable for several reasons. First, the premise of the soul of a mass murderer haunting, much less controlling and going on a murder spree in the guise of, a child's doll is so unbelievable that the character can almost only be interpreted as a figure of irony. Second, though, is the fact that Bushwick Bill, himself a dwarf, adopts the Chuckie persona as part of his own. He claims that "half [his] body is Chuckie, the other is Bushwick," but what he clearly means is that he, Bushwick, in the context of the song, has Chuckie's murderous nature within himself. The message is that dangerous people can come in all shapes and sizes, and that Bushwick should not be dismissed as innocuous just because of his small stature. Finally, with "Chuckie's" murder and cannibalism of children juxtaposed with verbal images of Iraqi children being killed by U.S. bombs, it is implied that large institutional forms of violence (as engaged in by the U.S. military) just might be psychotic as well.

In some cases, the Geto Boys' horror story narratives are overtly framed as simple instances of the exercise of free speech, made in order to point out that regardless of the extremity of the violence portrayed in these songs, equally (if not even more) violent things really do occur within our society, and not necessarily just in the inner-city ghetto. An example of such a framing device is used in another song that aims at telling a story of pure horror, from the album *Till Death Do Us Part*. "Murder Avenue" is claimed to have been "inspired by Jeffrey Dahmer." In this song, Bushwick Bill raps about the rape and murder of a law student who had been casing him, and the subsequent terrorizing of a newlywed couple. Although purportedly a song inspired by a real-life murderer, some of the crucial details of the real-world events are erased in the narrative that Bushwick performs—specifically, that Jeffrey Dahmer was a torturer, rapist, and murderer of other men. Heterosexuality is so normative within gangsta rap that it is almost inconceivable that any artist would attempt to lyricize possibly homosexual inclinations, even in a fictional story about committing atrocities against their fellow men. The rape in this song is directed toward the female law student ("Rosie") and newlywed bride ("Bridgett"), whereas the newlywed husband ("Ted") is merely tortured and murdered. In a later song ("The Bushwicken") from his solo album *Phantom of the Rapra*, Bushwick gives a further nod to the reality that inspires some of the lyrics in his music, claiming that in comparison to himself, Dahmer was a "minor case."

Psychological Breakdown

Some of the more extreme violence portrayed in the lyrics of the Geto Boys is intended to be taken much more seriously, however. In these cases, the presumed psychosis of the narrator is taken to be a natural outgrowth of the violence and chaos of the urban street life in which the narrator is (or has been) embedded. That is, the narrator is portrayed as reacting violently to a violent world over which he has no control.

A prototypical example of a song detailing the psychological breakdown of a narrator is "Mind of a Lunatic," which probes the psyche of men driven insane by the ghetto. This song, with its grisly details, is probably the most often cited example of the extreme lyrics of the Geto Boys. In it, Bushwick Bill raps about his rape and murder of a woman he had observed through an open window, and the paranoia he experienced after the deed when he remains with her bloody body. Scarface details getting into gunfights with drug dealers and the police, with his own insanity being exacerbated by the smoking of "fry," a marijuana joint laced with PCP. In a standoff with the police, Scarface begins to shoot innocent bystanders, but then he wakes up in a mental ward with slit wrists. Willie D warns the audience not to mess with him, because he is exceedingly dangerous and does not tolerate "bullshit"; he'll stab you, blow up your house, and other nefarious doings.

Songs like "Mind of a Lunatic" are particularly effective because of the street cred of their performers; although we presume that these stories are intentionally designed to have dramatic effect, they are delivered in such a way that the audience might well believe that the real-world rappers have the capability to do some of the things they rap about. As an example, Willie D overtly blurs the line between fantasy and reality, stating that what he is saying "is fact, not fiction." Fantasy also intrudes upon reality when the narrators, in the course of committing their crimes, invoke violent figures from popular culture (such as Jason, the hockey mask–wearing killer from the *Friday the 13th* movies, and Freddy Kruger, the killer who murders teens in their dreams in the *Nightmare on Elm Street* films). It is left to the audience to discern what is real and what is not, since we cannot trust the narrators themselves, they claim to have gone insane.

The narrators also claim that society should be blamed for the ills perpetrated by the characters in "Mind of a Lunatic," not only for causing their psychoses but also for allowing them to roam the streets. Bushwick raps that he ought to be bound by a straitjacket, and Willie D says that he should have been killed as a child before he had the opportunity to wreak havoc on society.

Paranoia, homicidal thoughts, and other forms of psychosis are also dealt with in one of the Geto Boys' biggest hits, "Mind Playing Tricks on Me."

Although these same issues are addressed in "Mind of a Lunatic," the former song is much less explicit than the latter. As a result, "Mind Playing Tricks" was actually able to be played on commercial radio, and it was, frequently, when it was released. Scarface describes paranoia and suicidal fantasies but relates that he cannot kill himself and leave his child an orphan. Willie D expresses the feeling of being well-known in the 'hood and feeling constant fear of being stalked by the people that he himself had victimized in the past. Bushwick delivers a particularly memorable tale of getting into a fight with the father of a child whose Halloween candy he and his friends had stolen, and then coming to the realization that not only is it not Halloween, but his friends are not with him, and he has not been beating a man but bashing his fists onto the concrete sidewalk.

World Politics

In some cases, the Geto Boys address geopolitical issues. The song "Fuck a War" features a very explicitly negative reaction to the dispatch of troops to repel Saddam Hussein's army from Kuwait in the First Gulf War, with Bushwick arguing that it would be better to simply nuke Iraq than send in "niggaz on the front line." Similarly, the politics of the ghetto are extended to the national level in "Damn It Feels Good to Be a Gangsta," in which the first George Bush, the president of the United States at the time, is portrayed as just another gang-banging hustler who only happens to be white and in possession of much more clout than the ghetto-bound gangstas featured in most gangsta rap music lyrics. "The World Is a Ghetto" discusses the similarities of U.S. inner-city urban environments like Houston's Fifth Ward to well-known hostile locales like Rwanda and discusses how poor (and especially black) people are neglected all across the world.

The Geto Boys engaged in larger political discourses outside the studio as well, with Bushwick Bill stirring up controversy for his use of the terms *bitch* and *ho* at a meeting of the National Association of Black Journalists in 1993. Scarface was among a variety of Rap-A-Lot rappers who recorded a song to benefit Texas death row inmate (and ultimately, executee) Gary Graham in 1993. Willie D's lyrics were almost always political, and in his later incarnation as a syndicated talk show host he addressed many issues relevant to urban and black America.

Sexual Politics

Like many rap groups that have been called gangsta, the Geto Boys, especially early in their career, produced songs about sexual relations, utilizing the well-known categories assigned to women in this genre (i.e., "bitches," "hos," etc.). Released in 1990, in the wake of N.W.A.'s song "A Bitch Is a Bitch" (1989), the Geto Boys' "Let a Ho Be a Ho" did not break any new lyrical ground. Even so, the issue of sexual politics from the gangsta perspective is addressed in such songs as "Gangsta of Love," "Bald-Headed Ho's," "Let a Ho Be a Ho," and "This Dick Is for You."

Other Themes

Of course, not all of the songs recorded by the Geto Boys can be topically compartmentalized, and many of their works crosscut the categories that have been proposed here. Among other notable topics covered by the Geto Boys' lyrics, "Cereal Killer" (from *Till Death Do Us Part*) is a satiric comedy, wherein Scarface raps about a crime spree involving various characters from the world of children's sugary breakfast cereals. His partner in crime is "Captain Crunch"; he murders a victim named "Fruity Pebbles," is chased down by a police officer named "Franken Berry," and so on. "The Unseen," from *Uncut Dope*, is an antiabortion song. "Bring It On" (from *Till Death Do Us Part*) is a tour de force mélange of the Geto Boys and various guest rappers (including the 5th Ward Boys) engaging in an old-school rap-off, testing their skills on the mic as they talk about their skills outside the studio.

THE LATER YEARS AND THE SOLO CAREERS

Perhaps not surprising for a group cobbled together as a business venture by an enterprising young rap mogul, the Geto Boys were never the best of friends outside the studio. In later years, they would always express respect for each other as individuals, while maintaining that their relationship as a group was for business only. Perhaps it is also not surprising that this perspective was conducive to a certain fluidity of group membership. Several lineup changes occurred over the years and, since this has been the case even from the very beginning, it might be said that fluidity is in fact the norm for the group, even though what has been called the classic lineup is still the prototypical arrangement of Geto Boys.

DJ Ready Red left after *The Geto Boys* was released in 1990, and Willie D would leave after the group released *We Can't Be Stopped* in 1991. For the recording of *Till Death Do Us Part* in 1993, Big Mike was added to the lineup, but he was gone when Willie D returned for a reunion with Scarface and Bushwick Bill on 1996's *The Resurrection*. For their next album, *Da Good Da Bad & Da Ugly* in 1998, Bushwick Bill was gone, replaced by the rapper DMG. In 1998, Bushwick Bill sued Rap-A-Lot Records for $20 million, for an alleged assault that occurred outside a comedy club, which he claimed had involved Rap-A-Lot employees attacking him for trying to break out of a recording contract. However, by 2005 all seemed to be forgiven, as Bushwick returned for yet another reunion with Scarface and Willie D, *The Foundation*, in 2005, and for *War and Peace* in 2006.

The later Geto Boys albums have met with relatively positive reviews and decent album sales, although their later work is generally regarded as only maintaining the legendary status that the group had already acquired. To date, two greatest hits compilations have been released. *Uncut Dope* was released in 1992, containing tracks from the first four albums (and mostly from *The Geto Boys* and *We Can't Be Stopped*), along with some otherwise unreleased material like "The Unseen" and "Damn It Feels Good to Be a Gangsta." A later package, *Greatest Hits*, released in 2002, includes tracks from those four albums plus songs from the later 1990s albums: *Till Death Do Us Part*, *The Resurrection*, and *Da Good Da Bad & Da Ugly*. The later package includes a bonus DVD featuring Geto Boys videos and live performances from the entire period covered by the collection.

Throughout the grand run of the Geto Boys, each of the members has worked on various side projects, and each has released various solo albums over the years. However, only Scarface has sustained a level of success as a solo artist that rivals (and possibly even exceeds) that of the Geto Boys as a collective entity.

Scarface

On October 26, 1991, the leading magazine observing the business side of the entertainment industry, *Billboard*, initiated a new category to track the success (measured in terms of album sales) of new musical artists. Unlike the other categories monitored by *Billboard*, the Heatseekers chart was designed to be open only to artists who had never broken into the top half of album sales for any given week (i.e., artists who have not appeared in the Top 100 on the *Billboard* Top 200 list). The number one album on that inaugural list was Scarface's first solo album, *Mr. Scarface Is Back*. While it might at first seem odd for a debut album to include the notion of returning, Scarface was already somewhat known from his work with the Geto Boys; in fact, on the album cover he is billed as "Scarface of the Geto Boys." This album graduated from the Heatseekers list (and into the *Billboard* Top 100) by the next week, having received critical accolades to go along with its commercial success. It would ultimately rise to number fifty-one on the *Billboard* Top 200 and number thirteen on the R&B/Hip-Hop list.

Lyrically, *Mr. Scarface Is Back* continued with the themes previously covered by the Geto Boys on their albums *The Geto Boys* and *We Can't Be Stopped*, but Scarface's performances were so well done that this solo effort quickly began to establish him as the standout performer of the group. This initial impression would be borne out by the later success of his solo albums, as compared to the solo output of Bushwick Bill and Willie D. Among the narrative-driven songs on *Mr. Scarface Is Back* were ones that dealt with the life of a drug dealer ("Mr. Scarface"); life in the urban jungle ("Money and the Power"); sexual politics ("The Pimp"); and mental psychosis brought on by the urban jungle ("Murder by Reason of Insanity" and "Mind of a Lunatic").

In 1993 Scarface released his second solo album, *The World Is Yours* (1993), which has been interpreted as a slight change of direction for him. On the song "Now I Feel Ya," Scarface expanded his thematic ground to cover the personal maturation that he had to undergo once he was able to see his own child growing up, and in trying to provide a better lifestyle for himself and his child Scarface draws a parallel between himself and the mother and grandmother who had raised him. It is only at this life stage that Scarface acknowledges understanding where they had been coming from when he was a troubled youth; as he states in the song's refrain, addressing his mother and grandmother, "*Now* I feel ya." Additionally, unlike his previous album (and much other music in hip hop up to that time), new legal issues prevented the indiscriminate sampling that had been such a focus of this genre in the past. Commercially *The World Is Yours* did better than *Mr. Scarface Is Back* and all previous Geto Boys efforts, rising to number one on the *Billboard* Top R&B/Hip-Hop albums chart. (That same year, *Till Death Do Us Part* would be the first Geto Boys record to reach that same level.)

Scarface's commercial success would only improve, as *The Diary* (1994) would reach number two on both the R&B/Hip-Hop and Top 200 lists. This album featured songs about murder ("The White Sheet"), death ("I Seen a Man Die"), vigilante justice ("No Tears"), gangstas defending their territory from rivals ("G's"), braggadocio over sexual prowess ("Goin' Down"), and a solo reworking of a Geto Boys classic ("Mind Playin' Tricks 94"), among others.

In 1997, Scarface's next album, *The Untouchable,* went all the way to number one on both *Billboard* lists. Although several Geto Boys and Scarface solo records would eventually be at the top of the *Billboard* R&B/Hip-Hop chart, to date *The Untouchable* is the only Geto Boys–related album to also reach the number one spot on the Top 200, which covers all musical genres. In 1998, Scarface released the double-length album *My Homies*, and in 2000 he released *Last of a Dying Breed*. Both of these albums would reach the Top 10 of both *Billboard* lists, giving Scarface a much better run of album sales than the other Geto Boys have been able to attain (either as a group or individually). To add to this commercial success, one of Scarface's biggest critical achievements was winning Lyricist of the Year honors from *The Source* magazine at the 2001 Source Awards for his work on *Last of a Dying Breed*.

Although at this point it is impossible to tell what may be in store for Scarface's future, one important milepost in any artist's career is the release of a worthy compendium chronicling their output up to that date. Scarface's collection *Greatest Hits* appeared in 2002, the same year that also saw the release of the Geto Boys' *Greatest Hits*. Scarface's collection included memorable tracks from all of his solo albums up to that time. However, this collection could hardly be said to have been a career-capper, as he almost immediately released another album, *The Fix,* in 2002, and has been actively recording ever since, subsequently releasing the further albums *Balls and My Word* (2003); *Scarface Presents the Product: One Hunid* (2006); and *My Homies Part 2* (2006). In addition, at this writing Rap-A-Lot Records has announced the imminent release of a collaborative album from Scarface and the late Tupac Shakur, *2-Face.*

Besides the commercial success evidenced by the numerical measurement of album sales and relative position on charts like the *Billboard* R&B/Hip-Hop and Top 200, one important sign of Scarface's major influence on hip hop and rap can be gauged by the number of important artists who have wanted to collaborate with him. The many artists who have recorded songs with Scarface over the years include Ice Cube, Dr. Dre, and Too $hort ("Game Over"); 2Pac and Johnny P. ("Smile"); Master P ("Homies and Thugz"); Too $hort, Devin "The Dude," and Tela ("F*** Faces"); Jay-Z and Beanie Sigel ("Guess Who's Back"); Nas ("In Between Us"); Faith Evans ("Someday"); the Game ("Never Snitch"); Mos Def and Common ("The Corner"); and also various Geto Boys such as Bushwick Bill ("Do What You Do") and Willie D ("The Geto"). Some of these and many other collaborations are featured especially on the albums *My Homies* and *My Homies Part 2* (as well as on *Greatest Hits*).

Beyond his success as a rapper, Scarface has also been a successful producer, producing not only various material of his own but also that of others. In 2002 he was named the president of Def Jam South, where he has been credited with the original major-label signing of Ludacris, who would turn out to be one of the Dirty South's most successful rappers. More recently, Scarface has formed a new company, the Underground Railroad Movement, and under a partnership with KOCH Records released *Scarface Presents the Product: One Hunid* in 2006. This record represents Scarface's effort to present and promote a new group of up-and-coming rappers to the world, rapping alongside Scarface himself. The Product features the vocal talents of Will Hen (from San Francisco) and Young Malice (from Jackson, Mississippi), in addition to Scarface.

In many ways, this new effort is a return to Scarface's roots with the Geto Boys, in that a rap mogul has formed a group to be promoted by his own independent record label. In this case, however, the man at the helm is one of the most respected rappers in the world. We will have to wait to see how successful (critically, commercially, and influentially) the Product will ultimately be; regardless, its appearance is yet one more footprint made by Scarface, who will always be remembered for originally establishing himself in his work with the Geto Boys.

Bushwick Bill

Although he originally wrote little of his own material with the Geto Boys, Bushwick Bill's stature has always allowed him to stand out in a crowd, and he has developed into a respected rapper with his own style, a flair for the outrageous, and a dark sense of humor. With such a strong personality, most people either love him or hate him. His first solo album, *Little Big Man*, met relatively positive reviews when it was released in 1992.

Perhaps the most well-known song on *Little Big Man* is "Ever So Clear," the title of which makes a pun on the high-alcohol grain liquor Everclear, which he was supposedly drinking on the night that is immortalized on the cover of the Geto Boys album *We Can't Be Stopped*. It was on that night that he got into a fight with his girlfriend, threatened her baby, and tried to coax her into shooting him after changing his mind about shooting her (according to the account told in this song). Bushwick details the pain, both physical and emotional, of being shot in the face and losing his eye, and he concludes that it was "fucked up" that he "had to lose an eye to see shit clearly." Another song on that album, "Letter from the KKK," implores "gangbangers" to abandon the violent gang life, since the inner city of that day was killing off the next generation of young black men, and that this was actually doing the work that white supremacists like the Ku Klux Klan would like to have been doing themselves. In "Chuckwick," Bushwick reprises his "half-Chuckie/half-Bushwick" role, for another round of lyrical killing.

According to one interview with the man himself, it was watching a *Ducktales* cartoon with his children that inspired Bushwick's mix of rap with opera on his next solo album, *Phantom of the Rapra*, in 1995. (It is not clear whence he adopted his new, short-lived pseudonym: Dr. Wolfgang von Bushwickin the Barbarian Mother Funky Stay High Dollar Bilstir). This album would be Bushwick's most commercially successful, rising to number three on the *Billboard* Top R&B/Hip-Hop Albums Chart, and number forty-three on the overall *Billboard* Top 200. Bushwick Bill's later solo albums include *No Surrender . . . No Retreat* (1998), *Universal Small Souljah* (2001), and *Gutta Mixx* (2005), all of which have had their fans and detractors.

Willie D

In an interesting twist of fate, Willie D may have started out as the strongest songwriter of the classic lineup of Geto Boys, but he has probably had the least successful solo career. This would not have been obvious to an outside observer in 1989, however, when he released his first album *Controversy*, thus becoming the only Geto (or Ghetto) Boy to record his own album before he joined the group. *Controversy* contained several songs that would later be recorded by the Geto Boys.

Willie D left the group, purportedly because of financial disagreements with Rap-A-Lot, for his second solo effort, which followed on the heels of his success with the Geto Boys with the albums *Grip It! On That Other Level* and *We Can't Be Stopped*. *I'm Goin' Out Lika Soldier* appeared in 1992, and was a *Billboard* number one Heatseeker for one week before peaking at number eighty-eight on the Top 200. This album was especially notable for its infamous song "Fuck Rodney King," in which Willie D calls Rodney King a "sellout" and an "Uncle Tom" for pleading for peace during the posttrial LA riots. At this time, Willie D also publicly called fellow rapper Eazy-E a sellout for supporting one of the four police officers on trial for beating Rodney King. Willie D's later albums, all of which have received mixed reviews and marginal attention, include *Play Witcha Mama* (1994), *Loved by Few, Hated by Many* (2000), *Relentless* (2001), and *Unbreakable* (2003).

Ironically, it is Willie D's other careers after the Geto Boys that make him stand out from the group, including a brief stint as a politically oriented syndicated radio talk show host, an amateur boxer, and the operator of a real estate business based in Azerbaijan. Nevertheless, Willie D will not be forgotten as a rapper and a songwriter, and he will always be recognized as the man whose bold lyrical invention propelled the Geto Boys into the limelight in their early days.

THE LEGACY OF THE GETO BOYS

The status of the Geto Boys as hip hop icons can be demonstrated by an examination of their legacy, within hip hop and rap music specifically, but also within popular culture more generally. With respect to their influence on other rappers, the Geto Boys showed early on that gangsta rap was a viable genre of music that could be applied outside of the already well-worn territories covered by LA-based groups. Like other gangsta rappers, the Geto Boys were able to infuse street credibility into their performances, and the subjects that they discussed were relevant to and caught on with urban audiences across the South and across the nation. In addition, the Geto Boys were also major innovators of the laid-back vocal performance that would come to be associated with the "Southern style," the Dirty South flow, and eventually Houston's Screwed and Chopped style (see sidebar: Sippin' on Some Syrup). Moreover, the extensive use of humor that permeated their music illustrated

"Sippin' on Some Syrup"
Jason D. Haugen

"Sippin' on Some Syrup" was recorded by Three 6 Mafia (featuring UGK), for their 2000 album *When the Smoke Clears*. The title of the song refers to the practice of drinking large doses of codeine-based prescription cough syrups, specifically Promethazine. The syrup is mixed with soda or fruit juice and Jolly Rancher candy. In lyrics, syrup is also called "drank," "purple drank," or "purple stuff," which references a series of television commercials for the fruit drink Sunny Delight. In the commercial, a group of thirsty kids searches through the refrigerator, bypassing soda, orange juice, and "purple stuff" for

Sunny D. In Three 6 Mafia's "Swervin'," the chorus from guest vocalist Mike Jones references drinking purple stuff.

The soporific effects of syrup change or enhance the experience of listening to music, and inspired the chopped and screwed method of production pioneered by Houston's DJ Screw. Chopped and screwed radically slows the backbeats and vocals of rap recordings to create a thick, sluggish sound. DJ Screw and other producers inspired by his style have created alternate chopped and screwed versions of full-length albums from major rap artists.

Drug use has been flaunted in rap music by such artists as Cypress Hill, Redman, Method Man, Ol' Dirty Bastard, Snoop Dogg, and Dr. Dre, whose extremely popular album *The Chronic* was named for a potent strain of Southern California marijuana. While marijuana has long been ubiquitous to many countercultural groups, getting high on codeine-based cough syrups has become specifically and uniquely identified with rap music, and in particular with artists from the Dirty South, such as DJ Screw and various others in the Screwed Up Click (from Houston) and Three 6 Mafia (from Memphis). DJ Screw died at the age of thirty in his recording studio, after suffering a heart attack that a Houston medical examiner attributed to an overdose of codeine.

---

that, although the subject matter was often very serious, it could also be treated in clever and witty ways.

In terms of the business aspect of rap and hip hop, Rap-A-Lot Records was one of the first independent music labels to make it big in the rap industry, and the Geto Boys were the featured artists associated with that label. Other artists to release records with Rap-A-Lot include, in addition to the various solo efforts of individual Geto Boys themselves, the 5th Ward Boys, Gangsta NIP, the Convicts, 2 Low, Do or Die, 3-2, Facemob, and Bun B. The success of Lil' J's Rap-A-Lot label allowed Houston to become one of the first major rap music scenes to emerge outside of New York or LA, and in turn led to the breakout of other major music scenes across the South (see sidebar: The Houston Rap Scene).

With respect to American culture at large, the Geto Boys were able to gain widespread notoriety through a popular acknowledgment that they were among the "hardest" of the hard-core gangsta rappers. The fact that they have been regarded as a bit too extreme may have led to the reality that they have not been able to maintain a consistent level of popular commercial success. Many of their songs have been assumed to be created merely to shock the audience; the controversies over the distribution and printing of their albums in the early years indicate that many people were in fact shocked by their music. The Geto Boys have been singled out and publicly criticized from various angles and from different sectors of American political life, from Republican Party presidential hopeful and Senator Bob Dole and William Bennett to C. Delores Tucker, the head of National Political Congress of Black Women.

The Houston Rap Scene
Jason D. Haugen

Until the breakout year of 2005, in which various artists from the Swishahouse record label (especially Mike Jones, Paul Wall, and Slim Thug) put "H-Town" on the map in a major way, the Houston rap scene had been thought of as a hotbed for promising but, financially speaking, ultimately disappointing talent.

With the exception of the solo career of Scarface, most Houston rappers could never quite make it onto the national stage for any sustained period of time. The Geto Boys, while well-respected among those in the know (including critics and other performers), perhaps pushed the envelope a bit too far for more mainstream tastes, and never hit it big at the national level. Some near-misses were derailed through offstage criminal doings (local rappers Fat Pat and Big Hawk were murdered, and the South Park Mexican was sentenced to forty-five years in prison for aggravated sexual assault on a nine-year-old girl), but most Houston rappers simply failed to catch any prolonged attention at the national level. However, in the wake of what success the Geto Boys did have, a number of well-received rap artists emerged from this city, including UGK (The Underground Kingz, composed of Bun B and Pimp C) and artists associated with DJ Screw.

Perhaps the most lasting single impact on the music industry is the legacy of DJ Screw's radically slowed down ("screwed") style of production. Influenced by the soporific effects of codeine-based cough syrups, DJ Screw single-handedly created a musical revolution that was wildly popular on the Houston underground scene from the early 1990s through the breakout success of Swishahouse in 2005. Although DJ Screw died in 2000 from a heart attack caused by an overdose of codeine, this tradition lives on through the work of many artists, including especially members of the Screwed Up Click from the early 1990s on, including E.S.G., Lil' Keke, Big Pokey, and Lil' Flip. Screw's signature method has been adopted by many artists from Houston and beyond, and remains the most notable contribution to the hip hop world developed in the Houston rap scene.

In terms of mainstream exposure, while many people have heard about the Geto Boys and their controversial lyrics, a lot of them have never actually heard or given serious consideration to the Geto Boys' music. One mainstream introduction to the group was provided by Mike Judge in his 1999 film *Office Space*, which utilized several songs of the Geto Boys in different contexts, albeit as an overt parody. Most notably, an extended scene highlights the song "Damn It Feels Good to Be a Gangsta." The main characters, portrayed as stereotypical white-collar types who are trying to break out of the corporate world, "get into some gangsta shit" with some office supplies, and in a "gangbang"-type effort involving a baseball bat they take out a hapless Fax machine, all while the Geto Boys play in the background.

An additional legacy of the Geto Boys is their secure place within American music generally. Songs that invoke murder are hardly unique to the Geto Boys or even to gangsta rap. Indeed, there is a long tradition of songs about murder in American popular music. In what was at the time the definitive collection of Johnny Cash's music, one of the three albums of his greatest hits collection covered the theme of murder (i.e., the album *Murder* appeared alongside the companion collections illustrating the two other great themes of Johnny Cash's music: *Love* and *God*). Motivations given for murder have varied widely within the canon, from Frankie murdering Albert because she caught him with another woman (in "Frankie and Albert") to the same crime being committed by Stagger Lee upon Billy Lyons, for whom it was all about the theft of the former's John B. Stetson hat. In one of his several classic contributions to this tradition, Johnny Cash's narrator in "Folsom Prison Blues" shoots a man in Reno, "just to watch him die."

What sets gangsta rap apart from the classical treatment of murder in American popular music is the fact that the narratives of gangsta rap are usually framed from the first-person point of view, and that the performers are African American and based in an urban context. Rap music performers who invoke murder, rape, drug dealing, and other crimes must adopt a position in their performance that alludes to some level of authenticity (street credibility) in the subjects of their raps. At the same time, the narratives (and the narrators) insist that the things being rapped about are true. This focus on authenticity is only enhanced by the real-world experiences of the artists, many of whom actually have been involved in the street lifestyle. Of course, this level of credibility is also not unique to gangsta rap or gangsta rappers. It is well known that country music legend Merle Haggard served time in San Quentin prison, supposedly even being in the audience when Johnny Cash performed there. Even earlier, Leadbelly (Huddie Ledbetter) served a couple different terms in prison (once for homicide, and a second time for attempted homicide), and he was (probably apocryphally) reputed to have won his pardon from a governor by the pleasing sounds of his musical performance.

In any event, murder and redemption are themes that permeate not only American music but also film (e.g., Alfred Hitchcock's *Psycho*, Oliver Stone's *Natural Born Killers*, etc.) and literature (e.g., Truman Capote's *In Cold Blood*, Cormac McCarthy's *Blood Meridian*, Bret Easton Ellis's *American Psycho*, etc.), and has even been the focus of a Broadway musical (Stephen Sondheim's *Sweeney Todd, the Demon Barber of Fleet Street*).

Tracing such themes as sin and redemption through the course of American popular song, and art much more generally, would be an interesting exercise but lies far beyond our discussion here. It should be sufficient to state that gangsta rap artists have not generally expended much lyrical energy on the redemption part, although Bushwick Bill does make a reference to changing his ways and "living for the Lord" in "Damn It Feels Good to Be a Gangsta."

THE FUTURE

As of this writing, Lil' J has changed his name to J. Prince, but he still owns and operates Rap-A-Lot Records, and he still owns the Geto Boys as a franchise. The classic lineup (Scarface, Bushwick Bill, and Willie D) have been more active as a group recently than at any time since their initial congregation, having released two albums. They also each pursue their own individual business interests and seem to be going strong.

For all of its massive popularity, hip hop and rap music can be a fickle game: New rappers come, strike it big overnight, and then disappear the next day, and this cycle repeats itself with a great deal of frequency. Regardless of what may happen down the road, the Geto Boys have solidified their place in rap music history and will always remain true icons of hip hop.

See also: Ice Cube, Dr. Dre, Outkast

FURTHER RESOURCES

Baker, Greg. Program Notes. *Miami New Times* (Florida) September 18, 1991: 60.
Illseed. "Searching for Willie D. of the Geto Boys." http://www.AllHipHop.com/features/?ID=845.
KOCH Records page for Scarface and the Product, http://www.kochentertainment.com/scarface.htm.
Mills, David. "The Geto Boys, Beating the Murder Rap: How Did Blood and Guts Get from the Street to the Top 40?" *Washington Post* December 15, 1991.
Official Def Jam Records page, http://www.defjam.com/defjamsouth.
Official Virgin Records page, http://www.virginrecords.com/geto_boys/home.html.
Rap-A-Lot Records, http://www.Rap-A-Lotrecords.com.

SELECTED DISCOGRAPHY

Making Trouble. Rap-A-Lot, 1988. Includes Bushwick Bill, but not Scarface or Willie D.
Grip It! On That Other Level. Rap-A-Lot, 1990. The "classic lineup."
The Geto Boys. Rap-A-Lot, 1990.
We Can't Be Stopped. Rap-A-Lot, 1991.
Uncut Dope: Geto Boys' Best. Rap-A-Lot, 1992.
Till Death Do Us Part. Rap-A-Lot, 1993. Willie D is replaced with Big Mike.
The Resurrection. Rap-A-Lot, 1996.
Da Good Da Bad & Da Ugly. Rap-A-Lot, 1998. Bushwick Bill is replaced with DMG.
Greatest Hits. Rap-A-Lot, 2002.
The Foundation. Rap-A-Lot/Asylum, 2005. Bushwick Bill returns.
War and Peace. Rap-A-Lot.
Screwed and/or chopped versions exist for the last six titles.

© David Corio.

The Native Tongues

Aine McGlynn

The Native Tongues are a collective of hip hop artists who emerged out of the burgeoning underground alternative rap scene in New York City in the late eighties and early nineties. The collective was pioneered by Afrika Bambaataa in the late seventies and early eighties, with Queen Latifah and the Jungle Brothers being the initial members. It expanded to incorporate De La Soul, A Tribe Called Quest, Chi Ali, and Black Sheep. A number of other artists, namely Common Sense (now Common), the Leaders of the New School, and Brand Nubian were also peripherally associated with the collective. The groups in the Native Tongues collective distinguished themselves from other rap artists of their day in three ways: their use of conscious, positive, uplifting rap, their allegiance to Afrika Bambaataa's Zulu Nation and the cosmic Afrocentric philosophy it advocated, and finally their sound, which relied on sampling widely and often from obscure jazz, blues, soul, gospel, folk, reggae, and rock records (see sidebar: R&B). Although the Native Tongues' heyday ended in the mid-1990s, many of the artists continue to record, although now less in connection with each other. They are a unique group of

R&B

Aine McGlynn

R&B covers a wide range of musical styles. The term *rhythm and blues* dates back to the late 1940s and refers to the sound that developed as the deep rural southern Memphis blues of such artists as Muddy Waters and Howlin' Wolf met an urbanizing black population. By the fifties it was already difficult to pin down what R&B referred to. It seemed to encompass soul, blues, doo wop, and jazz to some extent. By the 1990s, however, R&B was associated with superficiality, sentimentality, and overwrought romantic posturing. Several Native Tongues tracks feature disparaging comments about R&B singers. They are accused on *Black Star*'s "Thieves in the Night" of being devoid of any thought-provoking qualities whatsoever, while on A Tribe Called Quest's "Buggin' Out" Q-Tip rhymes about R&B trying to hone in on rap styling. Their critiques were for the most part well founded, as the early to mid nineties witnessed the success of acts such as Boyz II Men, Dru Hill, and Jodeci. These groups harmonized the fever-pitched strains of unfaithfulness, the pain of losing their women, and the hardships that go along with being a lover of ladies. The videos featured soft-focus lenses, yards and yards of billowing silk, and candlesticks in every corner of the ubiquitous bedroom. The critique of the R&B singer was multifaceted: The aesthetic was cheesy, the sound was a noxious and whiny neo-jazz, and the content was vapid.

The tune changed, though, later in De La and Tribe's careers as they began to incorporate R&B on such tracks as "Stressed Out" and "All Good." Initially they treated R&B with some tongue-in-cheek irony. For instance, De La Soul's "Baby, Baby, Baby, Baby, Ooh Baby" walks a fine line between parodying R&B and participating in the genre. By the end of the 1990s, R&B artists were working with more classically hip hop–oriented producers, which resulted in a sound that teetered between the two genres. The silk sheets had been folded up and put away, the candles were blown out, and R&B singers like R Kelly and Bobby Brown began to posture in a way that was more reminiscent of Snoop Dogg than Luther Vandross. Perhaps it was because the quality of production changed toward the end of the decade, or perhaps because De La and Tribe were trying to stay relevant and current by incorporating R&B sounds into their recordings; whatever the reason, such R&B staples as Faith Evans and Chaka Khan made their way onto albums by the Native Tongues artists who had so criticized R&B in the early 1990s.

artists whose presence continues to be felt whenever an MC rhymes about something other than guns, diamonds, and the size of his rims. The Native Tongues style lives on in tracks where the sample isn't an instantly recognizable tune from a fifteen-year-old hit single. Native Tongues music has a playful and enlightening message that can still be heard in such artists as Lauryn Hill, Mos Def, Kanye West, Talib Kweli, POS, and K-OS among others.

These artists are carrying a complex philosophy into the future of a genre whose mutated materialism takes it further and further away from its roots. The original Native Tongues cultivated a place for themselves on the margins of mainstream hip hop, where they cranked up the bass, turned up the Coltrane, and provoked an alternative sound. From hip hop's cradle in New York City, the collective wrote for themselves and for their community, a story of uplift through solidarity and positive thinking.

THE CONTEXT OF THE DEVELOPMENT OF THE NATIVE TONGUES

There was little to be positive about in the South Bronx in the early 1970s. The effects of deindustrialization and a crippling post-Vietnam recession were most deeply felt by the poorest members of New York City's population. The overpopulated, dilapidated slums of the Bronx River housing projects, the hallways and streets around Monroe High School, the subways flying by Prospect Ave., all sighed under the growing weight of hopelessness and despair. The unemployment rate had never been higher; drugs were never so cheap or easy to get. New York City was characterized by an ineffectual police force, an inadequate infrastructure, and a corrupt bureaucracy that didn't give a damn about its most vulnerable members (see sidebar: New York City: The Sixth Element).

New York City: The Sixth Element
Aine McGlynn

The first five elements of Native Tongues hip hop are the DJ, the MC, the b-boy, the graffiti artist, and knowledge of self. The sixth, unrecognized one is New York City. Aside from being the birthplace of hip hop, New York is a character that interacts with all the rhymes in the Native Tongues albums. The Jungle Brothers shouted out on "Belly Dancin' Dina" that they are from 113th Street and Seventh Avenue in Harlem, while Black Sheep's Dres mentioned that he wished he could get a cab in midtown Manhattan or a slice of pizza no matter where he happened to be in the city. The five boroughs are a central theme on all the Native Tongues albums. De La Soul shouted out their Long Island heritage as often as possible, while Tribe's Phife Dawg rapped about the New York Knicks, the Yankees, Mets, and Vinnie Testaverde, the quarterback of the New York Jets. In spite of the fact that Native Tongues philosophy was resistant to myths of American nationalism, the pride of being from New York City was always a part of their sound. This can be attributed to the varied textures of the city itself. It is more of a microcosm of the world than a place where American nation making occurs. It is home to representatives from all corners of the planet, and in its 321 square miles it holds infinite possibilities for shaping not only one's Saturday night but one's deepest sense of self.

> *Black Star*'s "Respiration" captures the beauty and depth of the life force that pulses through the city. It is like a body with a heart that beats out the pace of life. The kind of inclusivity that the Zulu Nation advocated and which the Native Tongues echoed could only have emerged from New York. Like all other cities, it undoubtedly has its ghettoes, and people wake up and go to sleep in segregation. But from 9 to 5, riding the subway puts a person into contact with every race, creed, color, shape, and size. It is in the flux of constant though unsustained contact among such varied people that the Native Tongues operated. The narrative of unity and inclusivity was always checked by raps that exposed the reality of a racist past and present. New York City's eclecticism, however, provided the potential space in which an integrated and equal future might be enacted.

In this environment, violence was a natural outlet for the frustration felt by the most abused and marginalized members of a crumbling outer borough. In the South Bronx, gang violence between such groups as the Black Spades, the Chingalings, and the Savage Nomads threatened to erupt into full-scale warfare. The sense of community and solidarity that might have existed after the heady days of the civil rights movement had grown thin and anemic. The prophets of equality and reform, JFK, Dr. King, Robert Kennedy, and Malcolm X had all been brutally exterminated, and in the void of social justice, the urban population experienced a collective, alienating grief that grew into an oppressive anger, which manifested in self- and community-directed violence.

After the tragic spring of 1968, gang life took on the quality of inevitability for young men in the South Bronx. To be outside on the street was to be vulnerable. Being associated with the gang that controlled a given street neutralized some of that vulnerability. The goal of inner-city gangs, of all violent collectives in fact, is to expand power and territory bases. Bronx gang territories were delineated by streets, schools, playgrounds, and bodegas. Intimate knowledge of the landscape was essential to any Bronx youth trying to negotiate the complex maps of belonging and conflict. As the city and state authorities were unable, or perhaps unwilling, to assuage the gang conflict, it became apparent that any kind of revolution of ideas would have to happen from within. It was up to the community to heal its own divisions. At the first truce meeting held in December 1971, Charlie Suarez, the infamous captain of the Ghetto Brothers, "opened the meeting with a command: 'I would like for the police to leave or we got nothing to say'" (Chang 58). A treaty was signed that depended on each gang respecting each other's turf. The streets in the Bronx were once again to become neutral environments where Latinos, blacks, and whites were, in theory at least, safe to interact with each other.

The record collection is an ideal metaphor for what the peacemakers were trying to achieve. Afrika Bambaataa, one of the founding fathers of hip hop and a former Black Spade, learned from his mother's eclectic record collection that South African spiritual music could rub up against northern soul, which could sit happily beside Motown doo-wop. An avid music fan, Bambaataa had no trouble finding a great drumbeat from a Monkees single that would make a crowd jump up and dance. When Bambaataa discovered and played those records for a Bronx crowd that would normally disdain them, he disrupted a whole set of stereotypes and limitations that kept kids from exploring a varied range of musical possibilities.

Bambaataa's most significant contribution to the renaissance that took place in the Bronx in the early 1970s was his undying faith in the power of a booty-shakin' good time to bring a group of people together. The block parties thrown by Bambaataa and his crew, the Organization, transformed the community's old associations between the street and violence. Instead of "beating each other upside the head like they used to do in the gang days," Jazzy J recalled, block parties saw kids "doing something constructive ... plugging into lampposts" and playing records until the early hours of the morning (Chang 97).

THE MEDIUM NEEDS A MESSAGE

The parties, as unifying as they were, were not something to believe in. There was still a void from the end of the civil rights movement that left these young hip hop heads without a directive, a policy, or a message that would give this energetic new outlet called hip hop the feeling of manifesto, of destiny. It took Afrika Bambaataa to shape the message. Bambaataa was the founder of the Universal Zulu Nation, which preached freedom, justice, wisdom, knowledge, and understanding. Bambaataa developed these principles into the Seven Infinity Lessons of the Universal Zulu Nation (see sidebar: The Infinity Lessons of the Universal Zulu Nation). At the heart of the Lessons is a drive toward empowerment through a process of coming to truth. This truth

---

The Infinity Lessons of the Universal Zulu Nation
Aine McGlynn

The Infinity Lessons were derived from the tenets of the Five Percenter faith and advocated by Afrika Bambaataa as a platform from which the Zulu Nation could spread their message. They formed a basic set of rules of behavior for members of the Zulu Nation but also packaged the movement for travel beyond the South Bronx. One of the most beautiful and appealing aspects of the lessons is the fact that they are never complete. They can always, at any time, by any member, be added to. Indeed, a visit to the Zulu Nation's Web site evidences the often complex and detailed additions that members make to the lessons. There is, however, a set of fundamental ideals around which

> they shift and develop. Among them is the focus on coming to know the self, recognizing that the Universal Zulu Nation is the "truth" and that any real change must come not from mere uncovering of the systems of power and oppression but from recognizing the god within oneself. The fact that the philosophy of the movement is open to improvement and innovation is one of the reasons that the Zulu Nation gelled so comfortably with the Native Tongues, and with hip hop more generally. Hip hop at its best is about the creativity that can happen within a specific moment; this is the legacy of the street corner ciphers, freestyle sessions where the beatboxer provided the rhythm and the rapper came up with rhymes right on the spot. In its purest form, hip hop is dynamic and constantly morphing in the same way as the Infinity Lessons do.

consisted of knowledge, wisdom, and understanding of the self, to the self, and by the self. It was up to the members of the Native Tongues collective to bring this message to a wide audience. Afrika Bambaataa and the Zulu Nation were the philosophical touchstone for all the early albums produced by the collective's core members. As a collective, they worked to promote not only the ideas of the Universal Zulu Nation but each other's albums as well, counting on the probability that success for one would translate into success for all. It was the philosophy of the Zulu Nation, which they held with such conviction, that gave them something meaningful to rap about and which, ironically, ended up forming the backbone of the posse's commercial success. Though each member of the posse was unique, they were bound together by what set them apart from every other rap group bursting onto the scene.

INTRODUCING THE MEMBERS

The Jungle Brothers

The Jungle Brothers were Afrika Baby Bambaataa, both a DJ and an MC or rapper; Sammy B, a DJ; and Mike G, also an MC. The Jungle Brothers (the JBs) emerged out of New York in the late eighties and released their debut, *Straight Out the Jungle,* in 1988. Theirs was a sound immediately distinguishable from those of their contemporaries. Their eclectic mix of samples from jazz, rock, soul, reggae, African spirituals, and blues produced a hip hop with an emphasis on musicality and melody. Not only was the album easy to listen to, the lyrics were unmistakably political, advocating sexual equality and unity within the African American community. Their next album, *Done by the Forces of Nature* (1989), is one of hip hop's most danceable albums. The hooks they used and the tunes they sampled were beautifully melodic and the bass was deeper and more compelling than on their debut. Their later efforts, *J. Beez Wit the Remedy* (1993) and *Raw Deluxe* (1997), did not achieve any notable success with hip hop audiences. These later efforts, along with *All That We Do* (2002), reestablished the JBs with a trip-house music audience.

De La Soul

De La Soul (De La) owed much of their sound and success to the Jungle Brothers. The group, made up of Posdnous (Plug One), Trugoy the Dove (Plug Two), and Pacemaster Mase (Plug Three), were the most commercially successful members of the Native Tongues collective. Their first album, *3 Feet High and Rising* (1989) was produced by Prince Paul and recalls the sound of the JB's debut. The liner notes feature a comic about the making of the album; the three members of De La are drawn stressing out about not being able to produce the album in time and calling in the JBs to help them out. The resulting album is a hip hop classic that reflects the inclusive, hippie-inspired roots of De La's D.A.I.S.Y. Age (Da Inner Sound Y'all) philosophy of spreading love and positivity. Their follow-up album, *De La Soul Is Dead* (1991), was more aggressive in its sound and its content. Gone were the songs about three being a magic number or tracks about washing yourself with soap to get rid of your stink, rhymed over a sample of the bass line from "Stand by Me." Instead the album pulsed with more aggressive tracks such as "Rap de Rap Show" and "Afro Connections at a Hi 5 (In the Eyes of the Hoodlum)," disparaging the "hard acts" who called their style soft. Because they had achieved a significant amount of commercial success, they were repeatedly accused of crossing over by rappers who didn't take kindly to De La's making fun of their ultra-macho gangsta personas. Their next two albums, *Buhloone Mind State* (1993) and *Stakes Is High* (1996), continued to express their frustration with fame and the accusations of selling out. These two albums attempted to distance the group from the mainstream by making references to hip hop history that only the most dedicated hip hop head would comprehend. Nonetheless, their flow, style, and Prince Paul's faultless production resulted in innovative albums that continued to achieve popularity outside of the typical rap audience (see sidebar: Prince Paul). The group released two albums, *Art Official Intelligence* (1999) and *AOI: Bionix* (2001), as part of

---

Prince Paul
Aine McGlynn

Prince Paul is the legendary hip hop DJ and producer who produced De La Soul's debut, *3 Feet High and Rising*, in 1989, as well as a couple of tracks on Queen Latifah's *All Hail the Queen*. He went on to produce De La's next two albums as well, and along with the influence of the Jungle Brothers, his playfulness and tight beats were a major shaping influence for the Native Tongues sound. Never one to be contained by genres, Prince Paul brought an open-mindedness to De La's sound that was uniquely his own. Paul introduced De La to the concept of album-unifying skits. The skits would carry some of the thematic weight of the album and create the sense of a singular work which Paul felt was vital to any album, and which is a distinctive characteristic of Prince Paul–produced albums. Paul produces conceptual albums that have a thought-out plan which articulates a single philosophy or idea.

Born in New York City, Prince Paul began his musical career with Stetsasonic, a hip hop group that got its start in the early eighties. Their live instrumentation and upbeat lyricism put them on the map and made Prince Paul the natural choice to be the producer for the positive, conscious rap that De La Soul was making at mid-decade. After working with De La, Prince Paul released two of his own albums before teaming up with RZA from Wu-Tang, Too Poetic, and Frukwan to form the Gravediggaz. Most recently, Prince Paul has teamed up with DJ Dan the Automator to form Handsome Boy Modeling School. Their albums *So . . . How's Your Girl* and *White People* showcase an innovative blend of trip hop, rap, rock, folk, nu metal, R&B, and comedy. It featured as disparate a lineup as Thom Yorke from Radiohead, Sean Lennon, Roisin Murphy, Del tha Funky Homosapien, Lord Finesse, Linkin Park, and comedian Father Guido Sarducci. Paul's post–Native Tongues days saw him continually articulating powerful critiques of the hyperconsumerism that began to plague hip hop from the early nineties. In a recent interview with *New York Magazine*, Paul insists that he will produce one more album as Prince Paul, and that it will be his last attempt to change the world. It is this type of ambitious optimism that Paul not only saw mirrored in the Native Tongues movement but also helped to inspire that movement.

---

an ambitious trilogy. The third album in the trilogy was never released, but De La's most recent album, *The Grind Date* (2004), redeemed them somewhat in the eyes of their critics and faithful fans. The opening track locates them in the past, present, and future of hip hop and reminds the listener right off the bat that this music is carrying a message, and a positive one at that. The rest of the album features musical samples, melodic tunefulness, and locates De La as successful, long-standing patriarchs of the hip hop family.

A Tribe Called Quest

A Tribe Called Quest, or Tribe, consists of Q-Tip and Phife Dawg as the MCs, Ali Shaheed Muhammed the DJ, and Jarobi, who appears only on their first album, *People's Instinctive Travels and the Paths of Rhythm* (1990). Tribe's sound was a jazzier version of the danciness that characterized the JB's albums, while Phife's raspy growl and complicated sports metaphors and Q-Tip's nasal, New York accent made Tribe a unique and vital addition to the underground hip hop landscape (see sidebar: Underground Hip Hop under Kool Herc).

They followed up the critical success of their first album with a second, equally acclaimed record, *The Low End Theory* (1991), which improved on their first album by combining thumping beats with an elegant jazz vibe. Critics have described this album as not only gracefully sampling jazz but also reflecting a similar kind of creative process. Like *The Low End Theory*, jazz recordings are a testament to a series of creative moments and interactions, rather than a singular act. The album was a unique blend of timely critical raps, innovative aesthetic considerations, and thumping bass breaks that moved the genre forward.

Their next album, *Midnight Marauders* (1993), kept the party going, but at the expense of some of the tight rhyme style and vexing content that made the previous two such standalone works of art. Nonetheless, the playfulness still pervaded the album. Unfortunately, by the time *Beats, Rhymes and Life* was released three years later, the sense of humor had all but disappeared and the rhymes were tight yet vacant boasts of their rhyme skills. The beats nonetheless still bounced. The last album the group released before the tribe dissolved was *The Love Movement* (1998). It bounced with the same tight production and booty-shakin' beats, but again the social and political urgency was missing, reflecting a general trend in hip hop at the turn of the century.

Black Sheep

Made up of Dres and Mista Lawnge, Black Sheep were the slightly more raunchy, slightly less peace loving, cousin to the tightly knit brotherhood of Tribe, De La, and the JBs. They came to attention touring with the JBs in the late eighties and through Dres's appearances on De La's *De La Soul Is Dead* (1991). Black Sheep had a massive hit with "The Choice Is Yours" from their debut album, *A Wolf in Sheep's Clothing* (1991). As a result, the album sold close to a million copies and was popular with both the traditional rap audience and the mainstream college radio stations. Unfortunately, the success didn't extend to their second album. *Non-Fiction* (1994) forwent the genuinely hilarious skits and raunchy playfulness of their debut for a more earnest autobiographical sketch of their transition from South Carolina to New York City. The failure of this album, somewhat attributable to the lack of marketing support from their record company, marked the end of Black Sheep.

Chi-Ali

The youngest member of the Native Tongues posse, Chi-Ali turned heads with his appearance on Black Sheep's "Pass the 40" and "Have U.N.E. Pull." At thirteen, he rapped about not being old enough to smoke joints or drink, but being old enough to attract the ladies. He gained enough attention to get a record deal out of his guest spots. *The Fabulous Chi-Ali* (1991) was the first album the Beatnuts ever produced, and it exists more as a testament to their early production talents than as evidence of Chi-Ali's MC skills. At fourteen, with a hit single in "Age Ain't Nothing but a Number," Chi-Ali might, if not for the fickleness of the market and perhaps a breaking voice, have had a lasting career. Unfortunately, like Another Bad Connection, Kriss Kross, and other such kiddie rap acts of the day, he was destined to remain a one-hit wonder. The appearance by Phife of Tribe and Mista Lawnge of Black Sheep were meant to legitimize him as a rapper, but their experienced flows merely revealed Chi-Ali's immaturity and ill-formed rhymes.

SELLING THE MESSAGE

Like every other genre of music, hip hop has a marketing hook, a saleable feature that convinces shoppers that they are buying more than an album. Rock and roll banks on its attitude, funk makes you hustle, jazz trades on its vibe, and the blues sells you your melancholy. Hip hop, on the other hand, promises a message. In fact in 1982, one of the earliest commercial successes of hip hop was the Furious Five's aptly titled "The Message." This track defined the genre in a number of ways. It told the story of a young man who is pushed to the brink by the degradation he witnesses in his neighborhood. "The Message" was an unusual track to emerge as a signal of the future of hip hop. It was downtempo, focused on the MC rather than the DJ, and was packed with consciousness-raising commentary on the state of the urban jungle. It diverged from how hip hop had been developing in the early 1970s. People went to block parties and listened to DJs spin records in order to dance, to gather together and forget the realities of their inner city lives. It took the release of "The Message" before hip hop achieved any mainstream music industry attention. This was not just about hedonism. This was, to the leftist liberal media especially, the kind of urgent wake-up call that needed to come out of the lowest class to challenge the conservatism of Reaganomics. This legitimating attention, not to mention a decent paycheck for Melle Mel and the Furious Five, shaped the future of the genre. Hip hop was no longer a careless grassroots movement for the community's enjoyment. It was a vehicle for talking about the needs and frustrations of a community, and in a revolutionary turn, this expression of anger could be lucrative. Thus the saleable myth of hip hop was born; its makers were urban, black, poor, and frustrated, and their music was patently designed to carry this message. The hip hop that moved records had a consciousness that moved minds toward activism and a break and bass line that moved asses as well.

It was the very fact of its ability to carry a philosophy that drew critical and thus industry attention to hip hop. This no doubt also influenced the Native Tongues' allegiance to Zulu Nation philosophy. The commercial pressures of the record industry versus the contradictory desire to pursue right knowledge and community uplift is a central tension in the Native Tongues narrative. The collective was ultimately united by its positive philosophy, its motivation to achieve success without selling out, and finally by a sound that called up the formative moments and ideas from the history of hip hop while also signaling the direction that the genre would take. Ironically, all three of these unifying aspects would contribute to the dissolution of the collective, but for a number of years at the end of the eighties and early nineties, the Native Tongues posse deeply influenced hip hop in one of its most formative moments.

DISRUPTING EXPECTATIONS

It was evident in the late eighties that one could make rap music and make money too. It was also becoming clear that rap could be violently aggressive and woman hating. The popularity of 2 Live Crew and N.W.A. attested to this fact. The Native Tongues emerged as a counteractive balance to the serious hatefulness in such tracks as "We Want Some Pussy," "A Bitch Is a Bitch," and "Get the Fuck Out of My House." De La Soul, Black Sheep, and A Tribe Called Quest brought serious playfulness on tracks such as "Similak Child," "The Magic Number," and "Ham and Eggs." The satirical skits and songs that peppered their albums played with the image of the rapper as a thug, a drug-taking urban boogeyman with a chip on his shoulder (see sidebar: Skits).

Skits
Aine McGlynn

As early as the Furious Five's 1983 hit "The Message," skits became a fairly common feature in hip hop tracks. For a precedent, one might even look back at Stevie Wonder's 1973 "Livin' for the City," in which Stevie arrives on the bus in New York City and is asked to carry a package across the street. When he does so, he is arrested and the track resumes. Similarly, the skit in the message depicts a conflict, not with the police, but with other people in the neighborhood. The Native Tongues picked up on the trend, using the skit format to speak to the ongoing conflict in their neighborhoods while also injecting some humor into their albums. Often, the more serious vignettes feature, as in the Stevie Wonder track, an encounter with the police. These skits depict the cops as abusing their authority, as dupes and racists. It is as though this depiction of the police must be stated explicitly; it cannot be rapped about. This conflict, because it is so central and common to the experience of being young and black in America, must be articulated as clearly as possible. The other type of conflict often highlighted in the skits is between people within the same neighborhood. This is the type of skit featured on "The Message" and on A Tribe Called Quest's "The Crew."

On the other hand, the skits can be hilarious. The format of the lighthearted skit echoes the comic book playfulness found in the liner notes of De La's *3 Feet High and Rising*. On this album in particular, the skits are about a mock game show that the abum comes back to again and again. On *Midnight Marauders*, a computerized host performs the interludes, unifying the album in a way similar to De La's game show. In a direct homage, the Black Eyed Peas' *Behind the Front* (1998) also features a series of game show–style skits, identifying that they are in conversation with the Native Tongues' sound and philosophy while also reaffirming the performative aspects of the genre.

Whether a skit is about conflict or humor, the emphasis is on performance. The format of the skit explicitly points out the distance between the album, the personas that are adopted, and the real-life identities of the performers. Nonetheless, what is being depicted in the skit, particularly the conflictual ones, is indicative of experiences based in social reality. The skit thus performs double duty; it highlights a very real American experience of racism and violent living, while also pointing to the plainly performative and inventive qualities of hip hop as a genre.

Their playfulness was a check to the narrative that was emerging about what an authentic rapper was to look like, sound like, and rap about. This "authentic" rapper was a man who had suffered and was damned if he wasn't going to let everyone know about it. It is a tendency of journalistic and scholarly writing about African American art forms to make an overly simplistic association between that community's suffering and their creative expressions. This connection between suffering and art is a reduction of the art to pathology. Pathology, defined as the essential nature of a disease, is a loaded word to use to speak about African American art. To read black art as being essentially about struggle and pain suggests that the natural or essential condition of a black person in America is to be plagued or diseased by the suffering that he or she endures. This reading often sells the artist short as it suggests that the art is not subject to aesthetic or stylistic concerns. To always suggest that the product of African American creativity is about suffering limits the possibility for expression on the part of the artist while also limiting the way in which that art object can be read. The attention that aggressive, violent, and misogynistic rap albums received in the late eighties and early nineties was, to some extent, the mainstream media looking for expressions of black art that confirmed the already entrenched association between black art and suffering. The Native Tongues, by contrast were quietly releasing albums that had little to do with gun play, gang allegiance, and beating women.

The Jungle Brothers' second album, *Done by the Forces of Nature*, for example, is an eminently danceable album. It is full of heady beats and celebratory melodies and messages, such as on the tracks "Good Newz Comin'" and "Beeds on a String." This album doesn't paint a picture of an abused race of people who are destined for further abuse. Rather, it is full of positive messages of solidarity among like-minded people. It compels the listener to move forward beyond pathological constructions of the black person as angry and downtrodden. This message of celebration and joy was, since Bambaataa rollicked through "Unity Part 1 (The Third Coming)," a specific strategy for moving a people beyond the idea of themselves as victims of marginalization.

WOMEN AND THE NATIVE TONGUES

The Princess of the Posse

The members of the Native Tongues posse also clearly set themselves apart from other rap groups in the 1990s in their attitude toward women. Queen Latifah was among the first members of Native Tongues. At eighteen, Latifah released her first album, *All Hail the Queen,* which achieved moderate commercial success. Nonetheless, on the cover Latifah, clad in a head wrap, took a proudly defiant stance with the African continent looming over her shoulder. This was an image of a female that stood out in contrast to the degrading references to women that were spilling so easily out of MCs' mouths. Queen Latifah, in the very fact of being a woman and an MC with unquestionable skills on the microphone, helped to cement the philosophy of the Native Tongues as inclusive, progressive, and far more respectful of women than their gangster counterparts. At a time when the controversy over 2 Live Crew's obnoxiously misogynistic lyrics was raging, Latifah appeared on the remix of De La Soul's "Buddy," which is one of only a few truly collaborative tracks that the Native Tongues produced.

The Native Tongues weren't the only collaborative acts in hip hop at the time. Producer Marley Marl brought together the Juice Crew to produce 1988's "Symphony." The track was a huge hit, leading to successful careers for its performers, Biz Markie, Kool G Rap, Masta Ace, and Big Daddy Kane, just some of the members of the Juice Crew. At the end of the 1980s the posse was becoming a widespread and well-proved method by which a group of rappers could achieve notoriety in the press, among listeners, and within the rap community. With the posse, though, came the attempt on the part of every member to outshine everyone else under the guise of creating music together.

"Buddy," one of the Native Tongues' early forays into collaboration, features Queen and De La, Q-Tip and Phife Dawg from A Tribe Called Quest, as well as the Jungle Brothers and Monie Love. Latifah and Monie Love participate in the track's playfully macho banter about having sex. The men refer to their penises as their "jimmies," and the women they pick up as their "buddies." Monie's rap, along with Latifah's skit with the French rapper Lucien at the end of the track, acknowledges that female sexual desire can be just as playful as that of their male counterparts. This is not a narrative of sex as a violent assertion of power, but rather a celebration of men and women as joyfully sexual beings.

The empowered female that Latifah portrayed on *All Hail the Queen* and on the collaborative tracks she produced with the Native Tongues is not all that remarkable. By 1989, Salt-N-Pepa and MC Lyte had achieved notably successful albums. What was unique about Latifah was the combination of Afrocentric solidarity that she derived straight from Bambaataa's Zulu Nation and the narrative of late-twentieth-century feminism. In the discourse that surrounds black femininity, there are pointed references to the choice that must be made between two allegiances, one based on gender and the other on race. It is often thought that in African or Afrocentric philosophy the female must occupy a subordinate role to her man. This suggests that a woman who is influenced by twentieth-century feminist thinking cannot take on the philosophy of Afrocentrism because the two systems contradict each other. Nowhere is this tension more evident in the hip hop community than in an infamous 1991 interview between Angela Davis, a professor of women's studies and African American studies at the University of California at Santa Cruz, and Ice Cube, a rapper who is often credited with coining the term "gangsta rap." Davis had been a Black Panther in the 1960s and had embraced the politics of black nationalism. Thirty years later, as she sat down with Cube, she was disturbed by what she saw as a new misogynistic Afrocentrism that was pervading youth culture. Davis's generation had somewhat successfully disrupted the connection between nationalism and patriarchy, and here in front of her was a young man who represented a whole generation's attempt to reestablish that destructive relationship.

Queen Latifah, who cites Davis as a major influence, collaborated with Monie Love on "Ladies First," a track which articulates a black feminism that engages not just with the reality of being a woman but also with the condition of the African diaspora. In the video for the song, Latifah aligns herself with the historical figures that are projected behind her and who saw no need to choose between fighting for their race and fighting for their gender. For them, and for Latifah, the challenge was to support not female over male or vice versa, but rather to recognize the larger difference between the haves and the have-nots.

The Boys Follow Suit

The rest of the Native Tongues posse, overwhelmingly male as they were, nonetheless took up this same Afro-feminist philosophy. A Tribe Called Quest recorded such tracks as "Description of a Fool," which includes in its description of a fool a woman-hating abusive man. De La Soul also pointed to respecting a sister by never violating her physically or emotionally on "I Be Blowin," and penned an anti-incest track called "Millie Pulled a Pistol on Santa." These tracks emphasize that the Native Tongues are on the opposite end of the spectrum from the aggressive gangsta and booty rap that was gaining popularity. Nevertheless, though the boys of Native Tongues might have been protofeminists, they also produced raunchy tracks about their sexcapades where the women they encounter are no more than conquests. Phife Dawg from Tribe was particularly raunchy in his tone on such tracks as "Electric Relaxation" and "Hot Sex on a Platter." Even the collaborations "La Menage" on *A Wolf in Sheep's Clothing* and "De La Orgy" on *3 Feet High and Rising* are bold-faced description of sex, wherein the men engage in hypermasculine boasts about how well endowed they are and how easily they can conquer a "bitch" or a "ho." There is, however, a difference between these tracks and, for example, 2 Live Crew's "Fuckshop." Not only is the raunch taken to a whole new level on the latter's recordings, but an unmatched level of scorn and aggression is directed toward women as well. In the Native Tongues tracks the emphasis is on bolstering masculinity and equating that with being an MC. This, for example, is why there are rampant metaphorical parallels between their dicks and their microphones. For 2 Live Crew, however, the emphasis is arguably entirely on the degradation of the woman, of reducing her to a receptacle rather than on shaping their conceptions of themselves as men. It would be a mistake even to refer to a personality in these tracks. They are devoid of a "she" or a "her" because the body that is being rapped about has been stripped of all identity and worth. Compare this to Black Sheep's (f/ Q-Tip) "La Menage," where there is at least a courting and some flirting before the sex is described. The woman is actually present beyond the description of her body parts.

In spite of the respect the Native Tongues generally afforded to women in their raps, it took Black Sheep to acknowledge the complexity of female-male relationships within the context of rap music as a genre. The skit "L.A.S.M." on Black Sheep's *A Wolf in Sheep's Clothing* embodies many of the complexities of the Afro-feminist position. The skit features Dres and Mista Lawnge being interviewed by the Ladies Against Sexist Motherfuckers. They parody the character of the conceited, sexist rapper and do nothing to improve their situation by telling the interviewer that *ho* is an abbreviation for *honey*. The interviewer explodes at them, telling them that they give men a bad name and refusing to let them defend themselves. In the skit, there is a subtle working out of the tension between the playful fiction of the characters Dres and Mista Lawnge, and the serious accusations of misogyny being launched against them by short-fused feminists. There is a suggestion that some feminism is misguided and that it mistakes the invented characters and situations of rap lyricism for literal stances on male-female relationships. The interviewer in the skit asks Dres and Mista Lawnge if they really think that people want to hear them refer to women so disparagingly. The answer that the two MCs are not allowed to give is, "Well, of course they do." To back up this claim, Dres would merely have to cite Ice Cube's record sales figures. On the album the track "U Mean I'm Not" is a parody of gangster rap, wherein Dres growls about shooting his sister for using his toothbrush and his mother for breaking his egg yolk. Black Sheep's position here is unique within the Native Tongues posse. They admit through these parodies that they are aware of, and to some extent complicit with, what was becoming the saleable myth of the macho, hyperaggressive masculine rapper. While the rest of the posse rapped about respect for women, Black Sheep discovered and pointed out a fundamentally patriarchal trajectory in the marketing and development of the genre.

The groups within the posse were able to make isolated critiques not only of a generalized society or system of oppression but of the specific way that those prejudices worked within the rap game. They could identify the points at which the record industry tried to shape their images and aesthetics in order to move albums. Whether or not they would be able to resist it remained to be seen.

THE ROLE OF THE COLLECTIVE

United They Rapped: In Defense of "Pease"

The effectiveness of the collective was only as strong as each group's record sales. The success of one group reflected on the success of the second group and encouraged the album sales of the third group. Put simply, the effectiveness of the Native Tongues collective (and others to come including Wu-Tang Clan, Diddy's Bad Boy Posse, Busta's Flip Mode Squad, the Quannum Collective, etc.) traded on the voracious nature of hip hop fans. Hip hop from its early days was not merely something that you listened to. Rap music was a felt experience that fans attuned their whole lifestyles to. You collected a group's records, sought out their remixes, dug through crates for the samples they used, and, most important for the Native Tongues in terms of sales and spreading the message, bought the albums that your favorite MC guested on.

As their album sales rose, particularly in the case of A Tribe Called Quest and De La Soul, they attracted a new white fan base. The Native Tongues were accused of crossing over, abandoning their black fans, and selling out to a mainstream audience. Curiously, no one accused Chuck D and Public Enemy of the same thing in spite of the fact their 1989 album, *It Takes a Nation of Millions to Hold Us Back*, competed toe-to-toe with De La Soul's and was also popular with white listeners. Both groups sold counterculturalism to their listeners but from opposite ends of the spectrum. This defiant stance was eminently marketable to a white suburban population schooled on their parents' reminiscences of Bob Dylan going electric and the Beatles' shaggy haircuts. While the gangster or hard-core version of counterculture involved finding violent individualistic solutions to a problem, conscious rappers such as De La and Tribe put their faith in the potential power of the collective struggle to effect community change over the long run.

At a time when such gangsta rap groups as N.W.A. were splintering, the Native Tongues were coming together. For the groups in the posse there was strength in numbers. They had to face major criticisms within the rap community about their record sales, the demographics of their fan base, and the playful, uplifting nature of their rap. Their response to these challenges was multifaceted. For De La it involved satire and straightforward lyrical defense of their position, while for Tribe, making as many heads bounce as possible was enough to legitimize their existence at the top of the record charts.

On their second album, De La chose to counter the accusations of being soft by parodying the haters who put their style down. Shaped by a more thumping beat and warnings about the strength of their crew, the album attempted to defend the Native Tongues philosophy while at the same time realigning them with some measure of what was becoming "authentic" rap music. Authenticity in rap music is a vexed issue. Simply put, to be real in the early nineties became equated with viciousness and hardness. The gang territories that had been made obsolete by the unifying principle of the beat were being redrawn between those acts who performed hardness and anger and those who performed the Bambaataa-like role of the missionary or proselytizer.

On *De La Soul Is Dead,* "Pease Porridge," a track about consuming peacefulness in the form of a bowl of porridge, exemplifies this tension between lyrically defending the ideals of the collective and coming across as hard enough to back up that defense. The track begins with two guys talking threateningly about how wack De La is. Posdnous begins his rhyme by calling out the names of the Native Tongues posse, evoking the strength of their numbers. He admits that their records are played on the radio as well as by the type of brothers whose malignant posturing opened up the track. He points out that in spite of De La being peace loving, the voices of the haters are getting more and more obnoxious, demanding an active response. From there the track moves on to a skit featuring two girls talking about witnessing De La, Tribe, and the Jungle Brothers beating up some kids who called them hippies. One of the girls is incredulous because she thought that the Native Tongues were peace-loving pacifists. Mase goes on to rap about the lack of contradiction between bringing peace and losing one's temper. For that reason, the track keeps returning to the choral loop where the title, "Pease Porridge," derived from a children's nursery rhyme, is repeated over and over by an innocuous male voice.

The fluctuation between the aggression and anger felt by Mase, Dove, and Pos and their desire to stay pea[s]eful by consuming the porridge is indicative of the double position that the Native Tongues were forced to take. Forced into this dual stance by criticisms from those who accused them of not being true to a so-called authentic conception of hip hop, much of the political and social urgency that fleshed out their earlier albums gave way to defensive posturing.

The track concludes with an imitation of Kermit the Frog talking about how always eating porridge keeps one peaceful. But the childishness of the reference undercuts the effectiveness of the strategy for grown men. Following Kermit, Tribe's Jarobi imitates a Hindi man who describes the peacefulness with which people eat porridge in his land and how perplexed he is by the violence that occurs between people in America. This becomes the conclusive statement for the track. It suggests that even when the desire to consume the porridge is present, the aggression and jealousy that surround the consumer don't allow him to eat peacefully. There is always someone or something that will irritate one enough to distract one from the act of physically taking in the principles of passivism and gentility. In contrast to ingesting peace, having it become part of one's essence, authenticity in rap music is put on like a Hilfiger sweater, strapped on like a .45 pistol; it is the performance of threat on the part of a black male who believes that no other identity is available to him.

The description of being interrupted while trying to eat porridge is as much a statement about De La Soul's desire to stick to positive rhymes and consciousness-raising rap as it is about the choice facing the record buyer. Presented with the choice between rap that offers a strategy for productive subversion of society, and a record that is more aggressive and overt (i.e., violent) in its image of resistance to the dominant, the tendency will be—record and concert sales attest to this fact—to choose the latter. As a collective, the Native Tongues could be more effective in countering the seductive image of the gangsta rapper. De La could put up the lyrical defense, the JBs could continue to make innovative beats and sounds that no hip hop fan or ignorant hater could resist moving to, and Tribe could bring the jazz-inflected party vibes that you could bump in your car. Taken together, they made up an encompassing sound, style, and politic that was as diverse as gangsta and booty rap were monolithic.

Speaking in Tongues: The Sound and the Posse

It was not merely their messianic proselytizing about the lessons of the Zulu Nation that compelled the Native Tongues to form a collective. They shared a sonic aesthetic that is still identifiable today and which, when paired with consciousness of self, marks Native Tongues–inflected hip hop as a unique subgenre. By the time Latifah's album came out and the Jungle Brothers had released *Straight Out the Jungle* (1988), rap music had been transformed from the live happenings of the early eighties. At block parties and clubs all over the country, the DJs took center stage spinning and scratching their way through funk, disco, and jazz classics. Once rap music became committed to wax, the MC's rhymes were foregrounded at the expense of the DJ's on-the-spot innovation, which was so central to the definition of a hip hop party in the early days.

In spite of the fact that on a record the lyricism of these MCs arguably occupied a more prominent role than the DJ's skills, the Jungle Brothers stayed true to the original block party format, wherein the DJ still had creative control. Sammy B dug deep into his crates of old records in order to sample reggae, calypso, African jive, James Brown, Parliament Funkadelic, and even some rock and roll classics. Sampling from a deep and wide collection of records recalled the early Bronx DJs Kool Herc, Grandmaster Flash, Grandwizard Theodore, and of course Afrika Bambaataa. This breadth and eccentricity became an identifiable central feature of the Native Tongues sound and arguably their politics as well. The samples they used were not merely about melody or tune; they carried much of the narrative weight for the track. In a poem, a word is chosen not merely because it rhymes but because of what it suggests about the overall theme. The samples that the Native Tongues chose similarly performed not only aural duties but also the task of telling the story and informing the theme on a given track. For instance, on the opening track of the JB's *Done by the Forces of Nature*, "Beyond This World," Mike G raps about being underground, being Afrocentric, and being sent to earth to educate his listeners. This reference to coming from outer space is about being marginalized, but it also calls to mind Zulu Nation metaphysics that see consciousness of self as unbound by the limits of earthly time and space. Mike G lyrically calls to mind this philosophy, but the sound transmits the message as well. He shouts out the Zulu Nation and immediately the track gives way to a classic Kraftwerk break that is singularly reminiscent of Afrika Bambaataa. This inclusive, electro-funk-infused album echoed Afrika Bambaataa's sound more directly than any other album produced by the Native Tongues collective. This referential tendency in the JBs was vital to the development of the Native Tongues sound because of the influence of the JBs on both De La and Tribe's prolific sound.

In the comic strip that illustrates the story of the making of the album *3 Feet High and Rising* (1989), it is revealed that De La Soul arrived from Mars to meet with a record executive who told them to make haste with the production of their album. While the extraterrestrial theme echoes Bambaataa's philosophy about the energy and power of life outside our galaxy, De La are also confirmed as members of the posse through the aural cues that pervade the album. In the same comic strip, Pos, Mase, and Dove call on the JBs to help them produce the album, and indeed tracks such as "Transmitting Live from Mars" and "The Magic Number" are inflected by the eclecticism that defined the JB's sound on their own debut. On the latter track alone, the samples include Led Zeppelin's "The Crunge," *Schoolhouse Rock*'s

"Magic Number," Johnny Cash's "Five Feet High and Rising," an Eddie Murphy sample, and a Bill Cosby one too.

These references taken together on a single track create a layering of meanings. The position and relationship between each of the samples on "The Magic Number" affect the way the track is interpreted. "The Magic Number" identifies each member of the group and defines what they as individual rappers, and as a group, stand for. Led Zeppelin's "The Crunge" is reminiscent of a classic funk record and Robert Plant parodies James Brown, calling out to the band for the bridge. De La, using such a parodic sample in their own parody of the kid's tune "Three Is a Magic Number" multiplies the level of interpretation. Their use of the Zeppelin tune locates them artistically within a conversation about stylistic borrowing and parody. In their form—two MCs and a DJ—they are firmly located within the hip hop community, but their willingness to call to mind Johnny Cash and Led Zeppelin, two decidedly un–hip hop acts, opens up the doors of possibility of hip hop sound. De La's innovation was noted throughout the rap community, as the free and wide sampling on the Beastie Boys' 1989 *Paul's Boutique* attests. In a single track on that album there are samples from as many as fourteen to twenty different sources, including Dylan, Zepplin, Afrika Bambaataa, and the occasional bong hit. This type of eclectic sampling harkens back to Grampa Bam's philosophy and sound. On "Unity Part 1," Afrika Bambaataa raps about listening to new wave, punk, and rock and roll in his urging to the audience to unify in the name of having a good time.

Similarly, A Tribe Called Quest's sampling of Lou Reed's "Walk on the Wild Side" on their track "Can I Kick It?" marked Tribe as advocating the same sort of block party eclecticism that defined the Bronx's epic street jams. In his rhyme, Q-Tip explicitly suggests that Tribe will not shy away from having funk beats meet rock and roll tunes. Adding a third level of sonic references, Tip tells listeners to do the jitterbug to this track if they want to dance. "The Jitterbug" was a hit for Cab Calloway in 1934. Calloway might be considered one of the ancestors of hip hop as his skat style pays attention to rhythmic lyricism in the same way that rap does. The lyrical and sonic cues used by the members of the Native Tongues posse united them as a collective with a shared aesthetic. Those samples contribute to the theme of the given song while also marking out the conscious choice on the part of the collective to call to mind the roots of hip hop not only in the Bronx, but in the entire catalogue of American music. This is the point at which aesthetics meet the inclusive politics of the posse.

Aside from a tendency to sample similarly, the posse was united in their rhyme style. The shared tendency to rap smoothly, without aggression, ending the rhyme right on the drumbeat, are features that are most recognizable on the early nineties albums. This rhyme style shifted to some extent later in the decade. The shift was evidence of the movement away from the roots or old-school style of rhyming and into the less message-heavy, more style-conscious new-school rap. Rapper Busta Rhymes in particular evidences this change. Busta Rhymes came to attention by appearing on A Tribe Called Quest's "The Scenario" on *The Low End Theory*. His raspy growl and breakneck flow attracted enough attention to launch Busta's group, Leaders of the New School, to a new level of popularity. LONS had produced a track for Elektra Records' fortieth anniversary compilation album and had toured with Public Enemy, but Busta was the breakout star, as his work with Tribe demonstrated. LONS released their own album, *A Future Without a Past*, in 1991, the same year as *The Low End Theory*. Their album featured the same playful quality that characterized the rest of the Native Tongues albums up until that point. They rapped playfully about teachers, girls, and trains. The group released a second album in 1993, but at that stage Busta was garnering the majority of the attention, and tensions over his popularity led to their dissolution.

Busta has been vocal about his audience being made up of hard-core or "real" hip hop fans. Part of ensuring that this remained the case was quickening the pace of his vocal delivery. Contrasted with Melle Mel's or Run-DMC's slow articulation of their lyrics, in which the line always ended on the beat, Busta's rhyme blistered. Particularly on tracks such as "P.T.A." on LONS's debut album, *A Future Without a Past*, Busta's tendency to rhyme around the contours of the beat distinguished what would be called new-school hip hop from classic old-school or golden age hip hop. The quickened rhyme pace and experimentation with line length was a feature that Tribe and De La picked up and which can be heard on their later albums. Busta's growl also signaled a "hardness" that countered the criticisms of Tribe as having sold out to suburbia, having bowed to the pressures of the censor, and generally becoming soft. This critique, also launched at De La Soul, would be nagging enough to form some early fissures in the connective tissue linking the Native Tongues.

THE BREAKUP OF THE COLLECTIVE: SUCCESS FOR SOME, OBSCURITY FOR OTHERS

Of the founding members, it was De La Soul and A Tribe Called Quest who blew up. They were big names in the music industry by the mid-nineties. Their positions on the Billboard Hot 100 list and the Rap Singles charts were secured. They maintained a loyal fan base who consistently bought their albums. Unfortunately, the success that they achieved did not extend to their fellow Native Tongues. The Jungle Brothers largely dropped out of the hip hop scene after the release of their second album and became more dance oriented in their sound. Black Sheep fell victim to record company mismanagement and faded away into relative obscurity, in spite of the fact that their first album sold close to a million copies. Chi-Ali got sent up on an attempted murder charge.

Completely on the other side of the coin is Latifah. Where there is a red carpet, there is Queen Latifah. Ironically, reflected in each of these disparate trajectories is an element of what defined the collective. De La used their lyrics to tell their story, to relate their message in the same way that Melle Mel did back in 1982. Though undoubtedly commercially successful as a group by the time *AOI: Bionix* was released in 2001, Pos, Mase, and Dove continued to question the value of the almighty dollar and to encourage positivity on such tracks as "Am I Worth You" and "Baby Phat." Tribe, meanwhile, kept up the party. 2000's *The Love Movement* featured, just like all the other Tribe records in the past, ample booty-shaking joints, like "Hot for You," "The Booty," and "Like It Like That." Tribe and De La exemplified the message and the party, the good-time street jam that introduced you to community you got down with, and your place within it. The Jungle Brothers, in their later forays into hip hop psychedelia, followed a direct line down from the cosmic Afro-universalism of the Zulu Nation. This is a difficult philosophy to sustain with any kind of vigor in a market that considered any such inventive conception of race, self, and history too radical to sell to a general public. Black Sheep also fell victim to the market, as Dres explained in a recent interview with Latin Rapper.com. Making pennies from every record that they sold, Black Sheep switched record companies after their first album and suffered the fate of being undermarketed and ignored by Mercury, a record label on the brink of bankruptcy. Their desire to be more than "slaves" to huge record label prophets contributed to their falling out of the public eye. Queen Latifah followed every path and opportunity that opened up to her. She developed her hip hop roots and her Native Tongues philosophy alongside her Hollywood career. She has never strayed very far from the eighteen-year-old woman on the cover of *All Hail the Queen*, fist raised and chest proudly lifted.

The message, the party, the wide-open universe of the Zulu Nation, the resistance to the record executives, the fame and fortune: the five fingers on the hand that was the Native Tongues collective. Of course, what united them drove them apart. The fame and fortune of some led to jealousy and envy among those not granted the same success. The techno-soul cosmic sound of Bambaataa became dated as bass lines deepened and that West Coast P-Funk whine captivated the expanding hip hop generation. Even the record labels couldn't be resisted. Eventually the reality of being under a lucrative contract exerted pressures on creativity that made the activist or resistant position from which the Native Tongues had proselytized a hypocritical one.

The party still happened, but even then, what was there to celebrate anymore? Back in the day, it was a novelty to be on the street after dark, partying among Spades and Nomads, Zulus and Gestapos. Where fear had been, and death had threatened, beats prevailed and decks revolved. These were community celebrations of youth, of potential, of a future for an embattled population. Now the party was about the size of the yacht that cruised around

Miami, how many crates of Crystal were on board, and how dental floss-thin the girls' thongs were. This was not the same kind of celebration. It was a showing off of capital gains, wherein women were part of that gain, and an indulgence in an image that aimed to provoke jealousy, emulation, and thus product sales. The party was no longer about observing the DJ or the MC, listening to his style and seeing how you could add your own innovation to it. The rarer the sample you found, the more original the track. Now a track is lifted, bass line and melody, a kick and a snare is added, and an MC "yo"s, "ugh"s, and "what"s his way through a vapid list of product endorsements. As for the message of empowerment and knowledge of self, in their last albums it was buried under De La's constant defending of their success and Q-Tip's self-aggrandizing rhymes about the smoothness of his flow. When they did attempt to recast the light on their early days of uplifting playfulness and positivity, the result was cringe-worthy tracks such as "The Love," which boasted an outdated multicultural inclusiveness that had failed to take on the authority of any real political movement.

THE LEGACY OF THE NATIVE TONGUES

Tracks such as "Buddy" on *3 Feet High and Rising*, "Mama Gave Birth to the Soul Children" on *All Hail the Queen*, "Black Is Black" on *Straight Out the Jungle*, and "La Menage" on *A Wolf in Sheep's Clothing*, among others, are truly Native Tongues collaborations. There is buoyancy, perhaps of youth, but also of a group of artists who were proud to know each other. They brought each other up from street corner ciphers, basement recording sessions, and record store crate digging to foist onto the hip hop community a sound and a politic that hadn't been heard before. By the mid-nineties everyone knew who Latifah was, had heard Black Sheep's "The Choice Is Yours," and was aware of a connection between De La Soul and A Tribe Called Quest. However, not everyone knew that they were connected through a network called the Native Tongues. De La and Tribe had begun to move huge numbers of records and no longer really needed the support of a wide network of peers to develop their already prolific careers. Many casual listeners of hip hop might recognize "Native Tongues" or "Zulu Nation" as mentions from a couple of tracks, but would not necessarily understand the implication of calling out these associations. Native Tongues–inflected hip hop had become strictly music to get down to. In a sense, there was a reversion to the pre–Afrika Bambaataa moment when the onus on the DJ was to move butts, not raise community consciousness. Though the political message might still have been there in Tribe's 1994 *Midnight Marauders* and De La's 1996 *Stakes Is High*, by the time *Beats, Rhymes and Life* and *Art Official Intelligence* came out, it was clear that nothing was as it had been. In fact, as early as 1993's *Buhloone Mind State*, Posdnous noted the changes that were happening to rap and to the collective. He rapped on "I Am I Be" about the dissolution of the collective, lamenting about broken promises of unity and the silence among what had been a tightly knit group of people. While members of De La and Tribe remained in contact (Phife appears on a track on *AOI*), it seems as though these two groups—and perhaps it is not coincidental that they were the most successful groups to emerge from the posse—were unique in their ability to stay connected.

The mid-nineties saw a shift in the market for conscious or positive rap. Though the message was still largely Afrocentric and related to the philosophy of the Zulu Nation, a quick scan of the faces of the audience at a Tribe or De La show revealed the nature of their demographic. It was largely white college kids listening to these albums. The Native Tongues had, to some extent, lost the war of authenticity that they had tried to avoid by fighting lyrically and stylistically. They were foreclosed on by black and urban populations as being crossover acts. However, this rejection of the Native Tongues by its traditional or intended audience says more about the marketing of hip hop and its accompanying image than it does about the legitimacy of either group's talent.

At mid-decade, the rise of violence glorifying gangsta rap and misogynistic booty rap were notable. These subgenres of rap came to bear the stamp of authenticity, in spite of the fact that the Native Tongues were closer to the roots of hip hop as it was created in the 1970s. The gangsta, however, had a far more marketable image. The hard-core thug in dark baggy clothes, wearing gang colors, gold in his teeth, and black shades, struck a fierce and immediately identifiable image of defiance and resistance. That same message of defiance and resistance existed on Native Tongues albums, but Native Tongues saw adopting a gangsta stance as a problem instead of a solution. Much of the hip hop that has sold well since the mid-nineties carries with it a message of violent conflict resolution, hypermasculine homophobia, and acquisition of wealth by any means. For the most part, major record labels are less interested in getting behind conscious hip hop because conscious groups tend to be less profitable. Nonetheless, there are still a very few hip hop artists who have managed to walk a fine line between promoting Native Tongues–style sounds and politics, and getting the support of the hip hop community and the record labels too.

Rawkus Records

Founded on borrowed money in 1995 by a couple of Jewish kids straight out of college, Rawkus Records was, for a decade at least, a refuge for hip hop that eschewed bling. Based in New York City, the label reinvigorated underground hip hop, making it easy to love rap music again. Rawkus provided an alternative sound to the ultrapolished, overproduced radio rap that was utterly divorced from any sense of hip hop history. Their timing was perfect.

In 1997, Big Pun, Jermaine Dupri, Jay Z, and Snoop were blowing up the charts. Rawkus, meanwhile, signed Company Flow and reinvigorated a hip hop sound that was rough around the edges and in touch with hip hop as a culture and not just a product. Two years later, Rawkus released *Lyricist Lounge* and *Soundbombing*, both albums that showcased the talented MCs that called Rawkus home. Tracks such as "Bring Hip-Hop Back," "Freestyle," "B-Boy Document," and "Da Cipher" evidenced a refocusing on the four elements that hip hop used to hold so dear. The MC, the DJ, the b-boy, and the graffiti artist were privileged once again on these Rawkus compilations. Not only were the four elements on display, but the fifth element, the one that Afrika Bambaataa added, knowledge of self, was there too. The raps were deeply political and critical of the industry, the American government, and rappers who were undeserving of their fame. De La Soul acted as host on *Lyricist Lounge*, introducing each group's track and confirming that the Native Tongues stamp was still one that carried underground credibility. Q-Tip also guests on a couple of tracks, which highlights the association between urgent, politically motivated hip hop and the Native Tongues as the forefathers of that type of rap.

A more cynical reading of De La and Q-Tip's presence on these Rawkus records would suggest that they appeared as a means to boost their credibility in the underground hip hop world right as their sound was becoming unpopular to the mainstream. High-profile guest appearances such as theirs work both ways though. Rawkus founders Brian Brater and Jarret Myer no doubt understood the marketing potential of having Tip and De La associated with their label. They also understood that the audience for what remained of the Native Tongues collective was largely white and that Rawkus was likely to attract a similar demographic.

Mos Def and Talib Kweli Are Black Star

Mos Def became a breakout star for Rawkus, thanks in part to his appearances on the compilation albums but mostly because of the album *Mos Def and Talib Kweli Are Black Star*, released in 1999. The reference to "Black Star" lines recalls the shipping line that Marcus Garvey established in 1919 and signaled that Afro-positive politics would be front and center on this record. The album picks up right where the Native Tongues left off (or sold out?). They sample widely from old hip hop flicks like *Style Wars* and update hip hop classics like Slick Rick's "Children's Story." The album even references Toni Morrison's *The Bluest Eye* and Alex Bradford's soul musical *Your Arms Are Too Short to Box with God*. Rather than merely speaking about knowledge of self, *Black Star* evidenced what kind of album could be made when knowledge of self was actually achieved. On the track "Thieves in the Night," *Black Star* managed to respectfully articulate the weaknesses within the Native Tongues philosophy. Mos raps about not being able to understand why men in the hip hop game have to choose between being "niggers" or "kings" while the women can identify only as "bitches" or "queens." What he gets at is a widespread disappointment that hip hop has become a polarizing institution where one of two oppositional positions must be taken up.

This is not an indulgent album that displays the kind of defensive posturing that plagued De La and Tribe's later efforts. Rather, the tracks directly attack what is wrong with the whole industry. Mos and Kweli go right after the marketing strategies that, purely in the name of profit, limit the definition of what it means to be black. Some tracks rejoice in the beauty of black women, others warn kids about the lucrative offers made by a corrupt rap industry, and all of them advocate self-education and knowledge of self. "K.O.S. (Determination)" in particular is an ode to old-school ideas about self-improvement. What makes it modern though, what moves it on from the collective movements of the Native Tongues, is that they never suggest that knowledge of self (k.o.s.) and determination will improve the community. The focus is squarely on what the individual can improve about himself. It is as though the fantasy of a struggle of collectivities has been abandoned. Mos Def and Talib Kweli, in their focus on the politics of the self, moved Native Tongues philosophy on from an outdated and commercialized politics of multiculturalism.

See also: Queen Latifah, Beastie Boys, Eric B. & Rakim, Kanye West

FURTHER RESOURCES

Allen, Ernest Jr. "Message Rap." *Droppin Science: Critical Essays on Rap Music and Hip-Hop Culture*. William Eric Perkins. Philadelphia: Temple University Press, 1996. 163-185.

Alridge, Derrick P. "From Civil Rights to Hip-Hop: Toward a Nexus of Ideas." *The Journal of African American History* 90.3 (2005): 226-253.

"Building with Dres of Black Sheep." LatinRapper.com. Posted March 21, 2006; visited February 4, 2006. http://www.latinrapper.com/featurednews53.html.

Chang, Jeff. *Can't Stop Won't Stop: A History of the Hip-Hop Generation*. New York: St. Martin's Press, 2005.

Hess, Mickey. "Metal Faces, Rap Masks: Identity and Resistance in Hip-Hop's Persona Artist." *Popular Music and Society* 28. 3 (2005): 297-313.

Rose, Tricia. *Black Noise: Rap Music and Black Culture in Contemporary America*. Hanover, TN: Wesleyan University Press, 1994.

Schloss, Joseph G. *Making Beats: The Art of Sample Based Hip-Hop*. Middletown, CT: Wesleyan University Press, 2004.

Shapiro, Peter. *The Rough Guide to Hip-Hop*. New York: Rough Guides Press, 1995.

Universal Zulu Nation. April 1, 2006. http://www.zulunation.com/.

SELECTED DISCOGRAPHY

Afrika Bambaataa

"Planet Rock." Tommy Boy, 1982.
"Looking for the Perfect Beat." Tommy Boy, 1982.

The Native Tongues

"Renegades of Funk." Tommy Boy, 1983.
Beware (The Funk Is Everywhere). Tommy Boy, 1986.

A Tribe Called Quest

People's Instinctive Travels and the Paths of Rhythm. Jive, 1990.
The Low End Theory. Jive, 1992.
Midnight Marauders. Jive, 1994.
Beats, Rhymes and Life. Jive, 1996.
The Love Movement. Jive, 1998.

Solo Albums from Members of A Tribe Called Quest

Q-Tip. *Amplified*. Arista, 1999.
Phife Dawg. *Ventilation: Da LP*. Groove Attack, 2000.
Ali Shaheed Muhammed. *Shaheedullah and Stereotypes*. Penalty, 2004.

Black Sheep

A Wolf in Sheep's Clothing. Mercury, 1991.
Non-Fiction. Mercury, 1994.

De La Soul

3 Feet High and Rising. Tommy Boy, 1989.
De La Soul Is Dead. Tommy Boy, 1991.
Buhloone Mind State. Tommy Boy 1993.
Stakes Is High. Tommy Boy, 1996.
Art Official Intelligence: Mosaic Thump. Tommy Boy, 2000.
AOI II: Bionix. Tommy Boy, 2001.
The Grind Date. Sanctuary, 2004.
The Impossible Mission: TV Series Part 1. AOI, 2006.

The Jungle Brothers

Straight Out the Jungle. Warner Brothers, 1988.
Done by the Forces of Nature. Warner Brothers, 1989.

Queen Latifah

All Hail the Queen. Tommy Boy, 1989.